FEAR NOT

Devotionals for Times Like These

Over 200 Stories of God's Faithfulness to
Men and Women Who Weathered the Worst

Dave and Neta Jackson

CASTLE
ROCK
CREATIVE

Evanston, Illinois 60202

Published in Evanston, Illinois. Castle Rock Creative, Inc.

Cover photo: © Gene Rhoden / Weatherpix. Used by permission.

ISBN: 978-0-9820544-5-1

Printed in the United States of America

For a complete listing of
books by Dave and Neta Jackson visit
www.daveneta.com and www.trailblazerbooks.com

FEAR NOT

Devotionals for Times Like These

Contents

Asterisks (*) indicate approximate dates

Part 2—The Reformation: Brother against Brother and Sister against Sister . . . 88

The Witnesses

Part 3—The Great Century: Missionary Outreach from 1793 to 1914 . . .160

The Witnesses

Part 5—Communism: Persecution by Design 291

The Witnesses

Introduction:

How These Stories Can Help You Through Hard Times

Threatening stories are all over the news. Natural disasters . . . ethnic hatred and genocide . . . suicide bombers . . . terrorist plots . . . poverty and homelessness . . . violent mayhem invading even our children's schools . . .

In all these situations, Christians are not immune from suffering and dying.

And it can hit close to home. Neta's mother lost her entire family in a devastating tornado at age thirteen. The nephew of a close friend recently shot his wife, and then killed himself. At times like these we think: *How much more can a person bear?*

We live in difficult times. Economic hardships roll over us like tsunamis. The national debt seems as out of control as a forest fire. We fear our country is losing its moral and ethical moorings. We lament media and political attacks on our religious liberties. "We surely are in the end times," another friend says, shaking her head.

Possibly. But in reality, most of us still lead relatively comfortable lives, enjoying incredible religious freedom, living on average twice as long as our great great grandparents. The hardships most of us experience today hardly compares to the widespread suffering, devastating loss, and waves of persecution of times past.

And yet . . . people of faith endured. Ordinary Christians all through the ages have faced tragic circumstances and even martyrdom with extraordinary courage and heroic faith. How? What can we learn from them to face the everyday hardships in our own lives—and even greater hardships still to come?

What we can learn from heroes of the faith—past and present

The root meaning of the Latin word *martyr* is "witness," first used to describe the early Christians who chose to "witness to their faith" with their willingness to die rather than deny Jesus as Lord and live. They personify those who believe that *something matters more than life*. They force us to think about our own convictions—for what would *we* be willing to die?—and help us clarify that it is not only a willingness to die, but whom we serve and why *he* died that gives ultimate meaning to life and death. The Apostle Paul said, "For to me to *live* is Christ, and to *die* is gain" (Philippians 1:21).

If given a blatant choice—"Deny Christ or die!"—most of us hope we would have the courage to remain true to our faith. But direct spiritual opposition is often com-

1

plicated by the layers of political, social, racial, and cultural differences that infect so much of our social expectations and personal interactions.

Did the Waorani ("Auca") Indians in Ecuador kill the five American missionaries *because* they were Christians? Not exactly. This primitive tribe feared "outsiders" who might take advantage of them. They thought white people were cannibals. Do these complicating layers invalidate the martyrdom of Jim Elliot and his fellow missionaries? No. They died in the cause of Christ, and the seed of their blood not only reaped a crop of new missionaries willing to take their place, but the eventual salvation of their Waorani murderers.

Even in the first century and beyond, it's important to note that many persecutors were motivated by what they believed was necessary to maintain order in society. Saul, for instance, thought he was doing "the right thing" to preserve the "traditional values" of the Jewish faith by rooting out the unruly sect of Jesus followers. In China, the Boxer Rebellion—which took the lives of so many dedicated missionaries and even more Chinese believers—grew out of a fear of Western colonialism, culture, and religion corrupting Chinese "traditional values" and self-determination.

Possibly the most difficult aspect of these stories are the ones in which the persecutors call themselves Christian: the Catholic Church's attempt to stamp out the Protestant Reformation; Protestants persecuting Anabaptists; the Spanish Inquisition; the ignoble Crusades to liberate Palestine; modern Ireland's bloody civil war between Protestants and Catholics; "ethnic cleansing" of Muslims in the former Yugoslavia; white supremacist groups like the Ku Klux Klan in the U.S. doing their dastardly deeds on Saturday and singing hymns in church on Sunday—to name a few.

At the same time, one cringes at the way some of the martyrs baited, scoffed at, and scorned their persecutors during the Reformation. In telling these stories, are we fanning the flames of hatred and intolerance all over again?

Martyr stories help us remember. But there is a "wrong remembering" and a "right remembering." The biblical record is a good example of right remembering. God instituted the Passover celebration, not to keep alive hatred of the Egyptians for their enslavement of the Hebrew people, but to remember God's faithfulness and deliverance. When the apostle Paul recalled Christ's suffering (Philippians 2:5-11), he did not focus on those who caused Christ's suffering and death but pointed out that because Jesus was "obedient to death," God exalted him to the highest place (vv. 8-9, NIV).

Wrong remembering focuses on the injustices done and incites hatred and revenge. Right remembering is a testimony that even suffering and death cannot extinguish the victory that is ours in Christ Jesus.

Looking back in order to move forward

The fact is, the persecution of Christians worldwide is on the rise, and we will not be exempt forever. Rather than fear the future or fight to maintain our comfortable life, we need to focus on Jesus' promise, "I am with you always, even to the end of the age" (Matthew 28:20).

What would persecution do to *our* faith? Are we so conditioned to comfort, our "rights," getting a fair deal, and protecting our interests that we can't comprehend "turn the other cheek" or "pray for those who despitefully use you"?

Meditating on the lives of the martyrs helps us remember that death is the worst the enemy can do to us—and it's ultimately impotent. Christ has conquered death on the cross! Our call to faithfulness doesn't depend on whether or not God stops the tornado of circumstances that is ready to envelop us. Suffering and death, while seemingly tragic in an individual instance, may well fertilize God's overarching plan for the salvation of the world. "The seed that dies . . . bears much fruit" (John 12:24 paraphrased).

The way Christian faith spreads departs so radically from other ideologies. Sacrificial love for our enemies has more power to storm the gates of hell than revenge, violence, hate, or weapons of destruction. After all, Christ's sacrificial death on the cross, paying the price for *our sin*, showed the world the depth of God's love. As followers of Christ, we are invited to share "the fellowship of his suffering"—not because suffering is desirable, but because the way of the cross leads to life.

We may not be called to witness to our faith as a martyr, paying the ultimate price, but we can be *thoroughly Christian* in the decisions and choices we make each and every day—in the lifestyles we choose, in the priorities we set, in the way we handle our relationships—to persevere, to *be faithful* to the One who poured out his own life for our redemption, to do what is right, to follow his call, to *live* for Christ . . . no matter how frightening the consequences.

Using this devotional

This devotional includes over two hundred stories of ordinary men and women who lived—and many who died—for Christ. It also includes **six essays** on the major eras of church expansion and the accompanying persecution. The stories basically run chronologically, from Biblical times until now, and generally fall into those six categories (with a few exceptions).

In addition to the individual stories of courage, trace in the Table of Contents the spread of the gospel across the face of the earth. Note the "hot pockets" of resistance and persecution in certain regions until the gospel ultimately becomes established and the front lines of the battle shifts elsewhere, and you'll see God's purpose unfolding through time until every tribe and nation has been reached (Revelation 5:9).

To give you a taste of the journey ahead, begin with the following five sample devotionals drawn from various eras . . . and then start at the beginning to walk through time with these men and women of faith, whose lives and deaths triumphantly echo *"that important line of angels: Do not be afraid."*[1]

---

1 "The Angel Gabriel," words and music by Jim Croegaert © 1986 Rough Stones Music. Used by permission.

The Witnesses

Daniel

Persia — ca. 537 B.C.

After King Nebuchadnezzar conquered Judah in 605 B.C., he took Daniel and thousands of his fellow citizens back to Babylon. Relocation, especially of the young and able-bodied, was a tactic to discourage rebellion. But he also siphoned off the most talented and incorporated them into his administration. Daniel served in this capacity about sixty years under Nebuchadnezzar and his successors, Belshazzar, Darius, and Cyrus. The following event, recorded in Daniel 6, took place when Daniel was in his eighties.

"May Your God . . . Rescue You"

Darius the Mede decided to divide the kingdom into 120 provinces, and he appointed a prince to rule over each province. The king also chose Daniel and two others as administrators to supervise the princes and to watch out for the king's interests. Daniel soon proved himself more capable than all the other administrators and princes. Because of his great ability, the king made plans to place him over the entire empire. Then the other administrators and princes began searching for some fault in the way Daniel was handling his affairs, but they couldn't find anything to criticize. He was faithful and honest and always responsible. So they concluded, "Our only chance of finding grounds for accusing Daniel will be in connection with the requirements of his religion."

So the administrators and princes went to the king and said, "Long live King Darius! We administrators, prefects, princes, advisers, and other officials have unanimously agreed that Your Majesty should make a law that will be strictly enforced. Give orders that for the next thirty days anyone who prays to anyone, divine or human—except to Your Majesty—will be thrown to the lions. And let Your Majesty issue and sign this law so it cannot be changed, a law of the Medes and Persians, which cannot be revoked." So King Darius signed the law.

But when Daniel learned that the law had been signed, he went home and knelt down as usual in his upstairs room, with its windows open toward Jerusalem. He prayed three times a day, just as he had always done, giving thanks to his God. The officials went together to Daniel's house and found him praying and asking for God's help. So they went back to the king and reminded him about his law. "Did you not sign a law that for the next thirty days anyone who prays to anyone, divine or human—except to Your Majesty—will be thrown to the lions?"

"Yes," the king replied, "that decision stands; it is a law of the Medes and Persians, which cannot be revoked."

Then they told the king, "That man Daniel, one of the captives from Judah, is paying no attention to you or your law. He still prays to his God three times a day."

Hearing this, the king was very angry with himself for signing the law, and he tried to find a way to save Daniel. He spent the rest of the day looking for a way to get Daniel out of this predicament. In the evening the men went together to the king and said, "Your Majesty knows that according to the law of the Medes and the Persians, no law that the king signs can be changed."

So at last the king gave orders for Daniel to be arrested and thrown into the den of lions. The king said to him, "May your God, whom you worship continually, rescue you." A stone was brought and placed over the mouth of the den. The king sealed the stone with his own royal seal and the seals of his nobles, so that no one could rescue Daniel from the lions. Then the king returned to his palace and spent the night fasting. He refused his usual entertainment and couldn't sleep at all that night.

Very early the next morning, the king hurried out to the lions' den. When he got there, he called out in anguish, "Daniel, servant of the living God! Was your God, whom you worship continually, able to rescue you from the lions?"

Daniel answered, "Long live the king! My God sent his angel to shut the lions' mouths so that they would not hurt me, for I have been found innocent in his sight. And I have not wronged you, Your Majesty."

The king was overjoyed and ordered that Daniel be lifted from the den. Not a scratch was on him because he had trusted in his God.

Barnabas the Apostle

Cyprus—61 or 64, honored[1] June 11

We learn a great deal about Barnabas the first time he is introduced by Dr. Luke in the New Testament (see Acts 4:36). His name was Joseph, a Levite from the island of Cyprus, but the apostles gave him a new name: Barnabas, "Son of Encouragement." His conversion to the gospel of Jesus was so complete that he sold some land that he owned and turned all the money over to the apostles for the needs of the church.

---

1 Days on which a person is "honored" is according to church tradition.

Everywhere Barnabas crops up in the New Testament, we see him speaking up on behalf of another. When Saul the Tormenter came back to Jerusalem as Saul the Transformed and wanted to join the believers, the disciples were afraid and flat-out didn't believe him (see Acts 9:26-28). But Barnabas took Saul in hand, brought him to the other disciples, and spoke on Saul's behalf. It's as if he said, "Now look. Do we believe Christ can turn a man around or not? At least listen to his story."

Barnabas's trust in Saul (who became Paul) paid off. Barnabas and Paul spent a year together teaching the new church in Antioch. Barnabas and Paul were chosen to carry aid from Antioch to the suffering church in Judea. Barnabas and Paul were set apart by laying on of hands for the first missionary journey. Barnabas and Paul, alone among the other apostles, worked at a trade to support themselves.

When the church of Antioch sent Barnabas and Paul on their first missionary journey, they took Barnabas's cousin, John Mark. For reasons unknown, Mark abandoned the journey at Perga in Pamphylia, their first stop. But it obviously annoyed Paul, because when Barnabas again wanted to bring his young cousin along on a *second* missionary journey, Paul would have none of it.

Let's listen in on what Paul and Barnabas *might* have said to each other....

Another Chance

"Take Mark? You've got to be kidding, Barnabas. He quit on us the last time."

"That was last time, Paul. Let's give him another chance."

"No. He let us down. How do we know he won't do it again?"

"I know. He made a mistake. But he is very eager to redeem himself. Mark has a lot of potential—but he needs mentoring. He would learn so much by coming with us."

"Just because he's your cousin, Barnabas . . ."

"It's not 'just' because he's my cousin. I see good qualities in Mark, if they could be developed. Please. Let him come with us. He could be a great help."

"No. We can't risk it. We need someone we can count on—and that's final."

"I'm . . . sorry you feel that way, Paul. Because I feel responsible for him. This is a critical point in Mark's life. If I stick close to him, I believe he will do great things for the church."

"What are you saying? That you won't go with me unless I take Mark, too?"

"Maybe . . . that would be best, Paul. We could cover twice as much territory if we make two missionary teams. Silas—he'd be a good choice."

"I can't believe this! You have too much faith in that boy, Barnabas."

"Too much? Did I have too much faith in you, Paul—taking a chance when the others didn't want to?"

"That . . . that was different."

"I see."

The Rest of the Story

The rift between Barnabas and Paul must have mended over the years, because Paul mentions him later in his first letter to the Corinthians as a close fellow worker. Ever concerned for his own people, Barnabas returned to Cyprus to encourage the budding church there. And like Paul, Barnabas paid the ultimate price for his faith. A mob killed him without even the pretense of a trial.

Seed of the Church

When someone has faith in us and encourages us, we tend to live up to that person's expectations. How many young people—people who have the potential to be the seed of the church—do we cut off too soon because they made a mistake? Seeds need watering, nurturing, patience. Can people call you an "encourager" like Barnabas?

John Wycliffe

England—December 31, 1384

John Wycliffe was one of Oxford University's last great medieval scholars, and because of the clarity and the popularity of his writings, he has been called "the father of English prose," doing much to shape our language today. In addition to being a priest and theologian, he was an English statesman, once representing King Edward III on the continent in negotiations with the legate of the pope. But he is also called the "morning star of the Reformation" because nearly two hundred years before the Reformation he challenged papal authority and criticized the sale of indulgences and published a series of strong attacks on corruption in the church, where the clergy were often immoral and illiterate and high offices were often bought or given out as political rewards. He also questioned the biblical basis for the doctrines of purgatory and transubstantiation (the belief that after consecration, the bread and wine turn into the actual body and blood of Christ during Communion).

In spite of the fact that Wycliffe declared himself a loyal Catholic, willing to submit his opinions to the judgment of the church, this was the time of the Great Schism (1378–1417) with two, and ultimately three, claimants to the papacy. Authority was uncertain, to say the least, and Wycliffe's positions were too threatening. Finally, church authorities banished him from Oxford University.

But his release from his teaching responsibilities at Oxford enabled Wycliffe to undertake his most lasting contribution, translating (along with some associates) the Bible into English by 1382. He then organized the religious order of the Lollards, itinerant laypreachers, who traveled throughout the countryside reading the Scriptures in English and preaching to the common people—for most, it was their first hearing of the Scriptures.

For Wycliffe, getting the direct message of God's Word into the language and hearts of the people held highest priority. He knew "God's words [would] give men new life." And it did. People thrilled at being able to hear the Scriptures in their own tongue and loved Wycliffe for it. Probably they also appreciated how he had challenged church corruption at a time when the common people often felt that the church had accumulated too much wealth.

Wycliffe's popularity with the people, however, was not enough to restore ecclesiastical goodwill. In 1382, the church banned all of his writing, but his enemies did not physically harm him. Finally, on New Year's Eve 1384, Wycliffe suffered a fatal stroke.

Seed of the Church

Wycliffe's influence was sufficient that forty-four years after his death his enemies succeeded in having him declared a heretic. His body was dug up from consecrated ground and burned, and its ashes were thrown into the Swift River . . . but not before John Hus, in Bohemia, had read Wycliffe's work and was moved to raise some of the same questions and go to the Scriptures for the answers (see John Hus). In turn, John Hus's writings profoundly influenced Martin Luther, known as the father of the German Reformation.

In 1942 a Cakchiquel Indian challenged missionary Cameron Townsend with this question: "If your God is so great, why doesn't He speak in my language?" Townsend recalled how important it had been for John Wycliffe to translate God's Word into English over five centuries earlier, and he the founded Wycliffe Bible Translators, which has since translated the Bible into four hundred languages.

In His Own Words

"God's words will give men new life more than the other words that are for pleasure. O marvelous power of the Divine Seed, which overpowers strong men in arms, softens hard hearts, and renews and changes into divine men, those men who had been brutalized by sins, and departed infinitely from God."

—John Wycliffe

It is the same with my word. I send it out, and it always produces fruit. It will accomplish all I want it to, and it will prosper everywhere I send it (Isaiah 55:11).

Jonathan and Rosalind Goforth
China—July 8, 1900

Born on a Canadian farm in February 10, 1859, Jonathan Goforth wore shabby clothes and didn't understand city ways when he arrived at Knox College in Toronto, Canada. But there he met and married Rosalind Bell Smith, an attractive and well-educated woman who had been raised in London, in a wealthy English family.

In 1888, the Goforths sailed for China where Jonathan found the Chinese language particularly difficult to learn as they attempted to adjust to a new culture. Over the years, they had eleven children only to suffer the sorrow of seeing five of them die very young.

A powerful evangelist, Jonathan became known as the "flaming preacher," sometimes speaking to as many as twenty-five thousand at a time. But the Goforths also used what they called "open-house" evangelism, inviting the curious Chinese people into their home to view their Western ways and kitchen stove, sewing machine, and organ. But before they would take a group of fifty people through the house, Rosalind would preach to the woman, and Jonathan would preach to the men. In this way, they made many converts.

The Fist of Righteous Harmony

By 1900 an organized uprising known to the West as the Boxer Rebellion and in China as the "Fist of Righteous Harmony" had spread throughout China. Its purpose was to drive all foreigners from the country. Even the Chinese empress encouraged it because Japanese and Western outsiders seemed to be taking over the country.

In June of that year, the Goforths had no sooner buried their fourth child, seven-year-old Florence, when they received a message from the American Consul in Chefoo saying, "Flee south. Northern route cut off by Boxers." The terrors and horrors of the infamous Boxer Rebellion were descending. The missionaries were in favor of staying at their post regardless of the consequences, but the Chinese Christians made it clear that their own chances of survival would be greatly reduced if the missionaries remained.

So the Goforths and other missionary families set out in ten heavily laden carts on the thousand-mile journey across China to safety. For a time they hooked up with a group of European engineers also fleeing the country, but when the missionaries couldn't travel fast enough, the engineers left them in the walled town of Hsintien. A mob gathered outside the door of their inn and battered it with stones, threatening to break in. Threats of "Kill! Kill! Kill!" continued all night. In the morning (July 8), the crowd was even larger. Jonathan had to sign a contract promising to pay for any injuries or damage to the carts or mules before the drivers would travel.

Outside the city, the crowd of thousands parted for their advance until they were in its middle. Then, led by the Boxers, they attacked the missionary caravan. Jonathan jumped out yelling, "Take everything, but don't kill! Take everything, but don't kill! Take everything, but—" He didn't get the last words out of his mouth before someone hit him on the head with a stick. A huge Boxer waded through the brawl swinging his two-handed sword from side to side. He didn't seem to have any particular target until the broad edge of his sword struck Jonathan on the side of his neck. Had it been the sharp edge, it would have cut off his head. Instead, it knocked the missionary to the ground. The next swing caught the brim of Jonathan's pith helmet, slicing right through it but not touching his head. Jonathan staggered to his feet and tried to lunge out of range, but the sword caught him on the back of the head, knocking him to the ground in a great cloud of dust.

As the attackers turned attention to raiding the wagons, the missionaries worked their way through the crowd—with Jonathan being the last one to crawl out of the melee—and made their way to a near-by Muslim village that finally took them in because, as the villagers reluctantly conceded, "Our God is your God."

Seed of the Church

When the Goforths returned to China about a year later, they changed their approach to a traveling evangelistic ministry that produced more than thirteen thousand converts by 1913. They remained in China until 1934 when poor health forced them to return to Canada. In addition to their many converts, they trained sixty-one full-time Chinese evangelists and Bible teachers and established thirty mission stations.

The Lord is my strength and my shield (Psalm 28:7, NIV; recited by Jonathan to encourage his family the night before the attack).

Ricky Byrdsong
Chicago—July 3, 1999

On the day Ricky Byrdsong was shot, he was in a spiritual zone of total dedication to God and willingness to die as a martyr if it came to that . . . and it did! July 4 weekend 1999, Benjamin Smith went on a three-day rampage across two states, shot at twenty-six people, hit twelve, and killed two before fatally turning his guns on himself.

Ricky Byrdsong, former head coach for the Northwestern University Basketball team and Won-Joon Yoon, a Korean Christian coming out of his church in Bloomington, Indiana, both died.

Some would say that Byrdsong was tragically in the wrong place (a block from his quiet suburban home) at the wrong time (walking with his kids) when a deranged person "went off." But most recognize that the shooting spree was more intentional than that—all the victims were either Jews or people of color, and Smith was an avowed white supremacist associated with the anti-Christian World Church of the Creator, a group linked to several other murders around the country.

While Byrdsong was absolutely dedicated to God, the WCOTC is just as dedicated to stamping out Christianity and all but the white race. (They hate Christianity because they think loving one's enemies weakens the white race.)

This set the stage for a spiritual battle with physical consequences. So, while Ben Smith may have thought he was shooting Byrdsong because he was black (and others because of their race), the Evil One—through willing, though possibly ignorant agents—launched an attack on Good in the form of God's servant, Ricky Byrdsong. In the spiritual realm, this also was no random act.

His wife, Sherialyn, left with three children to raise, could barely think about *why* Ricky had been shot. Just because he was *black*? It didn't make sense! Her husband was working at a job he loved, motivating kids to become all God meant for them to be. His kids needed their dad. They lived in a quiet, affluent suburban neighborhood. And just two weeks earlier a publisher had agreed to accept Ricky's book on parenting.

At the same time, she knew why. The stronghold of evil was in a spiritual war with the kingdom of God, and the Evil One had scored a victory by eliminating a man who was influencing others for good, who had gotten to the place in his life where "nothing else mattered" other than living for God. "In the twenty years I've been a Christian," Sherialyn Byrdsong said later, "all the Scripture I've studied and all the worship songs I've ever learned were like deposits into my heart. Now I'm making withdrawals big time."

An emotional and heartbroken congregation listened the following Sunday morning as the Byrdsongs' pastor said, "We're all asking, 'Why Coach?' I'll tell you why. Because Coach was *ready*." It was a reminder of the sermon Byrdsong had been asked to preach as a guest speaker . . . not that long before his death.

In His Own Words

"Don't you know that I had to come to that in my own life? Don't you know that they didn't want me talking about God to the basketball team? Don't you know that I had to say, 'But it doesn't matter now'? Don't you know that they didn't want me having Bible study in my own office with my own staff? But I said, 'It doesn't matter now.' Don't you know that they'd rather that I not quote any Scriptures to the newspaper? I was a coach of a major institution, and my words were going everywhere. They wanted me to keep that kind of talk in the church. But I had to get to the point where I said, 'It doesn't matter now.'"

—Ricky Byrdsong, September 21, 1998

Are *you* that ready?

When our perishable earthly bodies have been transformed into heavenly bodies that will never die—then at last the Scriptures will come true: "Death is swallowed up in victory. O death, where is your victory? O death, where is your sting?" For sin is the sting that results in death, and the law gives sin its power. How we thank God, who gives us victory over sin and death through Jesus Christ our Lord! (1 Corinthians 15:54-57).

Part 1

Into All the World: The Establishment of the Early Church

Before returning to heaven, Jesus told his disciples, "Go into all the world and preach the Good News to everyone, everywhere" (Mark 16:15).

Nothing has brought more persecution to Christians than their efforts to obey this command. In fact, except for the Reformation, all major waves of persecution of Christians throughout the centuries correspond to the church's evangelistic surges or a counter attack to earlier evangelism.

Jesus wisely warned his followers that this would be the case:

> Beware! For you will be handed over to the courts and beaten. . . . And you must stand trial before governors and kings because you are my followers. This will be your opportunity to tell them about me—yes, to witness to the world. When you are arrested, don't worry about what to say in your defense, because you will be given the right words at the right time. For it won't be you doing the talking—it will be the Spirit of your Father speaking through you.
>
> Brother will betray brother to death, fathers will betray their own children, and children will rise against their parents and cause them to be killed. And everyone will hate you because of your allegiance to me. But those who endure to the end will be saved (Matthew 10:17-22).

Jesus said, "*When* you are arrested" (emphasis added), with no question in his mind that this would be the fate of his followers. But he also identified the reason: "Everyone will hate you because of your allegiance to me" (v. 22).

In the book of Acts, we read that the church grew from 120 to 3,000, then 5,000 men (not including women and children). Then "crowds of both men and women" joined. At several points thereafter, we read, "the number of believers greatly increased." Some estimates suggest there may have been as many as 20,000 believers in Jerusalem at the time of Stephen's martyrdom and the subsequent persecution from which "all the believers except the apostles fled. . . . But the believers who had fled Jerusalem went everywhere preaching the Good News about Jesus" (Acts 8:1, 4).

Persecution followed them just as Jesus had predicted it would, first in the form of Saul of Tarsus and his posse tracking down and arresting Christians to bring them back to Jerusalem for imprisonment, and then as both

13

Jews and pagans resisted the gospel in the towns and cities around the Mediterranean to which the Christians had fled.

After Herod executed James (Acts 12:2), the apostles and other leaders also dispersed from Jerusalem. Tradition (and in some cases Scripture) identify these destinations:

- Andrew . . . . .Achaia
- Antipas . . . . .Turkey
- Barnabas . . . . .Cyprus
- Bartholomew . . . . . .Caspian Sea
- James the Greater. . .Spain
- John . . . . .Ephesus
- Jude Thaddeus. . . . .Persia
- Luke. . . . . .Greece
- Mark. . . . . .Egypt
- Matthew . . . . .Ethiopia
- Matthias. . . . . .Ethiopia
- Paul and Peter . . . . .Rome
- Philip . . . . .Hierapolis
- Simon the Zealot . . .Syria
- Thomas . . . . .India
- Timothy . . . . .Ephesus

Rome was remarkably tolerant of foreign religions but not of any perceived threat to its authority. Though law-abiding by precept, Christians faced two problems. First, Rome tested the loyalty of its subjects by requiring emperor worship, and faithful Christians refused to worship any false gods. Second, Christians went even further. They declared Jesus their King (Acts 17:7), which was seen as a direct challenge to Rome.

Nevertheless, intense persecution was not constant during the reign of the fifty-four Roman emperors from A.D. 30 to A.D. 311. Instead, it came in waves or at the whim of regional governors. In fact, it wasn't until A.D. 249–251 that Emperor Decius made an empirewide attempt to wipe out Christianity. The emperors most responsible for persecuting Christians were . . .

- **Claudius (A.D. 41–54).** Expelled the Jews from Rome in 52. Christians were seen at that time as a Jewish sect and therefore caught up in the purge.
- **Nero (A.D. 54–68).** This madman tried to blame the Christians for the fire that resulted from his own neglect and swept Rome in 64. A large number of believers were executed, possibly including Paul, Peter, Aristarchus, Epaphras, Priscilla and Aquila, Andronicus and Juina, Silas, Onesiphorus, and Porphyrius.
- **Domitian (A.D. 81–96).** John may have been describing Rome under this emperor as the "Mother of Harlots . . . drunk with the blood of the saints and with the blood of the martyrs of Jesus" (Revelation 17:5-6, NKJV).

- **Trajan (A.D. 98–117).** Wrote that Christians were "not to be hunted out. [Although] any who are accused and convicted should be punished, with the proviso that if a man says he is not a Christian and makes it obvious by his actual conduct—namely, by worshipping our gods—then, however suspect he may have been with regard to the past, he should gain pardon from his repentance."
- **Marcus Aurelius (A.D. 161–180).** Was responsible for the forty-eight "Martyrs of Lyons" in 177.
- **Septimius Severus (A.D. 193–211).** In 203, Perpetua and Felicitas were among the many believers martyred in the arena under this emperor.
- **Decius (A.D. 249–251).** In an attempt to shore up a faltering empire, he attempted to purge it of "disloyal" subjects by requiring pagan religious observances. That broad net, of course, challenged all Christians, including Fabian, the bishop of Rome, who was martyred in 250.
- **Valerian (A.D. 253–260).** Attempted to divert attention from Rome's decline by blaming the empire's troubles on the Christians. Following Decius's example, he required everyone to sacrifice to the gods. Origen, Cyprian, and Deacon Lawrence lost their lives during this persecution.
- **Diocletian (A.D. 284–305).** Mounted possibly the most organized attempt to wipe out Christianity in his attempt to restore the empire. The massacre of the Theban Legion and the martyrdom of Agape, Irene, and Chionia; Andronicus, Probus, and Tarachus; Alban; and Agnes were among scores of others that occurred during this period.
- **Maximinus (A.D. 308–313).** Was defeated by Emperor Licinius, with whom he had ruled the eastern half of the Roman Empire, and died soon after. By this time more than 700,000 Coptic Christians had been killed.[1]

Approximately a hundred years earlier, Tertullian in his *Apology* had written, "The oftener we are mown down by you, the more in number we grow; the blood of Christians is seed," and certainly that was proving true throughout the Roman Empire. By 311, many executioners had literally grown tired from all their work. Galerius, successor to Diocletian, finally admitted defeat in trying to stamp out Christianity.

The dousing of the flames was greatly aided by Constantine, who in an attempt to gain control of the empire, tried to eliminate his rivals. One night he had a vision of a glowing cross in the sky bearing the words, "Conquer by this." He interpreted it as a good omen and had the conjoined letters *P* and *X* (used by the early church to represent Christ) emblazoned on his imperial banner. On October 28, 312, he defeated Maxentius at the Milvian Bridge, a dozen miles up the Tiber from Rome, and thereby became sole master of the Western Empire. His victory favorably inclined him toward Christianity (though he resisted baptism until a few days before his death in 337), and he issued the Edict of Milan in 313, which mandated toleration of Christians.

Though Licinius, then emperor in the East, subscribed to the edict, he continued vigorous persecution of Christians in the East for a season. However, by A.D. 324, Constantine was sole emperor and the flames of persecution were almost out.

Coping with the Aftermath of Persecution

Believing that Christianity would die out if its leaders were killed, imprisoned, or banished, the Roman government initially targeted the bishops, pastors, and other leaders, leaving pagan mobs to attack the common church members. One report describes the fate of Quinta, a female convert: "Next [the mob took her] to the idol's temple and tried to make her worship. When she turned her back in disgust, they tied her feet and dragged her right through the city over the rough paved road, bumping her on the great stones and beating her as they went, till they arrived at the same place, where they stoned her to death. Then they ran in a body to the houses of the Christians, charged in by groups on those they knew as neighbors, raided, plundered, and looted."[2]

As has been true throughout the history of the church, some believers in the early church could not stand such pressure and compromised their faith. However, once the persecution subsided, many desired reinstatement in the church. What was the church to do with those who had lapsed in their faith?

During the first centuries, the church did not quickly grant forgiveness to those who had apostatized or committed such grievous sins as murder and adultery. Penance was public and lasted a long time, and those who were welcomed back into the fellowship were received "as though they had risen from the dead," said Origen. No clergy who sinned grossly were admitted again to their office.

However, during the "great persecutions" of the middle and end of the third century, thousands—possibly the majority of Christians—sacrificed to false gods and received a *libellus*, a receipt certifying their compliance with government edicts. Others bribed officials for a *libellus* even though they hadn't sacrificed. Consequently, the churches had to agonize over what policy to practice with those desiring reinstatement, especially after others had endured torture or death for refusing to apostatize.[3]

In Spain, where persecution had been severe and feelings ran high, the Council of Elvira excommunicated those who had actually sacrificed to pagan gods while they reinstated after penance some novitiates who had only purchased a *libellus*.

In Asia Minor the church was more tolerant, saying the laity could be readmitted after a period of three to five years of penance. Some lapsed clergy were allowed to keep their office but not to celebrate the sacrament.

In Rome a bitter struggle persisted between followers of Novatian—who had no mercy for those who had denied Christ under persecution—and Bishop Miltiades (and other bishops) who were more forgiving.

In Egypt, Bishop Peter of Alexandria recommended leniency so the church wouldn't completely lose those who had lapsed, while Bishop Meletius wanted severe punishment so the church wouldn't lose its integrity. This disagreement ultimately led to a split in the Egyptian church.

The North African church also split over the issue, though it was more sharply focused on those who had surrendered the Scriptures.

Seeds of Bloody Conflict

The seeds of bloody conflict were sprouting *within* the church as well.

The acquisition and preservation of wealth. By the end of the fourth century, the church was sufficiently accepted within the empire to become politically powerful and wealthy. Benefiting from imperial buildings donated to the church for religious use, this period began an extensive building program with impressive churches springing up throughout the empire.

The centralization of authority. The "Catechism of the Catholic Church" asserts, "The Pope, Bishop of Rome and Peter's successor, is the perpetual and visible source and foundation of the unity both of the bishops and of the whole company of the faithful. For the Roman Pontiff, by reason of his office as Vicar of Christ and as pastor of the entire Church, has full, supreme, and universal power over the whole Church, a power which he can always exercise unhindered."[4] However, in the New Testament church, it appears that though the apostles encouraged, debated, and even admonished one another (cf. Paul to Peter, Galatians 2:11), they did not presume to rule over one another.

While Bishop Clement of Rome wrote a letter correcting the church in Corinth in A.D. 96, it does not prove he had any more churchwide authority than did the apostle John or than Paul had some thirty years before, who exercised apostolic oversight far more actively than did Peter.

About a hundred years later, when Bishop Victor of Rome declared that Easter should be celebrated on Sunday rather than Nisan 14, whichever day of the week it fell, most other bishops went along, but not the churches in Asia Minor. They said no.

In fact, it wasn't until the issue of repentant apostates arose that the bishop of Rome really attempted to assert authority over the other bishops. However, their lack of responsiveness to Rome's authority is evident in the variety of regional policies previously outlined. Still, the authority of the bishop of Rome was consolidating and growing.

The reliance on force. The church also enjoyed the protection of the state and then began collaborating with the state in wielding the sword against "heretics."

All three of these seeds become bloody points of contention a thousand years later.

Notes

1. David Barrett and Todd Johnson, *World Christian Trends* (Pasadena, Calif.: William Carey Library, 2001), global diagram 4.
2. Eusebius of Caesarea, *Ecclesiastical History*, vol. 6, 40:1–42:6.
3. "Persecution in the Early Church," *Christian History* 27 (1997).
4. *Catechism of the Catholic Church*, par. 882, Vatican II.

The Witnesses

Azariah, Hananiah, and Mishael

Babylon—ca. 600 B.C.

Nebuchadnezzar, king of Babylon, conquered Judah in 605 B.C. To demonstrate his dominance, he took thousands of Jerusalem's wisest men and most beautiful women to Babylon as captives. Hananiah, Mishael, and Azariah were among them. Daniel 3 calls them by their Babylonian names: Shadrach, Meshach, and Abednego.

"I See Four Men"

King Nebuchadnezzar made a gold statue ninety feet tall and nine feet wide and set it up on the plain of Dura in the province of Babylon. Then he sent messages to the princes, prefects, governors, advisers, counselors, judges, magistrates, and all the provincial officials to come to the dedication of the statue he had set up. When all these officials had arrived and were standing before the image King Nebuchadnezzar had set up, a herald shouted out, "People of all races and nations and languages, listen to the king's command! When you hear the sound of the horn, flute, zither, lyre, harp, pipes, and other instruments, bow to the ground to worship King Nebuchadnezzar's gold statue. Anyone who refuses to obey will immediately be thrown into a blazing furnace."

So at the sound of the musical instruments, all the people, whatever their race or nation or language, bowed to the ground and worshiped the statue that King Nebuchadnezzar had set up.

But some of the astrologers went to the king and informed on the Jews. They said to King Nebuchadnezzar, "Long live the king! You issued a decree requiring all the people to bow down and worship the gold statue when they hear the sound of the musical instruments. That decree also states that those who refuse to obey must be thrown into a blazing furnace. But there are some Jews—Shadrach, Meshach, and Abednego—whom you have put in charge of the province of Babylon. They have defied Your Majesty by refusing to serve your gods or to worship the gold statue you have set up."

Then Nebuchadnezzar flew into a rage and ordered Shadrach, Meshach, and Abednego to be brought before him. When they were brought in, Nebuchadnezzar said to them, "Is it true, Shadrach, Meshach, and Abednego, that you refuse to serve my gods or to worship the gold statue I have set up? I will give you one more chance. If you bow down and worship the statue I have made when you hear the sound of the musical instruments, all will be well. But if you refuse, you will be thrown immediately into the blazing furnace. What god will be able to rescue you from my power then?"

Shadrach, Meshach, and Abednego replied, "O Nebuchadnezzar, we do not need to defend ourselves before you. If we are thrown into the blazing furnace, the God whom we serve is able to save us. He will rescue us from your power, Your Majesty. But even if he doesn't, Your Majesty can be sure that we will never serve your gods or worship the gold statue you have set up."

Nebuchadnezzar was so furious with Shadrach, Meshach, and Abednego that his face became distorted with rage. He commanded that the furnace be heated seven times hotter than usual. Then he ordered some of the strongest men of his army to bind Shadrach, Meshach, and Abednego and throw them into the blazing furnace. So they tied them up and threw them into the furnace, fully clothed. And because the king, in his anger, had demanded such a hot fire in the furnace, the flames leaped out and killed the soldiers as they threw the three men in! So Shadrach, Meshach, and Abednego, securely tied, fell down into the roaring flames.

But suddenly, as he was watching, Nebuchadnezzar jumped up in amazement and exclaimed to his advisers, "Didn't we tie up three men and throw them into the furnace?"

"Yes," they said, "we did indeed, Your Majesty."

"Look!" Nebuchadnezzar shouted. "I see four men, unbound, walking around in the fire. They aren't even hurt by the flames! And the fourth looks like a divine being!"

Then Nebuchadnezzar came as close as he could to the door of the flaming furnace and shouted: "Shadrach, Meshach, and Abednego, servants of the Most High God, come out! Come here!" So Shadrach, Meshach, and Abednego stepped out of the fire. Then the princes, prefects, governors, and advisers crowded around them and saw that the fire had not touched them. Not a hair on their heads was singed, and their clothing was not scorched. They didn't even smell of smoke! (Daniel 3:1-27).

The Innocent Children of Bethlehem

Judea—after the birth of Jesus, honored December 28

Seeing the star that announced the birth of Jesus Christ in Judea, wise men from the East came to pay him homage. But because they did not know the exact location, the wise men stopped in Jerusalem to ask King Herod where the child had been born. After consulting the leading priests, Herod told the wise men that the prophets predicted the Messiah would be born in the insignificant town of Bethlehem. Then, before sending the wise men on their way to find the child, Herod instructed them to return and inform him of the child's exact location, "so that I can go and worship him, too!"

The wise men found the child in Bethlehem, exactly where the prophets foretold and worshipped him, but they returned to their home in the East by a different route, avoiding Jerusalem and not informing Herod of Jesus' whereabouts because "God had warned them in a dream not to return to Herod."

Meanwhile, the Lord appeared to Jesus' father, Joseph, in a dream and told him to flee with Jesus and his mother to Egypt because Herod intended to kill the child. Matthew's Gospel then tells us in chapter 2, beginning with verse 16,

> Herod was furious when he learned that the wise men had outwitted him. He sent soldiers to kill all the boys in and around Bethlehem who were two years old and under, because the wise men had told him the star first appeared to them about two years earlier. Herod's brutal action fulfilled the prophecy of Jeremiah: "A cry of anguish is heard in Ramah—weeping and mourning unrestrained. Rachel weeps for her children, refusing to be comforted—for they are dead."

We do not know the number of innocent children exterminated nor the exact date. Ancient estimates range from 14,000 to 64,000 to as many as 144,000 babies massacred. While ruthless slaughter characterized Herod's paranoia— he murdered many people for political reasons, including his own son and other relatives—Bethlehem was a rather small village, so it is unlikely that the true numbers approached any of the ancient estimates, even when the surrounding countryside was included . . . unless Herod's wrath spread well beyond the what we might imagine as the immediate environs of Bethlehem.

While Bethlehem is about five miles south of Jerusalem, the scope of grief prophesied by Jeremiah reached as far as Ramah, five miles north of Jerusalem, the town where Isaac's wife Rachel had been buried. If this entire region was included in Herod's slaughter, then the carnage could have approached some of the ancient estimates. In any case, the devastation to the families and the magnitude of the crime were so great that a wail of inconsolable anguish spread like winter fog through the region.

These innocent children were the first to die explicitly because of the name of Christ. They may not have declared their allegiance to him or been given the opportunity to renounce him to save themselves, but they died for him, nonetheless. In fact, they died not only for him but also in his stead, just as he would later die in their place—and ours—on the cross.

God showed how much he loved us by sending his only Son into the world so that we might have eternal life through him. This is real love. It is not that we loved God, but that he loved us and sent his Son as a sacrifice to take away our sins. Dear friends, since God loved us that much, we surely ought to love each other. No one has ever seen

God. But if we love each other, God lives in us, and his love has been brought to full expression through us (1 John 4:9-12).

John the Baptist

Jerusalem — ca. 28, honored June 24

In dramatic content, the birth of John is an appropriate prelude to the miraculous virgin birth of his cousin, Jesus, Israel's long-awaited Messiah. John's father, Zechariah, a priest, was visited by an angel and told that he and his barren wife, Elizabeth, would have a child in their old age, and that this child would prepare the people for the coming of the Messiah. Because Zechariah did not immediately believe the angel (who could really blame him!), he could not speak until the child was born.

From the beginning, John was set apart. He prepared for his role in the desert, eating only what the desert provided, wearing rough clothes of camel's hair, learning to subject himself to God's leading. When it was time to begin his ministry, he preached repentance of sins and living justly: "Prove by the way you live that you have really turned from your sins! . . . If you have two coats, give one to the poor . . . [Tax collectors,] make sure you collect no more taxes than the Roman government requires you to. . . . [Soldiers,] don't extort money, and don't accuse people of things you know they didn't do. And be content with your pay" (Luke 3:11-14).

John was a practical preacher. He invited his listeners to make a public witness of their repentance by the rite of baptism—right there in the muddy Jordan River.

Some people thought John might be the Christ, but he clearly insisted he was only preparing the way. "I baptize with water. . . . But someone is coming soon who is far greater than I am. . . . He will baptize you with the Holy Spirit" (Matthew 3:11). When Jesus showed up on the riverbank one day to be baptized, John cried out, "Look! There is the Lamb of God who takes away the sin of the world!" (John 2:29). At this point, John had basically fulfilled his ministry, while Jesus' ministry was just beginning.

A Deadly Promise

John was nothing if not consistent. When he preached, he took on publicans and kings. King Herod Antipas to be specific. Herod had jettisoned his first wife and married Herodias, the wife of his half-brother Philip. John publicly criticized the king for his public adultery . . . and ended up in the king's prison.

Herodias was furious; she wanted John put to death. But Herod hesitated; what if the people were right and this man was a prophet, sent by God? So John languished in prison, caught in the middle of a lover's quarrel.

As weeks and months went by, John began to wonder. He *thought* Jesus was the Promised One of Israel. But maybe he had misunderstood. The Romans were still in control; he was sitting in Herod's prison; what was happening here? So he sent his disciples to respectfully ask Jesus, "Are you really the Messiah [the Savior] we've been waiting for, or should we keep looking for someone else?"

Jesus sent them back with the message: "Tell [John] what you have heard and seen—the blind see, the lame walk, the lepers are cured, the deaf hear, the dead are raised to life, and the Good News is being preached to the poor" (Matthew 11:3-5). John was satisfied.

An odd relationship developed: Herod often brought John out of prison to talk with him. The things John said disturbed him, but he developed a deep respect for John, and "kept him under his protection." But Herodias knew her husband's weaknesses. During Herod's birthday party, she sent her daughter to dance for him, knowing he would be dazzled. Sure enough, Herod foolishly told the girl, "Ask me anything you want up to half my kingdom—I'll give it to you!" At her mother's bidding, the girl asked for the head of John the Baptist . . . on a platter.

Herod was afraid to kill the prophet—but he was even more afraid to break his promise in front of all his guests. Soldiers were dispatched to the prison, who soon returned with the bloody head of the Baptist and gave it to the girl, who gave it to her gloating mother. When John's disciples heard what had happened, they came to the prison, took his body, and buried him with great sorrow.

In His Own Words

"He must become greater; I must become less."

—John 3:30 (NIV), John the Baptist, when his disciples complained
That more people were starting to follow Jesus than him.

Stephen the Deacon

Jerusalem—ca. 35, honored December 26

Stephen is often called the first Christian martyr, though the martyrdoms of John the Baptist and Jesus himself must also be counted among the first. His life and death are told in vivid detail in the Acts of the Apostles, chapters 6–8.

Like every religious group from the beginning until now, the mushrooming New Testament church soon broke into factions. The Grecian believers grumbled against the Jewish believers, saying that their widows weren't receiving the daily food baskets given to the needy. Wisely, the apostles delegated this responsibility, choosing Stephen and six other men who were "full of the Holy Spirit and wisdom" (Acts 6:3) to make sure no one got overlooked.

Stephen is described as a man "full of God's grace and power" (Acts 6:8). He knew the Scriptures well; he was an eloquent speaker; his ministry was accompanied by miracles and signs. Why was he assigned to wait on tables? Stephen did not complain. He accepted the responsibility as an opportunity, a time of training. His desire to serve Christ was translated into a willingness to serve others. At the same time, he was always ready to talk about Jesus. . . .

Ready with an Answer

The trouble began when a group of Jewish freedmen—former slaves who had formed their own synagogue—challenged Stephen to a debate. But Stephen always won. He had a passion for his proposition: that the promised Messiah had come!

Unable to talk him down, his disgruntled debaters persuaded some men (money is a great persuader) to tell lies about Stephen. "We heard him blaspheme Moses, and even God" (Acts 6:11). It didn't take long for Stephen to find himself arrested and on trial before the Jewish supreme court—the Sanhedrin. To their credit, the court gave Stephen an opportunity to speak in his own defense.

Once more Stephen turned an opening into an opportunity. Starting at the beginning, back when God gave a promise to Abraham, Stephen walked his listeners through the Scriptures, touching on the stories of Abraham, Isaac, Jacob, Joseph, slavery in Egypt, Moses the deliverer, the forty years in the wilderness, entering the Promised Land, King David, and the son of David who would one day rule on his throne. So far so good.

But when he called them "stubborn people" who were "deaf to the truth" (Acts 7:51), and accused them of resisting the Holy Spirit and murdering God's Promised One, the council members were filled with rage. *They* stood accused and the only way to escape the truth was to drown out the words of the accuser. Can you picture it? They stopped their ears with their fingers and, yelling at the top of their lungs, dragged Stephen out of the city and began throwing stones at him.

As the heavy stones beat upon his body, Stephen still had the last word. With a loud voice he cried out, "Lord, do not hold this sin against them!" and "Lord Jesus, receive my spirit!" (Acts 7:59-60, paraphrased).

How infuriating to be forgiven by the man you want to be wrong! Scripture says the whole city went berserk: "A great wave of persecution began that day" (Acts 8:1).

Seed of the Church

"The witnesses laid their clothes at the feet of a young man named Saul. . . . Saul began to destroy the church" (Acts 7:58; 8:3, NIV). Stephen's death was the beginning not only of a great persecution against the church but also of God's redemptive work in the life of one of the great apostles.

Always be prepared to give an answer to everyone who asks you to give the reason for the hope that you have (1 Peter 3:15, NIV).

James, "Son of Thunder"

Judea — ca. 44, honored July 25

We always hear them mentioned together in the Gospels: James and John, sons of Zebedee, partners in the fishing business with Simon Peter and Andrew. Though the brothers' names usually appear together, James is always named first, as the elder brother. Their mother, Salome, was possibly a sister or sister-in-law of Mary, mother of Jesus. She herself became one of the faithful women who followed Jesus and ministered to him.

These brothers had a nickname: *Boanerges,* or "sons of thunder"! What qualities earned them such a name? They were nothing if not bold, assertive, energetic, impetuous, once-committed-in-with-both-feet. Jesus obviously saw potential in these cousins of his: He called them to "come, follow me." James and John were not only counted among the twelve disciples but along with Peter also composed the "inner circle" that Jesus took with him up on the mountain to witness his transfiguration, into the house when he raised Jairus's daughter, and deeper into the garden of Gethsemane to "watch" with him, because his soul was "crushed with grief to the point of death" (Matthew 26:38).

Like many with strong character qualities, the "sons of thunder" succumbed to their own self-importance. We find a revealing story in Matthew 20.

A Mother's Appeal

Salome can perhaps be forgiven for making such a bold request. Wasn't her own sister the mother of Jesus, the Christ? Weren't her sons his cousins? Hadn't he called them to be among his chosen disciples? Weren't they two of his closest confidents?

When Jesus saw his kinswoman coming, flanked by her two strapping sons—grown men with the energy and enthusiasm of adolescent boys—he stopped to welcome her. She knelt respectfully at his feet, a traditional cue that she had come to make a request.

"What is your request?" Jesus said kindly.

The woman rose and spoke boldly. (Did the "sons of thunder" take after their mother?) In your Kingdom, will you let my two sons sit in places of honor next to you, one at your right and the other at your left?" (Matthew 20:21).

Oh, how Jesus' heart must have ached for the woman—not so much that she asked, but because *she had no idea what she was asking!* He turned to James and his brother John. "Are you able to drink from the bitter cup of sorrow I am about to drink?" (v. 22). What he meant was, *Are you able to suffer in the way I am about to suffer?*

It seemed like a requirement, a prerequisite. James and John didn't know exactly what Jesus meant, but hadn't they been faithful thus far? "Oh yes," they replied, "we are able!" (v. 22).

Jesus nodded. "You will indeed drink from it—but I have no right to say who will sit on the thrones next to mine. My Father has prepared these places for the ones he has chosen" (20:23) The other disciples were indignant. The nerve of those two! But Jesus had something to teach them all: "Whoever wants to be a leader among you must be your servant . . . even I, the Son of Man, came not to be served, but to serve and to give my life as a ransom for many" (20:26-28).

"You will indeed drink from it." It was a prophecy that came true for all of the disciples. But James, the elder "son of thunder," was the first to lay down his life for his Lord. In A.D. 44, he was beheaded by King Herod Agrippa, under orders from Claudius, the Roman emperor, to suppress the followers of Jesus. According to early historians, the executioner was so moved by James's steadfast faith in the Savior that he proclaimed his own faith in Jesus, the Christ, on the spot. The authorities were so enraged by this, that they executed the man along with James, right then and there.

In giving his life, James won another soul for God's kingdom.

[Jesus said,] "Whoever wants to be first must become your slave. For even I, the Son of Man, came here not to be served but to serve others, and to give my life as a ransom for many" (Matthew 20:27-28).

Philip the Apostle

Hierapolis — ca. 52, honored May 1

Philip was one of the first to be called by Christ to be a disciple (and should not be confused with Philip the deacon in Acts, known as "the Evangelist"). Unlike some of the "blue-collar" disciples, Philip was well educated in the law and had an expectant heart for the coming of the Messiah. When Jesus found him in Bethsaida, in Galilee (also Peter and Andrew's hometown) and gave him an invitation—"Come, be my disciple" (John 1:43)—Philip had an interesting reaction: He immediately hunted up his friend Nathanael (also called Bartholomew), with whom he had probably had many fascinating discussions about the prophecies of a Messiah. "We have found the very person Moses and the prophets wrote about! His name is Jesus, the son of Joseph from Nazareth!" (John 1:45).

Philip's mind knew the Scriptures; his spirit was hungry to see the Lord's promised One; his heart was ready.

Throughout the Gospels, Philip seems to have enjoyed a trusted position among the disciples and a close relationship with Jesus. When Jesus was preaching to a crowd of thousands near Philip's hometown, he turned to Philip with the question "Where can we buy bread to feed all these people?" (John 6:5). Jesus was testing his eager disciple, who knew good and well it would take a small fortune to feed all these people, even if he could find a bakery with enough loaves on the shelves!

Philip was also respected among the Greeks, several of whom came to him first when they wanted to meet Jesus.

Little is known about Philip after the death and resurrection of Christ, except that he took the Good News into Phrygia, where he encountered severe opposition. Early historians do not seem to agree on how he suffered his martyrdom. Some say his head was bound to a pillar, then stoned; others say he was crucified. Some combine the two sources and say he was first stoned and then crucified, or stoned while hanging on a cross.

Hungry for God

What a strange evening. Philip hardly knew what to make of it! He and the other disciples had celebrated the Passover meal with Jesus, and Jesus—of all people!—had washed their feet like a common servant. What perplexing things Jesus had said and done during the meal:

"Since I, the Lord and Teacher, have washed your feet, you ought to wash each other's feet" (John 13:14). (Philip was prepared to follow Jesus to the death if need be—but he wasn't so sure about washing the stinking feet of the other disciples.)

"The truth is, one of you will betray me" (John 13:21). (Betray Jesus? Unthinkable! Who among them could do such a terrible thing?)

Right in the middle of the meal, Jesus had given Judas Iscariot a piece of bread, then said, "Hurry. Do it now" (John 13:27). (Do what? They were right in the middle of Passover! Judas held their common purse—was he supposed to buy something? But all the shops would be closed!)

And Peter! Jesus outright told Peter, "Before the rooster crows tomorrow morning, you will deny three times that you even know me" (John 13:38). *(Not me, Lord, not me. I could never disown you . . . could I?)*

But what was Jesus saying now? "I am the way, the truth, and the life. No one can come to the Father except through me" (John 14:6).

Philip's heart was about to burst. All his life he had hungered to know God—really know him! And Jesus, this Jesus who kept talking about going away, had brought him closer to knowing God than he had ever dreamed possible. And yet . . . he knew there was more.

"Lord," Philip blurted, "show us the Father and we will be satisfied" (John 14:8).

Why did Jesus look at him so sadly? "Philip, don't you even yet know who I am, even after all the time I have been with you? Anyone who has seen me has seen the Father!" (John 14:9).

[Jesus said] Blessed are those who hunger and thirst for righteousness, for they will be filled" (Matthew 5:6, NIV).

Andrew the Apostle

Achaia—ca. 60, honored November 30

Every time we meet Andrew in the New Testament Gospel accounts, he is bringing someone to Jesus. A fisherman by trade, he was initially a disciple of John the Baptist, along with John, the younger son of Zebedee. When Jesus began his public ministry, the Baptist said, "Look! There is the Lamb of God who takes away the sin of the world! He is the one I was talking about" (John 1:29-30). Immediately Andrew and John ran after Jesus and spent several hours talking with him. Convinced that this was indeed the Promised One, Andrew hunted up his younger brother Simon (later called Peter) saying, "We have found the Messiah!" And he brought his brother to meet Jesus (see John 1:41-42).

Later, as one of Jesus' twelve disciples, Andrew was present when a huge crowd came to hear him speak (see John 6:1-15). "Feed these people," Jesus said, testing his disciples to see if their faith had grown after witnessing the many miracles he had already done. But, like most of us would be in that situation, they were astonished, and they thought he was asking the impossible. Andrew, however, brought to Jesus a young boy who'd brought a lunch. "There's a young boy here with five barley loaves and two fish. But what good is that with all this huge crowd?" (John 6:9). But that was enough for Jesus. He took what Andrew (and the boy) had brought him and fed the entire crowd of five thousand men *plus* women and children.

Toward the end of Jesus' ministry, during that fateful week before Passover, several Greeks who had heard about Jesus approached Philip, one of the Twelve: "Sir, we would like to meet Jesus." Philip told Andrew about it, and they went together to ask Jesus. Jesus didn't avoid what was ahead. He said, "The truth is, a kernel of wheat must be planted in the soil. Unless it dies it will be alone—a single seed. But its death will produce many new kernels—a plentiful harvest of new lives. Those who love their life in this world will lose it. . . . All those who want to be my disciples must come and follow me" (John 12:20-26).

Jesus had promised to make Andrew a "fisher of men"—a calling that Andrew embraced fully after witnessing the crucifixion and resurrection of Jesus, and being filled with the Holy Spirit at Pentecost. As the apostles scattered throughout the known world to preach the Good News of Jesus, Andrew preached in many different countries and Roman provinces, ending up in the city of Patras in Achaia around A.D. 60 (*Martyrs' Mirror* says A.D. 70). Maximillia, the wife of Aegeaes, the Roman governor, was converted to the Christian faith through Andrew's testimony. Outraged, Aegeaes had Andrew brought to him and threatened him with death by crucifixion if he did not stop preaching this Jesus.

Embracing the Cross

Andrew was not deterred. Wasn't the heart of his preaching *the cross* of Jesus where his Lord and Savior had suffered and died to take away the sins of the world?

27

The governor arrested the apostle and sentenced him to death by crucifixion. Tradition says he was bound—not nailed—to an X-shaped cross to prolong his suffering. But coming near to the place of execution, Andrew cried out, "O beloved cross! I have greatly longed for thee. I rejoice to see thee erected here. I come to thee with a peaceful conscience and with cheerfulness, desiring that I, who am a disciple of Him who hung on the cross, may also be crucified."

Andrew hung on that cross two—some say three—days. But he was not silent. As long as he could speak he taught the people who stood around the cross, telling them the truth about Jesus. At the end he cried, "O my Lord, my God! Whom I have known, whom I have loved, to whom I cling, whom I desire to see, and in whom I am what I am."

In His Own Words

"Had I feared the death of the cross, I should not have preached the majesty and gloriousness of the cross of Christ"—Andrew the apostle

---

If you refuse to take up your cross and follow me, you are not worthy of being mine. If you cling to your life, you will lose it; but if you give it up for me, you will find it (Matthew 10:38-39, spoken by Jesus when he sent out the Twelve).

James the Brother of Jesus
Jerusalem—ca. 63, honored October 23

We first hear about James, the brother of Jesus, in Matthew 14, when Jesus returned to his hometown of Nazareth (though tradition says that James was born either before Mary and Joseph fled to Egypt to avoid Herod's murderous plot or at least by the time they returned to Nazareth). The neighbors in Nazareth said, "Who does this Jesus think he is? Isn't his father a carpenter? Don't we know his brothers—James, Joseph, Simon, and Judas?" The implication was clear: common folks, nothing special.

His brothers didn't believe in him either—they scoffed! (See John 7:1-9.) Jesus admitted that "a prophet" is honored everywhere except in his own hometown and his own family. But the next time we hear about James, he had become a prominent leader among the Christians in Jerusalem (see Acts 12:17; 15:13-21), and Paul lists him among those to whom Jesus appeared after his death (see 1 Corinthians 15:7). James chose to *believe* that his own brother was the promised Messiah.

What kind of man was James? Historians of the early church portray him as a righteous man, a Nazarite who ate no meat, did not cut his hair, drank no wine. He spent so much time on his knees praying on behalf of the people that

28

his knees developed calluses that looked like "camel-knees." Even nonbelievers respected him for his piety and gave him the name "James the Just."

On His Knees

The Roman governor, Festus, was dead; Caesar was sending a new procurator. The son of Ananias the High Priest, also named Ananias, took office in Jerusalem about this time. The new high priest—a young and cruel man, eager to make his mark—took advantage of the civil uncertainty to confront one of his enemies. James, the brother of that rabble-rouser Jesus of Nazareth who had been put to death, was so respected not only among the people but also among the Jewish leaders that many were coming to believe that Jesus was the Christ!

During Passover, Ananias called a special session of the Sanhedrin (the religious "court") and brought serious charges of heresy against James the Just. Knowing that James was highly influential, Ananias took him to a high point on the temple and told him to deny that Jesus was the Christ where all the people could hear him. James did indeed speak to the people, but he boldly proclaimed that Jesus was the Christ, the Son of God, the Savior of all mankind to all who believe.

Infuriated that their plan had backfired, Ananias and his cohorts pushed James off the Temple. But though the fall broke his legs, it did not kill him. So Ananias incited others to stone him. But even as the stones rained down upon him, James struggled onto his knees and began to pray: "Lord, forgive them! They do not know what they are doing!"

One of the young priests, hearing his prayer, cried: "Stop! Why are we doing this? Can't you hear? He is praying for us!"

But one of the crowd, a dyer by trade, struck James in the head with the staff he used to wring out garments from the dying vats, killing him. He was buried on the spot where he fell, and a monument was erected to his memory, close to the Temple.

In His Own Words

"Dear brothers and sisters, whenever trouble comes your way, let it be an opportunity for joy. For when your faith is tested, your endurance has a chance to grow. So let it grow, for when your endurance is fully developed, you will be strong in character and ready for anything."

—James, in his letter to Jewish Christians scattered by persecution (1:2-4)

Prayer of the People

O God! How much time do I spend on my knees praying for my enemies—those who annoy me, abuse me, persecute me? Do I consider it "all joy" when trouble comes my way?

29

Mark the Evangelist
Alexandria, Egypt — ca. 64, honored April 25

It is presumed by most students of the Bible, as well as later historians, that the young man referred to as John Mark (or just Mark) in the book of Acts is the same person referred to as Mark by the apostles Paul and Peter in their letters to various churches. This is important because the references in the epistles (letters) give us clues to the maturing of a well-meaning but inconsistent young man.

When we first meet Mark in Acts, he could be called a "disciple of the apostles." A cousin to Barnabas, Mark accompanied Paul and Barnabas first to Antioch, then on the first leg of their first missionary journey. He was also Barnabas's choice for the second missionary journey, but Paul took Silas instead, and Barnabas took Mark to preach the gospel in Cyprus. Mark's family also assisted Peter. His mother, Mary, opened her home regularly as a meeting place for the disciples, and held an all-night prayer meeting for Peter when he'd been put in prison (see Acts 12:12-17).

Living Down Your "Rep"

Unfortunately, young Mark had a reputation for "cutting out" when things got tough. The Gospel of Mark tells a brief story about a "young man" (generally assumed to be John Mark himself) who was following along behind the disciples when Jesus was arrested. The mob tried to grab him, but he wiggled out of his clothes and ran away stark naked (see Mark 14:50-52).

Pretty understandable. The mob was hot for blood. (Even the disciples ran away that night.) But apparently the apostle Paul didn't understand when John Mark cut out on him and Barnabas after just a couple stops on their first missionary journey and went back to Jerusalem. "Deserted" was the word Paul used when arguing with Barnabas about whether to take Mark on the second missionary journey. (How would you like to go down in history as the reason the great missionary team of Paul and Barnabas split up?)

Barnabas, ever the encourager, took young Mark under his wing and sailed for Cyprus. That's the last we hear about Mark in the book of Acts. What happened to him? Did he deserve the "second chance" Barnabas gave him?

About ten years later, the church in Colosse received a letter from Paul, who was in prison. At the end of the letter Paul wrote: "Aristarchus, who is in prison with me, sends you his greetings, and so does Mark, Barnabas's cousin. And as you were instructed before, make Mark welcome if he comes your way" (Colossians 4:10). When Paul was released from prison, he wrote to Timothy: "Bring Mark with you when you come, for he will be helpful to me" (2 Timothy 4:11). And to Philemon, Paul wrote: "Epaphras, my fellow prisoner in Christ Jesus, sends you his greetings. So do Mark, Aristarchus, Demas, and Luke, my co-workers" (Philemon 23-24).

Whoa! Mark has gone from *persona non grata* to helping Paul while he was in prison, being sent on Paul's behalf to the Colossians, and described as "helpful to me" and "my coworker."

And when Peter writes to the scattered Jewish believers in his first letter, "Your sister church here in Rome sends you greetings, and so does my son Mark" (1 Peter 5:13), we can deduce two things: Mark had been traveling with Peter, and they had a very close relationship—like father and son. As Peter's assistant, Mark wrote down a compilation of Peter's teachings about Jesus and his ministry, which became known as the Gospel of Mark.

Mark is a good example of a young Christian who learned perseverance from others. According to early historians, Mark was sent out by Peter to preach the gospel in Egypt. Though he traveled numerous places in Africa, his primary ministry took root in Alexandria, where he nurtured a fledgling Christian church. "In the eighth year of Nero," the pagan priests of that city incited a riotous crowd that dragged Mark by ropes and hooks through the streets of the city until his skin had been ripped off by the stones. Thrown in prison overnight, he was dragged again through the city, and then his lifeless body was burned.

Don't let anyone think less of you because you are young. Be an example to all believers in what you teach, in the way you live, in your love, your faith, and your purity (1 Timothy 4:12).

Matthias, the Replacement Apostle

Jerusalem or Colchis, Ethiopia—ca. 63, honored February 24

Much of what we know about Matthias, the disciple who replaced Judas Iscariot as one of the Twelve after Judas's despicable betrayal of Jesus and subsequent suicide—is vague and sometimes contradictory. (Did some sources confuse Matthew and Matthias?) Some historians wrote that he was from the royal house of David, a resident of Bethlehem who studied the Scriptures diligently. We *do* know that he was an early follower of Jesus, was undoubtedly one of the seventy-two Jesus sent out ("two by two") to preach the Good News, and was a witness to Jesus' death and resurrection.

Let's join the disciples in Jerusalem shortly after the Ascension as the story unfolds in Acts 1. . . .

A Roll of the Dice

The upstairs room where the little band of believers had been meeting constantly to pray since the incredible events of Passover weekend was crowded and the air stuffy. Matthias eyed the closed windows and had an urge to open one—but he could never put this precious band in jeopardy. He glanced around the crowded room at the bowed heads and bodies; a low murmur lapped at the walls like gentle waves along the shore.

How privileged he was to be here! Peter—a chastened, humble Peter—often prayed with tears wetting his beard. Mary, the mother of Jesus, came early and stayed late. The rest of the Twelve—no, eleven—disciples . . . other faithful women . . . the brothers of Jesus, who now believed . . . and most of the seventy-two who had been sent out two by two by the Savior. Matthias guessed their number at a hundred and twenty. Day after day, praying and waiting. Hadn't Jesus' last words been, "Do not leave Jerusalem, until the Father sends you what he promised . . . in just a few days you will be baptized with the Holy Spirit" (Acts 1:4-5)?

Just then, Matthias saw Peter stand up and signal for their attention. "Brothers," boomed Peter in his Galilean accent, "it was necessary for the Scriptures to be fulfilled concerning Judas, who guided the Temple police to arrest Jesus. . . . This was predicted in the book of Psalms, where it says, 'Let his home become desolate' . . . and again 'Let his position be given to someone else' " (Acts 1:16, 20). Peter swept a hand across the room. "So now we must choose another man to take Judas's place. It must be someone who has been with us all the time that we were with the Lord Jesus—from the time he was baptized by John until the day he was taken from us into heaven. Whoever is chosen will join us"— Peter indicated the eleven—"as a witness of Jesus' resurrection" (Acts 1:21-22). A witness. No longer a *disciple*, a learner, but an *apostle*, a witness and messenger.

"I nominate Matthias," someone said.

Matthias was startled. His mind scrambled. What exactly would this mean?

"I nominate Joseph Barsabbas," said another.

There were no more nominations. Peter seemed satisfied. These two fulfilled his qualifications. "Now we must ask God to show us which one our *Lord* has chosen."

The eleven disciples gathered around Matthias and Joseph and began to pray. *O Lord, if I am chosen, make me worthy of your name*, Matthias prayed silently. The prayers were not long. After asking God for guidance, two small pebbles, or "lots," were cast on the floor. The lot indicated Matthias.

With "a roll of the dice," Matthias's life changed. He was now numbered with the twelve apostles. And like the other apostles, he would eventually pay for the privilege with his life.

According to the writings of Jerome, Matthias the apostle penetrated deep into Ethiopia with the gospel, then returned to Judea, Galilee, and Samaria. Some historians say Ananias the high priest—the same one who ordered that James, the brother of Jesus, be thrown off the temple—sentenced Matthias to be hung on a cross, stoned, then beheaded. The only detail that is important is that Matthias confessed Jesus as Lord and Savior to his last breath.

In His Own Words

"We must combat our flesh, set no value upon it, and concede to it nothing that can flatter it, but rather increase the growth of our soul by faith and knowledge."

—Attributed to Matthias the apostle
by the Nicolaitans (recorded by Clement of Alexandria).

Martyrs under Nero

Rome—64–67, honored June 30

Whether or not the fat little emperor with matchstick legs and light blue eyes sang his poem, "The Sack of Troy," as he watched Rome burn was not the issue. Nero had often made a fool of himself by publicly singing and playing the lyre at his famous orgies. The issue was had he *set* the fires that broke out in the merchant district of the city on the night of July 18, 64. That's what people were saying concerning the conflagration that roared for six days and seven nights, destroying 70 percent of the city and killing multitudes.

They said he had the fires lit so he could rebuild the city to his fancy with wide avenues and magnificent edifices in his honor. The rumors were harder to put out than the fires had been. Nero opened the Field of Mars, including Agrippa's public buildings, and even his own Gardens to house the homeless. He brought food from Ostia and neighboring towns and cut the price of corn to a fraction of its former rate. Still the rumors persisted, and the survivors— even the senators—were getting angry.

Nero was himself a survivor. His father had died when he was only three, and Emperor Caius Galigula had banished the family and seized its fortune. But when his mother's uncle, Claudius, became emperor, his mother connived to marry him and get him to adopt Nero, declaring him heir to the throne ahead of his own son. In A.D. 54, his mother murdered Claudius, and Nero became ruler at age seventeen. Within a year he evicted his mother and ultimately ordered her murdered for alleged treason in 59. Killing then became convenient as he poisoned his stepbrother, Britannicus, had his wife, Octavia, slain, and his teacher, Burrus, poisoned. He also kicked to death his pregnant second wife, Poppaea Sabina, and murdered Atticus Vestinus so he could marry *his* wife, Statilia Messalina. After all that killing, he wasn't going to let a little fire ruin his plans for fame.

In order to deflect accusations and placate the people, Nero laid blame for the fire on the Christians, several of whom were in his household (see Philippians 4:22). He issued a decree throughout the empire: "If anyone confesses that he is a Christian, he shall be put to death without further trial as a convicted enemy of mankind."

The eyewitness report of the Roman historian, Tacitus, in his *Annals* (ca. 116) is significant as one of the first mentions of Christianity in a non-Christian source. "First those were seized who admitted their faith, and then, using the information they provided, a vast multitude were convicted, not so much for the crime of burning the city, but because they were widely hated. In perishing they were additionally made into sports: They were killed by dogs by having the hides of beasts attached to them, or they were nailed to crosses or set aflame, and, when the daylight passed away, they were used as nighttime lamps. Nero gave his own gardens for this spectacle."

Among the "vast multitude," Peter and Paul are said to have been martyred in Rome under Nero. Thieleman J. van Braght in his *Martyrs' Mirror* claims the following familiar believers joined them in making their ultimate witness: Aristarchus, Paul's fellow prisoner (see Colossians 4:10); Epaphras, a fellow servant of Christ (see Colossians 4:12-13); Priscilla and Aquila, fellow laborers with Paul (see Romans 16:3-4); Andronicus and Juina, Paul's relatives and fellow prisoners (see Romans 16:7); Silas, who had been in jail with Paul and Judas (see Acts 15:27, 34; 16:19-39); and Onesiphorus, a friend of Paul (see 2 Timothy 1:16-18; 4:19).

Up from the Ashes

From the ashes of the city rose a more spectacular Rome. A city made of marble and stone with wide streets, pedestrian arcades, and ample supplies of water to quell any future blaze. In 68 A.D., the city was finally freed from Nero when he committed suicide.

But from the ashes of the martyrs rose a church that could never be destroyed.

Now I [Jesus] say to you that you are Peter, and upon this rock I will build my church, and all the powers of hell will not conquer it (Matthew 16:18).

Paul the Apostle

Rome—ca. 67, honored January 25

Saul, a Hebrew born in Tarsus with the privileges of Roman citizenship, was a *good* man. He was deeply religious, well-educated, dedicated, sincere. And wrong.

He tells the story in his own words:

> If others have reason for confidence in their own efforts, I have even more! For I was circumcised when I was eight days old, having been born into a pure-blooded Jewish family that is a branch of the tribe of Benjamin. So I am a real Jew if there ever was one! What's more, I was a member of the Pharisees, who demand the strictest obedience to the Jewish law. And zealous? Yes, in fact, I harshly persecuted the church. And I obeyed the Jewish law so carefully that I was never accused of any fault. I once thought all these things were so very important, but now I consider them worthless because of what Christ has done (Philippians 3:4-7).

What changed on the road to Damascus, when Saul the Pharisee was converted and became Paul the apostle? His *focus*. Jesus, whom he had been zealously persecuting, became Jesus, the Lord he served with his whole heart, soul, and mind.

From that point on, Paul's life reads like a modern thriller. "Five different times the Jews gave me thirty-nine lashes," Paul wrote. "Three times I was beaten with rods. Once I was stoned. Three times I was shipwrecked. Once I spent a whole night and a day adrift at sea. I have traveled many weary miles. I have faced danger from flooded rivers and from robbers. I have faced danger from my own people, the Jews, as well as from the Gentiles. I have faced danger in the cities, in the deserts, and on the stormy seas. And I have faced danger from men who claim to be Christians but are not. I have lived with weariness and pain and sleepless nights. Often I have been hungry and thirsty and have gone without food. Often I have shivered with cold, without enough clothing to keep me warm" (2 Corinthians 11:24-27). At the end of his life he could truthfully say, "My life has already been poured out as an offering to God" (2 Timothy 4:6).

A Prolific Letter Writer

Somewhere between getting arrested, thrown in prison, whipped, stoned, traveling for months by land and sea, and getting shipwrecked, Paul spent a good deal of time writing letters. Letters to churches he had planted all over the Roman Empire; letters to individuals he wanted to encourage.

Don't forget. This was before typewriters, word processors, and e-mail. Every letter was written by hand, with pens made from goose feathers and ink from berries, on heavy parchment scrolls. There were no copy machines or postal service. Every letter had to be carried by hand. Some were book length!

Why did Paul write so many letters under such difficult circumstances? *Because his lifework was to build up the church of God.* If possible, he visited or revisited the churches in person, even if it meant trips that took several years to complete. But if he couldn't be present in person to teach or encourage, he wrote a letter. Half of his letters were written from prison. (Doesn't this seem backward? Shouldn't the churches have been writing encouragement to *him* while he was incarcerated?)

But, oh, what a wealth of spiritual encouragement is in these letters. How many men, women, and children throughout the centuries have come to know the Savior from reading Paul's letters! (Did you?)

What about us? How many excuses do we give for not writing that note of encouragement to a friend or family member or missionary who is far away? What would Paul think of our excuses? Too busy? Don't have enough time? Too much trouble?

Paul's last letter was sent from a Roman prison to Timothy, a young man he had trained and who was now an elder in Ephesus. The book of Acts does not record how Paul's story ended, but in his letter to Timothy, it is clear that *Paul* knew the end was near. And several early church historians recorded that Paul was beheaded by order of Emperor Nero about A.D. 67, close in time to Peter's crucifixion.

In His Own Words
"The time of my death is near. I have fought a good fight, I have finished the race, and I have remained faithful. And now the prize awaits me—the crown of righteousness that the Lord, the righteous Judge, will give me on that great day of his return. And the prize is not just for me but for all who eagerly look forward to his glorious return."

—Paul the apostle in 2 Timothy 4:6-8

Peter the Apostle
Rome—ca. 67, honored June 29

You have to love Peter. At least, Jesus did. Jesus had a special fondness for the rash, brash fisherman. From the moment that Andrew urged his brother Simon to meet the Master, Jesus had a new name for him: Rock. (Well, that's the meaning of *Peter* in the Greek.) Not a polished rock or a dazzling diamond, but a rough rock. But Jesus knew. . . .

Peter tended to jump into things with both feet—sometimes literally. It was Peter who climbed out of the boat and wanted to walk on water to Jesus. It was Peter who enthusiastically suggested that they build three tabernacles for Jesus, Moses, and Elijah after witnessing Jesus' transfiguration. It was Peter who swore he would follow Jesus even to the death . . . only hours before he denied that he had ever known him.

But Jesus saw through the impetuousness to the zeal that would burn like a fire within Peter once he had become convinced of the truth. The risen Lord singled out Peter for a special message (see Mark 16:7) and appearance (see Luke 24:34) on the day of resurrection. Just before Jesus returned to heaven, he renewed Peter's call: "'Feed my sheep. The truth is . . . when you are old, you will stretch out your hands, and ohers will direct you and take you where you don't want to go.' Jesus said this to let [Peter] know what kind of death he would die to glorify God. Then Jesus told him, 'Follow me'" (John 21:17-19).

From that point on, Peter never wavered. On Pentecost he preached a sermon that won three *thousand* souls to Christ. When he was told by the jealous Sadducees to quit preaching about Jesus or suffer dire consequences, Peter shrugged. "We must obey God rather than human authority" (Acts 5:29). When he was whipped, he praised God that he had been counted "worthy to suffer dishonor for the name of Jesus" (Acts 5:41).

Peter survived imprisonment and beatings again and again as he and the other apostles declared the Good News throughout the known world. But when he was about seventy years old, according to numerous church historians, he was sentenced by the Roman emperor Nero to be crucified. Not counting himself worthy to die as his Savior died, Peter asked to be crucified upside down. His request was honored. Peter, the brash fisherman, had discovered something. . . .

More Precious than Silver or Gold
The three o'clock prayer service at the Temple . . . that was a good time for begging. Lots of traffic in midafternoon. The lame man waved off his friends who had laid him down beside the Beautiful Gate and shook his bowl. "Alms? Alms for a cripple?"

Two men were coming his way. Big, burly men. Didn't look wealthy, but that didn't matter much. Sometimes the poor put more in his bowl than the rich. "Alms? Do you have anything for a poor cripple?"

Hallelujah! They were stopping. But . . . why was the big guy looking at him like that? Not at his legs, but into his eyes. The beggar's eyes dropped, but jerked up again when the man commanded, "Look at us!" The beggar held out his bowl eagerly. "I don't have any money for you," said the man. "But I'll give you what I have." Before the beggar had time to be surprised, the man— whose name was Peter, he found out soon enough—reached out and took him by the hand. "In the name of Jesus Christ of Nazareth, get up and walk!" (Acts 3:4-6).

Strength began to flow into the useless limbs. Peter's strong grip pulled him to his feet. Astounded, the beggar just stood there for a few brief seconds; . . . then he began to move his feet. "I'm walking! I'm walking!" Laughter spilled out of his mouth; he began to jump around. Throwing away his bowl, the once- lame beggar waltzed into the Temple with Peter and John, praising God at the top of his lungs. *The name of Jesus* had done this awesome thing! He believed! He had asked for money, and received something far more precious than silver or gold.

In His Own Words
"You are the Messiah, the Son of the living God."
—Peter, in his heartfelt declaration of faith in Matthew 16:15-16

Antipas the Faithful Witness
Turkey—ca. 68, honored April 11
When Jesus dictated his evaluations of the seven churches of Asia Minor to the apostle John, he sent this message to the church at Pergamum (now Bergama in Turkey): "I know that you live in the city where that great throne of Satan is located, and yet you have remained loyal to me. And you refused to deny me even when Antipas, my faithful witness, was martyred among you by Satan's followers. And yet I have a few complaints against you. You tolerate . . . some Nicolaitans among you. . . . Repent, or I will come to you suddenly and fight against them with the sword of my mouth" (Revelation 2:13-16).[1]

There is no other mention of Antipas in the Bible or by ancient historians, but church tradition—along with known history of Pergamum—provides considerable detail.

Antipas is said to have been an accomplished dentist, who continued practicing medicine—along with faith healing—after becoming a Christian. His faith and compassion were sufficient for the apostle John (traditionally recognized as the overseer of the Asian churches) to install him as bishop in Pergamum.

Pergamum was regally situated on a lofty hill about sixteen miles inland from the Aegean Sea. Even though it was not on a major trade route, Pergamum was one of the most well-planned Greek cities of its time, with a theater, a temple dedicated to Athena, an amphitheater, a racetrack, and one of the finest libraries in the world. On the hillside was an awesome, forty-foot-high altar to Zeus that looked like a great throne surrounded by an impressive frieze depicting the epic world of heroes and gods (still visible today). All day this altar smoked with perpetual sacrifices to Zeus.

Pergamum considered itself the custodian of ancient Greek religion. Possibly this is why Christ said it was "where that great throne of Satan is located." In any case, church tradition tells us that the demons that the citizens of Pergamum worshipped had appeared to them and told them that they could no longer make Pergamum their home (or throne?) or accept the people's sacrifices because the power of Antipas was casting them out.

Antipas was therefore arrested and delivered to the governor, who tried to convince Antipas to toss just a pinch of incense into the huge, red-hot brass idol of an ox used for continual sacrifices. "After all," he argued, "the old ways are better than your new religion." Antipas refused, which angered the governor so much that he had Antipas cast into the oven himself. While the door was still open, Antipas could be heard praying to God, glorifying his great power, and thanking him for being worthy to suffer.

There is some controversy as to when all this occurred. Some sources say Antipas died under Nero's persecution, possibly about A.D. 68. Others say he wasn't martyred until about 95, during the reign of Emperor Domitian, who was the first emperor to officially title himself "God the Lord," certainly a satanic claim. However, John probably wrote his Revelation by 96, making it hard to imagine that the Pergamum church had gone so far off track as to tolerate the Nicolaitan heresy in only one year. The Scriptures identify Antipas as "faithful," so we know he had no part in the heresy. And the Scriptures also imply that he inspired the rest of the church not to "deny" Christ under persecution, demonstrating his influence. Therefore, it seems more likely that Antipas was martyred on the earlier date, which would have given some twenty- eight years for error to creep in.

Above all else, guard your heart, for it affects everything you do (Proverbs 4:23)

---

[1] The Nicolaitans apparently tried to introduce a false freedom and licentiousness into the church, thus abusing Paul's doctrine of grace. They echoed Balak, who induced the Israelites to eat things sacrificed to idols and to commit fornication.

Bartholomew the Apostle

Abanopolis on the Caspian Sea—ca. 70, honored August 24

The Bible tells us little about Bartholomew, though in the synoptic gospels (Matthew, Mark, and Luke) he was numbered among the twelve disciples of Jesus. Bartholomew is a patronymic name, meaning "son of Tolmai" (*bar* Tolmai), and he is generally presumed to be the same person called Nathanael in John's Gospel. The reasoning is that Bartholomew is often paired with Philip in the synoptic gospels, which never mention Nathanael; whereas in John's Gospel, Philip is paired with Nathanael (and Bartholomew is never mentioned). We might call him, "Nathanael *bar* Tolmai."

Early church historians generally agree that Bartholomew took the gospel as far as India, where he translated the Gospel of St. Matthew and preached to the people in their own language. But persecution drove him to Greater Armenia, where he brought King Polymius and twelve cities to the Christian faith. This inflamed the priests, who turned Polymius's brother, King Astyages, against the missionary. Astyages arrested Bartholomew and accused him of perverting his brother, to which Bartholomew responded that he preached the true worship of God and had not "perverted" but "converted" King Polymius.

Infuriated, King Astyages ordered that Bartholomew be suspended upside down on a cross and flayed alive. Some sources say he was beheaded with an ax to end his suffering.

What kind of man was Bartholomew, a.k.a. Nathanael, son of Tolmai? He wasn't famous like Peter or Paul, yet he paid the ultimate sacrifice for his faith. We find clues to the man in the brief story in John 1, when he first met Jesus. . . .

A True Son of Israel

Nathanael flopped down in the shade of a large tree and mopped sweat from his face with the sleeve of his robe. He couldn't rest long; he still had figs to pick and deliveries to make. People were counting on him. But it had been a long day already and the sun was hot. A few minutes in the shade would be welcome. . . .

"Nathanael! Nathanael!"

Nathanael's eyes jerked open. Who was calling him? He squinted against the sun at the figure running toward him. Looked like Philip. . . . What could make dignified Philip run like that? Unless something was wrong.

Nathanael had scrambled to his feet by the time Philip arrived, panting, his eyes alight. "We have found the very person Moses and the prophets wrote about! His name is Jesus, the son of Joseph from Nazareth."

What? Could it be? He and Philip had talked so many times about the prophecies in Scripture about the coming Messiah . . . but wait. This Jesus was from *where*?

Nathanael snorted, skeptical . . . yet disappointed, too. "Nazareth! . . . Can anything good come from there?"

But Philip wouldn't be put off, and Nathanael let himself be dragged along till they came to a small crowd listening to an ordinary-looking rabbi. But as they approached, the rabbi looked beyond the crowd, looked straight at Nathanael, and called out, "Here comes an honest man—a true son of Israel!"

Nathanael felt his face redden. He wasn't used to such attention. He preferred to live quietly with integrity, keeping the *spirit* of the Law, not just the outward show. He built his personal reputation on dealing fairly with everyone, rich or poor, even when it wasn't to his advantage. "How do you know about me?"

Jesus' gaze seemed to draw him closer. "I could see you under the fig tree before Philip found you."

Suddenly Nathanael *knew*. He said, "Teacher, you are the Son of God—the King of Israel!"

"Do you believe all this just because I told you I had seen you under the fig tree?" There was a hint of laughter *and* sorrow in Jesus' voice. "You will see greater things than this. . . . The truth is you will see heaven open, and angels going up and down upon the Son of Man" (John 1:45-51).

Nathanael didn't need to see these things to believe. He had seen *the Christ*. And from that day forward, he never turned back.

In His Own Words

"I would rather seal my testimony with my blood, than suffer the shipwreck of my faith or conscience."

—Bartholomew the apostle, according to *Martyrs' Mirror*

Jude Thaddeus the Apostle
Persia—ca. 70, honored October 28

There is no doubt in the lists of the twelve disciples (Matthew 10:2-4; Mark 3:16-19; Luke 6:14-16; Acts 1:13) that "Thaddeus" was the same person also called "Judas" (*not* Judas Iscariot) or "Jude." But there is difference of opinion whether Jude Thaddeus the apostle (as we shall call him) was (a) the *"son of* James" (NLT and NIV) or *"brother of* James" (KJV), and concurrently, (b) whether Jude Thaddeus is the same person as Jude, the writer of the Epistle and "brother of James" (Jude v. 1), whom most scholars agree refers to "James the Just, the brother of Jesus, head of the Jerusalem Church, and writer of the Epistle."

However, because John 7:5 clearly states that "even his brothers did not believe in him," it is completely reasonable to assume that Jude Thaddeus, one of the twelve disciples, is a different person than Jude, brother of Jesus and James, who later believed and rose to prominence in the early church. (But, Jude Thaddeus was "son" or "brother" of *which* James? Twice Thaddeus is mentioned right after James, son of Alphaeus, which implies a strong connection; when Simon the Zealot is mentioned in between the two, then he is designated "*son* [or *brother*] of James.")

Little is mentioned in Scripture about Jude Thaddeus, except for a critical question he asked Jesus during what became the Last Supper.

"Why Us?"

Jesus did a lot of talking that Passover night—like someone does who is going away or knows his "time" is near, reminding those he loves of what is most important. But the disciples were bewildered. First Jesus washed their feet like a common servant, said one of them was going to betray him, told Peter he would deny that he'd ever known Jesus, and said he was going somewhere to "prepare a place" for them.

Thomas blurted, "We don't have any idea where you're going, so how can we know the way?" Jesus told them *he* was the way to the Father. Philip said, "Okay, then, show us the Father." Jesus said they'd *already* seen the Father because they'd seen *him*.

Jesus said in a little while the world would not see him, but he was going to send his disciples the Holy Spirit, who would dwell in them and lead them into the truth—but the world wasn't ready to recognize or receive the Spirit of God.

Here Jude Thaddeus spoke up. "Lord, why are you going to reveal yourself only to us and not to the world at large?" (John 14:22).

Did he understand the significance—the glory—of Jesus' reply? "All those who love me will do what I say. My Father will love them, and we will come to them and live with them." Jesus was passing on the mantle of his ministry to his disciples. They would do "even greater works" than he had done (John 14:23). But, he said, the world would also hate them, just as it had hated him. A time was coming "when those who kill you will think they are doing God a service" (16:2).

As the evening came to a close, Jesus poured out his heart. "Oh, there is so much more I want to tell you, but you can't bear it now. [But] when the Spirit of truth comes, he will guide you into all truth" (16:12-13).

Oh, what a glorious burden knowing the truth is! It leads to obedience, which may lead to suffering for the name of Jesus. At the same time, the Holy Spirit makes *all God's resources* available to us, just as Jesus promised.

Like the other apostles, Jude Thaddeus was filled with the Holy Spirit at Pentecost, who indeed guided him into "all truth" and filled him with a passion to spread the Good News of God's salvation throughout Mesopotamia, Africa, and finally to Persia. Here, tradition states, he aroused the hatred of pagan priests because of all who were turning away from idol worship, and he was beaten with clubs and his head split with a broadax.

Surely Jude Thaddeus recalled Jesus' last words time and time again . . .

[Jesus said,] "I have told you all this so that you may have peace in me. Here on earth you will have many trials and sorrows. But take heart, because I have overcome the world"(John 16:33).

Matthew the Apostle

Possibly Ethiopia—ca. 70, honored September 21

In New Testament times, Roman rule had spread all around the Mediterranean Sea, gobbling up province after province. But there weren't enough Romans to administer the expanding empire, so local residents in each conquered province were employed to collect taxes from their fellow citizens for the coffers of Augustus Caesar, the Roman Emperor.

"Publicans," they were called—initially a form of flattery, for the Roman "publicanus" was a wealthy agent of State taxes, not a mere collector. But in Judea, Jews who sank so low as to betray their fellow citizens by collecting (and usually inflating) taxes for their enemies were called "publicans" in the same breath as the vilest "sinners"—thieves and harlots and adulterers and thugs. Social outcasts.

This is where Jesus found Levi (possibly from the tribe of Levi), a tax collector sitting in his custom house just outside Capernaum along the Sea of Galilee, situated so he could collect a road tax, as well as customs, as travelers passed from the territory ruled by Herod Philip into the territory ruled by his brother, Herod Antipas.

What happened next, however, startled everyone, from pious Pharisees to fellow publicans. . . .

Sinners, Not Saints

"Come, be my disciple!"

Levi wasn't certain he had heard right. But the rabbi was looking right at him, beckoning. The same rabbi who, that very day, had healed a man who had been paralyzed for years! The man had walked right past his booth, carrying the mat he usually laid on to beg. But now he was dancing and shouting and praising God.

The rabbi was still beckoning to him. Levi stood up. Most of his fellow Jews ignored him at best; others glared at him with hatred burning in their eyes. Still others called him vile names—even spat on him. He knew what they thought. It didn't do any good to argue that he was just doing his job, that it was just a way to make a living that used his mathematical mind.

But in that moment, the possibility of a new beginning presented itself, and the decision point was *now*. He knew if he walked out of that booth, he could never go back—not like those fishermen who were following this rabbi. The fish were always in the lake, waiting for them. But if he left this toll booth, the Romans would never give him another job. He wasn't sure anyone else would, either—except . . . this rabbi was calling *him*.

Levi chose. He left all that defined him and never looked back. But it didn't feel like loss. He felt so full, so happy, that he invited Jesus and his other disciples to come to a dinner at his house that evening. And he invited everyone he thought would come—other tax collectors and "friends" who weren't too worried about their already sullied reputations—to meet this amazing rabbi. If Jesus could heal a *paralyzed* man and *forgive the man's sins* . . . Levi was eager to share the hope he felt surging through his spirit.

During the meal, Levi heard a commotion outside. Some of Capernaum's religious leaders had their noses bent out of shape because Jesus, a respected rabbi, was eating with "publicans and sinners." For a moment, Levi may have feared that his party was over. He knew the value of a reputation. He couldn't blame Jesus if he left. But Jesus made no move to leave. He simply said, "Healthy people don't need a doctor; sick people do. . . . I came to call sinners, not those who think they are already good enough" (Matthew 9:12-13).

Levi's heart overflowed. From that point on Jesus called him Matthew, which means "gift of God."

The End of the Story

Matthew was "the son of Alphaeus" (Mark 2:14), so he may have been brother to James ("the less") and Thomas ("the twin"), who also became disciples of Jesus. After the death and resurrection of his Lord, Matthew wrote an account of the life and ministry of Jesus for his fellow Jews, "The Gospel according to Matthew." Tradition says that this apostle took the gospel to Ethiopia and died a martyr's death (beheaded). While we cannot prove beyond doubt all the details, we do know this disciple totally gave up his former life (it was Judas, not Matthew, who was treasurer for the disciples) for a new life where "birds of the air have nests, but the Son of Man has no place to lay his head" (Matthew 8:20).

Simon the Zealot

Syria—ca. 70, honored October 28

In the lists of the twelve apostles (Matthew 10:2-4; Mark 3:16-19; Luke 6:14-16; Acts 1:13), Simon is usually listed tenth or eleventh, and identified as "Simon the Cananean" or "Simon the Zealot." *Cananean* does not mean "from Canaan," but could mean "from Cana of Galilee." If so, some suggest that Simon may have been the bridegroom at the wedding feast where Jesus turned water into wine and became a disciple because of this miracle. But there are no additional facts to support this. *Cananean* (meaning "zealous" in Aramaic) was also the term given to members of a Jewish political party. The "Zealots," as they were called in the Greek, were part of a movement started by Judas the Galilean when Quirinius was governor of Syria (i.e., about the time of Jesus' birth—see Luke 2:2 and Acts 5:37) to resist Roman aggression. Was Simon looking for a political Messiah who would overthrow Rome? All of the disciples were a bit confused on this point—even after the Resurrection they asked Jesus, "Lord, are you going to free Israel now and restore our kingdom?" (Acts 1:6).

Whatever Simon's motives for initially responding to Jesus' call to follow him, or whether he, like the other disciples, did not grasp the full meaning of what Jesus meant by "the Kingdom of God is near!" (Mark 1:15)—he did respond to *Jesus* as *the Christ*, the Promised One, and allowed his understanding to change and grow with his relationship.

The implication of Simon's choice—and our choice—to put faith in the Son of God rather than human institutions or movements or political parties became apparent one day when the apostles found themselves in court for preaching about Jesus. . . .

Fizzle Out or Fight God

Jerusalem was in an uproar. The disciples of Jesus—the rabbi who had been crucified right after Passover—claimed that he had risen from the dead! They continued to preach in his name. The sick and the blind and people tormented by evil spirits crowded into the city from surrounding towns—and were healed! More and more people were calling themselves "believers."

The high priest and the Sadducee party (who claimed there is no such thing as resurrection after death) were downright jealous. Who was going to listen to them if people believed in this man's resurrection? They arrested all of Jesus' disciples and put them in the public jail overnight. The next morning they called together the entire Sanhedrin—the Jewish religious court made up of both Pharisees and Sadducees (somewhat analogous to our secular Congress, made up of both Democrats and Republicans)—and sent for the twelve rabble-rousers in the prison. A guard brought back disconcerting news: the jail was still locked but the men weren't there! In fact, they were back in the Temple teaching about Jesus!

Now the high priest was mad. He sent the captain of the Temple guard to bring these men to appear before the Sanhedrin. ("But don't use force, or we'll have a riot on our hands.") "We told you to stop preaching about this Jesus!" he stormed (see Acts 5:26, 28).

"Sorry," said the apostles. "We have to obey God" (see Acts 5:29). And once again they proclaimed that Jesus, whom this very court had condemned to death, was alive and sitting at the right hand of God.

At this point the Sanhedrin was furious and wanted to kill them. But Gamaliel, a respected leader of the Pharisees, asked that the guard remove the twelve from the room. "Be careful what you do here," he said to the Sanhedrin. "Some time ago there was that fellow Theudas, who pretended to be someone great. About four hundred others joined him, but he was killed, and . . . the whole movement came to nothing. After him, at the time of the census, there was Judas of Galilee [the Zealots]. He got some people to follow him, but he was killed, too, and all his followers were scattered. So my advice is, leave these men alone. If they are teaching and doing these things merely on their own, it will soon be overthrown. But if it is of God, you will not be able to stop them. You may even find yourselves fighting against God" (see Acts 5:35-39).

Simon the Zealot became zealous for God, and, like many of the other apostles, eventually suffered martyrdom by crucifixion, according to tradition. But Gamaliel's words were prophetic: "If it is of God, you will not be able to stop them."

Thomas the Apostle
India—ca. 70, honored December 21

One of the twelve disciples, Thomas was also called Didymus, Greek for "twin." Like the other apostles, Thomas was sent out to preach the gospel after Pentecost, when the disciples had been empowered by the Holy Spirit. Early church historians record that he evangelized among the Parthians, Medes, and Persians before reaching India, where he carried the Good News all the way to the Malabar coast. Today, a community of Christians in the Kerala district, the "Christians of St. Thomas," claim they are descendants of the first Christians converted by Thomas's preaching.

What we know about Thomas the disciple we find primarily in the Gospel of John. Say the name "Thomas," and the first thing that pops into people's minds is *Doubting Thomas*. But there is more to the man who was willing to live among the pagans of first-century India. To simply label him "Doubting Thomas" obscures the true character of a man who willingly endured being tortured with red-hot plates, thrown into a furnace, then speared to death by idolatrous priests.

Let us meet Thomas the man. . . .

"I Want to Know"

The disciples were confounded. What had Jesus just said?

"Let's go again to Judea."

Hadn't Jesus come *this close* to being arrested in Jerusalem a few days ago? Hadn't they just crossed the Jordan River—wise move!—to give time for things to cool off? Even when the message came from Mary and Martha of Bethany, saying their brother Lazarus was dying, Jesus had wisely, it seemed to the disciples, not rushed back into danger. So why now?

"Our friend Lazarus has fallen asleep, but now I will go and wake him up."

Asleep? Why, that was good! That meant he was probably getting better. No need to go now, was there?

"Lazarus is dead. And for your sake, I am glad I wasn't there, because this will give you another opportunity to believe in me."

The disciples didn't move. This all seemed pointless! Lazarus was already dead . . . Jesus was likely to get arrested . . . surely it was better to stay here.

Then someone stood and began putting on his cloak. Thomas, the twin. "Let's go, too—and die with Jesus." Resolutely, he turned his back on the others and turned his face toward Jerusalem (see John 11).

Fast forward to Passover. Thomas reclined at the table in the borrowed room where he and the others had prepared the Passover meal to eat with Jesus. As he often did when they were alone together, Jesus instructed them. But tonight was different. He seemed to be talking in riddles! Like now. Jesus was saying, "There are many rooms in my Father's home, and I am going to prepare a place for you. If this were not so, I would tell you plainly. When everything is ready, I will come and get you, so that you will always be with me where I am. And you know where I am going and how to get there."

"No, we don't know, Lord!" Thomas protested. He desperately wanted to understand. "We haven't any idea where you are going, so how can we know the way?"

Immediately Thomas felt foolish. What would the others think? Maybe *he* was the only one who didn't understand. But . . . he didn't care. He wanted to *know*.

Jesus didn't seem to be surprised at his question. "*I* am the way, the truth, and the life. No one can come to the Father except through me" (emphasis added).

Thomas clung to those words—though they were severely tested by the terrifying events of that weekend. When he heard that Jesus was alive again, he *wanted* to believe—but he had to know for himself. And when he saw the nail prints . . . (see John 14; 20).

When Thomas saw the risen Christ, he cried, "My Lord and my God!" Jesus said, "Blessed are those who haven't seen me and believe anyway" (John 20:28-29, paraphrased).

Luke the Physician

Greece—ca. 93, honored October 18

Luke, the author of the Gospel that bears his name and the Acts of the Apostles, is the only Gentile among the New Testament writers. Greek by birth, a physician by profession, a man of letters as well as medicine, Luke was probably a Jewish proselyte who met Paul in Antioch and became a Christian under his preaching. Luke was a consummate historian who wrote excellent Greek; together his two books—the life of Christ, and the lives of the apostles—comprise about one-quarter of the New Testament.

Luke does not mention himself by name in the book of Acts, though his prose switches to "we" in Acts 16, when he joins Paul and Silas in Troas and becomes a companion on their mission to Macedonia. He is mentioned by Paul in several of his letters as being one of Paul's faithful traveling companions (Colossians 4:14; 2 Timothy 4:11; Philemon 24).

Indeed, it was Luke who stood by Paul during his final imprisonment (Paul wrote to Timothy in 2 Timothy 4:6, 11: "The time of my death is near. . . . Only Luke is with me)." One by one all the apostles and many of the evangelists—Barnabas, Mark, Silas, Priscilla and Aquila, and many others—were laying down their lives for the gospel. Did Luke die a martyr's death? If so, it is not well documented, though *Martyrs' Mirror*, citing a few sources, says that Luke was "hanged by the ungodly to a green olive tree . . . in the eighty-fourth year of his age."

But whether or not he bears the label of "martyr," Luke endured many of the same hardships as the apostle Paul: he was present when Paul and Silas were arrested and beaten in Philippi (see Acts 16); was with Paul in Jerusalem when Paul was arrested by the Romans to keep him from being killed by a mob (see Acts 21); he accompanied Paul on the long voyage to stand trial before Caesar and was shipwrecked with him (see Acts 27). As a historian, Luke kept himself in the background, but as a writer Luke revealed his compassionate heart not only in *what* and *who* he wrote about but also in *how* he wrote about them.

The Compassion of a Good Doctor

For children: Luke's Gospel contains more stories about children than any of the other gospels, and he captures the heart cries of anguished parents: "My only child is dying!" "Please help my son!" While the other gospel writers use a nonspecific term for the children brought to Jesus to be blessed, Luke uses a Greek word that applied to both infants and the unborn (as when Elizabeth's unborn baby "leaped in her womb" at the voice of the pregnant Mary). Pastor Victor Shepherd says Luke's witness to the value of children, both born and unborn, is needed more than ever in our abortion-minded culture: "No society can finally be life-affirming and child-denying at the same time."

For society's misfits: Luke's Gospel abounds with stories of losers and outcasts. Some occur in Jesus' parables: the cocky, ungrateful son who blew his inheritance; the sinner praying in the Temple next to the virtuous religious leader; the homeless and jobless who were invited to a great feast when the invited guests didn't come. Other stories were about unsavory characters who came in touch with the Savior—Zacchaeus, the runty, conniving tax man; ten repulsive lepers; a common thief on a cross. With great compassion, Luke helps us see these people from God's perspective. "Today salvation has come to this house!" "The sinner went home justified." "Today you shall be with me in paradise."

For women: Luke's Gospel mentions thirteen women that none of the other Gospel writers mentions, as well as the many women who supported Jesus and his disciples financially, hosted them in their homes, and even traveled with them (see Luke 8:1-3). In Acts, Luke records women converts by name (e.g., Lydia, Dorcas) and tells the stories of faithful women who served in the church (e.g., Mark's mother, Priscilla).

Prayer of the People

O God, thank you for Luke, "the beloved physician," who recorded so many stories of ordinary people touched by the love of Jesus. Like Luke, give us the humility, grace, and courage to be loyal, faithful companions to those who are on the front lines today—pastors, teachers, speakers, ministers, evangelists—who need our love, care, and support.

Timothy, Bishop of Ephesus
Ephesus—January 26, 97

The region is called Turkey today, but in the time of the apostles, it was called Lycaonia. Chased out of the city of Iconium on their first missionary journey by a mixed mob of both Gentiles and Jews, Paul and Barnabas headed for Lystra and Derbe and continued to preach the gospel of Jesus Christ.

In Lystra, two women—a Jewess named Eunice, married to a Greek husband, and her mother, Lois—drank in the missionaries' words of life as soil sucks up the rain after a long drought. Bathing in the overflow of his mother's new faith, young Timothy also got an early education in the cost of discipleship.

Was he in the crowd when Paul spoke by faith to a man whose feet had been crippled since birth—and the man jumped to his feet and started walking? Did Timothy follow along when the market crowd, gaga at this display of godlike power, hurried Paul and Barnabas to the temple of Zeus and prepared to worship them as "gods in human bodies" (Acts 14:11)? The missionaries tore their clothes in dismay and cried out, "We are merely human beings like yourselves! We have come to bring you the Good News that you should turn . . . to the living God, who made heaven and earth" (Acts 14:15). Did young Timothy then feel the tide of public opinion turn as agitators stirred up the crowd, turning it into a murderous mob who picked up stones, threw them at Paul until he was unconscious, dragged him out of the city, and left him for dead? Eunice and Lois may well have been among the believers who gathered around Paul's wounded body, ministered to him, and sent him away with Barnabas the next day: "God be with you! Till we meet again!"

Seven years later, when Paul returned to Lystra with Silas on his second missionary journey, he was so impressed with the solid young man Timothy had become that he took him along as a helper and evangelist. Most of what we know about Timothy's character and mission can be found in Paul's writings:

Timothy, though young, lived his life with integrity. Today we might say he walked his talk. Paul told the Corinthian church, "When Timothy comes, treat him with respect. He is doing the Lord's work, just as I am. Don't let anyone despise him. Send him on his way with your blessings when he returns to me" (1 Corinthians 16:10-11). And later, when Timothy was serving the church in Ephesus, Paul wrote to him: "Don't let anyone think less of you because you are young. [Continue to] be an example to all believers in what you teach, in the way you live, in your love, your faith, and your purity" (1 Timothy 4:12).

Timothy not only lived what he believed but also taught what he believed. Again Paul encouraged him: "Teach these things and insist that everyone learn them. . . . Focus on reading the Scriptures to the church, encouraging the believers, and teaching them" (1 Timothy 4:11-13).

Timothy could be counted on. He had a heart to serve his mentor, Paul, and in turn was entrusted with the welfare of others. Paul wrote to the church in Philippi: "If the Lord Jesus is willing, I hope to send Timothy to you soon. Then when he comes back, he can cheer me up by telling me how you are getting along.

I have no one else like Timothy, who genuinely cares about your welfare. All the others care only for themselves and not for what matters to Jesus Christ. But you know how Timothy has proved himself. Like a son with his father, he has helped me in preaching the Good News" (Philippians 2:19-22).

Timothy's time of training with the apostle Paul prepared him to act boldly and stand firm when persecution arose. In his second letter to Timothy, Paul wrote: "I know that you sincerely trust the Lord, for you have the faith of your mother, Eunice, and your grandmother, Lois. This is why I remind you to fan into flames the spiritual gift God gave you when I laid my hands on you. For God has not given us a spirit of fear and timidity, but of power, love, and self-discipline. So you must never be ashamed to tell others about our Lord. . . . With the strength God gives you, be ready to suffer with me for the proclamation of the Good News" (2 Timothy 1:5-8).

According to the historian Eusebius, on January 26, in the year A.D. 97, Timothy, bishop of Ephesus and now in his eighties, went out into the streets to protest the orgiastic activities of Katagogia, a pagan festival in honor of the god Dionysus (some say the goddess Diana). Incensed that their "fun" was interrupted, the wild partygoers picked up whatever was at hand and clubbed the old man to death, faithful to the end.

John the Beloved Apostle

Ephesus—ca. 100, honored December 27

John was the younger brother of James, sons of Zebedee, nicknamed "sons of thunder." With Peter and James, he was part of the inner circle with whom Jesus shared his most intimate moments—the Transfiguration, the garden of Gethsemane. Formerly a disciple of John the Baptist and an eyewitness to the life and ministry of Jesus, John wrote one of the four Gospels, three pastoral letters (1, 2, and 3 John), and the book of Revelation during his exile on the Island of Patmos around A.D. 95. When his banishment was lifted in about A.D. 98, he is said to have returned to his adopted hometown of Ephesus. By then he is thought to have been the last survivor of the original apostles and the only one to have died a natural death.

If John could tell you one story from his extraordinary life, he might say . . .

The Right and Left Hand

"That Friday was the darkest day of my life. Night, day . . . they all blurred together after Jesus was arrested in the garden of Gethsemane. I hadn't slept at all—not since I fell asleep while Jesus was praying in the garden. 'Watch with me one hour!' he'd asked. But I didn't. If I'd stayed awake, would I have seen the torches coming? Would we have been able to hustle Jesus away before the temple police got there? The questions tormented me.

"But there was no time to think. Things were happening too fast. Jesus was hustled from high priest to high priest, then to Pilate, the Roman governor—the coward. He could have freed Jesus—custom allowed him to free a prisoner at Passover—but he freed that common thug, Barabbas, instead. And then they tortured Jesus! I didn't want to watch—but we had deserted him once already that night in the garden. I wasn't about to do it again. The soldiers shredded his back with that whip, and then they made a crown of thorns and pushed it onto his head, mocking him.

"I saw several of the other disciples mingling with the crowd—a mob, really, thirsting for blood. We didn't acknowledge one another. We knew our lives were in danger. But Jesus . . . Jesus . . .! They had actually condemned him to death! *For what?* All I could think about was the Last Supper we had with him, celebrating the Passover. He had washed our feet, like a common servant. *He* washed *my* feet! Oh, if I had only known. I would've given anything to wash his feet—his feet that were being nailed to that grisly wooden cross. Then his hands—oh, God! How does anyone stand the pain!

"The other disciples hung back among the crowd, my own terror and grief mirrored in their eyes. But then I saw my aunt, his mother, Mary, . . . and Mary Magdalen . . . and the other Mary, the wife of Cleopas—all standing at the foot of the cross. Their faces were awash with tears, holding each other up. And I felt so ashamed. These women were identifying themselves with Jesus, while we cowards were hiding in the crowd. I could stand it no longer. I moved forward, right to the foot of the cross, and put my arms around my aunt Mary. I felt her body sag against me for comfort. Little did she realize that it was she who was comforting me.

"As I stood there, I still battled with disbelief. This couldn't be happening! I wanted time to stop, to turn back. I felt so helpless, like an infant—not like a man. We men always want to *do* something. But there was nothing I could do.

"Suddenly the whole scene imprinted itself on my brain. Two common thieves were crucified on either side of Jesus. Jesus' arms were stretched out, nailed to the crossbeam. One man was crucified to his right hand, and the other was crucified to his left. A wave of horror came over me. Had my brother James and I *actually asked Jesus* if we could sit at his right hand and left hand when he came into his kingdom? What arrogance! He had asked *us* if we could "drink from the same cup" he was going to drink . . .

"I saw it then. I knew that "drinking from the same cup" meant suffering with him. Maybe not that day. But someday. And strangely, strength seemed to straighten my spine. Because I knew why Jesus was on that cross. Love. Everything he'd said at Passover was about love. The Father's love for him. His love for us. That we should love each other.

"Then I heard his voice, rasping through the pain. 'She is your mother now.' I looked up. Jesus was looking at *me*. I pulled Aunt Mary closer to show I understood. But how little I understood that day! Yet I knew that Love was on that cross . . ."

In His Own Words
"Dear friends, since God loved us that much, we surely ought to love each other" (1 John 4:11).

Ignatius, Bishop of Antioch
Rome—ca. 111, honored October 17
In the first century A.D, Antioch was a great city of 500,000 citizens, called "The Queen of the East" and considered the third ranking metropolis in the Roman Empire after Rome and Alexandria. "It was there at Antioch that the believers were first called Christians" (Acts 11:26). The church of Antioch thrived under the teachings of Paul, and sent him and his companions out on the first and second missionary journeys.

After the deaths of the apostles, Ignatius was appointed the second bishop of Antioch after Euodius. Because of his close relationship to Polycarp, Bishop of Smyrna, who was a disciple of the apostle John, it is generally assumed that Ignatius was John's disciple as well. Ignatius was also called *Theophorus*, which means "bearer of God," because the name of Jesus was often on his lips, whether in public or private.

God's Wheat, Ground Fine by Lion's Teeth
In the ninth year of his reign, the Roman emperor Trajan—fresh from victories over the Scythians and Dacians and hoping to consolidate the "universality" of his dominion—sent out an edict that the Christian sect should join their neighbors in sacrificing to the Roman gods. The penalty for refusing to do so was clear: "Sacrifice, or die."

Concerned for the health of the church, Bishop Ignatius inspired his flock to stand fast against the terrors of persecution with hope and courage. There were things worse than death. "The life of man is a continual death," he often said, "unless it be that Christ lives in us." He had no fear for himself. In fact, he looked forward to martyrdom that he might suffer with Christ and in so doing draw even closer to his Savior.

One ancient historian, Nicephorus, says that when Trajan stopped in Antioch to sacrifice to the gods, Ignatius showed up in the pagan temple and rebuked Trajan publicly for giving honor to mere idols that were powerless to help anyone. Arrested and brought before the emperor, Ignatius told Trajan: "You are in error when you call the demons of the nations gods. For there is but one God, who made heaven, and earth, and the sea, and all that are in them, and one Jesus Christ, the only-begotten Son of God, whose kingdom may I enjoy."

"Do you mean Jesus who was crucified under Pontius Pilate?" asked Trajan.

"I mean Jesus who crucified my sin," said Ignatius boldly.

Knowing that Ignatius was well-respected in Antioch, Trajan passed sentence that the bishop should be bound and taken to Rome "to be devoured by wild beasts." He hoped to terrify ordinary Christians by dealing harshly with their leader—but at a distance so that his followers would not rise up in rebellion.

Accompanied by ten soldiers, Ignatius set out on the long journey to Rome. Along the way, he wrote seven letters to churches and individuals, and encouraged groups of Christians in every city and port. In Smyrna, to his joy, Ignatius was briefly reunited with his beloved Polycarp, and they encouraged each other.

Ignatius even wrote ahead to the church of Rome, his destination. "I [already] fight with wild beasts, bound between ten leopards, who, the more I show myself friendly to them, the more cruel they become." But he wasn't complaining. In fact, he urged the Christians in Rome: "The time for my birth is close at hand. . . . Do not stand in the way of my birth to real life; do not wish me stillborn. My desire is to belong to God. Do not, then, hand me back to the world, do not try to tempt me with material things. . . . Give me the privilege of imitating the passion of my God." He declared, "I am God's wheat, ground fine by the lion's teeth to be made purest bread for Christ."

In His Own Words

"My dear Jesus, my Savior, is so deeply written in my heart, that I feel confident that if my heart were to be cut open and chopped to pieces, the name of Jesus would be found written on every piece."

—Ignatius, when asked why he repeated the name of Jesus so often.

At the name of Jesus every knee will bow, in heaven and on earth and under the earth, and every tongue will confess that Jesus Christ is Lord, to the glory of God the Father (Philippians 2:10-11).

Polycarp, Bishop of Smyrna

Smyrna—February 23, 155

The age of the apostles, which ended in Rome with the deaths of Paul and Peter about A.D. 67, was extended in Asia Minor by the apostle John, who lived until about A.D. 100. Church historians generally agree that Polycarp, born about 69 and raised by a Christian mother, was instructed by the apostle John. The writings of Irenaeus state: "[Polycarp] was not only taught by the apostles, and lived in familiar intercourse with many that had seen Christ, but also received his appointment in Asia from the apostles as Bishop in the Church of Smyrna."

As bishop of Smyrna (located in what is modern Turkey), Polycarp was strong and resolute when confronted with heresy in the fledgling Christian church, but gracious and peacemaking when it came to minor differences among church leaders (e.g., when to celebrate Easter). Without centuries of church tradition and Scripture interpretation to rely on when controversy arose, Polycarp had relied on imitating the life of Jesus. Ignatius, bishop of Antioch, told Polycarp, "Your mind is grounded in God as on an immovable rock."

Under Consul Marcus Aurelius, the persecution of Christians escalated in Asia Minor, but the church in Smyrna admired their bishop for not chasing after martyrdom, as some did. When the bloodthirsty crowds in the arena demanded, "Down with the atheists! Find Polycarp!" (Christians were called atheists because they did not believe in the pagan gods or worship Caesar), Polycarp was persuaded to go into hiding on a farm outside the city. He spent his time praying for everyone he knew. During his fervent prayers he had a vision that his pillow was on fire. From that time on he calmly accepted that one day he would be burned alive. And one day, the emperor's men came knocking on the farmhouse door. . . .

"Down with the Atheists!"

Polycarp could have tried to flee, since he was upstairs when the soldiers arrived. But the bishop came downstairs, greeted his captors, and insisted that they sit down to a good meal. "Just give me an hour to pray, then I will go with you." One hour turned into two, as Bishop Polycarp prayed once more for everyone he knew. The soldiers looked at each other uneasily. Why had they been sent to arrest such a gentle old man?

But they had their orders and delivered Polycarp to the arena on the Sabbath, February 23, in the year A.D. 155. The crowd roared when he was brought in, but those standing close to him heard a voice from heaven say, "Be brave, Polycarp, and act like a man!" The proconsul took pity on him because of his age and urged, "Just say, 'Away with the atheists!' and save yourself, old man."

Polycarp looked up into the stands full of men and women screaming for his blood, waved his hand in their direction, and said calmly, "Away with the atheists."

Startled, the proconsul pleaded with him to swear by the name of Caesar. Polycarp looked him full in the face. "If you think that I will swear by Caesar, you do not know who I am. Let me tell you plainly, I am a Christian."

Given the late hour, the wild beasts had been put away. "If you do not swear, you will die by fire!" Polycarp was unmoved. He knew that an hour in the fire here on earth was far better than eternal fire in hell. "For eighty-six years I have served Christ, and he has done me no harm. How can I then blaspheme my King, who saved me?"

People in the crowd were eager to help gather wood for a fire. But when the fire was lit, the fire seemed to arc over the old man, like a vaulted doorway. Bystanders said the smell was not burning flesh, but more like "golden bread baking." Seeing that Polycarp was not burning to death, the proconsul ordered that he be stabbed. The martyr's blood flowed with such abundance that it put out the fire.

In His Own Words

"Change of mind from better to worse is not a change allowed to us."
—Polycarp, when the proconsul said he would be torn apart by wild animals unless he changed his mind.

Justin Martyr
Rome—ca. 165–168, honored June 1

Born to Greek parents living in Samaria at the turn of the second century (about A.D. 100), Justin became a student of philosophy, studying in Alexandria and Ephesus. He eagerly studied Plato, believing that the Platonic philosophy would lead him to God. He was such a brilliant student that he soon earned the right to wear the traditional cloak indicating his stature as *Philosopher.*

But his inquisitive mind realized that not everything fit into the Platonic viewpoint. For instance, the Christians in Ephesus . . . they were accused of "living in evil and in the love of pleasure," yet they willingly embraced death rather than deny their Jesus, whom they called "the Son of God." It was true that they did not sacrifice to the gods, but they did not seem to deserve being denounced as "atheists" and "criminals." What philosophy gave them such courage, such joy?

A True Philosophy

Justin wrapped his cloak tighter around his shoulders and faced into the brisk wind coming off the Aegean Sea. He loved walking along the seashore. The waves and the wind shut out all the sounds of Ephesus's busy city life. Here he could think.

An old man seemed to have the same idea, walking along the shore with the help of a staff. When Justin caught his eye, he smiled invitingly. Always eager to learn from his elders, Justin fell into step with the old man and they began to talk. The old man was a good listener, and Justin found himself eagerly discussing Platonic philosophy and his belief that transcendent ideas could be known through the material world, and by careful reflection lead to knowledge of God.

The old man asked a few questions for clarification and listened respectfully. Then, gently, he told Justin that human knowledge alone could not lead to God, but that God had revealed himself in a Person, Jesus of Nazareth. Indeed, it wasn't philosophy that led to God, but a saving knowledge of the only true God that led to true philosophy—understanding of life—and happiness.

"How can I gain this divine knowledge?" Justin asked eagerly.

The old man pointed him to the Prophets of the Jewish Scriptures, who had faithfully recorded the works of God among his people and foretold the coming of the Messiah and whose prophecies were fulfilled in the life of Jesus. Later Justin wrote of this experience: "Straightway a flame was kindled in my soul, and a love of the prophets and those who are friends of Christ possessed me. Then only I became a true philosopher."

A prolific writer, Justin became an apologist for the Christian faith. Even today we have three well-documented writings by Justin: (1) An "Apology" written to the Emperor Antoninus Pius defending Christianity and describing current Christian ceremonies such as baptism and the Lord's Supper to counter distorted accounts; (2) a second "Apology" to the Roman Senate, refuting charges of immorality and misconduct among the Christians and arguing that Christians make good citizens; and (3) a "Dialog with Trypho the Jew" about whether Jesus was the promised Messiah spoken of by the Prophets.

A skilled debater, Justin was always willing to discuss his newfound "philosophy" whether in Ephesus or Rome. But Crescens, a Cynic philosopher, did not take kindly to losing these debates, and began to lay snares for Justin, accusing him of practicing an "unauthorized religion." Justin and six of his students (including a young woman) from his school of Christian philosophy were brought to trial before Rusticus, the Roman prefect. Each one affirmed: "We are Christians; we do not sacrifice to idols."

Sentenced to be whipped and then beheaded, Justin joined the ranks of those Christians he had admired in Ephesus, who faced death with the confidence that no trial on earth compared to the joy that awaited them in eternal life with God.

In His Own Words
"No right-thinking person falls away from piety to impiety."
—Justin, when urged to sacrifice to the Roman gods and save his life.

The law of the Lord is perfect, reviving the soul. The decrees of the Lord are trustworthy, making wise the simple (Psalm 19:7).

Blandina
France—177, honored June 2

Lyons (modern Lyon, France) was the Roman capital of Gaul and one of the most important cities in the empire during the reign of Marcus Aurelius. To it and nearby Vienne came a company of missionaries from Greece and Phrygia (central Turkey) under the leadership of the elderly Bishop Pothinus.

These industrious settlers prospered, and many acquired servants and became quite influential. But as often happens when one group thrives, lazy onlookers become jealous and hateful. They spread rumors charging the Christians with incest and cannibalism.

The pagans began to categorize Christians as outcasts, restricting them from certain social settings—the baths, markets, and finally all public places. They claimed that they worshipped their gods in all these places, and the presence of Christians defiled them.

Then in 177, while the governor was away, a mob—possibly inspired by a celebration in honor of the Roman goddess Roma—attacked the Christians openly. Their homes and businesses were vandalized, and many were beaten and stoned. In an attempt to restore order, city officials finally arrested and imprisoned the Christians.

When the governor returned, he set up public trials, and under torture many of the servants from the Christian homes testified that their masters were indeed guilty of incest and cannibalism. However, Blandina, a Christian servant girl, refused to sell out her masters. Apparently, she appeared physically weak and was rather plain, possibly even homely. But a letter later sent back to the churches of Greece and Asia about the incident said, "Blandina was filled with such power as to be delivered and raised above those who took turns torturing her in every manner from morning until evening. Finally, they acknowledged that they were conquered, and could do nothing more to her. They were astonished at her endurance, as her entire body was mangled and covered with gaping wounds. They even admitted that any one of the many tortures applied to her was sufficient to destroy life. But the young woman, like a noble athlete, renewed her strength and received comfort and relief from the pain through her consistent confession: 'I am a Christian, and we do nothing of which to be ashamed!'"

Bishop Pothinus, over ninety years old by then, was questioned and beaten, and thrown into a prison cell with a ceiling only three feet high, where he died two days later.

Other Christians were taken to the arena, and for the entertainment of the mob they were beaten and dragged about by wild beasts, finally being made to sit in a red-hot iron chair until their own smoke engulfed them. Still they kept confessing Christ.

Not knowing what else to do, Blandina's persecutors hung her on a post in the arena and released the wild beasts to eat her. But she looked as if she were on a cross, reminding the other martyrs—brought to witness and be intimidated by her torture—of Christ who had died for them all. Even the animals shied back and would not touch her. Some who had earlier recanted withdrew their denial and confessed Christ anew. Whoever had the rights of Roman citizenship the governor beheaded. The rest he fed to the wild beasts.

On the "games" went until forty-six Christians had died either in prison or in the arena. Then, on the last day of a sports event, Blandina was brought back into the arena, along with a fifteen-year-old Christian boy name Pontius. Blandina so encouraged him by her example that he remained faithful as they endured yet another round of tortures. Finally he died, leaving only Blandina, who—according to the letter reporting these events—was like a "noble mother who had encouraged her children and sent them on before her victorious to the King." After she had been scourged and exposed to the wild beasts again, and roasted in the iron chair, she was at last enclosed in a net and cast before a bull, which tossed her about like a ball until she was dead.

The mob burned the forty-eight bodies and tossed the ashes into the Rhone River, saying, "They despise dangers and are ready to even go to death with joy. Now let us see if they will rise again, and if their God can help them and rescue them out of our hands."

Jesus told her, "I am the resurrection and the life. Those who believe in me, even though they die like everyone else, will live again. They are given eternal life for believing in me and will never perish" (John 11:25-26).

The Scillitan Martyrs
Carthage, North Africa—July 17, 180

When Vigellius Saturninus was proconsul of North Africa, twelve Christians from the town of Scillitan were brought before him on July 17, 180. The exact location of Scillitan is not certain, but it was probably near Carthage. The following translation is based on a ninth-century manuscript, thought by some to be a copy of the original Roman transcript of the trial. Speratus acts as the spokesperson for the believers, but several others speak up as well. It is noteworthy that while the Christians faced death by the sword, a relatively humane form of execution, they were not tortured. Torture to extract recantations became more common in the empire later.

The Trial

Saturninus (the proconsul): You can win the indulgence of our lord the Emperor, if you return to a sound mind.

Speratus: We have never done ill, we have not lent ourselves to wrong, we have never spoken ill, but when ill-treated we have given thanks because we pay heed to Our Emperor.

Saturninus: We too are religious, and our religion is simple, and we swear by the genius of our lord the Emperor, and pray for his welfare, as ye also ought to do.

Speratus: If you will lend me your ears, I can tell thee the mystery of simplicity.

Saturninus: I will not lend mine ears to you when you begin to speak evil things of our sacred rites. But rather, swear by the genius of our lord the Emperor.

Speratus: The empire of this world I know not. I serve that God, whom no man hath seen, nor with these eyes can see. I have committed no theft, but if I have bought anything, I pay the tax because I know my Lord, the King of kings and Emperor of all nations.

Saturninus (to all the accused): Cease to be of this persuasion.

Speratus: It is an ill persuasion to do murder, to speak false witness.

Saturninus: Don't take part in this folly.

Cittinus: We have none other to fear, save only our Lord God, who is in heaven.

Donata: Honor to Caesar as Caesar but fear to God.

Vestia: I am a Christian.

Secunda: What I am is what I wish to be.

Saturninus (to Speratus): Do you persist in being a Christian?

Speratus: I am a Christian. (All the accused agreed with him.)

Saturninus: Would you like some time to reconsider?

Speratus: In a matter so straightforward, there is nothing to consider.

Saturninus: What are the things you are holding?

Speratus: Books and epistles of Paul, a just man.

Saturninus: Take thirty days and rethink your decisions.

Speratus: I am a Christian. (Again, all agreed.)

Saturninus (reading from the tablet): Speratus, Nartzalus, Cittinus, Donata, Vestia, Secunda and the rest, having confessed that they live according to the Christian rite, since after opportunity offered them of returning to the custom of the Romans, they have obstinately persisted, it is determined that they be put to the sword.

Speratus: We give thanks to God.

Nartzalus: Today we are martyrs in heaven. Thanks be to God.

Saturninus (to the herald): Declare publicly: Speratus, Nartzalus, Cittinus, Veturius, Felix, Aquilinus, Laetantius, Januaria, Generosa, Vestia, Donata, and Secunda, I have ordered to be executed.

All the condemned: Thanks be to God.

It is no shame to suffer for being a Christian. Praise God for the privilege of being called by his wonderful name! . . . So if you are suffering according to God's will, keep on doing what is right, and trust yourself to the God who made you, for he will never fail you (1 Peter 4:16, 19).

Felicitas and Perpetua

Carthage, North Africa—March 7, 203

Carthage was an ancient city in North Africa, now occupied by Tunis, the capital of Tunisia, situated between Libya and Algeria. In A.D. 202, persecution against the growing Christian "sect" intensified under Emperor Septimus Severus. Citizens of Carthage were required to carry a certificate stating that they had sacrificed to the Roman gods as a sign of loyalty to the emperor. Some Christians simply laid low, did not call attention to themselves, or even carried the certificates of their servants to avoid detection.

But it was hard to ignore Christians such as Vibia Perpetua, only twenty-two years old, married to a distinguished citizen (possibly a widow, since her husband is not mentioned), and mother of a nursing infant. Called before a judge along with Felicitas, her maid, who was pregnant, and three young men, all of whom were being discipled by one named Saturus, she boldly declared herself a Christian.

Although Perpetua's mother and brother were believers, her father was not. He begged his daughter to consider her son and his own gray hair, and renounce this dangerous name. "Father," Perpetua said, pointing to a common water pot, "can this pot be called by any other name than what it is?"

"No," admitted her father.

"Neither can I be called anything other than what I am, a Christian."

The judge had no choice but to confine Perpetua and her companions in prison. Saturus, their teacher, voluntarily gave himself up, so that he might join them in whatever fate awaited them.

Visions for Courage

The prison was dark, cold, and damp. Perpetua could not help being afraid— but her greatest sorrow was being separated from her child. Two Christian deacons gave money to the jailors so that they could visit and encourage the prisoners, and Perpetua's family brought her infant son to her so she could nurse him. To her joy, she was allowed to keep the child. She wrote in her journal: "The prison turned into a palace for me."

But their fate was not yet certain. One night Perpetua had a vivid dream. She saw a narrow ladder that reached all the way into heaven. All sorts of metal weapons were attached to the sides of the ladder—swords, hooks, daggers, and spikes—so that if anyone climbed carelessly, he would be cut and wounded. At the foot of the ladder lay an enormous dragon that terrified anyone who tried to climb the ladder.

In the dream, Saturus, her teacher, was first to go up the ladder. Looking back, he said, "Perpetua, I am waiting for you. But take care; do not let the dragon bite you."

"He will not harm me, in the name of Christ Jesus!" And using the dragon's head as the first step, Perpetua began to climb the ladder. At the top was a peaceful garden, where she was given fresh sweet milk to drink.

Waking from this dream, Perpetua knew that martyrdom would be their fate. But the fear was gone. At another hearing, the sentence was passed: all would face the wild beasts in the amphitheater.

However, the law did not allow the slaughter of an unborn child, and Felicitas, eight months pregnant, was afraid she would not be allowed to go with the others into the arena. Her companions prayed. Two days before they were slated to face the beasts, Felicitas went into labor and gave birth to a little girl, who was entrusted into the care of Christian sisters.

Now their joy was complete. The two young women would make their witness together. Saturus and the other men were attacked by a wild boar, a bear, and a leopard, but not mortally wounded. A rabid heifer tossed Perpetua and Felicitas to the ground, but Perpetua helped her loyal maid, friend, and sister in the Lord to her feet. Together they walked to the center of the arena, where they were beheaded.

Voice of the Hero
"Stand fast in the faith and love one another."
—Perpetua's last words to her brother

Our citizenship is in heaven. . . . Therefore, my brothers [and sisters], you whom I love and long for, my joy and crown, that is how you should stand firm in the Lord, dear friends! (Philippians 3:20; 4:1, NIV).

Hippolytus and Pontianus
Rome—236, honored August 13

Again and again the apostle Paul pleaded with the church to *avoid* quarrels and controversies. After nearly eighteen hundred years, it may be Monday-morning quarterbacking to say the controversies that caused Hippolytus to break away from the church were avoidable, but we can be sure that all divisions in the body of Christ grieve Jesus and delay the fulfillment of his prayer in John 17.

Hippolytus was a presbyter and theologian in Rome who strongly "contended" for the truth at the beginning of the third century. He had been a student of Irenaeus, who was a disciple of Polycarp, who was a disciple of John, the beloved disciple of Jesus. But Hippolytus also tended to be contentious. He fought most bitterly with a deacon named Callistus, whom he did not respect personally. They argued over absolution for certain sins—Hippolytus being more rigid and Callistus more forgiving—and the nature of the Trinity. Hippolytus was convinced of the "Logos" doctrine, which distinguished the persons of the Trinity, as opposed to Modalism, which believed they were simply different manifestations of the same person. At the time, his bishop, Zephyrinus, did not see the issue as much of a threat, and declined to take a stand. This infuriated Hippolytus, and he accused Zephyrinus of being an incompetent bishop manipulated by Callistus. The dispute broadened and the accusations flew.

When Zephyrinus died in 217, Callistus was selected over Hippolytus as the next bishop of Rome. That was too much for Hippolytus! He left the church and had himself declared bishop of Rome by his followers, thus dividing the church. He ended up saying he represented the true church while the great majority of Roman Christians were merely of the "School of Callistus." In retrospect, the Roman Catholic Church considers Hippolytus the first *antipope*. Some Protestants are not in agreement that the bishop of Rome was yet considered "pope" over the whole church. They maintain that not until Stephen (254–57), did the bishop of Rome try to claim authority over other bishops. And it wasn't until the 300s that bishops were sometimes called *pope*. But all agree that Hippolytus certainly divided the church of Rome.

Hippolytus maintained this division through two successors of Callistus: Bishop Urban (222–30) and Bishop Pontianus (230–35). However, when the Roman emperor Maximinus initiated his persecution of the church, directed primarily at the leadership, he rounded up both Hippolytus and Pontianus as bishops and sent them off to work in the "death mines" on the island of Sardinia. To make the election of a new bishop possible, Pontianus resigned his office immediately before departing.

Forced labor is humbling. Before Hippolytus and Pontianus died sometime in 236, they reconciled with one another. One can only imagine the circumstances or conversations between these two brothers. But Hippolytus— possibly through some correspondence or messenger—communicated his reconciliation to his followers in Rome and ended the schism in the church. One of the first things that Bishop Fabian of Rome did after being elected in 236 was retrieve the remains of both Hippolytus and Pontianus from Sardinia on August 13 and have them interred with honor in the catacombs he was restoring.

In spite of his schismatic influence, some historians consider Hippolytus the most important theologian and most prolific religious writer of the Roman church prior to Constantine. However, though there may be circumstances or issues with which we cannot live in peace with others in the church, Jesus' prayer for unity reveals God's perfect will: "My prayer for all of them is that they will be one, just as you and I are one, Father—that just as you are in me and I am in you, so they will be in us, and the world will believe you sent me" (John 17:21).

[Paul wrote,] "Again I say, don't get involved in foolish, ignorant arguments that only start fights. The Lord's servants must not quarrel but must be kind to everyone. They must be able to teach effectively and be patient with difficult people. They should gently teach those who oppose the truth. Perhaps God will change those people's hearts, and they will believe the truth" (2 Timothy 2:23-25).

Fabian
Rome—January 20, 250

It is said that Fabian became the bishop of Rome in a most unusual fashion. Upon the death of Bishop Antherus in A.D. 236, a council was convened to elect his successor, and Fabian, a visiting believer from his farm in the country and a man of no great notoriety, was in the assembly. According to the historian Eusebius, "A dove flew down from above and settled on his head as clear imitation of the decent of the Holy Ghost in the form of a dove upon the

Savior, whereupon the whole people, as if moved by one divine inspiration, with all eagerness and with one soul cried out, 'worthy,' and without more ado" selected him as their bishop.

Fabian turned out to be an excellent leader. He divided Rome into seven districts and appointed seven deacons to oversee these parishes—the same parish structure used by the Catholic Church to this day, and he supposedly organized the four minor orders. During his tenure the church flourished and there was a lull in persecution under Emperor Philip, but Fabian never forgot the martyrs and did considerable work restoring the catacombs and adorning them with paintings. He also retrieved the bodies Pontianus and Hippolytus from Sardinia where the Roman authorities had sent them to work in the extermination mines and had them entombed with honor in the catacombs. Then he commissioned fourteen historians to document the lives of the martyrs so their stories would not be forgotten.

Gregory of Tours, the historian of the Franks, also attributes to him the commissioning in A.D. 245 of seven missionary bishops to Gaul.

But the time of peace for the church did not last. When Emperor Philip died in 249, Decius, a man from a village near the Danube on the northern frontier, succeeded him. He recognized the military threat from the barbarians hounding the periphery of the empire and blamed Philip for military incompetence. But he also saw the social and economic decline in the cities and, along with many pagans, blamed the Christians.

His solution was to restore Roman customs and require all inhabitants of the empire to participate in the emperor's yearly sacrifice to the gods of Rome. The edict was probably issued in December of 249 along with a warrant for the arrest of leading Christians. Fabian was one of the first arrested in Rome.

Certificates (libelli) were published throughout the empire, which, when witnessed and signed by an official, would demonstrate the bearer's compliance with the edict. Several copies have survived, and one from as far away as Egypt reads: "To those appointed to see the sacrifices: from Aurelia Charis of the Egyptian village of Theadelphia. I have always continued to sacrifice and show reverence to the gods, and now, in your presence, I have poured a libation and sacrificed and eaten some of the sacrificial meat. I request you to certify this for me below."

The few years of peace preceding this had caused the church to grow soft, and many buckled under the threat of martyrdom. But Fabian, who was tried personally before the emperor himself, stood firm in his faith. He was executed on or shortly after January 20, 250, and is buried in the Cemetery of Calixtus that he helped rebuild and beautify. Today there remains a broken tombstone marking the place with the barely legible words, "Fabian, bishop, and martyr."

Turmoil in the Church

After Decius died in June 251 on a campaign against the Goths, the purge ended, and the church had to deal with all those who had denied Christ. Alexandria and Carthage had seen massive apostasies. In Smyrna, the bishop himself performed sacrifice. Bishop Cyprian, who had fled himself, returned to Carthage to aid demoralized and disorganized congregations. Some did not want to allow those who had given in to return to the church. Others were more ready to forgive.

> Jesus said to Simon Peter, "Simon son of John, do you truly love me more than these?" "Yes, Lord," [Peter] said, "you know that I love you." Jesus said, "Feed my lambs" (John 21:15, NIV).

Origen
Caesarea—ca. 254

Origen was raised by Christian parents in Egypt, where he received a sound education at home before studying under Clement of Alexandria. He was the eldest of seven children, and his father, Leonides, was very proud of learning. However, when Origen was only seventeen, his father was arrested under the persecution of Emperor Severus in 202, and Origen, who was very zealous for the faith, wanted to follow him in what he knew would be martyrdom. His mother wisely hid his clothes, preventing him from leaving the house until he cooled down. While his father awaited his execution in prison, Origen had to content himself with corresponding with his father.

After killing Leonides, the authorities seized his property, leaving the family destitute until Origen put his excellent education to use by teaching at the local catechetical school. There he became so popular that he had to divide his classes, letting an assistant teach the less advanced students. The persecution slackened for a time, but then it intensified, and some of Origen's students were martyred. He went with them to their trial, and stood by them in their sufferings, but he was allowed to go free.

He lived a very austere life, giving all extra money to the poor, eating only the poorest food, keeping only one coat for himself, and sleeping on the cold, stone floor. When he grew older and realized that he had hurt his health beyond repair, he regretted this behavior, considering it an impetuous mistake.

His learning was so extensive that many pagans went to hear him and were converted. He also was permitted to travel freely to Rome, Palestine, and Arabia, visiting churches and gaining the approval of many bishops. However, according to the historian Eusebius, he castrated himself in literal obedience to Matthew 19:12: "Some are born as eunuchs, some have been made that way by others, and some choose not to marry for the sake of the Kingdom of Heaven. Let anyone who can, accept this statement." That caused his own bishop, Demetrius of Alexandria, to refuse to ordain him. And so in

230, Origen moved to Palestine where the bishops of Jerusalem and Caesarea welcomed and ordained him.

Over the years he wrote prolifically, including letters, treatises in dogmatic and practical theology, apologetics, exegeses, and textual criticism—according to Jerome, over eight hundred works. Though many have been lost, others have come down to us today. Prior to Augustine, he is considered by many to have been the most influential theologian of the church. However, he created controversy when he tried to explain the gospel in terms his culture could grasp—particularly those influenced by Greek philosophy. He believed, for instance, in the preexistence of souls and that eventually everyone, including the devil, would be saved. In addition, he described the Trinity as a hierarchy, not as an equality of Father, Son, and Spirit. Also, though he taught against Gnosticism, he rejected the goodness of the material creation.

These deviations from orthodoxy caused many in the church to object to his teachings. Nevertheless, he was a strong Christian apologist and helped many endure persecution, something he endured himself in 250 under the violent reign of Decius.

At the age of sixty-five, he was imprisoned and, according to Eusebius, "He lay in iron[s] and in the recesses of his dungeon; . . . for many days his feet were stretched four spaces [apart] in that instrument of torture, the stocks. He bore with a stout heart threats of fire and everything else that was inflicted by his enemies." Yet he did not recant.

He was ultimately released, but his injuries contributed to his death in about 254.

In His Own Words

"In Psalm 116 there is written this rhetorical question: What shall I render to the Lord for all the things that He hath rendered to me? And then follows the reply . . . : I will take the chalice of salvation, and I will call upon the name of the Lord. The "chalice of salvation" is the usual term used for martyrdom, as we see from the Gospel. There the Lord answers them that wish for a higher honor in sitting on the right and on the left of Jesus in His kingdom, saying: Can you drink the chalice that I shall drink? He calls martyrdom a chalice, as is evident again from the words: Father, if it be possible, let this chalice pass from me. Nevertheless not as I will but as Thou wilt. And again we learn that he who drinks the chalice that Jesus drank will sit, reign, and judge beside the King of Kings."

—Origen, from *section 5:* "The Necessity, Essence, and Kinds of Martyrdom."

Cyprian
North Africa—September 14, 258

The eloquent trial lawyer glided gracefully through the streets of Carthage and spoke with poise to all who greeted him. At middle age, he lived with an elderly friend, Caecilianus, a priest who, knowing he was about to die, had asked Cyprian to care for his wife and family. Cyprian obliged and also accepted the gospel the priest shared with him. He then threw himself into serving Christ with as much vigor as he had previously applied to accumulating wealth—which he gave away to the poor.

In about 248, he was selected as bishop of Carthage, the largest church in Africa in one of the greatest cities of antiquity, poised on the continent's northern coast. However, in October 249, Decius became emperor with the ambition of restoring Rome's vitality and unity by requiring all inhabitants to participate in the yearly sacrifice to the gods of Rome. His first step was to put to death the Christian bishops and torture all other believers until they recanted. On January 20, 250, Bishop Fabian of Rome was martyred. Cyprian took warning and retreated to the hills outside his city. Though many criticized him for fleeing, he was able to conduct the affairs of the church from this hideout and thereby prevent his flock from being entirely scattered.

Once the proconsul arrived in April, the persecution in Carthage became severe. Children were tortured, women raped, and others burnt alive. Fifteen died of torture in prison. Some, after being tortured twice, were banished. Those who refused to recant were known as "confessors." Nevertheless, at Carthage the majority apostatized or "lapsed," and when the persecution let up after the death of Decius in 251, churches throughout the empire faced the dilemma of what to do with all the repentant members who had denied Christ just to save their skins.

Surprisingly, many of the confessors were more eager to grant quick pardons to those who had lapsed and repented than some of the elders at Carthage and Novatian, a leading theologian in Rome. They viewed apostasy as a "sin unto death" (1 John 5:16). Cyprian took a middle road. His concern was for church discipline and that the lapsed not end up in a better position than those who had stood fast under torture or exile and lost their property or health. He wanted repentant apostates to perform extended penance such as serving those in prison or ministering to the poor before being restored to good standing.

Nevertheless, at Carthage there were numerous reports of the dreadful state of those who had denied Christ. Reportedly, a man was struck dumb on the steps of the capitol where he had denied Christ. Another went crazy in the public baths and nearly bit off his tongue, with which he had tasted the pagan sacrifice. A lapsed elderly woman had a fit when she tried to receive communion unworthily. Fire was said to come forth from the sacrament when another lapsed woman reached for it. Another found the communion sacraments to be nothing but cinders when she tried to partake.

On the other hand, because they stood against apostasy, martyrs and confessors were held in high esteem in the church. The spiritual authority of confessors sometimes rivaled that of bishops. The anniversaries of martyrs' deaths began to be celebrated as feast days or heavenly birthdays, and numerous stories circulated of their seemingly miraculous feats of prayer during their lifetimes, so much so that people began to pray to them after their death to intercede on their behalf.

No Retreat

When Emperor Valerian ascended the throne, persecution of Christians was renewed. This time Cyprian did not flee and was arrested and tried before the proconsul Paternus, where he declared himself a Christian and a bishop. At first he was exiled to Curubis, but then he was brought back by a new proconsul, Galerius Maximus, and retried. When he refused to sacrifice to the Roman gods, he was condemned and beheaded on September 14, 258 A.D. He was the first African bishop crowned by martyrdom.

> [Jesus said,] "Whoever confesses Me before men, him I will also confess before My Father who is in heaven. But whoever denies Me before men, him I will also deny before My Father who is in heaven" (Matthew 10:32-33, NKJV).

Lawrence
Rome—August 10, 258

At the beginning of the month of August in 258, Emperor Valerian issued an edict, commanding that all Christian bishops, pastors, and deacons be put to death and that all church property should be confiscated.

Sixtus II, bishop of Rome at that time, was soon apprehended in the catacombs and summarily executed along with most of his clergy, two of which were Felicissimus and Agapitus. A few days later, on August 10, Deacon Lawrence was also martyred, possibly burned to death on a gridiron, though that would have been an unusual form of execution *if* he had been a Roman citizen. He was later buried in the catacombs of Cyriaca *in agro Verano* on the Via Tiburtina.

The Rest of the Story

The above facts have substantial historical documentation. But some interesting details about Lawrence and his martyrdom come down to us from Bishop Damasus, Ambrose of Milan, and the poet Prudentius, all writing in the fourth century probably from oral tradition. These details explain why Lawrence has been one of the most honored martyrs from the early church in Rome.

Lawrence supposedly saw his bishop, Sixtus II, being taken to his execution and called out to him, "Will you go to heaven and leave me behind?" To which the bishop replied, "Be comforted, you will follow me in three days."

The Roman prefect, knowing that Lawrence was responsible for the church's finances and thinking that the church had a great deal of gold, ordered Lawrence to tell him about the treasures of the church. Lawrence admitted that the church was very rich, and the prefect offered him this deal: Deliver the church's treasure, and you can go free. Lawrence reportedly agreed, saying that it would take him three days to gather it.

During that time he dispersed what money the church held to various stewards, and then gathered all the poor, widows, and orphans of the congregation and on the appointed day brought them before the prefect, saying, "These are the treasures of the church."

Threats frothed from the prefect's mouth, but Lawrence calmly explained. "These poor of ours are sick and lame, but beautiful and whole within. They bear with them a spirit fair and free from taint and misery. . . . [They are] not foul and shabby, or infirm, as now they seem to scornful eyes, but fair, in radiant vesture clad, with crowns of gold upon their heads."

Of course, the prefect was not amused and ordered Lawrence roasted alive on a gridiron. Lawrence submitted bravely, and, in the middle of his torture, is said to have told his executioner, "You may turn me over, now. I am done on this side." Then he used his last breath to pray for all the people of Rome.

The whole spectacle made a profound impression on the populace and many pagan Roman citizens were afterward converted to the Christian faith. Some of them are said to have been the people to rescue what remained of his body and convey it to the believers for burial in the catacombs.

But Lawrence's respect for the poor, lame, and sick—whether reported accurately in every detail or not—has remained in the memory of the church as an example of God's heart toward the needy for whom all deacons—indeed, all believers—are charged to care.

"Then the King will say to those on the right, 'Come, you who are blessed by my Father, inherit the Kingdom prepared for you from the foundation of the world. For I was hungry, and you fed me. I was thirsty, and you gave me a drink. I was a stranger, and you invited me into your home. I was naked, and you gave me clothing. I was sick, and you cared for me. I was in prison, and you visited me.' . . . 'I assure you, when you did it to one of the least of these my brothers and sisters, you were doing it to me!'" (Matthew 25:34-36, 40).

The Theban Legion
Greece—September 22, 286

The Theban Legion—over six thousand men in the Roman army—were said to have been recruited from around the city of Thebes in Upper Egypt, near the Valley of the Kings. They were almost entirely Christian, coming from what is now known as the Coptic church. Tradition holds that many—if not most— were black men.

Their captain, Maurice, was supported by Lieutenant Candid and camp doctor Exuperius. And in accordance with Roman custom, they were stationed far from home in what is now Switzerland during the time when Emperor Maximian and his colleague Diocletian ruled the empire.

When a rebellion arose in Gaul, Maximian marched his army—including the Theban Legion—north and quelled it. On the return route, Maximian ordered the whole army to sacrifice to the gods for their success. These rites included sacrificing their Christian captives.

Unwilling to take part in such horrendous celebrations, the Theban Legion removed itself from the rest of the army and made camp near the town of Agaunum.

When Emperor Maximian heard of this defiance, he became so angry that he ordered other army units to decimate the legion by executing every tenth man. Again he gave the order that they participate in the sacrifices to the pagan gods, but the Theban Legion refused. Enraged beyond all reason, Maximian ordered another mass execution of every tenth man.

Still the Thebans refused. But on the encouragement of Captain Maurice and his lieutenants, they drew up a response to their emperor.

Rather than bend to their appeal, Emperor Maximian's rage boiled over, and he commanded the remainder of the legion to be slaughtered.

In the Manner of Christ

True to their promise, the legion did not resort to their numbers or their weapons for protection but submitted willingly to the executioners. This barbarous slaughter took place on September 22, 286.

Some members of the legion were not at Agaunum at the time of the massacre. But Maximian's rage was so insatiable that he sent contingents to slaughter every member of the legion posted along the military highway linking Germany with Switzerland and all the way to Rome.

Some contemporary scholars doubt the authenticity of these events, but they are attested to by both the Coptic Orthodox and the Roman Catholic churches and in Foxe's *Book of Martyrs*, having been reported by Eucher, the bishop of Lyons, who died in 494. Rather than a town called Agaunum on the road from Rome to Geneva, one will today find the village of Saint Maurice.

In Their Own Words

"Emperor, we are your soldiers but also the soldiers of the True God. We owe you military service and obedience, but we cannot renounce Him who is our Creator and Master, and also yours, even though you reject Him. In all things that are not against His law, we most willingly obey you, as we have done so far. We readily oppose your enemies whoever they are, but we cannot stain our hands with the blood of innocent people. We have taken an oath to God before we took one to you. You cannot place any confidence in our second oath if we violate the first. You have commanded us to execute Christians, behold we are such. We confess God the Father, Creator of all things and His

Son Jesus Christ, God. We have seen our comrades slain with the sword, we do not weep for them but rather rejoice at their honor. Neither this, nor any other provocation has tempted us to revolt. Behold, we have arms in our hands, but we do not resist, because we would rather die innocent than live by any sin."

He was led as a lamb to the slaughter. And as a sheep is silent before the shearers, he did not open his mouth (Isaiah 53:7).

Agape, Chionia, and Irene
Greece—April 3, 304

Agape, Chionia, and Irene were the daughters of pagan parents living in Thessalonica, but they came to faith in Christ and collected copies of various New Testament books until Emperor Diocletian issued a decree in A.D. 303 making it a capital offense to possess any portion of the Christian Scriptures.

Dismayed, the girls fled to the mountains and lived in a cave where they could study the Scriptures in peace. An older Christian woman visited them each week, brought whatever they needed, took their handiwork back to town to sell, and distributed any excess to the poor. One day a spy followed her to see why she made so many trips up the mountain, and he discovered the girls praying in their cave. Somehow he overcame them, bound and dragged them down the mountain, and turned them over to Governor Dulcetius.

Suspecting that the sisters were Christians, Dulcetius tried to get them to eat food offered to the Roman gods. They not only refused; they also abandoned their former timidity and boldly announced that they were Christians. The governor then questioned them about why they wouldn't comply with the emperor's edict and the laws of the land. Agape said, "I believe in the living God, and will not by an evil action lose all the merit of my past life." Her sister Chionia replied in much the same way, and Irene explained that she disobeyed the laws because she did not want to offend God.

Then the governor tried to get the sisters to reveal where they had hidden their books and papers, but they would not tell him. "Who drew you into this persuasion?" asked the governor.

"Almighty God," answered Chionia.

"No, no. I want to know who induced you to believe this."

"Almighty God and his only Son, our Lord Jesus Christ."

"You think you can defy the just commands of our emperor, but you shall receive the punishment you deserve. I sentence Agape and Chionia to be burned alive for disobeying the emperor and professing this rash and false religion, Christianity."

The sentence on the two older sisters was carried out on March 25. Possibly because of her youth, Irene was returned to prison.

Within a few days, the authorities found the hidden Scriptures, and the governor again examined Irene. "Your madness is plain, girl, keeping so many Scriptures of the impious Christians. If you have not taken warning from the punishment of your sisters, your punishment is unavoidable. But even now I'll pardon you if you will worship the gods. What do you say? Will you obey the orders of the emperors? Are you ready to sacrifice to the gods and eat of the victims?"

"By no means, for those that renounce Jesus Christ, the Son of God, are threatened with eternal fire."

Then the governor, hoping to obtain the names of other Christians, tried to get her to reveal who had influenced her and told her to hide the Scriptures or even who knew that they possessed them.

Irene replied, "Nobody but the Almighty, from Whom nothing is hid: for we concealed them even from our own domestics, lest they should accuse us."

The angry governor then condemned her to a slower death, to be exposed naked in a soldiers' brothel with only one small loaf of bread per day. But Irene was miraculously protected from molestation until her sentence was changed and she was condemned to death. One version says she was burned as her sisters had been. Another says that before the flames reached her, she was shot through the throat with an arrow on April 3, 304.

They brought the apostles in before the council. "Didn't we tell you never again to teach in this man's name?" the high priest demanded. "Instead, you have filled all Jerusalem with your teaching about Jesus, and you intend to blame us for his death!" But Peter and the apostles replied, "We must obey God rather than human authority. . . ." At this, the high council was furious and decided to kill them (Acts 5:27-29, 33).

Alban
Britain—304, honored June 22

There was a Roman town in Britain known as Verulamium, some twenty miles northeast of London. There the Roman soldier Alban had been assigned. One day a Christian priest came banging on his door, seeking refuge from persecution that had broken out in the region. Alban admitted the man, who was supposedly named Amphibalus, and the two began to talk.

Alban was impressed by the priest's piety and wisdom and asked about the Christian faith, which was still a novelty in this Roman frontier. After hearing the gospel explained over two days' time, Alban became a Christian and was baptized.

In the meantime, the pagan governor of Verulamium heard that the priest was hiding at Alban's house and sent guards to apprehend him. When Alban saw the men coming, he threw on Amphibalus's habit and answered the door after instructing the priest how to escape out the back. Because the disguised Alban was hidden under the cowl, the guards immediately assumed that he was the man they sought and brought him bound before the governor, who was at that very time making sacrifices to Roman gods. Of course, when Alban's cloak was removed, it was obvious they had the wrong man. In a rage the governor ordered Alban to make sacrifices himself to the gods or suffer death.

According to the report by the Venerable Bede (ca. 760), when Alban refused, the governor asked, "Of what family and race are you?"

"How does my family concern you?" answered Alban. "If thou want to know what is my religion, I will tell you. I am a Christian and am ready to do a Christian's duty."

"But what is your name? Tell me immediately!"

Alban shrugged. "My parents named me Alban. But more important, I worship and adore the true and living God who created all things."

"Well, if you want to live, you'll sacrifice to the gods right now."

"These sacrifices which are offered to devils do no good. In fact, hell is the reward of those who offer them."

The governor then ordered Alban whipped, hoping to shake his faith with pain. But he endured it bravely, even acquiring new resolution from his suffering. So the governor sentenced him to death.

On the way out of town, across the river, and up to the hilltop where Alban was to be beheaded, Alban explained the reason and his new faith in Christ to his executioner and to a large number of spectators who accompanied them. So persuasive was his testimony that the executioner threw down his sword and resigned, asking to become a Christian on the spot, even if it meant death.

Another man was then detailed to take over, and both men were beheaded. According to some reports, the volunteer went blind after committing the deed.

The priest, upon hearing of Alban's predicament, hurried back to Verulamium hoping to intercede by turning himself in, but he was too late and was stoned to death a few days later about four miles from town.

These were the first three Christians known to have been martyred in Britain.

Seed of the Church

Alban's body was buried in a nearby cemetery, and after Constantine legalized Christianity in 313, the local community recalled Alban and erected a small church in his honor. Constantius, the first historical authority to mention Alban, tells us that St. Germanus visited it in 429 (Life of St. Germanus of Auxerre, 480). In 793, King Offa of Mercia built a monastery there, and during the Middle Ages, St. Alban's ranked as the premier abbey in England. In 1077, a great church was built on the site, which now serves as the cathedral of the diocese of St. Alban's. In time, the town that grew up around it was called St. Alban. Nearby Verulamium died out, though its excavated ruins can still be seen.

You must stand trial before governors and kings because you are my followers. This will be your opportunity to tell them about me—yes, to witness to the world (Matthew 10:18).

Andronicus, Probus, and Tarachus
Turkey—October 11, 304

Following the death of Emperor Valerian in 260, Christians enjoyed an extended period of relative peace. Christians could still be arrested and executed—particularly if they were discovered in the army—but churches grew and Christianity spread from the cities to the small towns and countryside.

However, beginning in 270, the philosopher Porphyry began an intellectual assault on Christians, claiming they "were the inventors, not the historians, of those things they record about Jesus." His attacks increased in the 290s.

Diocletian seized the throne in 284, determined to restore traditional values and order to Rome. Administrative uniformity and fiscal stability were achieved, but he soon discovered that the Christians stood in the way of reviving the old Roman values and religion. Caesar Galerius, his strongly anti-Christian lieutenant and successful military officer, pushed Diocletian to rid the empire of Christianity. He began by rooting all Christians out of the army and civil service by 302. Then on February 23, 303, the Feast of Terminalia, honoring the Roman gods of the fields, what became known as "the great persecution" began. Churches were destroyed, Christian services banned, and the Scriptures were seized and burned. Christians lost their jobs and their civil rights.

Diocletian at first attempted to bring off this purge without bloodshed. However, when Diocletian grew ill in 304, Caesar Galerius issued an edict that everyone in the empire was required to sacrifice to the gods on pain of death.

Three Christian Friends

In Cilicia, a province in what is now southern Turkey, three Christian friends were brought before Governor Maximus in Tarsus. The youngest of the three was Andronicus, who came from one of the leading families in Ephesus. Tarachus was a sixty-five-year-old retired military officer. Probus had left a rich lifestyle to serve Christ.

"I cannot renounce the law of God," said Tarachus when ordered to sacrifice.

Shocked, the governor said, "There is only one law, the one we obey."

"Oh, but there is another," replied Tarachus, "and you transgress it by adoring your own handiwork, statues of wood or stone." For this impudence, he was struck on the mouth and beaten with rods.

Probus also refused to sacrifice and was cruelly tortured. "Look at your torn body," said the governor. "The ground is covered with your blood!" "The more my flesh suffers for Jesus Christ, the more my soul acquires strength and vigor," responded Probus.

When the governor threatened the young Andronicus, he said, "I would rather see my body cut into pieces than lose my soul." He was tortured on the rack, and salt was put into his wounds.

The governor then moved on to Mopsuestia and then Anazarbus, bringing the three Christians with him and publicly examining them in each city with increasing tortures, hoping to intimidate other Christians. Finally, unable to walk, these faithful martyrs were thrown to the wild beasts in the amphitheater, but none of the ravenous animals would touch them. A large bear that had earlier that day killed three men was loosed on them, but neither it nor a ferocious lion would touch the prisoners. In exasperation, Maximus ordered gladiators to behead them, which they did on October 11, 303.

During this persecution the church grew all the faster. People began to reject the cruelty done in the name of their old gods and asked what was so good about Jesus Christ that his followers prefer him more than life?

On his deathbed in 311, Galerius realized that it was impossible to stamp out Christianity. He revoked the edicts of persecution and even asked that the Christians pray for him. His repentance was too late to save his life. He died six days later.

When he got there, [the king] called out in anguish, "Daniel, servant of the living God! Was your God, whom you worship continually, able to rescue you from the lions?" Daniel answered, "Long live the king! My God sent his angel to shut the lions' mouths so that they would not hurt me" (Daniel 6:20-22)

Agnes

Rome—ca. 304, honored January 21

In Greek, the name *Agnes* means "chaste," and in Latin, the word *agnus* means "lamb." On the walls of the catacombs near the road known as the *Via Nomentana* in Rome is a faded painting of a young girl with a lamb at her feet. The girl in the painting is Agnes, one of the most beloved martyrs of the primitive church.

By means of a military overthrow, Diocletian became emperor of Rome in 284 and immediately set about restoring the empire's former glory and unity. Christianity was well established by then, however, and hindered the revival of the pagan religious practices. Caesar Galerius, Diocletian's powerful lieutenant, convinced him that he had to purge the empire of Christians, and so in 303 he began the last and fiercest of the persecutions of Christianity by the Roman emperors.

A Virgin Dedicated to Christ

Agnes was a young believer of only about twelve or thirteen who it is said had determined to remain a virgin as the bride of Christ, a not uncommon vow among believers of that time. According to records from as early as the fourth century, suitors from prominent Roman families became angered by her refusal to wed and denounced Agnes to the prefect of Rome as a Christian.

The judge at first tried to cajole and entice her to recant, but Agnes paid no attention, repeating that she could have no other spouse than Jesus Christ.

He then threatened her, displaying such instruments of torture as iron hooks, racks, and fire, but the young woman expressed no fear.

Seeing that he was getting nowhere, the governor threatened to send her to a brothel. Agnes reportedly responded, "You may stain your sword with my blood, but you will never be able to profane my body, because it is consecrated to Christ." This so infuriated the governor that he immediately sent her to a public brothel with the instruction that anyone was free to abuse her. Tradition says many young men went to take advantage of this offer, but upon seeing her, they were all afraid to approach her—all except one, who when he reached out was instantly blinded by a flash and fell to the ground. Agnes, who had been singing hymns, took pity on him and by prayer restored his sight.

When the governor heard that all respected her, he was even more frustrated and condemned her to be beheaded. According to Bishop Ambrose, writing in 377, Agnes was transported with joy on hearing this sentence and still more at the sight of the executioner. She "went to the place of execution more cheerfully than others go to their wedding."

Her body was buried near the *Via Nomentana*, a short distance outside Rome. A church was built on the spot in the time of Constantine, and the body, which has been preserved, is that of a young girl about thirteen who suffered decapitation.

Seed of the Church

Ambrose wrote: "At such a tender age a young girl has scarcely enough courage to bear the angry looks of her father and a tiny puncture from a needle makes her cry as if it were a wound. And still this little girl had enough courage to face the sword. She was fearless in the bloody hands of the executioner. She prayed; she bowed her head. Behold in one victim the twofold martyrdom of chastity and faith."

God blesses you who are hated and excluded and mocked and cursed because you are identified with me, the Son of Man. When that happens, rejoice! Yes, leap for joy! For a great reward awaits you in heaven. And remember, the ancient prophets were also treated that way by your ancestors (Luke 6:22-23).

Habib the Deacon

Turkey—September 2, 313, honored November 15

Shortly after Emperor Licinius came to power in the East in 313 while Constantine was coemperor in the West, he issued an edict that all the altars of the gods be repaired, sacrifices be made, libations offered, and incense burned to Jupiter.

In the region around Edessa (now Sanliurfa, Turkey), Christians were at this time more numerous than pagans, and when word reached them that even Constantine in the West had become Christian and did not sacrifice, they presumed that they could ignore the edict. Habib, a devout and active deacon of Telzeha, a village near Edessa, went privately among the churches in the surrounding villages encouraging the Christians not to comply.

But when Lysanias the governor of the region heard of Habib's activities, he became enraged and sent a report to Emperor Licinius, asking him what should be done to those who would not sacrifice, especially anyone who encouraged others to disobey. Licinius wrote back that instigators were to be burned to death and all others who followed their counsel should be beheaded.

By the time this command came to Governor Lysanias, Habib had gone across the river to the people of Zeugma encouraging them to hold true to their Christian faith and not sacrifice to any pagan gods. When the governor's men couldn't find Habib in his home village of Telzeha, they arrested his family and many of the people of the village and dragged them in irons to Edessa and put them in prison.

Following His Own Counsel

When Habib heard the news, he was stricken and decided he couldn't remain in hiding with his loved ones held hostage. So he went to Edessa and turned himself in to Judge Theotecna.

"Did anyone see you come?" asked Theotecna.

"No. I don't think so."

"Then be gone. Remain in hiding until this time of persecution passes."

"What about my family and the villagers?"

"Don't worry about them. They will be in prison a few days, and all this will blow over. The governor has not entered charges against them. He's just looking for you."

Habib thought for a moment. "It's not really about my family and friends. As I think about it, it is about my faith. Am I going to run and hide, just because I have the opportunity, or stand up for what I believe, no matter the consequences—just like I've been advising others? So, if you won't take me to the governor, I'll go by myself."

"You fool," snarled the judge and had an assistant escort him to the governor.

When the governor discovered that Habib surrendered himself willingly to judgment, rather than respect his courage, he thought Habib was behaving with contempt.

After Habib acknowledged his name and that he was a Christian and a deacon, the governor said, "Wherefore have you violated the command of the emperors, ministering in this religion of yours and refusing to sacrifice to Zeus, whom the emperors worship?"

"We are Christians. We do not worship the works of men, which are nothing. We worship God, who made the men who carved your idols from wood or stone."

For insulting Zeus and the other gods, the governor had Habib whipped piteously by five men, but he still would not submit. More tortures were heaped on until no place on Habib's body lacked a wound. Still, he remained faithful to Jesus Christ. While the governor's men were tearing at his body, Habib cried out, "The sufferings of this time are not equal to that glory which shall be revealed in those who love Christ."

Exasperated, the governor had Habib burned to death by a slow, lingering fire. The most complete report of these events comes from Theophilus, an eyewitness. He says the day was September 2. The Orthodox Church honors Habib on November 15. Before 313 ended, Constantine got Licinius to join him in issuing the Edict of Milan, mandating toleration of Christianity throughout the empire. By 324 A.D. Constantine was sole emperor.

What we suffer now is nothing compared to the glory he will give us later (Romans 8:18).

The Forty Martyrs of Sebaste
Armenia—320, honored March 10

In A.D. 320, coemperors ruled the Roman Empire—Constantine in the West and Licinius in the East. Constantine embraced Christianity in 312; Licinius, in spite of agreeing to the Edict of Milan (313), which mandated toleration of Christians, persecuted them in the East.

When Licinius ordered that all his legions offer sacrifices to the pagan gods, there was a unit stationed near Sebaste, in Lesser Armenia (Sivas, Turkey, today), in which there were forty devout Christian soldiers who refused to comply. At first, their general, Lysias, tried to reason with them. Then, because he valued their fighting prowess, he offered bribes for their cooperation with promises of preferential privileges and rewards. Still, they maintained their steadfast commitment to Christ, and the general turned to force, causing them to be whipped and torn with hooks in their sides.

Finally, enraged by their unwavering faith, the general devised a plan he thought would surely melt their resolve. It was early March, and the north wind rolled down from Russia, across the Black Sea, cutting anyone deprived of shelter like a hawk's talons. On the banks of a frozen pond outside town, the general set up bathing tents with tubs of hot water and welcoming fires. Then he ordered the forty Christians stripped naked and thrust out onto the ice where they were to be kept until they recanted or froze.

Without waiting to be stripped, the forty believers undressed themselves and marched out onto the ice, singing songs and praying loudly: "Lord, we are forty who are engaged in this combat; grant that we may be forty crowned, and that not one be wanting to this sacred number."

The hours passed as guards on shore, assigned to keep the baths warm and the fires blazing, waited to see if any on the ice would be tempted. In the middle of the night, as the singing carried through the crisp air, one lone naked man came crawling to the shore. On seeing this, the guards called for others to follow, but no more would recant. So they helped the poor apostate into his bath, where he promptly died from the shock.

Then, as one of the guards stared out at the shivering faithful, he saw brilliant beings coming down out of heaven, placing crowns on the heads of each of the faithful. So overcome was the guard by this vision, that he stripped off his clothes and ran out onto the ice, fulfilling the prayers of the others that their number remain forty to the end.

The next morning as the guards were retrieving the stiff bodies and loading them onto a wagon to be taken away and burned, they discovered that the youngest of the martyrs was still breathing slightly. They set him aside, thinking that once he revived, he would surely recant. But it so happened that his mother was present. As she watched closely, her son made a small hand signal indicating his wishes. "Go, go, my son," she cried. "Proceed to the end of this happy journey with your companions, so you will not be missing from those who present themselves before God." Then with uncommon strength, she picked him up and put him into the wagon with his brothers.

Seed of the Church

When the bodies had been burned, local Christians retrieved the ashes and remains and distributed them to the fledgling groups of converts in the surrounding cities and towns. As dramatic reminders of the faithful witness offered by the forty martyrs of Sebaste, these relics encouraged and inspired the believers to preach the gospel more boldly than ever, and soon numerous churches were erected in honor of these men, firmly establishing Christianity in the whole region. Their martyrdom is usually honored on March 10.

Blessed is the man who perseveres under trial, because when he has stood the test, he will receive the crown of life that God has promised to those who love him (James 1:12, NIV).

Oswald, King of Northumbria

England—August 5, 642

When Roman administrators withdrew from England in 410, nominally Christian warlords ruled small, unstable kingdoms. However, beginning in 449, historian James Keifer explains that pagan Germanic peoples known as Angles, Saxons, and Jutes invaded Britain and drove the native Britons north and west into Wales, Scotland, Ireland, and Cornwall. In their place, the Anglo-Saxons (as they came to be called) set up seven kingdoms: the Saxon kingdoms of Essex, Wessex, and Sussex; the Angle kingdoms of East Anglia, Mercia, and Northumbria; and the Jute kingdom of Kent (in southeast England, the London area). But they were turbulent realms, always subject to conquest or coup.

The Christian King

Oswald, born about 605, was one of the sons of King Ethelfrith, who was grandson of Ida, the first king of Northumbria (north of the Humber River). Oswald spent his youth at home until 617, when Redwald, king of East Anglia, slew his father in battle. Oswald and his brothers escaped to Scotland, where they were cared for at the Iona monastery. There Oswald accepted Christianity and was baptized.

In 633, Oswald returned from exile to claim the throne from King Cadwallon of Wales and the pagan king Penda of Mercia who had invaded Northumbria. In spite of facing a much larger army, Oswald set up a wooden cross the night before the battle and asked all those in his mostly pagan army to join him in prayer. They not only joined him but also promised to accept Christ and be baptized *if they won.*

Their victory the next day against a superior force, and the death of the celebrated warlord Cadwallon, surprised everyone. King Oswald united Northumbria into the most powerful of the seven kingdoms and paved the way for Christianity. Immediately, he appealed to the monastery of Iona, where he had received the gospel, asking for a Christian missionary. Corman, the first missionary, was rude and selfish and a failure, but his replacement, a monk named Aidan, had a heart for the people.

Because Aidan spoke only Gaelic, King Oswald often accompanied him to interpret his sermons into the Anglo-Saxon language. Soon other missionaries joined Aidan, and the church flourished in Northumbria.

Then King Oswald created an alliance with Wessex, the second most powerful kingdom, by marrying the king's daughter, Cyneburh, who, along with her father, became a Christian, thus opening southwestern England to the gospel.

By 638, the kingdom was sufficiently secure that Oswald sent his army north to besiege and capture Edinburgh. Then, according to historian David Nash Ford, Oswald arranged for his brother, Prince Oswiu, to marry Princess Rhiainfelt, the last remaining heiress of North Rheged. This peaceful takeover reunited the old Celtic kingdom.

But Penda, the pagan king of Mercia, still held a grudge against Oswald for conquering Northumbria; killing his old ally, Cadwallon; and for spreading Christianity. In 640 with the help of former followers of Cadwallon, Penda resumed war with Northumbria. Indecisive skirmishes continued until 642, when Penda killed Oswald in a great battle near what is now Oswestry (Oswald's Tree) in Shropshire, on the border between their kingdoms. Nevertheless, Christianity thrived in the land thereafter.

Seed of the Church

It may feel uncomfortable to celebrate the gospel spreading in the wake of political alliances or violent conquest. Yet some of these stories are not too different from those in the Old Testament. Perhaps we do not need to explain or justify why and how God uses world events but only thank him that he is in control, working everything for good.

> When the Most High assigned lands to the nations, when he divided up the human race, he established the boundaries of the peoples according to the number of angelic beings. . . . "Look now; I myself am he! There is no god other than me! I am the one who kills and gives life; I am the one who wounds and heals; no one delivers from my power!" (Deuteronomy 32:8, 39).

Boniface
Friesland—June 5, 754

Born as Winfrid or Winfrith in England in about 675 into a noble family, Boniface was inspired to become a missionary by some missionary monks who stayed in his home when he was a boy. He excelled in his education at the monastery in Nursling, Hampshire, and finally, after becoming a respected priest and Bible scholar, he convinced the abbot to let him go preach to the pagan Saxons on the Continent.

But as soon as Winfrid crossed the channel, hoping to join the famous missionary Willibrord, who was already working among the Saxons, Winfrid discovered that Radbod, king of Friesland (now a part of the Netherlands), had declared war on all Christians, destroying churches and monasteries and driving Willibrord into exile and the believers into hiding. Nothing Winfrid said persuaded King Radbod to let him preach in Friesland. Finally, he returned to England in defeat.

Not to be deterred from his call to missions, Winfrid accepted that he had gone to Friesland with more enthusiasm than wisdom, so he started planning his second missionary journey. This time he went first to Rome and sought Pope Gregory II's counsel and support. On May 15, 719, Gregory commissioned him as a missionary to all the tribes of Germany and christened him with a new name: Boniface.

Some mission work had been done in these remote regions, but the church was isolated and peppered with superstition and heresy. Boniface traveled through Thuringia, Bavaria, Saxony, and finally Friesland—after King Radbod died—reviving the church and restoring orthodoxy. Multitudes of Christians who had abandoned their faith under the persecution by King Radbod turned back to Christianity. Thousands of others came to faith in Christ for the first time. Many of these became members of religious communities and chose to live their lives according to the Rule of St. Benedict.

Finally, he ventured into the unreached region of Hesse (west central Germany). Although the people there found the teachings of Christianity attractive, they would not abandon their pagan gods and superstitions—maybe because they were afraid of how those "gods" would respond if the people chose to follow Christ. Recalling Elijah's contest with the prophets of Baal,

Boniface called the tribes to a display of power. As the people watched, Boniface attacked with an axe the Sacred Oak, an ancient tree of immense size, sacred to the god Thor. With every blow, the crowd expected Thor to annihilate Boniface with a thunderbolt. Instead, after only a few strokes, the tree trembled and split in four parts that, it is said, fell to the ground in the shape of a cross. Boniface stepped back, triumphant over the old gods and strong in the power of the one true God.

The old tree revealed itself to have been rotten to the core. This was the beginning of a highly successful missionary effort, and the planting of a vigorous Christian church in a region where Boniface was named bishop. To assist him in his effort, he sought support from Christian Saxons in England. In response to his request, they provided books, supplies, and financial resources. They also sent monks to share the teaching and preaching responsibilities.

After his success in Hesse, Boniface returned to Thuringia, where some of the old problems of a decadent church—as well as many difficult questions remained: What was the status of someone whose baptism was not done in the proper way? How should he respond when members of the clergy were living immoral lives? The lesson he had learned by going to Friesland on his own was not lost on Boniface, and this time he approached the pope in Rome for answers to these questions, gaining him increased credibility and a closer bond between Europe and Rome.

Still, the strength of paganism in the region was strong. On June 5—the eve of Pentecost—754, as he prepared a group of new converts for confirmation, heathen warriors attacked and murdered not only Boniface but all fifty-two who were with him.

Seed of the Church

Nevertheless, the church thrived, and historian Christopher Dawson suggests that Boniface may have influenced the course of history in Europe more than any other Englishman.

And when the people saw [that the fire of the Lord had flashed down from heaven and burned up Elijah's sacrifice according to his prayer], they fell on their faces and cried out, "The Lord is God! The Lord is God!" (1 Kings 18:39).

Wenceslaus, the Good King
Bohemia—September 28, 929

> *Good King Wenceslaus looked out*
> *On the Feast of Stephen. . . .*

We often sing this song at Christmastime, about the good king who took pity on a poor man struggling in the snow and, taking his page with him, personally delivered food, drink, and fuel for the man's fire. But who is the "good king" who inspired the song?

Wenceslaus was the son of Vratislas and Drahomira, Duke and Duchess of Bohemia (now part of the Czech Republic). His Christian grandmother, Ludmilla, educated the boy and taught him to love God. Wenceslaus was still young when his father was killed in battle, so his mother took over as regent. A Christian in name only because of her marriage, Drahomira easily caved to pagan counselors, plunging the country into a civil war between Christians and non-Christians.

Discovering that Ludmilla was urging Wenceslaus to claim his rightful title as Duke of Bohemia and end persecution of Christians, Drahomira sent two of her nobles to her mother-in-law's castle to strangle her. However, in 922, when Wenceslaus finally "came of age" at fifteen and took his rightful place as ruler, he declared every person would have "liberty of conscience" to worship God freely. "If God bores you," he supposedly told the pagan nobles, "why forbid others to love him?"

A deeply compassionate young man, Wenceslaus honored the clergy, built churches, defended widows and orphans, tried to abolish the death penalty, visited prisoners, fed and clothed the poor, and tried to end oppression of the peasants by the nobility. Politically he desired to maintain peaceful coexistence with surrounding rulers, and in 926 acknowledged King Henry I of Germany as his overlord.

This was the last straw for his enemies within his own court and household, who had power plans of their own. . . .

O Brother, What Are You Doing?

Some of the pagan nobles began to feed the ambitions of Wenceslaus's younger brother, Boleslaus. He could become Duke of Bohemia if Wenceslaus were out of the way. What kind of country gave the poor and the Germans and the Christians so much leeway? Boleslaus would know how to be a powerful ruler. Now that Wenceslaus was married and had a son, Boleslaus must act now if he wanted the succession.

It was Wenceslaus's habit to visit various churches on their feast days. Hearing that the duke had come to his city in late September, Boleslaus urged his brother to stay the night at his palace. Uneasy in his spirit at his brother's intentions, Wenceslaus nonetheless dined with Boleslaus and went to bed. Unknown to Wenceslaus, a plot to assassinate him at the banquet table had fizzled when his enemies hesitated.

When the bell for morning prayers rang at the chapel on September 28, Wenceslaus said, "Praise to you, Lord! You have allowed me to live to this morning!" He rose quickly to attend the prayer service and ran into Boleslaus at the church door. The duke smiled. "You were a good subject to me yesterday, my brother."

But Boleslaus was not going to let his opportunity slip past again. "And now I intend to be a better one!" he said, drawing his sword and swinging at his brother.

The blow only glanced off Wenceslaus's head, and he cried out, "What are you trying to do, Brother?" He grabbed Boleslaus and the two brothers began to wrestle. But several of Boleslaus's coconspirators ran up and ran the duke through with a sword.

As he lay dying on the steps of the church, Wenceslaus murmured, "Brother, may God forgive you."

Many people, rich and poor, mourned the death of the good king. And many years later, in 1853, an Anglican minister, John Mason Neale, penned the words we sing to commemorate this good man:

> *Therefore Christian men, be sure,*
> *Wealth or rank possessing;*
> *Ye who now will bless the poor*
> *Shall yourselves find blessing.*

Stop oppressing the helpless and stop making false accusations and spreading vicious rumors! Feed the hungry and help those in trouble. Then your light will shine out from the darkness, and the darkness around you will be as bright as day (Isaiah 58:9-10).

Alphege
England — April 19, 1012

Square-sail ships, manned by horn-helmeted, warrior-oarsmen known as Vikings, were raiding England unchecked in 953 when Alphege was born to a noble Saxon family near Bath (Somerset). While still very young, he renounced the world and, against the wishes of his widowed mother, became a monk at Deerhurst, in Gloucestershire.

After a time, he moved on to Glastonbury, where he was selected as prior. But the distractions of this position were too many, and he left to become a hermit near the hot springs in Bath. So many of his disciples followed him that Dunstan, the primate of all England, asked him to become abbot of a nearby community. Following the death of Aethelwold, bishop of Winchester, in 984, Dunstan again prevailed on Alphege, this time to quit his solitude and accept the bishopric of Winchester. He provided so liberally for the needs of the poor that there were no beggars in the whole diocese of Winchester.

At the same time, the Vikings marauded England's coast, sometimes with fleets of over three hundred ships.

Recognizing Alphege's gifts, King Ethelred of England commissioned him to negotiate with Anlaf and Swein, the Danish invaders. The king was ready to pay tribute to ward off the raids, but Alphege thought it better to try to convert the Vikings with the gospel of Christ. He succeeded with Anlaf, who became a Christian and never invaded England again. Alphege also brought the newly baptized King Olaf Tryggvason of Norway to a peaceful meeting with King Ethelred and to his confirmation at Andover.

So Far, So Good

In 1006, Alphege was appointed Archbishop of Canterbury, but shortly after that more Viking attacks ensued, as Danish raiders, who had not been party to the previous peace agreements, overran much of southern England. In 1011, they laid siege to Canterbury itself. The English nobility tried to get Alphege to flee to safety, but he refused. Saying it was the part of a hireling to abandon his flock in the time of danger, Alphege remained and personally conducted the city's defense. The city held out for three weeks against overwhelming odds until a traitor opened the city gates. Led by Earl Edric, the Vikings burned the cathedral, plundered the city, and took many of its citizens as slaves, including Archbishop Alphege.

The captives were held near Greenwich for seven months as their captors tried to extort the highest ransom possible for their release. During this time, the Viking army suffered an epidemic of fatal dysentery that they came to believe was God's judgment for how badly they had treated the archbishop. When they released him from the dungeon in which he had been held, he went about praying for them and giving his enemies bread. It is said that whoever ate the bread recovered, and the epidemic ceased. Finally, the English paid forty- eight thousand gold crowns in ransom for the release of the prisoners. But when the Vikings demanded an additional three thousand for Alphege's release, he refused to allow this added extortion of his people.

Incensed at Alphege's defiance, the Danes got drunk and on April 19, 1012, dragged him to the scaffold, pelting him with ox bones and stones. Their leader, Thorkell the Tall, tried to save Alphege, but by then it had turned into a mob scene. Weakened, Alphege fell, and Thrum, a Dane who had come to faith in prison and been baptized, killed him with an ax to end his suffering.

Later, Alphege's body was transported to London and buried in Saint Paul's Cathedral with great reverence. After the Dane Cnut (Canute) became King of England in 1016, his pious wife persuaded him to make reparations by moving the remains of Alphege from London to Canterbury, where he built a high and costly altar over Alphege's new grave.

The good shepherd lays down his life for the sheep. A hired hand will run when he sees a wolf coming (John 10:11-12).

Olaf, King of Norway
Norway—July 29, 1030

Olaf Haraldsson was born to King Harald Grenske of Norway in 995. From age twelve, he joined various Viking expeditions, some under Thorkell the Tall, who brought him to England where he became interested in Christianity. Later he traveled to France and became a Christian. Archbishop Robert of Rouen baptized him in about 1014.

When the Danish king Canute conquered England, Olaf joined his service, and the two men struck up a fast friendship. However, when the English bishop Sigfrid showed favoritism to Olaf and persisted in calling him "King Olaf," King Canute became jealous. Bishop Sigfrid defended this epithet by saying, "He was chosen and crowned by the highest Lord and Ruler, the King of all kings, the one almighty God, to rule and govern that kingdom to which he is born, and this special destiny awaits him."

This declaration of divine appointment made Canute all the more jealous, and Olaf was forced to flee England.

A Bold Endeavor

In 1015, Sigfrid, who brought Christianity to Sweden, accompanied Olaf back to his homeland of Norway, where with the support of his relatives and after distributing financial incentives and conquering the country's principal chieftains, Olaf finally seized control of the kingdom. Things went relatively well for about ten years while he unified the country. Olaf not only established peace and security for his people, he also revised or restored old laws and insisted on their enforcement, unaffected by bribes or threats.

In addition to reorganizing the governmental infrastructure of the nation, Olaf brought English missionaries into the country, demolished the pagan temples and customs, and built Christian churches in their place. He outlawed all other faiths except Christianity. But the old clans resented his reforms, which had eroded their powers.

When King Canute of Denmark and England heard of their discontent, he sent them a large sum of gold and silver, asking them to discard Olaf and submit to him. They agreed, and so in 1028 King Canute sailed to Norway with fifty ships and drove out King Olaf, installing himself in his place.

After two years of exile in Sweden, during which he contemplated various options, Olaf had a dream in which the old king of Norway, Olaf Tryggvason, appeared to him and said, "Why are you are thinking of laying down the kingdom God has given you? Back to your kingdom that you have taken as your inheritance and have long ruled over with the strength God has given you, and do not let your underlings make you afraid. It is to a king's honor to win victories over his foes, and an honorable death to fall in battle with his men. Or are you not sure whether you have the right in this struggle?"

"God Help Me!"

He returned to Norway with an army of over three thousand men and at Stiklestad on July 29, 1030, met his rebellious subjects—an army of over fourteen thousand men loyal to King Canute, though Canute did not take part in the battle.

In spite of being outnumbered four to one, Olaf, like Gideon, decided to reduce his numbers by choosing only Christians to fight in his army. Before the battle was joined, Olaf had a vision that he would be defeated and lose his own life. Then an eclipse took place, and though Olaf fought with great courage, he was mortally wounded and fell, praying, "God help me!"

Immediately, a sense of dread spread through the rebel army, and when night fell, a light was seen over the place where Olaf fell. Miracles of healing were reported by those visiting his grave.

Soon, the Norwegians repented of resisting Olaf and expelled King Canute. Then they recalled Olaf's son Magnus from Russia to be their king.

The Lord Most High is awesome. He is the great King of all the earth. . . . Praise him with a psalm! God reigns above the nations, sitting on his holy throne. The rulers of the world have gathered together. . . . For all the kings of the earth belong to God. He is highly honored everywhere (Psalm 47:2, 7-9).

Raymond Lull
Tunisia—June 30, 1315

Born into a prominent family on the island of Majorca, Spain, about 1235, Raymond Lull spent his early adulthood as a page, tutor, poet, and troubadour in the court of King James of Aragón until age thirty. By then he was married with two children.

One evening as Raymond sat on a couch, strumming his lute and composing an erotic song to a married woman who had ignored him, he suddenly saw a vision of Christ hanging on the cross. The expression on Jesus' face appeared so disappointed that Raymond became conscience-stricken and could not continue. He went to bed as though ill for eight days. When he finally arose and attempted to finish the song about his unrequited love, the vision returned. It was Jesus' true love for *him* that he had not returned.

In that moment, he surrendered his life to Christ, and his conversion was so dramatic that he forsook his life of ease and wealth in the king's court to become a hermit and afterward a lay member of the Order of St. Francis.

Within his heart grew a desire to become a missionary to the Muslim world. He particularly wanted to become a Christian apologist who could persuade unbelievers of the truth of the gospel. For nearly ten years he studied Arabic and engaged Muslim and Jewish scholars in debate as preparation for this ministry.

However, in about 1291, as he was about to set sail for Africa, Lull became so overwhelmed with terror at the thought of imprisonment or torture that might await him that he could not control his emotions. He let the ship sail without him. But such bitter remorse for his failing faith seized him that he boarded the next ship. According to him, from that moment on, he became a new man and peace of mind returned.

He landed in Tunis where he arranged to debate the relative merits of Islam and Christianity with the local Islamic leaders. He announced that he had studied the arguments on both sides of the question and was willing to submit the evidences for Christianity and for Islam to a fair comparison. He even promised that, if he was convinced, he would embrace Islam. The Muslim leaders responded to the challenge and came in great numbers to the conference. After much debate, Lull brought his primary philosophical charge against Islam: *lack of love in the being of Allah, and lack of harmony in his attributes.* These, Lull claimed, were not characteristics of the God of Christianity.

Some accepted his arguments, but others turned fanatical and cast him into prison. Only the efforts of a less prejudiced leader saved him from death by reminding the ruler that a Muslim with as much courage would be highly honored. Reluctantly the ruler commuted Lull's death sentence to banishment and put him on a ship, warning him that if he returned, he'd be stoned. Lull escaped before the ship sailed and hid out, witnessing privately.

However, unable to debate publicly (his primary means of evangelism), he finally traveled to Naples where he continued to study and refine his methods. From 1301 to 1309, he made several missionary journeys, which are remarkable considering that he was over sixty years old and the primitive and dangerous traveling conditions of the Middle Ages.

During all this time, he wrote prolifically—about three hundred works—as a philosopher, poet, novelist, writer of proverbs, keen logician, deep theologian, and fiery controversialist. But Christian apologetics were his major theme.

At about eighty years of age, he returned to North Africa and worked secretly among his little band of converts. After about ten months he emerged to preach in the marketplace. Filled with fury at his boldness, and unable to reply to his arguments, the populace dragged him out of the town where they stoned him on June 30, 1315.

In His Own Words

"As the needle naturally turns to the north when it is touched by the magnet, so is it fitting, O Lord that Thy servant should turn to love and praise and serve Thee; seeing that out of love for him Thou wast willing to endure such grievous pangs and sufferings"

—Raymond Lull, from his work,
Liber Contemplationis in Deo, cxxix., 19

Part 2

The Reformation: Brother against Brother and Sister against Sister

The many causes of the Reformation are too complex for this venue, but the elements that enabled those claiming to be Christians to torture, murder, and go to war with one another are directly relevant to any discussion of persecution. Blaise Pascal, the French mathematician, physicist, and theologian, converted in 1654, wrote, "Men never do evil so completely and cheerfully as when they do it from religious conviction." And yet, it was more than deep convictions that made the Reformation so bloody. Most of the 5.5 million Christians killed over the centuries by other "Christians" died during the period of the Reformation, which lasted from the early 1500s to the mid-1600s.[1]

Three temptations planted within the church over a thousand years earlier had gone to seed: the love of riches, the corruption of absolute power, and the reliance on the sword.

The Love of Riches

In addition to accumulating significant property from the state as Christianity became more favored in the declining Roman Empire, the Catholic Church continued to accept property bequeathed to it by dying childless people as well as penitent sinners. By 580, King Chilperic, ruler of the Frankish kingdom of Neustria in northern France, complained that the royal treasury was exhausted because all the wealth of the kingdom had been transferred to the church.

Believing that the wealth of the church really belonged to the poor, Pope Gregory the Great (540–604) saw himself as the administrator of that property. However, though he was very generous with the church treasury when it came to helping the poor, he was shrewd enough to retain, manage, and expand the church's property holdings. He served during a time when famine, plague, and war raged through the land. Lombards, Franks, and Imperial troops pillaged the towns and farms unchecked. Gregory believed that the four horsemen of the apocalypse were coming and claimed a "divine revelation" that the "end of the world" was near, further spurring people to transfer their property to the church in order to "store up treasures in heaven."

By the thirteenth century, the vast tax-free possessions of the church constituted, by varying estimates, between one fifth and one third of the land in all Europe, and Gregory's successors did not necessarily inherit his integrity or generosity toward the poor. While the wealthy were often able to negotiate an exemption, the common people paid heavy church tithes, dues, and fees—further enriching the church's coffers—while the poor had to work off such obligations as laborers on church properties. Everywhere people were saying that the clergy were always hunting for money and legacies.

Eager for deliverance from the intolerable yoke of the church as well as freedom from their feudal overlords, Martin Luther's revolt against Rome ignited the Peasants' War in 1524. Luther denounced the peasants for resorting to violence, and they were defeated within a year, but not before thousands died in the conflict.

If James is correct in identifying the greed, selfishness, and other evil desires as the primary cause of conflict—even war (James 4:1-2)—that would certainly explain one reason why the Reformation became so bloody. There was a lot of property and power at stake, but the fact that it was held by the church did not exempt the church as an institution from the same dynamics which tempt individuals.

The Corruption of Absolute Power

The strength of the medieval Catholic Church was its powerful centralized government. Its weakness was the same. While it preserved orthodoxy at many turns during centuries when literacy was low, it did little to help educate common people and did not entrust them with the Scriptures. The great power of the bishops and the popes—many of whom were poorly educated themselves—was subject to widespread corruption and confusion as seen in the following examples:

- Pope Honorius I (625–638) was pronounced a heretic after his death by the Sixth General Council in Constantinople in 680 and confirmed by his successor, Pope Leo II.
- Pope Sergius III (904–911) introduced the decades known as the "pornocracy" of the papacy. Some authorities, however, dispute that Sergius III obtained the papal office by murder and fathered an illegitimate son by Marozia, a fifteen-year-old girl.
- Pope John XII (955–964) is described by the Catholic Encyclopedia as "a coarse, immoral man, whose life was such that the Lateran was spoken of as a brothel."
- Pope Benedict VIII (1012–1024) bought the papal office with open bribery.
- Pope Benedict IX (1033–1045), made pope when merely a youth, was a disgrace to the office according to the Catholic Encyclopedia. Other sources charge him with openly committing adultery and murder.
- Pope Boniface VIII (1294–1303) "scarcely [omitted] any possible crime: infidelity, heresy, simony, gross and unnatural immorality, idolatry, magic" (the Catholic Encyclopedia).
- Pope Eugene IV (1431–1447) condemned Joan of Arc as a witch and had her burned alive. Later, Pope Benedict XV declared her a saint in 1919.

- Pope Alexander VI (1492–1503) won election by bribing the College of Cardinals. Prior to this—while he was still a cardinal—he had fathered four illegitimate children. When he was pope, rumors continued to circulate of his rampant illicit sexual relationships, including claims that he had an incestuous affair with his daughter, Lucrezia Borgia.

Perhaps the crisis of authority came to a climax in 1378 with the Great Papal Schism that lasted for forty years during which time at first two and later three popes vied for supremacy.

While the confusion in the Catholic Church contributed to the *need* for reform, it was the corruption that signaled a leadership too often willing to do anything—including martyring dissidents—to maintain its power.

Reliance on the Sword

Constantine's declaration that Christianity was to be tolerated in the empire was a great blessing to the church. Public worship was possible without constant fear. Evangelism could go forth in the cities and provinces, and missionary efforts advanced on the frontier, howbeit not without danger from pagan barbarians. But support from the government brought the temptation to call upon the power of its sword.

From the beginning of the Christian movement, there were tendencies for heresies and cults to arise. Paul, Peter, John, and even Jude contended with false teachers in their epistles. But they dealt with false teachings with persuasion and, in the most grievous cases, expulsion from fellowship (Titus 3:10; see also Matthew 18:17). In addition to false teachings, the postapostolic church came to consider outright rebellion heresy, especially if it divided the church, even if deviant doctrine, per se, had not fueled the division.

In the spring of 251, persecution subsided for a time as Rome paid more attention to raiders from the north, and the church had to decide how to deal with repentant Christians who had renounced their faith under persecution. Bishop Fabian of Rome had died a martyr, and the obvious successor seemed to be Novatian, a leading churchman and brilliant theologian. However, he held a hard line toward lapsed believers, stating that he would never readmit them to the church. Consequently, the more merciful Cornelius was elected bishop of Rome.

However, rather than accept the will of the majority, supporters of Novatian declared him bishop. Both bishops then sought the recognition of church leaders abroad. Bishop Cyprian of Carthage in North Africa, for instance, supported Cornelius, but the conflict worsened and evolved into two separate churches, with competing bishops and congregations throughout the empire.

What was the church to do in the face of heresy (as Novatian's rebellion was considered)? Whether the threat was false doctrine or a schismatic movement, how was the church to preserve its unity and authority? In the case of Novatian, the church was not able to preserve unity. His church endured for about four centuries, until Muslim invaders swept westward and slaughtered those who refused to convert to Islam. One might say God brought correction in his time, but the church was not willing to be so patient.

Once the government withdrew its sword of coercion from the throat of the church and actually endorsed Christianity, there was the possibility of enlisting it to help suppress heretical movements. It was none other than the great Augustine, bishop of Hippo, who wrote in A.D. 408 the following rationale for using coercion on heretics:

> The thing to be considered when any one is coerced, is not the mere fact of the coercion, but the nature of that to which he is coerced, whether it be good or bad: not that any one can be good in spite of his own will, but that, through fear of suffering what he does not desire, he either renounces his hostile prejudices, or is compelled to examine truth of which he had been contentedly ignorant; and under the influence of this fear repudiates the error which he was wont to defend, or seeks the truth of which he formerly knew nothing, and now willingly holds what he formerly rejected. Perhaps it would be utterly useless to assert this in words, if it were not demonstrated by so many examples. We see not a few men here and there, but many cities, once Donatist, now Catholic, vehemently detesting the diabolical schism, and ardently loving the unity of the Church; and these became Catholic under the influence of that fear which is to you so offensive by the laws of emperors. . . .
>
> Originally my opinion was that no one should be coerced into the unity of Christ, that we must act only by words, fighting only by arguments, and prevail by force of reason, lest we should have those whom we knew as avowed heretics feigning themselves to be Catholics. But this opinion of mine was overcome not by the words of those who controverted it, but by the conclusive instance to which they could point.[2]

By the time Pope Urban II launched the First Crusade in 1095 to free the Holy Land from the Muslims, there was little compunction against using force in the name of Christ. For two hundred years, this bloody baptism continued initiating most European families—from peasants to knights, from children to women—into the practice of "killing for Christ" and searing their consciences so that it wasn't that hard to turn the sword on other Christians when Reformation ideas threatened the power structure.

It was a violent era in the whole world. In the east, far more were *dying* for Christ. In 1214, Genghis Khan martyred as many as 4 million Christians. In 1258, Hulaku [or Hülegu] Khan massacred another 1.1 million more in his capture of Baghdad. And in the fourteenth century, Tamerlane martyred 4 million Nestorians, a Christian sect that had spread across Asia.[3] (We in the West seldom appreciate that over the centuries nearly 40 million Christians have died for their faith in the East.[4])

The Fourth Crusade (1202–1204) wasn't even directed against the Muslims. Instead, crusaders attacked Constantinople, the capital of eastern Christendom! When the city fell, the crusaders marched in and sacked the city. They plundered the churches of millions of dollars of booty, killed men, and raped women—even some Orthodox nuns in their convents. Upon hearing the news, Pope Innocent III (1160–1216) rejoiced over this victory over the Eastern Church, which had so far refused to accept the primacy of his office.

In the essay on Islam (Part 6 in this book), we will take up other implications and consequences of the Crusades. However, before the end of the Crusades for the Holy Land, a cult—with undeniably heretical, dualistic beliefs—developed in southern France known as the Albigenses, named after the town of Albi where it started. When the Roman Catholic Church could not stop it, Pope Innocent III launched the Albigensian Crusade (1208–1229) against them. When his army arrived at the first large town and soldiers asked how they could distinguish between heretics and orthodox, the commanding Cistercian abbot thundered: "Kill them all. God will know his own," and they slaughtered all forty thousand men, women, and children.

Pope Innocent III later boasted that his armies took five hundred towns and castles from the heretics, butchering every inhabitant. Small groups of Albigenses survived in isolated areas and were pursued by the Inquisition as late as the fourteenth century.

In the meantime, Peter Waldo, a wealthy French merchant, had been criticizing the pope and preaching publicly from the Bible. Though his beliefs were generally orthodox, the archbishop banned him and his increasing number of followers from preaching. Then he excommunicated them and began persecuting them. This persecution increased and developed into the Inquisition (which targeted many other "heretics"). In 1487, Pope Innocent VIII organized a crusade against the Waldenses in Dauphiné and Savoy (both now part of France). Finally, the remaining Waldenses took refuge in Switzerland and Germany, merging gradually with the Bohemian Brethren, and the group survives today.

This reliance on the sword was not limited to the Roman Catholic Church. In Switzerland, the reformer, Ulrich Zwingli, found it "necessary" to execute his former friend and colleague, Felix Manz, in 1527 for practicing believer's baptism. Before the century ended, Anabaptists ("rebaptizers") had been persecuted all over Europe by Protestants and Catholics alike. In England and Wales, Protestants executed over three hundred Catholics and persecuted fellow non-Catholics such as John Bunyan and others who departed from the Church of England. Even in America where many had fled for religious freedom, liberty was too often denied those of a different persuasion, for example, leading in the case of Quaker Mary Dyer to her execution by Puritans in 1660.

How could the followers of a nonviolent, Jewish rabbi who rebuked his disciple for taking up a sword in his own defense have come to this bloody end? Perhaps our sorry history will foster the compassion of Jesus within our hearts toward those who even now seek our destruction so we, too, can say, "Father, forgive these people, because they don't know what they are doing."

Notes

1. David Barrett and Todd Johnson, *World Christian Trends* (Pasadena, Calif.: William Carey Library, 2001), global diagram 16.
2. Augustine to Vincentius, *Epistle 93* (A.D. 408).
3. David Barrett and Todd Johnson, *World Christian Trends* (Pasadena, Calif.: William Carey Library, 2001), part 11.
4. Extracted from David Barrett and Todd Johnson, "Global Top Ten Lists on 145 Major Missiometric Categories," *World Christian Trends* (Pasadena, Calif.: William Carey Library, 2001), "Martyrs," list 5

The Witnesses

John Hus
Bohemia—July 6, 1415

Honored to be assigned the rector of Prague's Bethlehem Chapel (large enough to hold three thousand people), John Hus applied himself to his most popular gift: preaching. This drove him to more intense Bible study and subsequently to the works of John Wycliffe, especially as they emphasized the centrality of the Bible as the rule of life and practice and questioned papal authority and the sale of indulgences. Wycliffe's writings had found their way from England into Bohemia (later Czechoslovakia) after England's Richard II married Anne of Bohemia in 1382.

Consequently, Hus began to stress personal piety and purity and the Bible's supreme authority in the church. This came after a period of particularly conspicuous excesses, immorality, and such confusion in the Roman clergy and hierarchy that at one point there had been three claimants to the papal office. Matters came to a head when one claimant (later declared unfit) proclaimed a sale of indulgences to raise money for a war against his rivals, something that incensed Hus, and he said so in his sermons.

The archbishop told Hus to stop preaching and asked the university of Prague to burn all of Wycliffe's writings. Hus refused to comply. Finally, in 1412 his archbishop excommunicated him, not for heresy, but for insubordination.

When word got to Rome, the pope confirmed Hus's excommunication and effectively excommunicated the whole city of Prague by prohibiting the people from receiving the sacraments. To spare the people, Hus left the city but continued to preach in the countryside, sometimes even in the open air.

In 1414, he was ordered to appear before the Council of Constance. Though the emperor guaranteed Hus's personal safety even if he was found guilty, as soon as Hus arrived, he was thrown into a most dismal cell where he soon became sick. The council condemned Wycliffe's teachings and Hus for supporting them and for preaching against the often immoral and extravagant lifestyles of the clergy and the pope. They also condemned Hus for having said that Christ is the sole head of the church and that no pope or bishop could rightly to establish doctrine contrary to the Bible. But Hus had gone further in claiming that no one had to obey a clergyman's order if it was plainly wrong.

In his defense, Hus refused to renounce the beliefs the council claimed were errors unless the Bible demonstrated he was wrong. Then he announced, "I would not, for a chapel full of gold, recede from the truth."

The council, having only recently united the Roman Church under a single pope after years of chaos, could not afford to have the pope's authority questioned. Therefore, it found John Hus guilty of heresy, and he was burned at the stake on July 6, 1415.

In His Own Words

When Hus was brought to his place of execution, he was asked whether he would retract his views. He responded, "God is my witness that the evidence against me is false. I have never thought nor preached except with the one intention of winning men, if possible, from their sins. Today I will gladly die."

Seed of the Church

John Hus's heroic death only increased his popularity among the laypeople. His followers rebelled against the Catholic Church and the empire. Fierce persecution of the "Hussites" followed, but the movement survived as an independent church, known first as the Unity of the Brethren and later as the Moravians. The Moravian Church survives to this day, and is well-known for missionary efforts around the world. The Moravians were some of the most respectful and effective missionaries among North American Indians.

Jesus replied, "Every plant not planted by my heavenly Father will be rooted up, so ignore them. They are blind guides leading the blind, and if one blind person guides another, they will both fall into a ditch" (Matthew 15:13-14).

Felix Manz

Switzerland—January 5, 1527

Sadly, Felix Manz was the first "Protestant" martyred by Protestants. Martin Luther in Germany and Ulrich Zwingli in Switzerland were the leading church reformers in 1519 when Felix Manz returned from university in Austria and joined Zwingli's Bible study and discussion group. Conrad Grebel, the son of a Zurich city council member, also joined, as did others. At first all was congenial, and they were in considerable agreement about the need for reform in the church—even to the point of breaking with Rome and declaring the Scriptures the sole rule for life and practice.

Shortly, however, Manz and Grebel rejected Zwingli's inclination to rely on the city council to determine and enforce ecclesiastical changes. Believing the two hundred city council members to all be Christians, Zwingli envisioned a reformed state church backed by the power of the civil magistrate. Manz and Grebel renounced the sword—the power behind the state—considering the marriage of church and state dangerous, possibly leading to the same symbiotic excesses and abuses of power from which they were breaking away. They wanted a simple spiritual reformation and a church made pure because the members joined and submitted voluntarily, not because they feared the state.

Also, though Zwingli admitted that he saw no clear examples of infant baptism in the Scriptures, he felt a state church necessitated infant baptism as the means of including and controlling the whole population. Manz and Grebel renounced this concept, claiming that infants could not freely choose.

At first these disputes—some held publicly—were relatively academic, except that Manz and Grebel and their followers did not have their *own* children baptized. But one day in 1525 as several of these "Swiss Brethren," as they came to be called, gathered at Manz's house, they realized that if faith needed to precede baptism, their own baptism had been invalid. George Blaurock, one of those present, fell to his knees and asked Conrad Grebel to baptize him with Christian baptism based on his *personal* faith, not that of his parents or the demands of church and state. Grebel complied, and then he and the others asked Blaurock to baptize them.

As the practice spread, Zwingli's new church and the city council issued an edict ordering everyone to forsake Anabaptism. Lamentably, Zwingli, whose church was only about five years old at this time and still in danger of retribution from Rome, quickly turned to threats to control those who disagreed with him. Of course, the Anabaptists preached and practiced their doctrine all the more. Manz was imprisoned for a while, and Grebel was too. But Grebel contracted plague while in a damp dungeon and died in 1526. Once Manz was freed, he went back to baptizing, hundreds, if not thousands.

Finally, in parody of a "third baptism," Felix Manz was condemned and drowned in the River Liemat on January 5, 1527. Four years later in a war with Catholic cantons (districts), Zurich was defeated, Zwingli was killed, and the Swiss reformation stalled.

In Their Own Words

In the fourth verse of his hymn "I Sing with Exultation," still sung today by many Mennonites and other Anabaptist congregations, Manz summarized his convictions.

> *Christ bids us, none compelling,*
> *To His glorious throne.*
> *He only who is willing*
> *Christ as Lord to own,*
> *He is assured of heaven*
> *Who will right faith pursue,*
> *With heart made pure do penance,*
> *Sealed with baptism true.*

"Put away your sword," Jesus told [his follower]. "Those who use the sword will be killed by the sword" (Matthew 26:52).

Michael Sattler
Germany—May 21, 1527

In 1517, Martin Luther posted his ninety-five theses against papal indulgences, but the Roman Church violently resisted change. Farther south a group of believers, sometimes known as the Swiss Brethren and influenced by Conrad Grebel and Felix Manz, concluded that the state church was beyond reforming. Claiming church membership needed to be a voluntary, adultlike decision, they baptized each other and then others into independent congregations. Disparagingly they came to be called Anabaptists (rebaptizers).

Michael Sattler, who had been educated at the University of Freiburg and was a prior of the cloister of a Roman Catholic monastery, joined these early Anabaptists, and by 1527 had become a prominent leader, especially after the death of Grebel (from plague in 1526) and Manz (drowned as a "heretic" in 1527). Summarizing a number of agreements reached by a conference of Swiss Brethren at Schleitheim, Switzerland, Sattler penned "The Schleitheim Confession." It was not a comprehensive theology but contained seven articles that distinguished these new gatherings of Christians, addressing (1) baptism, (2) the ban, or excommunication, (3) breaking of bread, (4) separation from the abomination, or state church, (5) pastors in the church, (6) the sword, and (7) the oath.

Sattler's treatise was widely read and contributed to his being hunted by the authorities. He was soon arrested and held in prison until his trial on May 21, 1527. After answering an number of charges against him, he concluded: "Ye ministers of God, I admonish you to consider the end for which God has appointed you, to punish the evil, and to defend and protect the pious. Whereas, then, we have not acted contrary to God and the Gospel, you will find that neither I nor my brethren and sisters have offended in word or deed against any authority. [However, if you] prove to us with the Holy Scriptures, that we err and are in the wrong, we will gladly desist and recant and also willingly suffer the sentence and punishment for that of which we have been accused, but if no error is proven to us, I hope to God, that you will be converted, and receive instruction."

The judges only laughed. After disputing with him a little further, they withdrew to deliberate. When they returned, they sentenced that his tongue be cut out, his body be torn twice and pinched five times with red-hot tongs, and then that he be burned to ashes.

Steadfast to the End

There were in the courtroom eighteen other brothers and sisters—including Sattler's wife—on trial as well at that time, and Sattler was very concerned about them. The records suggest that they were required to witness his execution, possibly to encourage their recantation.

While in prison, Sattler wrote a long letter to the brothers and sisters of his church, encouraging them in the faith. He knew that how he endured his trial and execution could encourage them to stand firm as well. He promised to give them a sign from the burning stake to show that he remained steadfast to the end, enduring it all willingly for Christ. When the fire finally severed the cords that bound him, he lifted up his hand and pointed toward heaven.

Two of those on trial with Sattler recanted. The others remained steadfast to the end. The men were beheaded and the women drowned, including his wife.

In His Own Words

"Beloved brothers and sisters, this letter shall be a farewell to all of you who truly love and follow God, and also a testimony of my love which God has given into my heart toward you for the sake of your salvation. I did indeed desire, and it would have been profitable, I trust, if I had labored a little while longer in the work of the lord, but it is better for me to be released and to await with Christ the hope of the blessed. The Lord is able to raise up another laborer to finish this work."

—Michael Sattler, written in the tower at Binzdorf

Patrick Hamilton
Scotland—February 29, 1528

Born of noble birth in Scotland in about 1503, Patrick Hamilton studied for a religious career at Paris University where he became acquainted with Martin Luther's writings. Earlier, Hamilton had been made abbot of Ferme, undoubtedly because of his political connections, but when he returned to Scotland at the age of twenty-three, he chose not to conduct "business as usual." Instead, he decided that politics, corruption, and pastoral neglect in the Catholic Church needed reform.

Archbishop Beaton, however, did not like the tone of what young Hamilton was saying. In 1525 parliament had passed an act forbidding the importation of Luther's writings, but Hamilton, a local abbot, was espousing similar views. Fearing retribution, Hamilton fled to Germany. While there he furthered his studies and was able to meet Martin Luther and Philip Melanchthon (another Reformation theologian) in person. Hamilton also met Francis Lambert, a converted Franciscan whose example influenced him strongly. Apparently, these direct exposures to the Reformation lit a fire in Hamilton's heart. He wrote *Patrick's Places*, setting forth the doctrine of justification by faith and soon returned to Scotland, boldly preaching what was essentially Lutheran theology, quickly gathering a large following. Hamilton's activities did not escape the attention of Scotland's Catholic leaders, and in 1528, he was invited by Archbishop Beaton, two bishops, and five abbots to a conference at St. Andrews, on the pretense of debating topics related to Hamilton's new beliefs.

The Trap

Archbishop Beaton assigned Friar Campbell, a Dominican, to meet with Hamilton and pretend he was persuaded by his ideas, so he could ascertain the scope of Hamilton's "heresy." Once Campbell had gathered sufficient evidence, Hamilton was arrested in the middle of the night and thrown into prison. The next day, he was brought before the archbishop and his entourage and placed on trial with Campbell as his primary accuser.

It took very little time for this hastily assembled "court" to find him guilty of heresy and strip him of all dignities, honors, orders, offices, and benefits of the church and hand him over to the secular authorities for punishment. Fearing that even the king or other influential friends might intervene, Beaton recommended an immediate execution.

Consequently, that very afternoon (February 29, 1528), the executioner bound Hamilton to the stake outside the gate of Saint Salvator's College in Saint Andrews and lit the fire. As the flames rose, Friar Campbell called for him to convert.

But Hamilton replied, "Wicked man! You know I am not a heretic and that it is the truth of God for which I now suffer. You confessed as much to me in private. For this you will answer before the Judgment Seat of Christ!"

Soon after Hamilton's death, a dreadful remorse of conscience seized Friar Campbell for his part in Hamilton's murder, and he could not shake the chilling apprehensions that he faced eternal wrath. Within a year, he died in agony of soul.

Seed of the Church

Archbishop Beaton intended the example of Hamilton's execution to quell the spread of Reformation thought in Scotland. Instead, everyone began discussing why he had been killed and whether the Catholic Church possibly needed reform. One witness to the execution said, "The smoke of Patrick Hamilton had infected as many as it blew upon."

One of those upon whom it blew (though not literally) was John Knox, the Scottish chaplain to Edward VI of England. He picked up Hamilton's "torch" and opposed the rule of the Roman Catholic Mary, Queen of Scots, successfully helping to found the Presbyterian Church of Scotland in 1560.

You have suffered so much for the Good News. Surely it was not in vain, was it? (Galatians 3:4).

Thomas Bilney

England — August 19, 1531

Thomas Bilney is sometimes called the father of the English Reformation because he was one of the first martyrs for that cause and because he led several others to faith, including one of King Henry VIII's senior advisers, Hugh Latimer. Nevertheless, Bilney at first recanted his convictions.

Bilney was born in Norfolk in 1495 and studied at Trinity Hall in Cambridge. He was a shy but tenderhearted young man who became anxious about his salvation. He went to the priests and humbly confessed all his sins, even those he only suspected were sin. The priests prescribed fasting, prolonged vigils, and costly masses and indulgences, but Bilney experienced no peace in his heart. Growing weak from the fasting and penniless from paying for all the indulgences, he finally said, "My last state is worse than the first."

However, one day he came across a Greek New Testament, recently produced by Erasmus. At first, Bilney held back because the priests strictly prohibited Greek and Hebrew books, "the sources of all heresies," and Erasmus's New Testament was particularly forbidden. And yet he wondered whether this book—after all it was the Testament of Jesus Christ—might have within it the word that would reassure his soul. At last, he secretly purchased the volume and returned to his room to peruse it in private.

Opening it, he read 1 Timothy 1:15: "This is a faithful saying, and worthy of all acceptation, that Christ Jesus came into the world to save sinners; of whom I am chief" (KJV). How could the great St. Paul consider himself the chief of sinners and yet be so confident of his own salvation? The answer was not in who Paul was or in the church or the penance its priests prescribed, but in Christ's work. "Yes, it is Jesus Christ who saves!" realized Bilney. "*Christ* saves sinners. At last I have heard of Jesus." He believed and immediately found release from his doubts. "Now I see it all. My vigils, my fasts, my pilgrimages, my purchase of masses and indulgences were destroying instead of saving me."

In 1525, Bilney became a preacher of this basic gospel in the diocese of Ely. He denounced the worship of saints and attendant ceremonies and pilgrimages. They could not save, only Jesus. Before long, there developed a small group of Reformation-minded theologians who met for periodic discussions at the White Horse Tavern. They included Thomas Bilney, William Tyndale, John Frith, and possibly Hugh Latimer, among others.

Meanwhile, King Henry VIII's advisor, Cardinal Wolsey, presided over a massive burning of Lutheran books in 1526. He was determined to purge the land of "heretics." He arrested Thomas Bilney in 1527 and confined him to the Tower of London.

Losing Courage

"Recant what you have been preaching or die at the stake!" he was told when brought before the Bishops' Court at Westminster. Cuthbert Tunstall, Bishop of London, who oversaw the proceedings, was reluctant to find Bilney guilty and tried to persuade him to recant. For two days, under intense pressure from Tunstall and well-meaning friends, Bilney stood resolute. Then finally, in a confused and weary state of mind, he recanted, reasoning that by saving his life he could still serve God. After being marched before the Council of Bishops, he was led back to prison to serve his sentence.

There he was overcome with regret. After two years he was released, but it was another year before, like Peter restored after his denial of Christ, Bilney regained his courage and purpose. Off he went again, preaching and distributing New Testaments and declaring that never again would he deny the truth of God's Word. When Richard Nix, the blind, eighty-year-old bishop of Norwich heard of it, he informed Sir Thomas More, who had Bilney arrested, brought to London, and shut up in the Tower.

This time there was no recanting . . . and no saving him, though influential friends tried. He was burned at the stake on August 19, 1531.

> Peter was grieved because [Jesus] said to him the third time, "Do you love Me?" And he said to Him, "Lord, You know all things; You know that I love You." Jesus said to him, "Feed My sheep" (John 21:17, NKJV).

John Frith
England—July 4, 1533

John Frith was such a brilliant scholar at Cambridge that Cardinal Wolsey invited him to his college at Oxford, and Henry VIII tried to recruit him as one of his court theologians. But the mysteries of the Word of God and questions of conscience prevailed, and Frith remained at the college (now known as Christ's Church) where he began to teach and preach Protestant doctrines. He also joined with a small group of Reformation-minded theologians who met for periodic discussions at the White Horse Tavern.

Possibly it was the combination of his Protestant sermons and the fact that he had declined the king's court that initially got Frith arrested for heresy and thrown in prison. He was released on the condition that he would remain within ten miles of Oxford until his trial. But knowing that a conviction for heresy could mean death, he fled to Germany, where he met William Tyndale, who was translating the Bible into English. This association confirmed Frith in his Protestant convictions, and he joined in helping Tyndale with his project.

Captivated by Tyndale's vision to provide "an English Bible that can be read by king and plowboy alike," Frith returned to England in 1532, intent on circulating the gospel in person. But Sir Thomas More, chancellor of England, had already issued a warrant for his arrest. Frith was soon apprehended and thrown into the Tower of London.

While there, he engaged in a dialog by letter with More about purgatory and the sacrament of communion. Frith's letters were always moderate, calm, and learned. Where he was not forced to argue, he tended to give in for the sake of peace. Later, Frith wrote to his friends, "I cannot agree with the divines and other head prelates that it is an article of faith that we must believe—under pain of damnation—that the bread and wine are changed into the body and blood of our Savior Jesus Christ while their form and shape stay the same. Even if this were true, it should not be an article of faith."

101

In addition, Frith wrote to Rastell, Sir Thomas More's brother-in-law and a distinguished theologian of the day, hoping specifically to convert him. Frith's words, well founded in Scripture, persuaded Rastell. The conversion of Sir Thomas More's brother-in-law made a great sensation in England.

A Brief Reprieve

After King Henry's secret marriage to Anne Boleyn in January 1533, persecution of Protestants lessened for a time. Frith was released from his chains and permitted to receive whatever he asked for. He was even granted furloughs from the Tower at night, taking the opportunity to visit Christian friends and encourage them in the faith.

However, under the malicious influence of Dr. Curwin, Henry VIII's chaplain at the time, the king ordered, "I am very much surprised that John Frith has been kept so long in the Tower without examination. I desire his trial to take place without delay, and if he does not retract, let him suffer the penalty he deserves." From that point on, no one could save Frith from the consequences of what the assembled bishops of London ruled to be heresy.

On July 4, the sheriff led him to the stake, where Frith willingly embraced the wood and fire, giving a perfect testimony with his own life. For two hours, the wind blew the fire away from him and toward Andrew Hewet, who was also being burned that day for "heresy." This prolonged Frith's suffering, but he seemed glad that Hewet went quickly.

A Lasting Legacy

One might wonder why Frith and so many other reformers were willing to go to the stake over issues such as the nature of the sacrament, which he, himself, said, "should not be an article of the faith." After all, no one was requiring him to renounce Christ, as has happened to so many Christians on pagan frontiers. But the issues were not so simple as mere doctrinal differences. They were asked to say they believed something they could not, in good conscience, affirm. These were the early battles for the freedom of religion.

For instance, a direct descendent of Frith's associate, Rowland Taylor, was James Madison, who successfully strengthened the Virginia Constitution (on which the U.S. Constitution was modeled) by adding the clause that "all men are equally entitled to the free exercise of religion, according to the dictates of conscience."

Forty Roman Catholic Martyrs

England and Wales — Sixteenth and Seventeenth Centuries, honored October 25

Rather than ranting over the 288 Protestants Mary Tudor burned at the stake in her brief five-year reign as she tried to restore Catholicism to England, Protestants should weep that Roman Catholics count over three hundred martyrs in England and Wales executed by Protestants, most in the years following Mary Tudor's reign. Though politics played a big role in their persecution—as it did for many Protestants—these people died for being Catholic and furthering the Catholic religion in England.

Political Complexities

After the death of Mary Tudor in 1558, her half sister Elizabeth came to the throne. For a time, she successfully ruled as a "moderate" Protestant, but then Pope Pius V officially excommunicated her and decreed that: (1) English Roman Catholics could no longer receive the sacraments in the English-speaking services throughout England, but must instead receive them from priests smuggled in from the mainland who would say the Mass in Latin; (2) Elizabeth was no lawful monarch, and Roman Catholics had a duty to replace her with her Roman Catholic cousin Mary of Scotland.

The English government took this as a virtual declaration of war and declared that the saying of Mass in Latin was treason. This set the stage for more than a hundred years of religious martyrdoms with political undercurrents. The politics was complicated and the times were treacherous. Still, no true Christian—Protestant or Catholic—can justify persecuting and killing other believers for their faith. We rightly repent.

Remembering in Sorrow

On October 25, 1970, Pope Paul VI designated a representative forty of these martyrs to commemorate all the Catholics killed for the sake of conscience in England during this period. They are as follows. Read them prayerfully.

Laywomen: Margaret Middleton Clitherow (a wife, mother, and schoolmistress in York), 1586; Margaret Ward (a gentlewoman who engineered a priest's escape from prison), 1588; Anne Higham Line (a widow who harbored priests), 1601.

Laymen: Richard Gwyn (a Welsh poet and schoolmaster), 1584; Swithun Wells (a Welsh schoolmaster) died in prison, 1591; Philip Howard (Earl of Arundel and Surrey) died in the Tower, 1595; John Rigby (household retainer of the Huddleston family), 1600.

Ordinary parish priests not in monastic orders: Cuthbert Mayne, 1577; Ralph Sherwin, Alexander Briant, 1581; John Pain, Luke Kirby, 1582; Edmund Gennings, Eustace White, Polydore Plasden, 1591; John Boste, 1594; John Almond, 1612; John Southworth, 1654; John Lloyd (Welsh), John Plessington, John Kemble, 1679.

Monks and friars from religious orders:

Carthusians: John Houghton, Augustine Webster, Robert Lawrence, 1535.
Brigittine: Richard Reynolds, 1535.
Augustinian friar: John Stone, 1539.

Jesuits: Edmund Campion, 1581; Robert Southwell, Henry Walpole, 1595; Thomas Garnet, 1608; Edmund Arrowsmith, 1628; Henry Morse, 1645; Philip Evans (Welsh), David Lewis (Welsh), 1679.
Jesuit laybrother: Nicholas Owen, 1606.
Benedictines: John Roberts (Welsh), 1610; Ambrose Barlow, 1641; Alban Roe, 1642.
Friar observant: John Jones (Welsh), 1598.
Franciscan: John Wall, 1679.

[Nehemiah prayed,] "I confess the sins we . . . including myself and my father's house, have committed against you. We have acted very wickedly toward you. We have not obeyed the commands, decrees and laws you gave your servant Moses" (Nehemiah 1:6-7, NIV).

William Tyndale
Antwerp, Belgium — October 6, 1536

As a student of Scripture at both Oxford and Cambridge, William Tyndale grappled with "Lutheran ideas"—the current hot topic in the early 1520s. Leaving Cambridge, he took a position as a tutor in the household of Sir John and Lady Anne Walsh at Little Sodbury Manor in Gloucestershire, where many of England's nobility and clergy were often guests. Tyndale was disturbed that even the priests barely knew what the Word of God said. He determined that he was going to translate and print the Bible in English so that ordinary people could read God's Word for themselves.

Tyndale first sought church approval, but the English church strongly opposed putting the Bible into the hands of the common people. So in 1524, he left England and settled in Germany to work on a translation of the New Testament from the original languages. (The only English version prior to this was the hand-copied Wycliffe, 1380.) Fifteen thousand printed copies were smuggled into England between 1525 and 1530. A copy was given to King Henry VIII, but he would not sanction it. Church authorities did their best to buy up and burn Tyndale's New Testament, but their money simply financed more printings!

Tyndale, meanwhile, was considered an outlaw by English law, and he had to go into hiding even as he worked on translating the Old Testament. He was given sanctuary by an English merchant in Belgium—but he was betrayed by a spy and thrown into prison on May 21, 1535. Condemned as a heretic, he was strangled and burnt at the stake on October 6, 1536. His last words were, "Lord! Open the eyes of the King of England."

His prayer of faith was answered. Using Tyndale's work, Miles Coverdale published the first-ever complete Bible in English and King Henry VIII gave it his stamp of approval!

Table Talk

The talk around the table at Little Sodbury Manor was always lively. This particular evening, the discussion turned to the pope's denial of King Henry VIII's request to divorce Queen Catherine.

"The king may not get his male heir after all," said one guest.

"Rubbish!" snorted another. "King Henry will get his son—even if he has to leave the Catholic Church and marry again to do it."

A visiting abbot, the head of a local monastery, eyed William Tyndale, a young priest who tutored the Walsh children. "Master Tyndale, I hear that you picked up some 'reform' ideas at Cambridge. What do *you* think?"

"It's not what I think," said Tyndale. "Tell me, Abbot, what the Bible says about divorce."

"Well, I . . . I . . . it's up to the pope!"

"We know what the pope says. What do the Scriptures say?"

The abbot grew red. "I will not have a country priest question me!"

Tyndale's eyes narrowed. "You don't answer because you don't read the Bible. And the people can't read it because all we have is the Latin Vulgate. We need an English Bible that can be read by king and plowboy alike!"

In His Own Words

"If God spares my life, before many years pass I will help the boy behind the plow to know more of the Scriptures than you do!"

—William Tyndale to an abbot of the church at Little Sodbury

Prayer of the People

O God! Thank you for translators like William Tyndale, who was willing to risk death so that I can read your Word in my own language. Help me not to take the Bible for granted, but to read it, feed on it, hide it in my heart. Amen.

Maria van Beckum

Netherlands—November 13, 1544

When Maria van Beckum's mother kicked her out of the house because of her faith, she went to live with her brother, John van Beckum, and his wife, Ursula. But the authorities soon tracked her down and came in the middle of the night demanding that she surrender. Her brother wanted to hide her, but the house was surrounded, and her pursuers had heard her cry out when they called her name.

"Give her time to put on some clothes," John replied, still looking for some escape.

Seeing that her captors were all men, Maria asked her sister-in-law, Ursula, to accompany her.

"I will if John permits. We will rejoice in the Lord together."

Even though he knew that this could easily lead to his wife's indictment as well, John nevertheless agreed for the sake of his sister.

Indeed, both women were tried for heresy and sentenced to death.

Singing Sisters-in-Law

On November 13, 1544, they were led, singing, to the stake. When they realized that many in the crowd were crying, they said, "Don't weep for us. We are not being punished as witches or other criminals but because we adhere to Christ and will not be separated from God. Therefore, be converted, and it shall be well with you forever."

When the time for their execution arrived, Maria said, "Dear sister, heaven is opened for us. We will suffer only for a little while; then we will forever be happy with our bridegroom." They then gave each other the kiss of peace and prayed together, that God would forgive the judges their sins, since they didn't know what they were doing. "O Lord, have compassion on us, and receive our souls into your eternal kingdom."

Maria was taken to the stake first, and as the flame was kindled, one of the officials tried to turn Ursula away so she would not have to watch. "No," she said, turning back. "Let me witness the end of my sister-in-law, for I also desire to receive the glory into which she shall enter."

After Maria was burned, they asked Ursula if she would finally recant. "No," she said, "I will not forsake my eternal riches." Then, feeling some mercy, they offered her death by the sword, but she said, "My flesh is not too good to be burned for the name of Christ." But when she stepped upon the wood, her foot slipped, and she said, "I think I am falling off."

"Stop!" cried one of the officials. "She wants to recant."

"No, no," said Ursula, "the block merely slipped under me. I will not faint in the Word of God, but constantly adhere to Christ."

In this manner, both remained steadfast to the end.

Seed of the Church

Two young men, named Bartel and Gerrit, were present at this execution, and heard Maria say before she was burned, "You will see this stake at which I am to be burned grow green, by which you may know that it is the truth for which we here suffer and die." Some time later they happened by the site and saw that the stake had indeed budded and was growing.

Modern skeptics say that if this was the case, there are some woods that can suffer considerable flame and still sprout, but the consequence was that both young men went directly and sought out a group of believers and committed their lives to Christ. Gerrit resided in Amsterdam as a faithful Christian until his natural death. Bartel, however, also became a martyr for the faith.

A white robe was given to each of them. And they were told to rest a little longer until the full number of their brothers and sisters—their fellow servants of Jesus—had been martyred (Revelation 6:11).

Hans Blietel

Bavaria—June 25, 1545

Not every one who claims to be a believer is faithful.

Hans Blietel had been sent by the church in Moravia on a fraternal mission to Ried, Bavaria. He presumed the pleasant couple who welcomed him into their home were true believers, but they had been seduced by the ransom on Blietel's head and betrayed him to the authorities.

When Brother Hans had lain in prison for four or five weeks, he was sentenced to death by burning, on about St. John's day. As he was led through town toward the place of his execution, the local priest attempted to convince him to deny his faith. "I cannot do that," Blietel said. "Today I have something else to do. I must follow Jesus Christ, my Lord and God, and fulfill what I have promised."

Then Blietel recognized in the crowd that lined the street an acquaintance named Michael Dirks. As he was led past, Blietel warmly smiled at the onlooker and pointed toward heaven.

When Blietel arrived at the place of his execution, he thought about his church back at home in Moravia. They should be told what had happened to him, that he had died as a martyr but that he did not deny his faith. So he called out to the crowd that had gathered for his burning. "Is there anyone here who would go to Moravia and tell the church there that I was burned here on this date for the gospel of Christ?"

In spite of the risk to himself, a man in the crowd called back, "Yes. I will go!"

"Praise God," said Blietel, encouraged by the response, even as the fire was kindled around him. "Tell them that my faith is in the divine truth." And then to the crowd, he said, "Repent, reform, and desist from your unrighteous and wicked life!"

By this time, the fire was crackling around him. "Today," he cried, "God will give a sign in the heavens to testify that this is the way of eternal life. And my spirit and the smoke from my fire will ascend straight up to heaven."

Within minutes, the sun became dark—even though the sky was clear—and cast no shadow. Seeing the fulfillment of the sign, Blietel began to sing and praise God and pray for those who were torturing him until the fire overcame him. And as the people stared in silence, the smoke did go straight up into the sun-darkened sky. Some later claimed that they saw a white dove come right out of the flames and go up with the smoke.

A Convert Who Could Not Be Stopped

But Michael Dirks, the man on whom Blietel had smiled on the way to the stake, was so utterly shocked that a man could smile in those circumstances that he became contrite and told his wife. Her reaction was so intense that she didn't eat anything for three days. Finally, they went together to seek out the local church and became devout members.

The historical records do not say, but it is quite possible that Michael Dirks and his wife were the same couple that had betrayed Blietel in the first place. And maybe, just maybe, Dirks was the man in the crowd who found the courage to expose his sentiments and volunteer to report Blietel's faithful witness to the church in Moravia.

Can you imagine the burning zeal in his heart as he trudged across country toward Moravia? He may have caused one of the faithful to fall, but now he had been given the privilege of rising in his place. Nothing could stop him!

"And zealous?" [wrote Paul.] "Yes, in fact, I harshly persecuted the church. . . . But now I consider [that] worthless because of what Christ has done. . . . As a result, I can really know Christ and experience the mighty power that raised him from the dead. I can learn what it means to suffer with him, sharing in his death, so that, somehow, I can experience the resurrection from the dead!" (Philippians 3:6-7, 10-11).

Anne Askew
England—July 16, 1546

In *The Prince and the Pauper,* Mark Twain wrote, "One summer's day [Tom Canty] saw poor Anne Askew and three men burned at the stake in Smithfield, and heard an ex-Bishop preach a sermon to them which did not interest him." Twain's book may have been fiction, but the martyrdoms of Anne Askew and her three companions were real enough.

As the youngest daughter of Sir William Askew of Kelsey, in Lincolnshire, Anne was well educated for a woman of that time, and through studying the Scriptures, came to a strongly held faith of a Protestant persuasion. However, when her oldest sister, who had been engaged to marry a harsh and bigoted old man, died, Anne's father required her to take her sister's place. Out of obedience, Anne tried, but the arrangement was a disaster, and she finally fled to London to sue for divorce.

While in London, Anne became involved in the circles of John Lascelles, a Protestant leader and gentleman of the court and household of King Henry VIII. Through him Anne became acquainted with some of Queen Catherine Parr's ladies and may even have attended some of Catherine's Bible studies.

Henry's Sixth Wife

Though King Henry had instigated his break with the pope—to pursue his matrimonial capers—he still considered himself a faithful Catholic in doctrine. When he set out to invade France in 1544, he named Queen Catherine, his sixth wife, as regent, an expression of great respect and trust. However, Catherine was not inclined to submit to the influences of Lord Chancellor Thomas Wriothesly and his ally, Stephen Gardiner, the conservative Catholic

Bishop of Winchester. So when the king returned, they set about undermining his trust in his wife. Their intent was to prove Catherine's Protestant leanings.

Anne Askew spoke freely of her own biblical convictions, and it was not long before she was arrested on the charge of holding heretical opinions against the Six Articles, especially concerning the sacrament of the Lord's Supper.

Under many examinations, Anne acknowledged her doctrinal variance from the Six Articles, especially her doubt that the bread and the wine turned into the actual body and blood of Christ. During one bizarre grilling, the Lord Mayor of London asked her, "What if a mouse were to eat the sacred bread after it was consecrated? What shall become of the mouse, thou foolish woman?"

"What say you, my lord, will become of it?"

"I say that mouse is damned!"

"Alas, poor mouse," Anne replied quietly, but she would not name or implicate anyone else. And that was what Wriothesly and Gardiner were after.

They put her on the rack and nearly pulled her apart, Wriothesly himself turning the wheel and threatening her. Finally, they gave up and sentenced her to death.

At the age of twenty-five, she was burned at the stake on July 16, 1546, along with John Adams, a tailor; John Lascelles, a courtier of King Henry; and a minister from Shropshire, Nicholas Belenian. Maybe Mark Twain's Tom Canty was not there, but a very large crowd witnessed her peaceful surrender and later read the final prayer she wrote just before being taken from her cell to the stake.

In Her Own Words

"O Lord, I have more enemies now than there be hairs on my head. Yet, Lord, let them never overcome me with vain words, but fight thou, Lord, in my stead! For on Thee cast I my care. With all the spite they can imagine, they fall upon me, who am Thy poor creature. Yet, sweet Lord, let me not set by them that are against me, for in Thee is my whole delight. And, Lord, I heartily desire of Thee that Thou wilt, of Thy most merciful goodness, forgive them that violence which they do and have done unto me. Open also Thou their blind hearts that they may hereafter do that thing in Thy sight, which is only acceptable before Thee and to set forth Thy [truth] aright without all vain fantasies of sinful man. So be it, O Lord! So be it!"

Martin Luther
Germany — February 18, 1546

When Martin Luther appeared before Emperor Charles V and the Imperial Council in the City of Worms on April 17, 1521, he knew death threatened. His accuser, the renowned Catholic scholar, John Eck, was out to get him and had forbidden any discussion. "Just answer the questions put to you and make no other statements. Is that understood?"

Eck read off the titles of a stack of Luther's books. "Did you write them, and are you willing to renounce them?"

"Yes, I wrote them, but as to whether I can renounce their content, that would take some discussion, and you do not want any debate."

"Why must there be discussion?"

"First of all," answered the stocky Luther, "no one in this room would argue against the majority of their content. To deny that material would in itself be heresy . . . . As for the other content, the material which you and the Church of Rome might object to, I cannot deny anything unless it is shown to me to be in conflict with the Scriptures. That would require discussion."

"The Just Shall Live by Faith"

Martin Luther was born on November 10, 1483, in Eisleben, Germany. Soon after Martin's birth, his peasant parents—Hans and Margarethe— moved to Mansfeld to find employment in the mines. His industrious father rented a forge where he could smelt copper ore into raw copper and thereby went into business for himself.

Luther attended school there, in Magdeburg, and in Eisenach, and finally entered university in Erfurt. One day when twenty-two-year-old Martin was returning to the university, he reportedly was caught in a severe storm and nearly struck by lightning. In terror, he cried out and pledged to become a monk if only his life would be spared.

Within two weeks, he made good on his promise and entered a monastery. There he made another vow: "Henceforth I shall serve you God, you Jesus, you only." And he did. On April 3, 1507, Luther was ordained a priest. In 1512 he earned his doctor of theology degree and became a professor in the University of Wittenberg.

But in spite of his professional success, Luther felt tormented by his sins and did not feel he had found favor with God. The harder he worked to be "good," the worse he felt until one day he was studying Romans 1:17: "Therein is the righteousness of God revealed from faith to faith: as it is written, The just shall live by faith" (KJV).

Even though he was a teacher of religion, he had not realized that one cannot *earn* God's favor. It is a gift from God, received by faith alone. After Martin accepted God's gift, his first question was, "Why didn't I learn this from my church?"

He looked around. The people were told that to please God they must buy "indulgences" (written pardons for sin) and obey church rules. This brought money into the church treasury and kept the people under control for the government. But it was a fraud.

Writing about these and other abuses had landed him on trial before the Imperial Council. And he probably would have been burned as a heretic had not some friends "kidnapped" and taken him to Duke Frederick of Saxony's Wartburg Castle where Luther was "confined" until it was politically safe for him to move about and later become the most influential leader of the Reformation before his death on February 18, 1546.

In His Own Words

Possibly while enjoying the protection of the Wartburg Castle, Luther reflected on God's greater defense mentioned in Psalm 46 when he penned his well-known hymn:

> *A mighty fortress is our God,*
> *A bulwark never failing;*
> *Our helper He, amid the flood*
> *Of mortal ills prevailing.*

God is our refuge and strength, always ready to help in times of trouble. . . . The Lord Almighty is here among us; the God of Israel is our fortress (Psalm 46:1, 11).

Luis Cáncer de Barbastro

Florida—June 26, 1549

From the outset, missionary efforts in the Americas were contaminated by and sometimes almost indistinguishable from the Spanish conquest of the New World . . . and, of course, the search for gold. The Catholic Church supported Spain's imperial expansion based on the Spaniards' responsibility to spread Christianity. But because of mixed motives, the methods were mixed as well. At the very least, gospel preaching enjoyed military protection, but in too many instances the indigenous people were offered one choice: convert or die.

Bartolomé de Las Casas took exception to advancing the cross with the sword and finally obtained a commission by King Ferdinand V of Spain as "Protector of the Indians." Through his tract, "The Only Method of Attracting All Peoples to the True Faith," he argued in favor of peaceful means of evangelism.

Disciple of Peace

One of the many Europeans influenced by Las Casas's campaign to defend the New World Indians was Luis Cáncer de Barbastro, born in Aragón, Spain, about 1510. He is thought to have entered the Dominican Order in the Priory in Huesca, but his calling was that of a missionary. Sometime in 1518, he left to join the newly formed Province of the Holy Cross of the Indies on the island of Hispanola (now shared by the Dominican Republic and Haiti).

In 1542, Cáncer initiated a preaching mission in the territory of Guatemala then known as *Tuzulutlán* (the Land of War, because of the Mayan's continuing battles against the Spanish). After mastering various Mayan dialects, Cáncer composed songs that presented the gospel in the native languages. When, after spreading the songs by means of merchants who had access to the territory, he discovered that the people liked them, he volunteered to go in alone, not with a group of priests and certainly not under the protection of a military guard. This brave and risky tactic opened the area for the establishment of a full-fledged mission. Within four years, the territory became known as *La Tierra de la Verapaz,* "the Land of the True Peace." Thus Cáncer proved the peaceful approach to evangelization advocated by Las Casas was valid and effective.

Florida

Near the end of 1547, Cáncer gained permission to lead a peaceful missionary expedition to Florida. He departed early in 1549 with three other priests, a lay brother, and an Indian woman interpreter, named Magdalena. The abduction of a few "savages" from the coast was a common tactic of the conquistadores, who believed that after a period of indoctrination in the Spanish language, culture, and the Catholic faith in a nearby colonial capital, they would become loyal interpreters. Cáncer's intentions, however, were to return Magdalena to her people.

On May 29, Louis waded ashore near Espíritu Santo Bay with two Dominican brothers and Magdalena. They received such an open welcome that Cáncer returned to the ship for more gifts, but before he could return, the Indians killed the two Dominican brothers, and Magdalena deserted to the Indians. These facts were reported by a Spaniard who had been captured during the Fernando de Soto expedition of 1539–43 and escaped to the ship.

Cáncer instructed the ship's captain to move on but not to stop at any place where the conquistadores had previously visited. However, against Cáncer's orders he brought the ship to Tampa Bay, where he knew he could find fresh water.

Against the warnings of one of the two survivors, Cáncer swam ashore alone on June 26. Shortly after he arrived, an Indian grabbed him by the arm. Then other Indians approached. One yanked off Cáncer's hat while another clubbed him in the head. His last words, heard by those still on the ship were, "*Adjuva me, Domine!*" ("Help me, Lord!")

Help me, O Lord my God! Save me because of your unfailing love (Psalm 109:26).

Elizabeth Dirks

Netherlands—March 27, 1549

To elude the authorities, young Bible teacher Elizabeth Dirks took up residence in the town of Leeuwarden in the home of Hadewijk, a brave older woman who risked everything to harbor her. But the day finally came when the authorities smashed in the door and found Elizabeth with her Latin New Testament, a sure sign of what she had been doing. The council followed this evidence when interrogating her the following day.

Lords: "We say you are a teacher, and that you seduce many. We have been told this, and we want to know who your friends are."

Elizabeth: "My God has commanded me to love my Lord and my God, and to honor my parents; for what I suffer for the name of Christ is a reproach to my friends."

Lords: "We will let you alone in regard to this, but we want to know whom you have taught."

Elizabeth: "Oh, no, my lords, don't ask me that. Interrogate me concerning my faith, which I will gladly tell you."

Lords: "We shall make you so afraid that you will tell us. . . . What persons were present when you were baptized?"

Elizabeth: "Christ said: ask them that were present, or who heard it."

Lords: "Oh, quoting Scripture, huh? Now we know you are a teacher."

When she would not betray any of her fellow believers, they applied thumbscrews.

"Help me, O Lord," she cried. "For you are a helper in time of need."

The lords all exclaimed: "Confess, and we will relieve you your pain; for we told you to confess, not to cry to God the Lord." But as she refused to give up the names of other brothers and sisters, the Lord took away her pain.

Finally, on March 27, 1549, the magistrates condemned her to be drowned in a bag.

Not Tempted beyond What We Can Bear

Hadewijk was arrested with Elizabeth and held in the same prison, though in another cell. As the guard escorted Elizabeth to her interrogation he told Hadewijk that her test would come the next day.

Terrified that because she could not read, she would not be able to give good answers or that she could not withstand the pain, she spent the day pleading with God. "O loving Father, you know that I am weak and unfit for such a test." Then recalling 1 Corinthians 10:13, she said, "Please do not try me beyond my ability, but deliver me by your mighty hand."

113

While she was praying she heard a voice call, "Hadewijk!" But looking around, she saw no one, so she continued praying. A second time she heard her name called, but again there was no one in her cell.

Finally, the same voice said, "Hadewijk! I tell you, come out!"

This time when she looked up, she found that the door to her cell was open, so she put on her hooded cape and walked all the way out of the prison unimpeded. But she didn't know where to hide, so she went to the church.

There she heard that the gates of the city had been closed because a woman had escaped from prison, and a search was being made for her. She hid for a night in the attic room of an old acquaintance, who arranged her escape from the city the next day in a boat through the floodgate. Hadewijk then fled to Emden, where she lived out the rest of her days in peace in the meeting-houses of the believers.

"If we are thrown into the blazing furnace, the God whom we serve is able to save us. He will rescue us from your power, Your Majesty. But even if he doesn't, Your Majesty can be sure that we will never serve your gods or worship the gold statue you have set up" (Daniel 3:17-18).

Jacques Dosie
Netherlands — 1550

The lanky, pallid youth hesitated when the guard opened the door to the great hall and pushed him in to where the lord and lady of Friesland were holding court with their nobles and ladies in all their finery.

"Ah, here's that young lad I asked about," said the lady. "Don't mind your appearance, son. We know you've been languishing in prison. But maybe we can do something about that. No, no. Don't be afraid. Come forward. . . . Now, what is your name?"

"Jacques Dosie, my lady."

"And how old are you?"

"I am fifteen years old, my lady."

"A mere child. What a shame!" She shook her head. "Why does the inquisitor say you are guilty of heresy?"

Jacques looked around. Had she brought him here just to entertain her guests? Nevertheless, he recalled the Scripture that said, "if you are asked about your Christian hope, always be ready to explain it. But you must do this in a gentle and respectful way." So he said, "This was done only because I believe in Christ, cling to him alone, and will never forsake him."

The lady raised her eyebrows. "Devotion to our Lord is commendable, so . . ." Her eyes narrowed. "You don't belong to the people who rebaptize themselves, do you? . . . the ones who are creating rebellion in our country, banding together and claiming to be scattered for the faith? I hear they boast of being the church of God, even though they do wicked things and stir up a commotion among the people."

The bored nobles and ladies ceased their idle chatter and turned to listen.

"My lady, I don't know any rebellious people, nor am I one of them. In fact, according to the teaching of the Scriptures, we would much rather help our enemies, giving them food and drink if they are hungry or thirsty. Nor do we resist them with either revenge or violence."

"A likely claim," snorted one of the guests. "If they had the power, they'd kill us all."

Jacques glanced at him and then turned back to the lady. "Oh no, my lady. We believe it is of the devil to resist the authorities with the external sword. We would much rather suffer persecution and death than turn to violence."

The lady leaned back in her chair, a smile teasing at the corners of her lips. "I'm inclined to believe you, but tell me, in what way do you still differ from the inquisitor?"

Jacques honestly reviewed the points where he differed, answering other questions put to him by the nobles. Finally, the lady said, "My dear boy, won't you repent and come over to our side? Then you'll be out of this trouble, and I promise to secure your release."

"My lady, thank you very much for your affection and favor, but I cannot change my faith to please anyone unless my err be shown me with the Scriptures, for I have given myself entirely to God. Herein I hope to live and die."

The lady shook her head. "I find many good things in you, Jacques, but your greatest error I consider to lie in your view of baptism—that you will not have the children baptized. For all Germany and every kingdom regards your doings as heresy."

She dismissed him then, but brought him before her on other occasions in a genuine attempt to convince him to give up his faith. She used grave threats and grand promises, but nothing would sway him. Finally, in spite of her efforts, he was condemned and put to death in 1550 in Leeuwarden, capital of the Dutch province of Friesland.

[Jesus said,] "You will be dragged into synagogues and prisons, and you will be accused before kings and governors of being my followers. This will be your opportunity to tell them about me. So don't worry about how to answer the charges against you, for I will give you the right words and such wisdom that none of your opponents will be able to reply!" (Luke 21:12-15).

Jerome Segers

Belgium—September 2, 1551

February 14 is Saint Valentine's Day, commemorated by sending affectionate notes to our beloved as Valentine supposedly did from prison. Early records mention three different people named Valentine who were variously martyred for their faith sometime before 312. But there is little, if any, evidence for this myth of sending love notes.

Nevertheless, some *true* love letters were sent between a Christian husband (Jerome Segers) and his wife (Lijsken Dircks) as they waited in prison for their chance to witness for their faith.

Background

Jerome Segers, along with his wife, Lijsken Dircks, and a man known as Big Henry (probably Hendrick of Deventer) were arrested for their testimony at Antwerp, Belgium, in 1551. Antwerp had the scandalous distinction of executing over 1,648 "heretics," more than any other European city.

In His Own Words

My most beloved wife, Lijsken Dircks, whom I wedded before God and his holy church, and thus took to wife according to the command of the Lord, may consolation, gladness, and joy be increased to you.

I earnestly pray that our Lord will comfort you and protect you from anything too hard. I know, my chosen lamb, that you are very sorrowful on my account, but lay aside your grief and look to Jesus, the Captain and Finisher of our faith.

My mother brought me your letter, and I read it with tears of joy. Thank you for your affectionate comfort. I'm glad that you are holding up so well.

Also, I want you to know, my chosen and beloved wife, that I have been before the military governor. He had with him two priests, two judges, and the clerk of the criminal court. He asked me whether I had changed my mind yet and added that he had prevailed upon the priests to try and win my soul if I would repent. I replied that I would not forsake my faith since it was the truth.

They then tried to convince me otherwise, and the governor tried to manipulate me by saying such things as: "I have hope you'll change because you came to these ideas in the innocence of youth, and you come from such a good family, and your mother is almost dead with grief."

But it was to no avail. Then the governor changed his tact and said, "I shall cause you to be burned alive if you will not hear."

I laughed at that and said, "All that you inflict upon me for my faith, I will willingly suffer."

Then he said that you, my dear, are the greatest heretic in the city. What an honor, coming from him.

I can't thank the Lord enough for all the great strength and power he gives us. He is such a faithful Captain. As Paul says, "Who shall separate us from the love of Christ? Shall trouble or hardship or persecution or famine or nakedness or danger or sword?"

Well, my most beloved wife, we're certainly into it now, but nothing can separate us from Christ. As he admonished us: "He who stands firm to the end will be saved." Therefore, let us continue faithful to the Lord unto death; for the crown is not at the beginning, nor in the middle, but at the end.

We must realize, my dear Lijsken, that if he wipes away all tears, tears must first be shed. If he heals us from sufferings, we must first suffer in this world. Therefore, defend yourself diligently with prayer and hold fast to the teachings of Jesus Christ our Savior. Fight with Paul the good fight. Herewith I commend you, my dearly beloved wife and sister, to the almighty, eternal, and strong God.

—Your loving husband, Jerome Segers

If we die with him, we will also live with him. If we endure hardship, we will reign with him (2 Timothy 2:11-12).

Hans van Overdam
Belgium—July 9, 1551

The bailiff and his deputies and even a few judges were waiting in ambush when the house church of Ghent, Belgium, gathered in the woods outside of town on Sunday morning for worship. A traitor in their midst had betrayed them.

Twenty or so believers were arrested, shackled, and loaded into wagons. But before being delivered to the lords of the Imperial Council, they were held together in one room in a castle outside town. This gave them time to encourage and admonish one another and to agree on how they should respond to their interrogation. If separated, they would give strong testimony concerning their faith but avoid arguing with anyone concerning the *grounds* for their faith. "It requires a special gift to debate, as well as much maturity in the Lord," advised their pastor, Hans van Overdam. He knew because three youths from his congregation had been arrested earlier and questioned separately only to be bated into controversy. They had become confused and finally denied their faith.

Pastor Overdam did not want this to happen to the rest of his flock.

When they had been moved to the prison in Ghent, they were brought one by one before the Imperial Council. Overdam was questioned closely with the intent of gathering more names of the faithful. "We know that you people don't lie, so tell us," said the clerk.

Overdam said, "That you know that we don't lie, is a testimony to our salvation, but your appeal for me to betray others has no power with me." He had actually been careful to not know the names of many people among his flock so that if he were apprehended, he could not reveal their identities.

The council members threatened to torture him if he did not tell them everything, but he simply said that he could not tell what he did not know. During the days that followed they tried to entice each brother and sister individually to debate the grounds of their faith, but each one held fast to their agreement.

After that, Overdam lay in a dark dungeon for a month and was then moved to a deep round hole where there was a little more light. While there he was able to write a letter to the believers on the outside. In it he described the events of his capture and interrogation and then provided the following encouragement.

In His Own Words

My most dearly beloved,

Grieve not on my account, but praise the Lord that he is so good a father to me that I can suffer bonds and imprisonment for the testimony of Christ, for which I also hope to go into the fire. The Lord give me strength through his Holy Spirit. . . .

I hope to offer up my sacrifice this week, if it is the Lord's will, together with those whom the Lord has foreordained thereto, for if it does not take place this week, it will no doubt be deferred for two months yet, because no court will be held for six weeks. Know that our brothers and sisters are of good cheer and courage through the grace of the Lord; God be praised. They greet you all with the peace of God. We pray for you daily.

Please circulate this letter throughout Friesland as soon as you can, making copies as necessary.

—With brotherly love, Hans van Overdam

Thinking Ahead

On July 9, 1551, the day van Overdam was burned at the stake, van Overdam's friend and fellow believer, Hans Keeskooper, agreed to create a delay by taking off his stockings and climbing onto the scaffold by himself. This was so that Overdam would have more time to preach to the large crowd that had assembled for their execution.

[Jesus said,] "Behold, I send you out as sheep in the midst of wolves. Therefore be wise as serpents and harmless as doves" (Matthew 10:16, NKJV).

Adrian Corneliss

Netherlands—1552

Hearing that two sisters and three brothers had been arrested in Leiden, Adrian Corneliss, probably a pastor, walked the nine or ten miles from Delft to check on them. When he arrived in Leiden, he stayed at the home of Stephen Claes and heard that the bailiff's servant at the prison might be sympathetic. Reportedly he had once said to one of the prisoners, "Shall I leave the door open sometime so you can escape?"

The brother had warily asked, "Why should you do that?" and the servant seemed confused by such a reply, but there was a chance . . .

So when Adrian went to the prison, he asked to see this servant, who was named Jan Jans. They spoke cordially, and Adrian inquired in the most general terms as to whether those arrested for heresy several months before had yet been tried and sentenced. Jan Jans did not know, but he seemed to warm to mention of the prisoners and finally said, "Would you like to speak with them?"

Thinking this might be a divine opportunity similar to Paul and Silas's witness to the jailer in Acts 16:29-30, Adrian said yes.

First he visited briefly with the women, taking care not to reveal that he knew them. Then the servant escorted him upstairs to visit with the men, where their joy at seeing one another could not be concealed. While they spoke, the servant slipped away on an errand.

The errand turned out to be arranging for Adrian's arrest. It had all been a trap.

Soon the whole council was assembled to interrogate Adrian because they had heard that there were many secret believers in the city, and they thought he was some great leader among them and might be able to reveal everyone's identity.

The Need-to-Know Principle

While awaiting execution, Adrian managed to write and smuggle a letter out to the believers. In addition to recounting the torture to which he had been put, he offered this principle for times of persecution: Don't try to know more than you need to know!

"Dear friends," he wrote, "I have always been careful not to know much, so that in case I should be arrested, I might not have much to tell. This issue is sadly overlooked by some of you, who continually inquire after this or that person, and have your feelings hurt if you are not given the desired information. Oh, dear friends, if you only knew what suffering it can mean if you are imprisoned. You would not make such inquiries. Accept this admonition in a good spirit, for I write it in love. All the torture I have suffered was inflicted upon me, to make me inform on others. Believe me—the less you know, the less you have to answer."

Then he explained that the bailiff's servant who had betrayed him was the one who brought him his food each day. Adrian often talked to him as

119

kindly as he could and one day asked forgiveness if he had offended him in any way. The man said, "You have not offended me; none of your people have." The love that Adrian showed to him caused him to feel ashamed that he had betrayed him. Maybe his conviction brought him to faith.

In His Own Words

Christ has gone this way before us and his beloved apostles likewise, and we his servants are not above our Lord. . . . They think by killing us to exterminate the God-fearing, but for [every] one whom they kill, a hundred others shall arise. With this testimony, Adrian Corneliss made his witness.

[Jesus said,] "I tell you the truth, unless a kernel of wheat falls to the ground and dies, it remains only a single seed. But if it dies, it produces many seeds. . . . Whoever serves me must follow me; and where I am, my servant also will be. My Father will honor the one who serves me" (John 12:24, 26, NIV).

Lijsken Dircks
Belgium—February 9, 1552

Lijsken Dircks was pregnant when she and her husband, Jerome Segers, were arrested. In a letter, Jerome wrote, "Do not worry about the child, for our brothers and sisters in the Lord will take good care of the baby; yea, the Lord will care for it." The fact that they do not mention other children and speak at one point of the "short time" they had together suggests that she was pregnant with their first child and that they were relative newlyweds.

In another letter, Jerome apologized that they did not depart from Assuerus—apparently the place of their capture—since Lijsken had often asked him to do so. Then he wrote, "This has cost me many a tear, and I am very sorry. Yet I can do nothing against the will of the Lord, and had it been his will, he would have provided a deliverance for us."

Finally, Lijsken finds the words with which to reply.

In Her Own Words

My beloved husband, Jerome.

Grace and peace be to both of us from God the Father, and the love of the Son, and the communion of the Holy Spirit be with us.

At first, the time in prison seemed so long, but that was because I was not used to being imprisoned and was constantly tempted to depart from the Lord. But your letters of encouragement and God's Word have helped sustain me.

Sometimes my captors would say to me, "Why do you trouble yourself with the Scriptures; attend to your sewing. Who do you think you are, trying to follow the apostles? If you're so great, where are your signs? They spoke with different tongues after they received the Holy Spirit. So where is your special language?"

This mocking was hard to receive, but it is sufficient that we have believed because of the words of the apostles even if we don't express their signs. Our sign is that God gave us his dear Son. And the Scriptures promise that "if we die with him, we will also live with him; if we endure, we will also reign with him. If we disown him, he will also disown us; if we are faithless, he will remain faithful, for he cannot disown himself." Therefore, as it says in the book of Hebrews: "Since we are surrounded by such a great cloud of witnesses, let us throw off everything that hinders and the sin that so easily entangles, and let us run with perseverance the race marked out for us. Let us fix our eyes on Jesus, the author and perfecter of our faith, who for the joy set before him endured the cross and scorned its shame." And as Peter says, "when he suffered, he made no threats."

In this same way, my most beloved husband, I commend to both of us the crucified Savior as our everlasting joy and strength.

My dear husband in the Lord, whom I married before God and his church, they are saying that we lived in adultery because we did not marry in the Roman church. This greatly pains me, but I try to rejoice that they speak evil of us falsely, because as Jesus promised, "great is your reward in heaven."

I'm sorry that you heard that I was upset because we didn't move away from Assuerus when I suggested it. I want you to know, my most beloved, I wasn't upset about that. I know that if it had not been the will of the Lord, we would not have been arrested. The Lord's will must be done, and he will not allow us to be tested beyond what we can endure. Be glad that he has chosen us worthy to be imprisoned for his name's sake.

I pray, my beloved, that you will be of good cheer in the Lord.

—Your faithful wife, Lijsken

Reunited

In his last letter Jerome wrote, "I go with a glad heart, to offer up my sacrifice to the praise of the Lord." Their sole goal was to hold fast to their faith until the very end. And this they did. Jerome was burned at the stake the next day, September 2, 1551. Lijsken's life was preserved until her child was born. Then on February 9, 1552, she was tied in a bag and drowned in the Scheldt River before dawn so that the public would not see. Nevertheless, some did witness her death and testified that she remained steadfast until she departed to be with her Lord . . . and Jerome, her "valentine" on this earth.

John Bradford
London—July 1, 1555

"There, but for the grace of God, go I." John Bradford was the first person on record to have made this now familiar confession. He was in prison at the time for his faith. But his comment concerned a condemned criminal he observed on his way to execution.

Bradford knew firsthand about God's grace.

Born in 1510, he received a good education and earned a good living serving under John Harrington, the paymaster to King Henry VIII's forces fighting in France. However, at some point Bradford helped Harrington cheat the king out of a large sum of money. He did not profit personally but was somehow party to the swindle.

While Bradford was studying law, a fellow student presented the gospel to him, and Bradford converted to the Protestant Christian faith. Unwilling to take any further role in the money scheme, he quit working for Harrington and enrolled at Cambridge to study theology. Still, his conscience was not at peace, and he made every effort to make restitution, at one point proposing to hire himself out as a bondsman to repay the sum.

So distraught was he that he sold his personal jewelry and gave his money to the poor. He became a much-loved preacher throughout the London, not harsh or condemning as one might think, given his own sense of guilt, but compelling.

In 1550, during the reign of Edward VI, Bishop Ridley commissioned Bradford to be a "roving chaplain." However, when Edward died in 1553, the springtime for Protestantism in England crashed under the reign of "Bloody Mary" Tudor. (In the five years that she reigned, nearly three hundred people were condemned to death for heresy.)

Within a month, Mary's agents arrested Bradford on an insignificant charge and threw him into the Tower. In the two years following, he wasted no time but preached to all who would listen and wrote encouraging letters to believers throughout England. He so gained the trust of his jailers that they regularly gave him passes from the prison to go visit the sick and needy, knowing that on his word he would return by evening.

For a time he shared a cell with three fellow reformers who also became martyrs: Hugh Latimer, Nicholas Ridley, and Thomas Cranmer. It was in this fellowship, spent studying the New Testament and encouraging one another, that Bradford found peace for his soul. The Scriptures made it clear that the sacrifice of Christ upon the cross was perfect, holy, and complete. God did not require any other, not even the restitution that he could not pay. At last he understood grace and was able to say when he saw others going to execution for crimes like he'd committed, "There, but for the grace of God, go I."

Finally, in January 1555, he was condemned for heresy with no mention of the ancient financial affair. He was burned at the stake along with another martyr, John Leaf, on July 1, 1555. The authorities planned the execution for four in the morning to avoid the crowds of those who loved Bradford. But word spread, and thousands showed up, delaying the event until nine o'clock.

In His Own Words

Bradford wrote the following inscription in a friend's New Testament: "This book is called The Word of the Cross because the cross always accompanies it, so that if you will be a student thereof, you must needs prepare yourself for that cross, which you began to learn before you learned your alphabet. And Christ requires it of every one that will be His disciple, therein not swerving from the common [manner] of callings or locations, for no profession or kind of life wants its cross. So that they are [much mistaken] who think that the profession of the gospel, which the devil most envies, the world does hates, and the flesh most [complains] at, can be without a cross. Let us therefore enable us to take up our cross by denying ourselves."

—John Bradford, from prison, February 18, 1555

By grace you have been saved through faith, and that not of yourselves; it is the gift of God, not of works, lest anyone should boast (Ephesians 2:8-9, NKJV).

Robert Ferrar

Wales—March 30, 1555

One of the five bishops executed by Queen Mary Tudor in her effort to restore England to Catholicism, Robert Ferrar is often overlooked because he was in Wales.

Early on, Robert's mentors at the Augustinian monastery in Yorkshire recognized his intellectual abilities and sent him to the universities of Cambridge and Oxford, but his curiosity about "Lutheran books" soon got him into trouble.

When Henry VIII started dissolving the monasteries in England, Ferrar actively began spreading reformed principles in northern England and emphasized the need for biblical preaching. Through his association with Archbishop Thomas Cranmer and to the Protector Somerset, Ferrar was made bishop of St. David's in Wales some time after Edward VI came to the throne in 1547. From this position he did much to reform the church with Protestant teaching and practice.

Ferrar got into a series of disputes not only with his own clergy but also with some of the local gentry. One of these clashes led to a lawsuit before the Privy Council, where he was almost deprived of his office.

Still, his Reformation influence was clear and significant enough that Mary Tudor set her henchmen on him as soon as she came to power in 1553.

Ferrar was brought before Lord Chancellor Stephen Gardiner along with John Hooper, John Rogers, and John Bradford, where the records show that he was in full agreement with them on the questions of faith. In an attempt to stamp out his influence among the people, he was ultimately condemned to be burned at Carmarthen in Wales, the place where he was best known.

"He Opened Not His Mouth"

A few days before his execution, Ferrar told a friend, "If you see me once stir in the fire because of the pain, you do not need to believe any of the doctrines I have taught. But do not worry, God will give me strength."

When the awful time came, he did not forget his promise, and, by God's grace, he kept it well. He stood in the flames holding out his hands until they had burned to stumps. Then with a stroke of mercy, one of the sheriff's men struck him on the head and put an end to his sufferings.

Contending for the Faith

In preaching on Jude 3, John Piper, pastor of Bethlehem Baptist Church in Minneapolis, Minnesota, explained why it is so important to contend for the faith. He said, "The faith that we cherish was preserved for us with the blood of hundreds of reformers. From 1555 to 1558 Queen Mary, the Catholic ruler in England, had 288 Protestant reformers burned at the stake—men like John Rogers, John Hooper, Rowland Taylor, Robert Ferrar, John Bradford, Nicholas Ridley, Hugh Latimer, and Thomas Cranmer. And why were they burned? Because they stood by a truth."

On November 25, 1984, in the Bethlehem Baptist Church in Minneapolis, John Piper noted, "The blood of the martyrs is a powerful testimony that the faith once for all delivered to the saints is worth contending for. . . . When the faith is at stake our salvation is at stake. If the truth is lost salvation is lost. The apostles and reformers were willing to die for the sake of the faith because they cared about whether the message of salvation would be preserved—they cared about people and about the glory of God."

I felt I had to write and urge you to contend for the faith that was once for all entrusted to the saints (Jude 1:3, NIV).

John Hooper and Rowland Taylor

England—February 9, 1555

It was Archbishop Thomas Cranmer who installed Dr. Rowland Taylor as the rector at Hadleigh in Suffolk during the reign of Edward VI. There Taylor preached the gospel boldly, and the people loved him greatly. Though he was a married man, he never sat down to dinner with his family without first asking whether the poor wanted anything. He was an indulgent, tender, affectionate husband, and brought up his children in the fear of God.

But when Edward died and Queen Mary ascended the throne, everything changed.

One day Dr. Taylor heard the bells of his church ringing unexpectedly. He went to investigate and found that a Catholic priest with a guard—swords drawn—had taken over the church. When Taylor ordered them to leave, they charged him with heresy, after which Lord Chancellor Stephen Gardiner ordered Dr. Taylor to London for trial.

His friends begged him not to go, to flee instead to Geneva or some other safe place. But Taylor replied, "God will either protect me from sufferings, or he will enable me to bear them. Besides, if I must, my dying for the truth will serve the cause of Christ more than fleeing the malice of my persecutors."

Meanwhile ...

Queen Mary removed John Hooper from his bishopric in Gloucester and imprisoned him in London to be tried for heresy because of his Protestant messages.

Hooper had been born in Summerset and educated in Oxford where he entered the monastery. When Henry VIII abolished the monasteries for political reasons in 1536, Hooper went to London where he encountered and adopted Reformation ideas. After his installation as the bishop of Gloucester, his work was exemplary. He preached regularly, visited parishes, helped the poor, sought to correct social injustice, and encouraged the habit of Bible reading. But then came Queen Mary.

In His Own Words

The grace of God be with you. Amen.

Now is the time of trial, to see whether we fear God or man. It was an easy thing to hold with Christ while the Prince and world held with Him, but now the world hateth Him; it is the true trial who be His. Wherefore, in the name and in the virtue, strength, and power of His Holy Spirit, prepare yourselves in any case to adversity and constancy. Let us not run away when it is most time to fight. Remember, none shall be crowned but such as fight manfully, and "he that endureth to the end shall be saved."

You must now turn all your cogitations from the peril you see, and mark the felicity that followeth the peril—either victory in this world of your enemies or else a surrender of this life to inherit the everlasting kingdom. Beware of beholding too much the felicity or misery of this world, for the consideration and too earnest love or fear of either of them draweth from God. . . .

Imprisonment is painful, but yet liberty upon evil conditions is more painful. The prisons stink, but yet not so much as sweet houses where the fear and true honor of God lacketh. I must be alone and

125

solitary; it is better so to be, and have God with me, than to be in company with the wicked. Loss of goods is great; but loss of God's grace and favor is greater. . . .

I can do no more but pray for you; do the same for me, for God's sake. For my part (I thank the heavenly Father), I have made mine accounts, and appointed myself unto the will of the heavenly Father; as He will, so I will, by His grace. . . . Fare you well.

Your bounden, John Hooper

—A letter from John Hooper, in prison,
to his friends, January 21, 1555

Both men were burned at the stake on February 9, 1555. Dr. Taylor was executed at his home in Hadleigh while Bishop Hooper died in Gloucester.

Hugh Latimer and Nicholas Ridley
England—October 16, 1555

When King Henry VIII of England died in 1547, he left three heirs: his son, Edward, and two daughters, Mary and Elizabeth. Edward, who had been raised by Protestants, ascended the throne. Under his rule, church services, previously in Latin, were translated into English, Thomas Cranmer's *Book of Common Prayer* was introduced, the Bible was to be read, and other changes were made. But when Edward died, the throne passed to his sister Mary, who was firmly Roman Catholic and determined to return England to union with the Pope. She failed, but for burning 288 martyrs, she is remembered as "Bloody Mary." Hugh Latimer and Nicholas Ridley were two of the five bishops she burned. The others were John Hooper, Robert Ferrar, and John Bradford.

The Unlikely Convert

Educated at Cambridge, Hugh Latimer was at first antagonistic to the Reformation. But he got involved with the Reformation though Thomas Bilney, one of the leaders of a group of reformed theologians who met for discussion at the well-known White Horse Tavern. Bilney asked to make confession to Latimer. Latimer thought he was going to confess his Protestant convictions, and indeed, Bilney told him all about how he had come to complete faith in the perfect sacrifice of the spotless Lamb of God. This testimony so moved Latimer that he humbled himself before God and embraced the Reformation movement.

After King Henry broke with Rome, Latimer became one of his senior advisers, and in 1535 became bishop of Worcester, but resigned in protest against the king's refusal to allow what Latimer considered essential Protestant reforms. He maintained a low profile until Edward came to the throne in 1547.

His eloquence as a preacher then earned him the bishopic of Rochester, and he assisted Thomas Cranmer in creating the *Book of Common Prayer*. When Mary Tudor became queen, however, she promptly moved him to the Tower of London, after which he was tried for heresy (technically, sedition) with Nicholas Ridley and Thomas Cranmer and condemned to death.

Nicholas Ridley

In 1534, while a proctor of Cambridge, Nicholas Ridley signed the decree against the pope's supremacy in England. But otherwise, throughout the 1530s, he demonstrated little inclination toward Protestant thinking. However, after becoming chaplain to Thomas Cranmer in 1537, his thinking began to change. In 1541, he became chaplain to Henry VIII and canon of Canterbury. After Edward came to the throne in 1547, and Protestant reform swept the land, Ridley served as a commissioner in the examination that resulted in the deposition of bishops Stephen Gardiner and Edmund Bonner because of their adherence to the doctrines of Rome. Afterward, Ridley was made Bishop of London in Bonner's place.

Ironically, it was the reinstated bishops, Stephen Gardiner and Edmund Bonne, who tried and condemned Nicholas Ridley, Hugh Latimer, and Thomas Cranmer. Ridley and Latimer were burned at the stake together before Balliol Hall, Oxford, on October 16, 1555. Cranmer's execution was delayed until the following March.

In Their Own Words

Latimer's parting words to Ridley as they awaited the blaze are often quoted: "Be of good courage, brother Ridley, and play the man; for we shall this day light such a candle by God's grace in England, as I trust shall never be put out."

Therefore, my dear brothers, stand firm. Let nothing move you. Always give yourselves fully to the work of the Lord, because you know that your labor in the Lord is not in vain (1 Corinthians 15:58, NIV).

John Philpot

England—December 18, 1555

John Philpot was the son of an English knight, educated at Oxford, and served—during the Protestant reign of Edward VI—as the archdeacon of Winchester. When Edward died and his sister, Mary Tudor, took the throne in 1553, attempting to restore the Roman church, some clergymen fled. Philpot, however, stayed in England and took part in a debate with Roman apologists in a convocation after being assured that he could speak freely.

After the debate, his words were turned against him, and he was arrested. Philpot endured fourteen examinations by various church officials, especially the Catholic bishops Gardiner and Bonner. The following transcript from an 1833 edition of John Foxe's *Book of Martyrs* begins with Philpot's opening statement. The names Gloucester and Worcester refer to the bishops from those locations.

The Fourth Exam

Philpot: I have, my lords, been these twelve months and a half in prison without any just cause, and my living is taken from me without any lawful order, and now I am brought (contrary to right) from my own territory and ordinary, into another man's jurisdiction, I know not why. Wherefore, if your lordships can burden me with any evil done, I stand here before you to purge me of the same. And if no such thing can be justly laid to my charge, I desire to be released.

Bonner: There is none here that goeth about to trouble you, but to do you good, if we can. For I promise you, you were sent hither to me without my knowledge. Therefore speak your conscience without any fear.

Philpot: My lords, it is not unknown to you, that the chief cause why you count me, and such as I am, for heretics, is because we be not at unity with your church. You say, that whatsoever is out of your church is damned, and we think verily, on the other side, that if we depart from the true church, whereon we are grafted by God's Word, we shall stand in the state of damnation. . . .

Gloucester: Why, Mr. Philpot, do you think that the universal church hath erred, and that you only are in the truth?

Philpot: The church that you are of was never universal, for two parts of the world, which are Asia and Africa, never consented to the supremacy of the bishop of Rome, neither did they follow his decrees.

Gloucester: Yes, in the Florentine council they did agree.

Philpot: It was said so by false report, after they of Asia and Africa were gone home, but it was not so indeed, as the sequel of them all proved the contrary. . . .

Worcester: Thou art the arrogantest fellow that ever I knew.

Philpot: I pray your lordship to bear with my hasty speech; it is part of my corrupt nature to speak somewhat hastily, but for all that, I mean with humility to do my duty to your lordship.

Bonner: Mr. Philpot, my lords will trouble you no further at this time, but you shall go hence to the place whence you came, and have such favor as in the mean while I can show you. And upon Wednesday next you shall be called upon again, to be heard what you can say for the maintenance of your error.

Civil though these exchanges may sound, they had only one goal: to convince John Philpot to recant. When he proved immovable after fourteen encounters with the most adept Catholic scholars in England, he was condemned to death. On the morning of his execution, December 18, 1555, he met the sheriff's men joyfully at eight o'clock and proceeded to Smithfield. There he kissed the stake and said, "Shall I disdain to suffer at this stake, seeing my Redeemer did not refuse to suffer the most vile death upon the cross for me?" Then he quoted Psalms 106–108 and submitted to the flames.

O give thanks unto the Lord, for he is good: for his mercy endureth for ever. Let the redeemed of the Lord say so, whom he hath redeemed from the hand of the enemy (Psalm 107:1-2, KJV).

John Rogers
England—February 4, 1555

King Henry VIII (who reigned in England from 1509 to 1547) is said to have executed about sixty people for "religious" reasons. Personal ambition (to have a male heir) and ruthlessness drove him far more than principle. His revolt against the pope had nothing to do with sympathy for the Reformation invading England at that time. Still, there were some in his court—Hugh Latimer, Nicholas Ridley, Thomas Cranmer, Matthew Parker, and possibly Queen Anne Boleyn—who had Protestant leanings.

After his death, Henry was succeeded by his sickly teenage son, Edward VI, who had been raised Protestant by the Dukes of Somerset and Northumberland. It was during his reign that the Church of England became Protestant. Edward died six years later, and Mary Tudor became queen in 1553. She became known as "Bloody Mary" because of her vicious efforts to restore Roman Catholicism. In five years she burned 288 Protestants at the stake—1 archbishop, 4 bishops, 21 clergymen, 55 women, and 4 children.

The Bible Man

John Rogers was born in Aston, near Birmingham, and went to Pembroke Hall, Cambridge, where he graduated in 1526. Six years later, he became rector of Holy Trinity in London. However, in 1534 he resigned to take the position of chaplain to the British merchants in Antwerp, Belgium. There he met William Tyndale (see his story) who had fled England to finish translating the Bible into English. (He had been smuggling thousands of copies of his English New Testament into England since 1525.)

Their conversations together led Rogers to adopt Protestant convictions, and he joined Tyndale along with Miles Cloverdale in the translation project. After Tyndale was arrested, Rogers and Cloverdale continued the work and published the first-ever complete Bible in English on October 4, 1535, just two days before Tyndale was burned at the stake. Surprisingly, King Henry VIII gave it his stamp of approval, fulfilling Tyndale's last prayer, "Lord! Open the eyes of the King of England."

In 1537 John Rogers printed the second complete Bible in English. Since a significant portion of his Bible was Tyndale's translation, which was still condemned by the English authorities, Rogers printed it under a pseudonym: Thomas Matthew. Known as the Matthew's Bible, it combines the 1534–1535 edition of Tyndale's Pentateuch and New Testament, the Coverdale Bible, and Rogers's own translation and marginal notes, making it the first English commentary.

Rogers returned to England in 1548 when Protestantism thrived under Edward VI and ultimately became the divinity lecturer at St. Paul's Cathedral in London.

In 1553, Queen Mary came to power, trying to restore Catholicism in all of England. Of the fifteen hundred monks, nuns, and friars she found, less than a hundred were willing to return to celibacy, so Mary went after the most vocal Protestant leaders.

At first, she put Rogers under house arrest, but then she sent him to Newgate Prison. He went on trial in January 28, 1555, before a commission appointed by Cardinal Pole with Lord Chancellor Stephen Gardiner presiding. The commission convicted Rogers of heresy because he did not recognize the infallibility of the pope or agree that bread and wine became the actual body and blood of Christ upon consecration.

When Gardiner passed the sentence of death on him, Rogers begged to speak a few words to his wife. Gardiner refused, telling Rogers he was not legally married because he had once been a priest. However, on February 4, as Rogers walked to the stake singing psalms, he passed his wife and their eleven children. He had never seen the youngest, whom she held in her arms.

At the stake, Rogers was given one more opportunity to recant his beliefs and return to the Roman Catholic Church. He refused. The sheriff lit the fire, and Rogers washed his hands in the flames as though they were cool water.

He was the first of many martyrs under Queen Mary.

It is no shame to suffer for being a Christian. Praise God for the privilege of being called by his wonderful name! (1 Peter 4:16).

Thomas Cranmer
England—March 21, 1556

Serving as the archbishop of Canterbury under the reign of Henry VIII must have been something like sailing through a typhoon. At one minute, the wind is at your back, then dead calm, then it's in your face. So was the experience of Thomas Cranmer, born in 1489 as the son of a squire in Nottinghamshire. His early schooling was harsh, but by the time he arrived at Cambridge he was a good student.

He had been married only a year when his first wife died in childbirth. Still Cranmer became a priest in 1523 and served as a fellow at Jesus College, where he was known as a solid biblical scholar. When King Henry VIII heard of Cranmer's idea to poll the universities concerning their opinion of Henry's desire to divorce Catherine of Aragon and marry Anne Boleyn, Henry said, "That's the man for me!"

He sent Cranmer to Europe to do the survey, hoping it would rally support for his divorce. While there, Cranmer met some of the reformers and married Margaret, the niece of Andreas Osiander. Then he learned that Henry wasn't so Reformation-minded as he appeared. Henry required celibacy for all his priests. Consequently, for fourteen years, Cranmer kept his wife in Germany a secret while, at one point, Henry insisted that he punish married priests in England.

In 1533, Henry finally convinced Cranmer to accept the office of archbishop of Canterbury. That anchorage may have saved Cranmer's life. When Cranmer's enemies wanted to try him for treason, Henry appointed Cranmer the head of the commission to investigate the charges. Moving very carefully, Cranmer set about rooting out superstition and ecclesiastical abuses in the church, and he encouraged Henry to approve an English translation of the Bible, which he did in 1535.

But "typhoon" Henry was a fickle man. In 1536, he had Anne Boleyn beheaded for supposed unfaithfulness. In January 1540, Henry got Cranmer to approve of his marriage to Anne Clever. But when Henry wanted a divorce in July, Cranmer approved it, too, saying the original marriage was unlawful. Such compromise.

Probably his greatest contribution came after Henry's death, when he was freer to express his Protestant convictions. Under Edward VI (1547–1553), he wrote the *Book of Common Prayer*, still used today in the Anglican, Episcopal, and other liturgical churches.

However, when the Catholic Mary Tudor came to power in 1553, Cranmer's enemies descended like hailstones, charging him with sedition and treason for his Protestant views. Through a protracted trial, he vigorously defended his views until he cracked under intense psychological pressure and the strain of prison—or maybe it was his accommodating habits, established under Henry. In any case, he recanted. It did not, however, save his life.

Courage Rallied

At the very end, Thomas Cranmer repudiated his recantation in a final letter, announcing that he died a Protestant. He said, "I have sinned, in that I signed with my hand what I did not believe with my heart. When the flames are lit, this hand shall be the first to burn." Indeed, when Cranmer faced the fire, he kept his word. Before the fire had moved farther than his feet, he reached down and placed his right hand in the flames, refusing to remove it until it had been consumed. Apart from that action, he neither spoke nor moved except to use his left hand to wipe sweat from his face.

Seed of the Church

We praise thee, O God, we knowlage thee to be the Lorde.
All the earth doeth wurship thee, the father everlastyng.
To thee al Angels cry aloud, the heavens and all the powers therin.
To thee Cherubin, and Seraphin continually doe crye.
Holy, holy, holy, Lorde God of Sabaoth.
Heaven and earth are replenyshed with the majestie of thy glory,
The gloryous company of the Apostles, praise thee.
The goodly felowshyp of the Prophetes, praise thee.
The noble armie of Martyrs, praise thee.

—From "Morning Prayer,"
Book of Common Prayer, 1549

Julius Palmer

England—July 15, 1556

Julius Palmer was born in the city of Coventry, the son of a respected merchant. He first went to the free school and then was educated at Oxford, where he obtained a fellowship at Magdalen College. However, he was so contentious that he was expelled.

Upon her enthronement, Mary, Queen of Scots, purged the college of all non-Catholics. Palmer took advantage of the vacancies to get his job back. However, he became interested in the reasons the Protestants were expelled and why some were willing to suffer martyrdom rather than recant. His inquiries persuaded him of the correctness of their beliefs. He attended the examination of Bishops Ridley and Latimer as well as their execution, where he was heard to say, "O raging cruelty! O barbarous tyranny!"

From that day on, he became a student of the Scriptures and as a matter of integrity, resigned his fellowship at Magdalen College. Subsequently some of his friends helped him obtain a position as a teacher at the grammar school at Reading, in Berkshire. However, when some of his fellow teachers discovered his Protestant convictions, they threatened to expose him to the queen's commissioners unless he resigned quietly and gave his position to one of their friends. Fearful of death, he complied with their demands.

Without any means of support, he returned to his mother's home to collect his inheritance from his father. However, having heard of his religious beliefs, his mother cursed him and kicked him out. Upon leaving, he said with tears, "Mother, you have cursed me. I beseech God to bless you and prosper your undertakings as long as you live."

Being destitute, he returned to Reading School to collect his back pay and some of his personal belongings. His old enemies, however, had him arrested on a number of false charges of a political and civil nature, which he later disproved. But when they found that their plot against him had failed, they accused him of heresy.

Again he was taken before the magistrate and, of course, did not deny his religious convictions. During his trial he was held in Newberry Prison with two other believers accused of heresy: Thomas Askin and John Gwin.

After his hearing, court was adjourned, and one of the justices took Palmer aside. "Listen, Palmer, set aside these opinions of yours and save your life. I don't want to see you condemned. I'll take you into my own family as . . . as a chaplain and give you a handsome salary. Or, if you choose to cease being a cleric, I'll procure a farm for you. But just give up these ideas." Palmer thanked him warmly for his kind offer but assured him that he had already renounced his living twice for the sake of Christ and was ready to give his life for the sake of Christ if God, in his providence, should call him to do so.

When court resumed and he refused to recant, he was sentenced to death, as were the other two believers with whom he had shared prison.

In Their Own Words
On the day of their execution, about an hour before they were led to the stake, Palmer addressed Thomas Askin and John Gwin as follows: "Brethren, be of good cheer in the Lord and don't faint. Remember the words of our Savior Christ, who said, 'Happy are ye, when men shall revile and persecute you for my sake. Rejoice and be exceeding glad, for great is your reward in heaven.' Fear not them that kill the body, but are not able to hurt the soul. 'God is faithful and will not suffer us to be tempted above what we are able to bear.' We shall end our lives in the fire, but we shall exchange them for a better life, Yes, for coals we shall receive pearls; for God's Spirit witnesses in our spirits, that He hath prepared for us blissful mansions in heaven for His sake, who suffered for us."

When they were chained to the stake and the fire was kindled and began to reach their bodies, they lifted up their hands toward heaven and cheerfully, as though they felt very little pain, said, "Lord Jesus, strengthen us! Lord Jesus, assist us! Lord Jesus, receive our souls!" In this way they continued without struggling, holding up their hands and sometimes beating upon their breasts and calling on the name of Jesus till they expired.

Jan Hendricks
Rotterdam, Netherlands—March 28, 1558
At twenty-eight, Jan Hendricks descended the steps of city hall as gingerly as a ninety-year-old arthritic, leaning heavily on the constable on his right and the executioner on his left. That's what the rack will do to every joint

in your body. What it does to one's spirit depends. Jan had not recanted his faith, but when the pain had become too great, he had given up the name of Leenert, the famous evangelist who had baptized him.

Leenert had baptized thousands, Hendricks had reasoned, why suffer more to protect the name of one who was already well known to the authorities? And yet, was that betrayal? Would God consider him faithful? "O Lord, help me," he prayed.

Three large stakes had been driven into the hard-packed earth in front of city hall—for Hendricks and two other condemned "heretics." A corral had been constructed around the stakes at a distance of about twenty feet to keep back the rowdy crowd.

A bell sounded, and one of the assistant constables announced in a loud voice that anyone hindering the justice of the day by word or act could forfeit life and property.

Jan Hendricks was then escorted to one of the stakes and helped up on to a small stool at its base. The constable wrapped a cord around the prisoner's neck and through the hole that had been bored in the top of the stake. The cord was tied snugly, and then the constable put a stick through it and twisted it tight.

The executioner piled wood around the base of the stake then put a bundle of dry straw in a basket and emptied a cask of gunpowder onto it. He would ignite it before the prisoner's face to flash-burn him before dropping the burning straw to light the wood.

When everything was ready, the executioner stepped back. The constable kicked the stool out from under the man's feet—the heretic hung, choking from the top of the stake. Quickly the constable threw his arms around the man's legs, and pulled down with all his might. If that did not dispatch him quickly, there would be the "mercy" of the flash.

The Misfire

The rowdy crowd grew ugly, yelling insults and shaking their fists. Most were out-of-towners, just in for the "festivities." It was wise the authorities put up the barricade.

The executioner stepped forward with his basket and dropped in a red-hot coal. The straw smoldered, but the gunpowder remained dormant. Again and again he tried.

"You throw the fire badly," yelled an onlooker. The crowd roared. "You'll make the man die a thousand deaths before you're done," called someone else. "Yeah," hooted another. "Stone the constable instead!"

Soon the mob picked up the refrain, and first a slipper and then stones began to fly. The executioner and constables regrouped, then backed up the steps of city hall to protect the judges who were overseeing the event. When the corral broke under the press, they panicked and retreated inside, barricading the door after them.

The riot raged, someone cut the strangle rope, and Hendricks' limp body crumpled onto the pile of wood. On pushed the insurgents, storming city hall and rescuing the two condemned prisoners and two other women whose cases had been postponed until after Easter. Fearing for their lives, the city officials retreated up into the tower and did not come down for several hours.

Later, a man named Avicenna Jans dragged Hendricks' body into the nearby house of Kors Goverts where he discovered that Jan Hendricks was still alive.

That night some of the believers put Hendricks into a boat and took him out of the city to a place of refuge where he finally recovered.

None of the rioters were shown to have any connection to the condemned, nor were they part of the outlawed Christian house churches, but sometimes God raises up strangers to accomplish his purposes.

When the children of Israel cried out to the Lord, the Lord raised up a deliverer for them (Judges 3:15, NKJV).

Joris Wippe
Netherlands — October 1, 1558

Joris Wippe was a cloth dyer in Dortrecht and was well liked by all who knew him, including the town magistrates. Agents of the Inquisition, however, who discovered that he had converted and were determined to make an example of him, insisted on his arrest.

The magistrates finally issued a summons but did not follow through to apprehend Joris, hoping that he would flee to safety. Joris however, trusting in their goodwill, responded voluntarily. The magistrates even tried to ignore his presence in court, but the bailiff, who supported the Inquisition, seized Joris and announced, "Here's your man. He has come to forfeit his life and property."

Trying to save him, the magistrates sent Joris to The Hague, but the officials there returned him, saying he had to be tried in the place where he had been arrested. There was no way around it. When at his trial Joris Wippe openly acknowledged that he had been rebaptized and held "heretical" views, the magistrates could do nothing but sentence him to death since the agents of the Inquisition were watching over their shoulders.

It so happened that the executioner—the most menial civil servant—was a neighbor of Joris Wippe. Upon hearing of Joris's sentence, he declared, "I would rather forfeit my job than put to death a man who has so often fed me and my wife and children. He always gives to the poor and has never harmed anyone."

Indeed, many in the city were upset over the sentence. Dortrecht had never before executed anyone for religious reasons. Knowing that Joris had written letters from The Hague, and fearing that he might write more and in so doing stir up the populace, the bailiff confiscated Joris's ink bottle and ordered that he be given no ink.

For seven weeks the executioner avoided—even refused—his duty. In fact, he may have been the one who smuggled some mulberries in to his friend. Finally, the bailiff had one of his henchmen drown Joris Wippe in a wine cask of water during the night when the executioner was absent. The next morning, October 1, 1558, Wippe's body was hung by the feet from the public gallows. Later, the grief-stricken executioner was required to flog some thieves before expelling them from the city. When he finished, he cried out to all present, "They have crucified Christ, and released Barabbas."

But a final letter remained, written with mulberry juice.

The Mulberry Letter

My dearly beloved and obedient children,

I wish you an honorable, virtuous, and godly life in the Lord. You are well aware now that I am in bonds for the testimony of Christ our savior. And I wait patiently for the time when it pleases him for me to offer up my body in sacrifice to his holy name.

Please honor your poor bereaved mother, who is deprived of everything for the name of the Lord, for she suffered great pain in your births and has worked hard to raise you so far.

But now it is God's will that we part. I admonish you to obey God's commandments all your life, and we will meet again in the hereafter. I urge you to share your bread and money with the poor. In short, I commend the Bible as your guide. Spend time in prayer that God will keep you from evil. Have no fellowship with the evil of this world. And don't be afraid, for the Lord your God is with you wherever you go, and he will be your protector. Always speak the truth.

Herewith I take my leave of you forever, my dear children, until we meet at the resurrection.

—Joris Wippe, imprisoned at Vuylgate in Dordrecht for the testimony of Jesus Christ

---

The King will say to those on the right, "Come, you who are blessed by my Father, inherit the Kingdom prepared for you from the foundation of the world. For I was hungry, and you fed me. I was thirsty, and you gave me a drink. I was a stranger, and you invited me into your home. I was naked, and you gave me clothing. I was sick, and you cared for me. I was in prison, and you visited me" (Matthew 25:34-36).

Jacob de Roore and Herman van Vleckwijck

Belgium—June 10, 1569

Before condemning them to death, serious attempts were sometimes made during the sixteenth century to convince Anabaptists, Protestants, and others to recant their disaffection from the Roman church. Such was the case when Friar Cornelis spent two days debating with Jacob de Roore and Herman van Vleckwijck. Though de Roore was a candlemaker by trade, he was an eloquent teacher among the Anabaptists—but as was common with many of the reformers, his boldness sometimes overwhelmed common tact.

Van Vleckwijck was a common member in the local congregation, but he, too had studied the Scriptures carefully and was able to give an apt answer when questioned.

Friar Cornelis was university trained at Louvain and had studied theology a long time. Their "disputations" were recorded verbatim on May 9 and 10, 1569. The following are excerpts from the debate with de Roore, showing the kinds of issues in question.

The Dispute

Friar Cornelis: "Well, I've come here to see whether I can convert you, Jacob, from this false and evil belief in which you are erring."

Jacob: "With your permission, sir, I deny that I have an evil, false belief. But I do confess that I have apostatized from the Babylonian church to the true church of Christ."

Friar Cornelis: "You dare to call our mother, the holy Roman Church, the whore of Babylon? And you call your devilish sect of Anabaptists the true church of Christ? Who the devil has taught you this!—your accursed Menno Simons, I suppose."

After debating the authority of the Pope, the priesthood of the believers, the taking of oaths, the sacraments of holy and extreme unction, confession and confirmation, holy chrism, marriage, and holy communion, they continued:

Friar Cornelis: "Let us now dispute about Anabaptism and infant baptism and be done with it. Let us hear why the sacrament of baptism is not necessary to children for their salvation."

Jacob: "In the Gospel of Mark, Christ says: 'He that believes and is baptized shall be saved; but he that believes not shall be damned.' Now, if one of the two were necessary to children for their salvation, faith is more important than baptism."

Friar Cornelis: "Would you exclude from heaven innocent children that die unbaptized?"

137

Jacob: "No, we believe that infants are nevertheless saved though they die unbaptized, for Christ says of the children: 'Of such is the kingdom of heaven.'"

Friar Cornelis: "Since you Anabaptists esteem baptism so little that you allow children to die unbaptized, why do you have yourselves rebaptized? Is this not madness?"

Jacob: "We baptize the believing, but you baptize the unbelieving."

Friar Cornelis: "Indeed, Anabaptist? Bah, though the children are not believing, they must nevertheless be baptized if they are to be saved. In John's Gospel Christ said to Nicodemus: 'Except a man be born again of water and of the Spirit, he cannot enter into the kingdom of God.' Doesn't this say plainly that children must be baptized?"

Jacob: "Water baptism signifies the washing of regeneration in which Christ baptizes with the Spirit. John the Baptist said, 'I baptize you with water, but one comes after me who shall baptize you with the Holy Spirit.' From this we understand that water baptism does not give an entrance into the kingdom of God, but only the baptism by the Holy Spirit with which Christ baptizes."

Friar Cornelis: "Never in my life have I heard the Scriptures expounded so strangely. I have no desire to dispute with you any longer. I shall go my way and let the executioner dispute with you with a burning fagot—and afterwards the devil in hell, with burning pitch, brimstone, and tar!"

Friar Cornelis left the cell, followed by the recorder and clerk. Still angry, Cornelis disputed the next day with Herman van Vleckwijck, also an Anabaptist, who answered him in much the same way. Both Jacob and Herman were sentenced to be burned to ashes at the stake. The sentence was carried out on June 10, 1569.

Dirk Willems
Netherlands—May 16, 1569

Whereas, Dirk Willems, born at Asperen, at present a prisoner, has, without torture and iron bonds (or otherwise) before the bailiff and us judges, confessed, that at the age of fifteen, eighteen or twenty years, he was rebaptized in Rotterdam, at the house of one Pieter Willems, and that he, further, in Asperen, at his house, at divers hours, harbored and admitted secret conventicles and prohibited doctrines, and that he also has permitted several persons to be rebaptized in his aforesaid house; all of which is contrary to our holy

138

Christian faith, and to the decrees of his royal majesty, and ought not to be tolerated, but severely punished, for an example to others; therefore, we the aforesaid judges, having, with mature deliberation of council, examined and considered all that was to be considered in this matter, have condemned and do condemn by these presents in the name, and in the behalf, of his royal majesty, as Count of Holland, the aforesaid Dirk Willems, prisoner, persisting obstinately in his opinion, that he shall be executed with fire, until death ensues; and declare all his property confiscated, for the benefit of his royal majesty. So done this 16th of May, in presence of the judges, Cornelis Goverts, Jan van Stege Jans, Adnaen Gerritts, Adnaen Jans, Lucas Rutgers, Jan Jans, and Jan Roefelofs, A.D. 1569.

Between Fire and Ice
The death sentence of this dear believer might have been lost among the dusty legal records of the town of Asperen in South Holland had it not been for an event that distinguished him from the four thousand to twelve thousand other Christian martyrs of this era.

After his initial apprehension, Dirk escaped, but not cleanly. Hot on his trail, his guard followed Dirk across the thin ice on one of the many canals in the region. Dirk, being light—possibly as a result of deprivations while in prison—made it across safely. But his pursuer, called a "thiefcatcher" in the old records, broke through the ice into the frigid water.

As Dirk scrambled up the bank to safety, he looked back and saw that his nemesis was drowning. Even though he had a clear shot at freedom, Dirk turned back and at considerable risk to himself, ventured back out onto the cracking film and rescued the man. The grateful thiefcatcher wanted to let Dirk go, but the mayor, who had apparently arrived on the scene by this time, demanded that the thiefcatcher remember his oath to uphold the law and insisted that Dirk be taken into custody again. "Let the court decide his fate!"

And it did!

The day of Dirk's execution was blustery, and the wind whipped the blaze to the side so that it did not quickly engulf his whole body. Consequently, he suffered severely and cried out over seventy times, "O my Lord; my God," so loudly that that he was heard in the nearby town. But he never recanted or cursed his persecutors.

Dirk's suffering was so great that the judge assigned to oversee his execution turned his horse around so he did not have to watch and finally ordered the executioner to dispatch Dirk more quickly.

Seed of the Church
Possibly no other story coming out of the Reformation has inspired more Christians to love their enemies than this simple tale recorded in full detail in Thieleman J. van Braght's seventeenth century volume, *Martyrs' Mirror.*

> When we were utterly helpless, Christ came at just the right time and died for us sinners. Now, no one is likely to die for a good person, though someone might be willing to die for a person who is especially good. But God showed his great love for us by sending Christ to die for us while we were still sinners (Romans 5:6-8).

Huguenots: The Saint Bartholomew's Day Massacre
France—August 24, 1572

Before dawn, August 24, 1572, the "St. Bartholomew's Day Massacre" began with the assassination of the admiral of France, Huguenot leader Gaspard de Coligny. After stabbing him in his bed, the soldiers of the Duke of Guise threw his body out the window, where a mob later mutilated it, cutting off the head and hands, and dragged it through the streets of Paris. Soldiers then killed all the Huguenot (Protestant) nobles who had gathered in Paris for a royal wedding celebration.

In the terrible days that followed, estimates extend to as many as 100,000 Huguenots killed in all of France before the killing stopped.

The crafty queen mother, Catherine de Médicis, had unquestionably wanted to destroy the Protestant movement for many years. The Reformation's rapid spread across France, accompanied by bloody civil strife between Protestants and Catholics, threatened her weak sons—successive kings Francis II, Charles IX, and Henry III. But when nobles and high officials like Admiral Gaspard de Coligny converted, they introduced a supposed political threat of alignment with pretenders to the throne or even foreign interests. Multiple written communications document plans to execute various Protestant leaders summarily. In fact, in 1559 the French Parliament promised a reward of 50,000 écus to whoever would apprehend Admiral Coligny, dead or alive.

In 1570, however, the French court and the Protestants signed a peace agreement. Ostensibly to seal this peace, Catherine's daughter, Margaret of Valois, married Protestant, Henry of Bourbon on August 18, 1572. Most of the Huguenot nobles, including Admiral Coligny, attended the wedding in Paris. Catherine used the occasion to order Coligny's assassination. The assassin's bullet—fired on August 22—wounded Coligny only slightly, and the Huguenots demanded an investigation. Knowing an investigation would have implicated her, Catherine persuaded her son, King Charles IX to order the murder of all the Huguenot nobles in Paris and to officially organizing a massacre of Protestants. This was the time to "clean house." The royal troops were commissioned to kill the Huguenot nobles; a mob was also mobilized to threaten the bourgeois troops in case they should venture to side with the Huguenots.

While Catholics admit that the assassination of Coligny was premeditated, they claim that the massacre was the result of Catherine's rash—possibly panicky—impulse. In the context of that cruel era, they maintain that it was not the result of any religious disturbances and did not even have religious incentives.

Protestants, however, saw the whole event—wedding, assassination, and massacre—as a premeditated plot to eliminate Protestants, a plot not only masterminded by Catherine but also done at least with the Vatican's foreknowledge. Pius V (1566–May 1, 1572) had considered the Huguenots "a party of rebels" who undermined the stability of France and had encouraged the king to "fight the enemies of the Catholic Church unto their utter destruction." Earlier he had said to the Spanish ambassador, "The masters of France . . . want to destroy by underhand means the Prince of Condé and the Admiral."

But more telling was the response of his successor, Pope Gregory XIII, who, upon hearing of the massacre celebrated openly and had a medal stamped (now in the British Museum) to commemorate the event. On one side of the medal is a profile of the pope surrounded by his name and title and on the other side an angel is depicted bearing in one hand a cross and in the other a sword with which he is killing a fallen host of Huguenots. The wording on this side reads, "Slaughter of the Huguenots, 1572."

Repentance, the Key to Reconciliation

In 1997, Pope John Paul II made this public statement before a million people gathered in Paris: "On the eve of August 24, we cannot forget the sad massacre of St. Bartholomew's Day, an event of very obscure causes in the political and religious history of France. . . . Christians did things which the gospel condemns. I am convinced that only forgiveness, offered and received, leads little by little to a fruitful dialogue, which will in turn ensure a fully Christian reconciliation. . . . Belonging to different religious traditions must not constitute today a source of opposition and tension. On the contrary, our common love for Christ impels us to seek tirelessly the path of full unity."

Jan Block
Netherlands—ca. 1572

Again and again one finds a strange eagerness in the words of the martyrs, looking forward to "when I shall offer up my sacrifice" or "when I make my witness." These sentiments expressed by Jan Block were no death wish. He had been a wealthy playboy who spent most of his time with prostitutes or in the taverns of Nijmegen.

He had every opportunity to continue that life, but one of his companions, Symon van Maren, a furrier from Hertogenbosch, suddenly ceased carousing. "I have given my life to Christ," he told Block. "Here, read this New Testament, and you will see why."

Jan Block followed the advice, and the Lord opened his heart. He, too, converted and joined a local house church. Not being the quiet type, he began telling everyone. Soon, officials seized all his property and put a price of seventy gold coins on his head.

He fled to a country village and asked a mason for a job as his hod tender since he had never learned a trade with which to support himself. The mason, fearing that the authorities would soon be on Block's trail, said no, fearing any aid to a "heretic" would get him in trouble, too.

Not knowing what else to do, Block returned to Nijmegen and stayed with some friends, but someone saw him on the street and turned him in for the reward. When the bailiff came to the house, the woman of the house warned Block to stand on the bed behind some curtains so he would not be seen. The bailiff, who was not very eager to make an arrest on religious grounds, looked into the room briefly and then closed the door. He then left the house and announced to the bounty hunter, "Jan Block's not there, so forget the money."

"Oh yes he is. I saw him go in. He's in there."

Finally, the bailiff sent one of his assistants back to check again, and he found Block behind the curtain and marched him off to prison, where Jan Block was condemned to be burned at the stake.

Going to a Wedding Feast

As he was escorted to the scaffold to be put to death, Block's face looked as joyful as if he were on his way to a wedding feast, and once on the scaffold, he fairly leaped toward the stake in eagerness. "Say, my man," he said to the executioner, "you have put the holes in the wrong place on the stake. Next time you must be more careful."

His spirit was so indomitable that several of the lords who had sat in judgment over him were moved to tears at his execution.

In His Own Words

Dear brothers and sisters in the Lord,

O how great was the spiritual food in your letters with which you fed and comforted my poor hungry soul from the holy Word of the Lord. It incited me to take undaunted courage, for which I cannot thank you enough. By the help of our dear Lord, I still have the will to do well. I hope and trust in God our heavenly father, who shall strengthen me to finish my race to his holy praise when I shall offer up my sacrifice. As you write to me of many prophets and apostles, yes, of Christ Himself, who for the sins of us all and out of love for us all was led to the slaughter as a dumb lamb, how much more ought I, poor miserable sinner, to deliver up my life for his holy name's sake, of which I sincerely

deem myself unworthy. . . . My mind is firm and of good cheer in
the Lord, and I am as courageous as a young lion. I cannot thank
God enough for his great goodness.

—Jan Block

Let us be glad and rejoice and honor him. For the time has come for
the wedding feast of the Lamb, and his bride has prepared herself (Revelation 19:7).

Maeyken Wens
Antwerp, Belgium—October 6, 1573

Maeyken Wens was the God-fearing wife of a faithful lay minister,
Mattheus Wens, a mason by trade, in the city of Antwerp. These "Brethren," as they called themselves, rejected infant baptism as a means of
salvation, practicing "believers' baptism" on confession of faith instead.
They were derisively called anabaptizers or "rebaptizers" by their detrac-
tors. Their insistence upon reading and teaching the Word of God among
laypeople, refusal to bear the sword, and forbidding the swearing of oaths
guaranteed their persecution from a state church that found these beliefs
akin to treason.

Maeyken Wens was arrested in the month of April 1573, along with Hans
and Janneken van Munstdorp, and two other women, Mariken and Lijsken.
While in bonds, Maeyken wrote several letters to her husband and oldest son,
assuring them of her steadfastness in the Lord, and encouraging her son to
"fear the Lord" in spite of her imprisonment.

She was burned at the stake in Antwerp, Belgium, October 6, 1573, along
with three other godly women.

A Witness

A boy of fifteen clung tightly to his little brother's hand as they pushed
through the festive crowd. Wooden benches had been brought out for the
spectators. Adriaen Wens saw an empty one and stood upon it, peering desperately past the broad shoulders and big hats. Would he be able to see his
mother? If only Father were here! But a knock at the door last night, a whispered word: "They will be on the lookout for sympathizers tomorrow. I beg
you! Do not come!"

But Adriaen could not let his mother die without a witness. A boy caring
for his baby brother . . . they would not be noticed. There! They were bringing
the prisoners out. Dread and longing clashed in his breast. Was his mother among them? He had not seen her for six months, not since the terrible
day soldiers had burst into the home of Hans and Janneken van Munstdorp,
where his mother had gathered with other friends.

143

But she had written. Several times. In his pocket was a letter she had written to him, delivered only yesterday. "Oh, my dear son, though I will soon be taken from you, begin now in your youth to fear God. . . ."

Then he saw her, passing by the crowd with soldiers on either side, heading for the four stakes in the center of the square. Adriaen stared in horror. The mouth of his mother was contorted, her tongue pierced with a cruel screw to keep her from speaking to the crowd.

Darkness rushed at Adriaen and he felt himself falling. . . .

Adriaen opened his eyes. Little Hans was sitting by his side, whimpering. The crowd was gone. All that remained were four charred stakes in the center of the town square. Trembling, Adriaen took a stick and poked in the still-smoking ashes. The stick caught on something and he bent to pick it up. A tongue screw . . .

"Oh, Mother, Mother," he cried. "I have heard you speak. I *will* follow our Lord, just as you have done."

In Her Own Words

"My dear son, do not be afraid of this suffering. It is nothing compared to the suffering which endures forever. The Lord has taken away all my fear. I cannot fully thank my God for the grace which he has shown me."

—From a letter written by Maeyken Wens to her fifteen-year-old son, Adriaen, on October 5, 1573, from prison

---

What we suffer now is nothing compared to the glory he will give us later. For all creation is waiting eagerly for that future day when God will reveal who his children really are (Romans 8:18-19).

Twenty-six Martyrs of Japan
Japan—February 5, 1597

When Francis Xavier, a Portuguese Jesuit missionary, landed in Japan in 1549, he called it "the delight of my heart . . . the country in the Orient most suited to Christianity." The Jesuits were followed by the Spanish Franciscans, and by the end of the century, 300,000 Japanese had converted to the Christian faith.

But western missions—whether Protestant or Catholic—often got entangled with competition for trade and political power. In 1587, after decades of civil war, Shogun Hideyoshi issued an edict to banish foreign missionaries in an attempt to unify the nation. The edict was rarely enforced and the missionaries were tolerated for another decade. But in 1596, the *San Felipe*, a Spanish trade ship, ran aground off the coast of Shikoku with a cargo of ammunition, which was immediately confiscated by the Japanese. The ship's captain, angry at the loss of his cargo, threatened the Japanese with conquest by Spain—which, he said, normally followed in the footsteps of missionaries who "prepared the way."

The Franciscan missionaries, who worked primarily among the poor, denied being "spies for Spain," but six missionaries and twenty Japanese Christians were immediately rounded up for execution. (The Jesuits were temporarily reprieved because they worked among the ruling classes and had more ties to the shogun's court—but only temporarily.) These twenty-six were just the beginning of a major persecution against Christians in Japan, both foreign and national. But there was one way out. . . .

Stepping on the Fumie

It was so simple. All a Christian had to do was step on a *fumie*—a small square tile inlaid with a picture of the Madonna and Child—and he would be declared apostate and be free to go. One didn't have to outright deny Christ or turn against his brothers. Just step on the icon. What did the icon mean, anyway? It was only an outward symbol. Not what was true in one's heart. Just step on it and go free. Just a step . . .

The twenty-six Christian prisoners were given the opportunity to step on the fumie. Not one did—even though two of the believers were mere boys, ages twelve and thirteen. (At other times, some Christians did recant under torture.) All chose instead to take step after weary step on a long march to the city of Nagasaki—a journey that took thirty days during winter—where they would be publicly executed by crucifixion.

Terazawa Hazaburo, the executioner and a brother of Nagasaki's governor, was waiting on the hill of execution as the martyrs finally arrived, their feet bloody but their hearts and voices still singing. This would be a difficult task; Paul Miki, one of the prisoners, was one of Terazawa's friends. Twenty-six crosses were laid on the ground, waiting. The prisoners were tied to the crosses, then each cross was raised and dropped into a hole. The shogun's sentence was read: "As these men came . . . under the guise of ambassadors, and chose to stay in Miyako preaching the Christian law, which I have severely forbidden all these years, I decree that they be put to death, together with the Japanese that have accepted that law."

Paul Miki, a preacher at heart, took his cue from that last phrase, transforming his cross into a pulpit. "I am Japanese by birth," he called out, "and a brother of the Society of Jesus. I have committed no crime, and the only reason why I am put to death is that I have been teaching the doctrine of our Lord Jesus Christ. I am very happy to die for such a cause, and see my death as a great blessing from the Lord. At this critical time . . . I want to stress and make it unmistakably clear that man can find no way to salvation other than the Christian way."

The witnesses, even the soldiers, were spellbound. When Miki's last sermon was over, the brothers encouraged one another from their respective crosses and joined in song. And then the final execution began. Two soldiers with lances thrust them into the chest of each man on the cross . . . and the

145

voices of the martyrs were silent. Several noticed that, as Terazawa turned away, his grisly task done, he was crying.

> Dear friends, don't be surprised at the fiery trials you are going through, as if something strange were happening to you. Instead, be very glad—because these trials will make you partners with Christ in his suffering, and afterward you will have the wonderful joy of sharing his glory when it is displayed to all the world (1 Peter 4:12-13).

Antoine Daniel

Canada—July 4, 1648

Antoine Daniel, who took his vows as a Jesuit in 1621 at the age of twenty-one, was teaching at the College of Rouen, France, when he was given a special assignment. A promising boy named Amantacha from the Huron Nation in New France (Canada) had been selected by Jesuit missionaries there to be educated "in the mother country." Baptized Louis de Sainte Foy, Amantacha's care and education were assigned to Daniel.

No doubt this relationship inspired Daniel's desire to be sent to New France as a missionary. But even after he had been ordained, he had to wait, because the English had captured Quebec and sent all the Jesuit missionaries back to France. But in 1632, he and a companion, Ambroise Davost, sailed for Canada in the company of Jean de Brebeuf, the veteran missionary among the Hurons, who was returning to his post.

Daniel was eager to set off for Huronia, but Samuel de Champlain, founder and governor of Quebec, would not let the missionaries travel. An Indian who had killed a Frenchman was being held prisoner in Quebec, and his relatives had vowed to kill any "Black Robes" who attempted to come "up river." But the waiting time was well spent studying the Huron language under Brebeuf, a skilled linguist.

Even before the journey began, difficulties piled up. Because of the Iroquois threat, river parties had to travel in great numbers. Even friendly Indian tribes, such as the Algonquins, were anxious about possible repercussions if any of the missionaries met a violent death—natural or otherwise. Sickness delayed their departure. But finally, on July 7, 1634, Antoine Daniel and Jean de Brebeuf stepped into Huron canoes for the eight-hundred-mile journey by river to Lake Huron.

A month later the party arrived at their destination. At the Ihonatiria—or St. Joseph—mission, Daniel met his former protégé, Louis de Sainte Foy. But to Daniel's great disappointment, the Huron boy had rejected not only French culture on his return but also the Christian faith.

But Antoine Daniel continued to believe that reaching the Hurons with the gospel began with the young. At St. Joseph he formed a youth choir to assist at worship services. In 1636, he accompanied three Huron boys back to Quebec, where he took charge of a new boarding school for native boys. The trip downriver was in no way as difficult as the original trip, but one of his fellow Jesuits was taken aback at Daniel's appearance: "His face was bright and happy, but greatly emaciated; he was barefooted, had a paddle in his hand, and was clad in a wretched cassock, his Breviary suspended from his neck, his shirt rotting from his back."

A few years later, Ambroise Davost took charge of the school and Daniel headed back to Huronia. His mission expanded to the "People of the Rocks" or the Rock Nation, one of the four nations of the Huron Confederacy, focusing on two villages: Cahiague (St. Jean Baaptiste) and Teanaostaiaë (St. Joseph II). From here he visited neighboring villages, preaching the gospel.

The Blackrobe Barrier

Antoine Daniel had just returned to St. Joseph II from a spiritual retreat in early July, 1648, when an Iroquois war party attacked the village. As the battle raged, Daniel gave comfort and aid to the wounded and dying. When the war party finally penetrated the stockade surrounding the village, the Jesuit missionary in his big black robe walked boldly toward the intruders, putting his body between the invaders and the fleeing villagers. Struck by volley after volley of arrows, he finally fell, calling on the name of Jesus. Even after he was dead, the warriors kept abusing his body, finally throwing it into the log church and setting it on fire, along with the rest of the now empty village.

By putting himself in harm's way, Antoine Daniel had given his flock precious time to escape from their enemies.

In His Own Words

"The more I saw myself abandoned and removed from human comforts, the more God took possession of my heart."

—Antoine Daniel

Francisco Fernandez de Capillas

China—January 16, 1648

Some historians have called China the "land of the martyrs," and with good reason given the waves of persecution of Christians that have swept over the land since the gospel was introduced.

Giovanni de Montecorvino, an Italian Franciscan, established the first Christian mission in Beijing in 1234. He founded three churches, baptizing thousands of converts. Other Franciscans, including bishops, arrived in the next century, and the number of Catholics swelled to thirty thousand.

Ignatius of Loyola sent Francis Xavier to China in 1549, and within fifty years a total of twenty-five Jesuits, twenty-two Franciscans, two Augustinians, and a Dominican were in the country.

Mission administrators selected who would be sent to China not only for their spirit of faith and love but also for their cultural talents and scientific knowledge, particularly in mathematics and astronomy, sciences that were highly respected in China. Some of these early missionaries even helped correct the Chinese calendar.

The missionaries' cultural and scientific qualifications opened many doors to them, and the quality of their religious life led many upper class people to convert.

Visiting the Sick

Francisco Fernandez de Capillas was born on August 14, 1607, in Palencia, Spain. He joined the Dominican Order in Valladoid, and in February of 1632 his superiors sent him to Manila, where he was ordained a priest. He worked in the Cagayan Valley in Luzon, where he ministered zealously among the poor and sick for nine years.

In 1641, he volunteered to go to Taiwan, and then on to Fujian Province, China, in 1642. He carried on an itinerant ministry of preaching the gospel, comforting, and administering the sacraments among the fishermen, farmers, and sick. He also organized the Third Order of St. Dominic among the Christians.

His compassion, especially for the sick, was noted by one of his coworkers, who later wrote, "Francisco would go to a hospital every day after prayers to serve the sick, with much love and care, embracing them, consoling them, feeding them and even fixing their beds."

In 1644, invaders from Manchuria swept into China, reaching Fujian Province in 1646. At the height of a riot on November 13, 1647, Father Capillas's superior sent him to assist a dying Christian. On the way, some soldiers captured him and threw him into prison.

"I am here with other prisoners," he later wrote, "and we have developed a fellowship. They ask me about the gospel of the Lord. I am not concerned about getting out of here because here I know I am doing the will of God. They do not let me stay up at night to pray, so I pray in bed before dawn. I live here in a great joy without any worries, knowing that I am here because of Jesus Christ. The peers I have found here these days are not always easy to find outside."

Father Francisco Fernandez de Capillas was condemned to death on January 15, 1648. He was beheaded the next day while praying, the first Christian martyr in China. Two months later, local Christians found his remains when Ming troops overran the region.

The King will say to those on his right, "Come, you who are blessed by my Father; take your inheritance, the kingdom prepared for you since

148

the creation of the world. For I was hungry and you gave me something to eat, I was thirsty and you gave me something to drink, I was a stranger and you invited me in, I needed clothes and you clothed me, I was sick and you looked after me, I was in prison and you came to visit me. . . . I tell you the truth, whatever you did for one of the least of these brothers of mine, you did for me" (Matthew 25:34-36, 40, NIV).

Jean de Brebeuf and Gabriel Lalemant
Canada — March 16, 1649

They were called "Black Robes," Jesuit missionaries who followed French explorers to the New World. Their mission: to bring the gospel of Jesus Christ to the Indian tribes in what is now Ontario and Quebec. French explorers had generally been assisted by the Huron Nation, so the first Jesuit missionaries headed to "Huronia." But tribes in the Iroquois Confederacy were mortal enemies of the Hurons. The Jesuits knew that to be friends of one was to be considered the enemy by the other. Most were prepared to lose their lives in their mission—and many did.

One of the earliest Jesuit missionaries was Jean de Brebeuf, who arrived in Canada in 1625. A robust man, this "gentle giant" was skilled at languages, learning first Algonquian and then the Huron languages. His mission was interrupted when his superior recalled him to France shortly before Quebec fell to the English in 1629. But in 1633, with "New France" back in the hands of the French, he returned at the request of Huron converts eager to be taught, making the long, arduous journey along the St. Lawrence and Ottawa rivers to Lake Huron, establishing missions at Ihonaturia and Ossossane near Georgia Bay.

Mission work was often discouraging, beset by Iroquois marauders, natural disasters, sickness, and religious superstitions of the Hurons. But finally in 1637, two of the leading Hurons, Pierre Tsiouendaentaha and Joseph Chiwatenha, converted to Christianity. With their steadfast example, other Hurons came to faith in Christ.

In 1638, Jerome Lalemant relieved Brebeuf as Superior of the Huron Mission. But the veteran missionary was restless in the relative comforts of Quebec, and with great joy was allowed to return to Huronia in 1644. These were golden years, as more and more Hurons listened to the Black Robes and asked for baptism. By 1647 the converts numbered in the thousands.

By 1648, however, the relentless Iroquois attacks threatened to destroy not only Huron trade with the French but also the very existence of the Huron Nation. Nonetheless, new Jesuit missionaries were arriving, among them Gabriel Lalemant, eager to follow in his uncle Jerome's footsteps. The young man was described as "frail," but he was so eager that he was assigned to assist the veteran Jean de Brebeuf in the villages of St. Ignace and St. Louis,

149

arriving in February 1649. Brebeuf was delighted to have the enthusiastic Gabriel, little knowing that martyrdom awaited both only a month later.

Shoulder to Shoulder

On March 16, 1649, a war party of twelve hundred Iroquois escaped detection of Huron scouts and overwhelmed the village of St. Ignace, subduing five hundred Hurons, mostly women, children, and elders. Three managed to escape and warned the village of St. Louis; the majority of that village fled. But eighty warriors remained to fight, buying precious time for the others to escape. The two Jesuit missionaries also remained. When the Iroquois attacked, they moved among the fallen, ministering to the wounded and dying.

One of the Huron warriors realized the battle was futile and urged his fellows to escape. "What?" said another. "Could we forsake these two good fathers who have exposed their lives for us? Their love of our salvation will be the cause of their death. They cannot escape now over the snow, so let us die with them, and we shall go to heaven with them."

The few Huron warriors who were not killed were captured, along with the two Black Robes, and marched to St. Ignace. The prisoners knew what faced them, for among the Indian tribes great value was placed on courage in the face of pain. Torturing prisoners was a kind of competition to see who could endure the most without flinching. Stripped and tied to stakes along with their Huron brothers, Jean de Brebeuf and Gabriel Lalemant endured hours of agony, including a mockery of Christian baptism when boiling water was poured over them. The robust Brebeuf died from his tortures that same day, but the frail Gabriel lived to see the morning light. Amazed at his fortitude, his torturers tore out his heart and ate it, hoping to absorb some of his courage.

In His Own Words

"Sustain with courage the few remaining torments. They will end with our lives. The glory which follows them will never have an end."

—Jean de Brebeuf to his beloved Hurons and fellow captives in their last hours

Mary Dyer

Boston—June 1, 1660

Even though the English Separatists and later the Puritans took the perilous journey to the New World in search of religious liberty, in Massachusetts Bay Colony "religious liberty" was defined as liberty for Puritan beliefs. A challenge to their beliefs—which encompassed a theocratic government as well as manner of dress, manner of worship, and manner of behavior—became a challenge to the entire social structure.

Early on, Mary Dyer and her husband, William, had fallen on the wrong side of Puritan sensibilities by being open supporters of Anne Hutchinson during the "antinomian controversy." Mary gave birth to a hideously deformed stillborn child, which Governor John Winthrop considered "God's divine judgment" for her errors. Excommunicated and banished to Rhode Island in 1637, William Dyer became a respected landowner and one of the founders of Portsmouth, serving as the first clerk, then secretary, general recorder, and attorney general.

On a political trip to England with Roger Williams, Mary Dyer became a follower of George Fox, founder of the Society of Friends—derisively called "Quakers" because they were said to tremble with religious zeal—with their emphasis on the "Inner Light" of Christ within each person in contrast to a system of "rules" for salvation. Unaware that the Boston general court had recently passed laws forbidding this "heresy"—the sentence for breaking these laws included "banishment upon pain of death"—Mary Dyer returned to New England via Boston Harbor and was immediately arrested. She was kept incommunicado in a dark cell, and it was two and a half months before William heard of his wife's imprisonment. Because of William's prominent position in Rhode Island, Governor John Endicott released Mary under the condition that she would never set foot in Massachusetts again.

Religious Liberty . . . or Death

After her banishment from Boston, Mary Dyer became a prominent Quaker minister. But along with several other Quakers who had suffered imprisonment, Mary refused to accept that people could be imprisoned, whipped, banished, and even killed simply for what they believed. Learning that several Friends had been imprisoned in Boston, middle-aged Mary went to visit them and was promptly arrested. This time she and the others were banished and threatened with execution if they ever returned to Boston again.

This made the Quakers only more determined. Again Mary and two others returned to Boston in a deliberate attempt to challenge these unjust laws. On October 27, 1659, they were condemned to die by hanging.

"Yea, and joyfully I go," Mary responded.

Even as the noose was around her neck, Mary was given a last-minute reprieve. But even though she could have assured her own safety by staying obediently in Rhode Island, Mary let it be known that she intended to return to Boston to force the repeal of "that wicked law against God's people," even if it meant offering up her life there.

In late April 1660, Mary again returned to Boston and was arrested. This time there was no mercy. She appeared before the court on May 31 and made her testimony: "I came in obedience to the will of God . . . desiring you to appeal your unrighteous laws." The following day she was hanged.

In death Mary Dyer became an example—a "witness"—for freedom of conscience in matters of religion. Her execution hastened the repeal of laws against the Quakers, which had been her desire and her intention all along.

In Her Own Words
"My life not availeth me in comparison to the liberty of the truth."
—Mary Dyer, quoted on a bronze statue erected in her memory
on the grounds of the State House in Boston, Massachusetts,
three hundred years after she was hanged in that same city

[Jesus said,] "They will lay hands on you and persecute you. They will deliver you to synagogues and prisons, and you will be brought before kings and governors, and all on account of my name. This will result in your being witnesses to them" (Luke 21:12-14 , NIV).

John James
London—November 26, 1661
When Oliver Cromwell died in 1658, the British government teetered toward instability. In desperation, Parliament retrieved exiled Charles II and restored him to the throne. He promised religious toleration, but all who did not support the Church of England were soon persecuted. The Fifth Monarchists, a quasi-political religious party, intent on ushering in the millennium based on King Nebuchadnezzar's dream recorded in Daniel 2:44, were banned, and those who supported them were regarded as rebels.

The Reverend John James was not a Fifth Monarchist, but he was a preacher among the fledging and often persecuted Seventh-Day Baptists, and he did expect Christ to literally return to earth displacing all earthly government to establish the Millennium. On October 19, 1661, he was in the middle of preaching a fiery message on this subject to his congregation at Bull-Stake Alley, Whitechapel Road, London, when officers of the law rudely interrupted him twice, commanding him to come down out of his pulpit. Finally they dragged him down and charged him with preaching treason against the king. The witnesses against James were so disreputable that the justice at his arraignment nearly dismissed the case, but he was nonetheless sent to Newgate Prison.

At his trial on November 14, he was charged with "endeavoring to levy war against the king, with seeking a change in government, with saying that the king was a bloody tyrant, a blood sucker and a bloodthirsty man, and that his nobles were the same; and that the king and his nobles had shed the blood of the saints at Charing Cross, and in Scotland."

While no one could produce any evidence to the truth of these charges, he was still convicted and "sentenced to be hanged at Tyburn, near Hyde Park, and while still alive to have his entrails drawn and his heart taken out and burned, his head to be taken off and placed . . . on a pole opposite his church in Bull-Stake Alley; his body to be cut in quarters and placed on four of the seven gates of the city."

Twice his wife presented a petition to King Charles II, proving his innocence and appealing for mercy. The first time the king said, "Oh! Mr. James, he is sweet gentleman!" but walked away. The second time he declared, "He is a rogue and shall be hanged."

When James was brought to the scaffold, on November 26, he addressed the crowd in a calm and noble manner. "I do own the title of a baptized believer, and I own the ordinances and appointments of Jesus Christ and all the principles in Hebrews 6:1-2." But he denied every charge related to treason or having spoken against the king. When he finished his address, he knelt down and thanked God for his mercies, and then he prayed for those who given witness against him falsely and for his executioner. He prayed for the people of God, for the removal of divisions among Christians, for the coming of Christ, for the spectators, and for himself, that he might enjoy a sense of God's favor and presence, and an entrance into glory. When he ended, the executioner said, "The Lord receive your soul," to which Mr. James replied, "I thank thee." To a friend nearby he said, "This is a happy day." And then after thanking the sheriff for his courtesy, he said, "Father, into thy hands I commit my spirit."

The executioner was so moved by the power of James's testimony that he refused to draw and quarter the man until he was completely dead, a small mercy, but all he could do.

In the next three years, Parliament passed a series of acts that excluded Baptists and other Nonconformists from holding public office, forced them out of schools, and penalized them for not attending Anglican services and for preaching without a license. These laws put the Baptist preacher, John Bunyan in jail in 1678, where he penned *The Pilgrim's Progress*, the second most widely read English book of all time.

[Jesus said,] "You have heard that the law of Moses says, 'Love your neighbor' and hate your enemy. But I say, love your enemies! Pray for those who persecute you! (Matthew 5:43-44).

Elizabeth Hooton
Jamaica—January 8, 1672

George Fox, founder of the Society of Friends that later came to be known as the Quakers, had no qualms when it came to the equality of men and women. His first known convert was a middle-aged woman named Elizabeth Hooton, whom he met in 1647 in Nottinghamshire and described in his journal as "a very tender woman." Little did Fox, or Hooton herself, envision just how tough the "tender woman" would need to be to face the hostility and persecution showered on this Christian "sect" on both sides of the Atlantic.

In 1650, Elizabeth was given the official "gift of the ministry" as a Quaker minister and began making visits to meetings of Friends to encourage and exhort them. She wasn't as welcome in other Christian congregations, however, and found herself occupying a series of rude prisons for months at a time during the next ten years for "exhorting a congregation" at Rotheram, for "reproving a priest" at Derby, for "disturbing a congregation" at Lincoln. In April 1660, the graying woman in her sixties, wearing the plain garb of the Quakers, was attacked on the road near Selston, Nottinghamshire, by the village minister "who abused her, beat her with many Blows, knockt her down, and afterward put her in the Water," even though no words had been exchanged.

Missionary Journeys

Adversity only seems to have strengthened this grandmother. Setting out for New England in 1661 on a "missionary journey," Elizabeth was not allowed to disembark in Boston because she was known as a Quaker. Undeterred, she got off the ship in Virginia and set out on foot to visit several Friends in Boston's prison. But because of the new laws against Quakers, people refused to sell her food or give her a place to stay. Arrested for visiting the Quaker prisoners, Governor John Endicott demanded, "Why are you here?"

"To do the will of Him that sent me," she said simply—which didn't save her from landing behind prison bars as well. But that was not enough: A few days later she was taken out of the prison, marched two days' journey into the wilderness, and left to fend for herself—or starve.

Somehow the indomitable woman made her way to Rhode Island, where Roger Williams had provided a safe haven for the persecuted Quakers. But Elizabeth Hooton—like many other Quakers—was not content to "preach to the converted." On a return trip to England, she obtained a license from King Charles II which gave her permission to settle anywhere in New England. The Boston authorities ignored the licenses. This time she was thrown in prison and given no food or water for two days, then taken out and publicly whipped in three different towns, and once again taken deep into the surrounding forest—in the middle of winter—and left to die.

Befriended by an unknown "Good Samaritan," Elizabeth once again made it back to Rhode Island and eventually England—where she landed in prison once again "for disturbing a congregation." She even "disturbed" King Charles II, asking for an audience so that she could "witness for God, whether he would hear or not."

What kept this woman going in the face of such adversity? Nearing seventy, she said, "The love I bear to the souls of men makes me willing to undergo whatsoever can be inflicted to me." Her love for the "souls of men" inspired her to join George Fox on another missionary journey—this time to the West Indies. On board ship, Elizabeth fell ill; she died shortly after the ship landed in Jamaica the first week of 1672, surrounded this time by Friends. But it would not have mattered how or when she died. To Elizabeth Hooton, every trial had been an opportunity for witness.

In Her Own Words
"The Lord hath given me peace in my Journey, and God hath so ordered that the takeing away of my Cattle hath been very serviceable, for by that mean have I had great priviledge to speak to the faces of the great men."
—Elizabeth Hooton

[Jesus said,] "On my account you will be brought before governors and kings as witnesses to them and to the Gentiles" (Matthew 10:18, NIV).

Donald Cargill
Scotland—July 17, 1681

Many seventeenth-century Scottish Presbyterians were known as "Covenanters" for signing covenants in 1557 and 1581 pledging themselves to maintain Presbyterianism as the sole religion of Scotland. When Charles I tried to impose Anglicanism on Scotland in 1638, the Scottish Parliament reaffirmed the covenant of 1581.

Various rounds of civil war ensued as the Covenanters, Parliamentarians, and Royalists jockeyed for power. But when Charles II came to the throne in 1660, he reestablished the episcopacy and cruelly persecuted the Covenanters, as did his Catholic brother James II. The Scottish succeeded in restoring Presbyterianism as the state religion of Scotland only after the revolution of 1688 deposed James II.

Field Preacher

Donald Cargill was born to respectable parents in Rattray, Scotland, in about 1610. He said that as a youth he was naturally hasty and fiery and often felt troubled about his soul and whether he had any purpose in life. These thoughts so troubled him that he decided to take his own life and would have done so by drowning himself had not people kept coming by and interrupting him.

Next he decided to get up early in the morning before anyone was about and throw himself into a deep coal pit. But as he stood on the brink, he heard a voice from heaven say, "Son, be of cheer, thy sins be forgiven thee!" That not only stopped him but also cured him of his anxious thoughts.

He later pursued studies at the University of St. Andrews and, after his ordination, became minister of the Barony Parish in Glasgow. He continued ministering effectively in this position until 1660, when Charles II issued an edict restoring the Anglican Church in Scotland. When Cargill would not accept the appointment from the archbishop or celebrate the king's birthday, the authorities were incensed and banished him to north of the river Tay. Though he was no longer the official minister of the Barony Parish, he didn't let their edict interfere with his ministry until 1668 when the council summoned him and commanded him to obey their former order and especially avoid coming near Glasgow.

In response, Cargill chose to preach in open fields, gathering crowds that would listen wherever he could. Often he denounced what he considered the evil of clergy submitting the church to secular powers and the secular authorities using the clergy to control the people. In 1679, he even took part in the futile revolt at Bothwell Brig (Bridge) where thirteen were killed, though he escaped with only wounds. Government agents continually tracked him and on several occasions attempted to apprehend him without success.

In September of 1680, Cargill preached to a large gathering in Torwood. Using 1 Corinthians 5:13 as his text ("Therefore put away from among yourselves that wicked person"), he "excommunicated" King Charles II, the dukes of York, Rothes, Lauderdale, and Monmouth; Sir Thomas Dalzell and Sir George Mackenzie.

This message of defiance brought down a bounty on his head of five thousand merks. Finally, in May 1681, Irving of Bonshaw captured him at Covington in Lanarkshire and took him to Lanark to claim his reward. Cargill was convicted of treason in Edinburgh and hanged and beheaded on July 27, 1681, along with four other Covenanters: Walter Smith, James Boig, William Thomson, and William Cuthill.

In His Own Words

"I had a sweet calmness of spirit, and great submission as to my taking, the providence of God was so eminent in it; and I could not but think, that God judged it necessary for his glory, to bring me to such an end, seeing he loosed me from such a work.

"As to the causes of my suffering: the main is 'Not acknowledging the present authority, as it is established in the Supremacy and Explanatory Act.' This is the magistracy that I have rejected, that was invested with Christ's power. And seeing that power taken from Christ, which is his glory, and made the essential of the crown."

—Donald Cargill, in his final written testimony

Margaret McLauchlan and Margaret Wilson
Scotland—May 11, 1685

Persecution of Scottish Covenanters did not end with the execution of Donald Cargill, one of their most outspoken preachers, and his four associates on July 27, 1681. Before the revolution of 1688, which deposed James II, Scotland endured what many called, "The Killing Years," 1684–1685.

During this period, suspected Covenanters were executed on the spot by bands of vigilantes or troops of soldiers—some 31 were killed in Edinburgh itself and another 113 in the countryside. Another of the government's solutions to ridding the country of Covenanters was to transport them to the colonies. However, when the *Crown of London* wrecked off Orkney, 211 more Covenanters were drowned. George Wood, a sixteen-year-old from Sorn, Ayrshire, was the last Covenanter executed, shot down in the fields near his village in June 1688.

The execution of two women in 1685, one a young girl and the other an old widow, demonstrates the fury with which these early Presbyterians were persecuted.

Old and Young Alike

Margaret Wilson was daughter of Gilbert Wilson, farmer in Wigtonshire. Gilbert had a good farm, well stocked with cattle and sheep. Both he and his wife had conformed to the government's religious edicts and regularly attended church at Penningham. Their children, however, were sufficiently outspoken in their sympathy for the persecuted Covenanters that the government put them on the wanted list, and they had to flee and hide in the upper barren part of Galloway.

Government agents warned Margaret's parents to have no contact with their children, whatsoever. They even fined Gilbert Wilson for the nonconformity of his children. Scores of soldiers billeted themselves at his house and commandeered his supplies as they pleased. To this were added various fines levied by the court because of his children. So heavy were these demands, that Gilbert and his wife were reduced to relative poverty.

In the meantime, Margaret McLauchlan, the widow of the carpenter John Mulligen, from the shire of Galloway, had reached the age of seventy. Though blameless in her life and piety, she was a Presbyterian and refused to attend church in Kirkinner but sometimes snuck off to hear the forbidden preachers and gave shelter to "wanted" Covenanters, like eighteen-year-old Margaret Wilson and her younger sister, Agnes.

One Sunday when the young Margaret was visiting, a supposed friend, Patrick Stuart, betrayed them, and the authorities broke in and arrested the widow and the two girls.

When the three would not swear an oath renouncing their religious convictions, they were accused of being traitors and participants in the battle of Bothwell Brig (Bridge) in 1679 (no matter that the girls would have been only twelve and seven). All three were found guilty and sentenced to death by drowning. They were to be tied to stakes out on the beach near Wigtown at low tide. Then, as the sea rose, it would do the dirty deed of executing them.

Because of her tender age, Gilbert Wilson, upon appealing to Edinburgh, was allowed to purchase the life of his younger daughter for one hundred pounds sterling. However, on May 11, 1685, the two Margarets were conducted to the shore by a company of soldiers and tied to stakes in the sand. The old woman was tied out farther than the eighteen-year-old with the obvious intent of terrifying the girl into recanting, but they both remained steadfast.

As the tide advanced, Margaret Wilson sang from the words of Psalm 25:7-9: "Remember not the sins of my youth, nor my transgressions: according to thy mercy remember thou me for thy goodness' sake, O Lord. Good and upright *is* the Lord: therefore will he teach sinners in the way. The meek will he guide in judgment: and the meek will he teach his way" (KJV, emphasis added).

John Bunyan
England—August 31, 1688

John Bunyan was born in 1628 to Thomas Bunyan and Margaret Bentley in Bedfordshire in southern England. He was the son of a tinker. At age sixteen, John joined the army. One day, his unit was called to besiege Leicester. Just as he was ready to go, another soldier asked to go in his place. While on guard duty, his comrade was shot in the head and died. John later wrote about this event and other times when God spared his life, saying, "Here . . . were judgments and mercy, but neither of them did awaken my soul to righteousness; wherefore I sinned still, and grew more and more rebellious against God, and careless of mine own salvation."

After John married, his Puritan wife inspired within him a powerful religious conversion. This led to his becoming a lay preacher in the nonconformist congregations of Bedford. His style was powerful and direct, and he became a favorite preacher in the surrounding towns.

After giving birth to four children, John's wife died in about 1658. John was very lonely and needed help raising his small children. Mary, the oldest, was only eight years old and blind. Before long John remarried. Elizabeth was a loving wife and mother and bore two more children.

During John's youth, civil war had torn England. King Charles I was killed and his son, Charles II, was driven out of the country. Oliver Cromwell then took over the government. He ruled well, but when he died (the same year John's first wife died), Charles II was brought back and made king.

When the kings were in power, the official Church of England controlled most religious life and supported the king. But when Oliver Cromwell ruled, he encouraged the independent churches—Puritan, Baptist, Presbyterian, and Quaker. Naturally, when King Charles II returned to power, he wanted to get rid of these independent churches, fearing that they might be disloyal to him. But it was in these independent churches that John Bunyan preached. When he was told to stop, he refused to obey the king's law. He said he had to obey God. So he was thrown into prison, the specific reason being he had been preaching without a license. Of course, being a nonconformist, John could not get a license, even though he had pastored a church for several years.

The prison to which John was sent in 1661 was just down the street from the Bunyan home, and every day his blind daughter, Mary, brought him a jug of soup.

Bunyan spent nearly twelve years there, but he did not waste his time. He wrote many articles and books. The most well-known book is *Pilgrim's Progress*, an imaginary story of a young man traveling toward heaven. John was released from prison in 1672 (the formal pardon was dated September 13) and returned to his life as a pastor.

He died in London in 1688 from pneumonia, caught after riding far out of his way through a chilling rainstorm to help settle a quarrel between a father and son.

In His Own Words

The prison very sweet to me
Hath been since I came here,
And so would also hanging be,
If God would there appear.

Here dwells good conscience, also peace;
Here be my garments white;
Here, though in bonds, I have release
From guilt, which else would bite.

When they do talk of banishment,
Of death, or such like things,
Then to me God send heart's content,
That like a fountain springs.

—John Bunyan, from *Prison Meditations*, 1665

Don't forget about those in prison. Suffer with them as though you were there yourself (Hebrews 13:3).

Part 3

The Great Century: Missionary Outreach from 1793 to 1914

Ever since the Celtic missionary monks of the sixth century, Roman Catholic missions have flourished with a particular surge following the discovery of the New World in 1492 and again in the middle of the nineteenth century when many new missionary institutions were established and the old societies revived.

However, both Protestant[1] and Orthodox[2] historians identify the nineteenth century as the "Great Century" of missions. For Protestants, William Carey struck the spark in 1792 with his small book, *An Enquiry into the Obligation of Christians to Use Means for the Conversion of the Heathens*. It won over a group of Baptist ministers in England who formed an innovative mission society, strategy, and structure. Under the Baptist Missionary Society's sponsorship, Carey went to India in 1793, ending up at Serampore, a Danish colony, since the British East India Company at first refused to allow him to work in their jurisdiction.

While in India, Carey translated the entire Bible into five languages, partial translations into another five languages, and translated smaller portions into twenty-three additional dialects. Starting from virtually nothing, Protestants numbered half a million Indian believers by the middle of the nineteenth century. Carey helped outlaw the common practice of *sati* or widow burning in 1829 and secured for them the right to remarry in 1856. He also worked vigorously against female infanticide and child sacrifices. Through these and many other contributions, Carey helped the modernization and reform of India, culminating in the country's eventual independence.

These efforts not only earned Carey the title, "father of modern missions," but also inspired a proliferation of evangelistic organizations such as the London Missionary Society, Church Missionary Society, Netherlands Missionary Society, Basel Mission, American Bible Society, American Board of Commissioners for Foreign Missions, American Baptist Missionary Board, and many others.

Certainly, the age of enlightenment and the heightened role of the individual in society fueled an adventurism that fed missionary expansion. What could be more exciting than following in the steps of David Livingstone in Africa, Ann and Adoniram Judson in Burma, Hudson Taylor in China, or Barbrooke Grubb in South America? But there was more. Spanning some fifty years, from the 1790s to the 1840s, the Second Great Awakening turned the hearts of millions to sacrificial service for God, many of whom declared with Paul, "My life is worth nothing unless I use it for doing the work assigned me by the Lord Jesus" (Acts 20:24).

These eager and often ill-prepared volunteers were willing go anywhere, face any dangers, often sacrificing comforts, country, prospects for marriage, family, and health to spread the gospel. William Carey and American missionary Adoniram Judson, for instance, both buried two wives and several little children on the field. When men weren't available, women like Scotland's Mary Slessor went alone into such remote jungles as Calabar, Africa.

As had happened when Christianity encountered the pagan culture of the Roman Empire, missionaries taking the gospel into other hostile cultures sometimes faced violent resistance. John Williams, Pierre Louis Chanel, and George and Ellen Gordon are typical of those slain by South Sea islanders, many of whom were cannibals. But stories of these dangers often served to recruit quick replacements ready to face the challenge for Christ.

Beginning with Hudson Taylor's founding of the China Inland Mission, the major independent "faith" missions emerged, including

- China Inland Mission, 1865
- Christian and Missionary Alliance, 1887
- Central American Mission, 1890
- The Evangelical Alliance Mission (initially the Scandinavian Alliance Mission), 1890
- Sudan Interior Mission, 1893
- African Inland Mission, 1895

The Cover of Colonialism
There was a geopolitical reality that gave these brave ambassadors for Christ entrée to most lands as well as a semblance of protection once they got there. It was the network of trading companies that stretched to the four corners of the globe as well as the pattern of colonialism that supported them. In addition, many mission societies adopted the organizational structure of the trading companies.

Initially, the trading companies and colonial governments were opposed to missionaries entering their arenas. Missionaries were, after all, green, ignorant, prone to need rescuing, and sometimes "meddled," that is, complained about how the trading companies and colonial governments treated the local people. Nevertheless, both trading companies and colonial governments came to provide an umbrella of protection and support for missions and in some cases facilitated the spread of the gospel.

For instance, it was Hudson's Bay Company agents who brought Garry (later known as Chief Spokane Garry) and Kootenai Pelly, young sons of two Columbia plateau chiefs, 1,850 miles up through Canada and all the way east to the Red River Mission where they received the gospel, accepted Christ, and studied the Bible.

Four years later, at age eighteen, Garry returned to his tribe along the Spokane River with the Bible and a prayer book to tell them about Jesus. When the tribe gladly responded, he built a small church, complete with a bell, where he called his tribe together on Sundays for worship. On weekdays, Garry held school in the little building where he taught English, simple agriculture (growing potatoes and vegetables), and the Christian life. During the winter, when the tribe was not busy hunting and gathering, he had as many as a hundred adults and children in attendance at his school. He also evangelized the surrounding tribes.

In the summer of 1834, when Captain Bonneville made a trip through the region, he recorded his Sunday experiences this way:

> Sunday is invariably kept sacred among these tribes. They will not raise [move] their camp on that day unless in extreme cases of danger or hunger; neither will they hunt, nor fish, nor trade, nor perform any kind of labor on that day. A part of it is passed in prayer and religious ceremonies. Some chief . . . assembles the community. After invoking blessings from the Deity, he addresses the assemblage, exhorting them to good conduct, to be diligent in providing for their families, to abstain from lying and stealing, to avoid quarreling or cheating in their play, to be just and hospitable to all strangers who may be among them. Prayers and exhortations are also made early in the morning on weekdays.[3]

Two years later, Dr. Marcus and Narcissa Whitman along with Rev. Henry and Eliza Spalding arrived in the region, proving that white women could cross the Continental Divide. Work by the Spaldings with the Nez Perce, one of the tribes influenced by Chief Spokane Garry, went well, but against the advice of trading company agents and other scouts, Marcus Whitman insisted on locating among the Cayuse, ultimately losing sight of his ministry purpose as he chose to serve first the thousands of settlers coming west on the Oregon Trail. It was a choice that proved disastrous as he and his wife along with twelve others were massacred by Indians resentful of losing their land and contracting disease from the passing settlers.

Regional authorities and volunteer militia tracked down and killed those responsible for the massacre . . . along with most of the rest of the tribe. But the mission work in the region was largely ruined.

Sometimes, however, the "support" from the trading companies and colonial governments wasn't welcome as in the case of John Paton and the HMS *Curaçoa*. Paton, a missionary on the island of Tana, Vanuatu (known then as the New Hebrides), had been driven off his island by warring natives, many of whom were cannibals. He had hoped to return, but while he waited at a mission station on a neighboring island, the HMS *Curaçoa*, a British man-of-war, arrived in response to a mission leader's petition for an investigation of the murder of two other missionaries and the violence that had driven Paton from his island.

Paton hadn't called for the warship and didn't like the idea of force, but since he was the only English speaking person who knew the native language of the people on Tana, he agreed to act as interpreter for the captain. Discussions with the natives started out reasonably well, but when, after three days of negotiations, the natives refused to surrender the ringleaders, the captain backed off in his ship to shell the island villages with his cannons. Paton pleaded for patience, but the captain replied, "If I leave without punishing them now, no vessel or white man will be safe at this harbor." And he dismissed Paton from his warship.

Having received sufficient warning to escape, only one villager was injured, but their huts were blown to pieces and trust among the people was so damaged that Paton had to relocate to another island, and years passed before mission work on Tana resumed.

The involvement of trading companies and colonial force was even more questionable in China. Missionaries of the "Great Century" arrived in a China already bitter toward the West, primarily for smuggling opium into their country. In payment for losing the Opium Wars (1839–1843, 1856–1860) to British and French military might, China ceded Hong Kong to Britain as well as opened up five more Chinese ports to the British. Although China was never formally colonized, it appeared all the western powers intended to carve up the country, and Chinese resentment ran high. Perhaps the first large-scale reaction to colonialism followed: the inevitable rise of nationalism.

This nationalism crescendoed in the Boxer Rebellion of 1900. When the Chinese rioted against all foreigners in Shanghai and elsewhere in 1900, it became a campaign of terror against Christian missionaries, particularly in the northeastern provinces. Hundreds of foreign missionaries—Protestant, Catholic, and Orthodox—were murdered; others barely escaped with their lives. But Chinese Christians suffered even more for having associated with foreigners. Over thirty thousand Chinese Christians endured mutilation, torture, and death. Again, Western powers steamed in to put down the revolt and imposed huge fines on China to cover the cost of losses and damage, and missionaries were allowed to return.

This—rather than the occasional martyr killed by those who hated the gospel—was the true price of missions in the "Great Century." In many regions of the world that price would not be collected until the last half of the twentieth century. It was not a cost in direct reaction to the gospel, nor was it invited or even understood by most missionaries, but it came with the territory. Colonialism provided the opportunity for spreading the gospel, an opportunity that could not be passed up, but it also created the backlash of nationalism that would turn African rivers red and create a vacuum ripe for Communism and Islam.

The good news is, missionaries and mission agencies *unaligned* with state churches (whether Catholic or Protestant) were able to maintain more distance from the "covering" colonial powers, sometimes even criticizing them. Extensive research by sociologist Robert Woodberry has found the impact of these independent missions profoundly advanced the spread of democracy in those regions of the world. Woodberry demonstrated: "Areas where [independent] missionaries had a significant presence in the past are on average more economically developed today, with comparatively better health, lower infant mortality, lower corruption, greater literacy, higher educational attainment (especially for women), and more robust membership in nongovernmental associations." Even Woodberry's secular critics admit that the legacy of these missionaries was amazingly positive and lasting.[4]

Notes

1. Kenneth Scott Latourette, *The History of Christianity*, vol. 2 (New York: HarperCollins, 1953, 1975).
2. Metropolitan Philip (Saliba) of New York and North America, "The Orthodox Church in North America: Mission and Evangelism," *Word Magazine* (Antiochian Orthodox Christian Archdiocese of North America, January 1985). http://www.orthodoxresearchinstitute.org/articles/mission/saliba_mission_evangelism.htm
3. Captain Bonneville, quoted in Washington Irving, *Adventures of Captain Bonneville* (Philadelphia: Carey, Lea, and Blanchard, 1837), chap. 45, http://www.gutenberg.org/files/1372/1372-h/1372-h.htm#link2H_4_0047.
4. Andrea Palpant Dilley, "The World the Missionaries Made," *Christianity Today*, January/February 2014, 40, 41.

The Witnesses

The Hochstetlers

Pennsylvania — September 19, 1757

Indian raids were common in the frontier settlements in eastern Pennsylvania during the years 1755–58. It was, after all, the middle of the French and Indian War. Jacob Hochstetler, his wife and four of their children lived in the Northkill Amish settlement in Berks County. Two older children—Barbara and John—had already married and lived on nearby farms.

Mixing a little socializing with their work, some of the young people in the settlement gathered at the Hochstetler's house on the evening of September 19, 1757, to pare and slice apples for drying. After they had finished and said their good-byes and the Hochstetlers had gone to sleep, the incessant barking of the family dog woke Jacob Jr., the eldest son. Dutifully, he went to see what was wrong. No sooner had he opened the door, than a bullet hit him in the leg. He instantly realized Indians were attacking and managed to lock the door before they could enter.

Everyone awoke from the commotion and went to peer through the windows. Outside they saw several Indians and at least three French scouts talking near the outdoor bake oven. Before Jacob Hochstetler realized what was happening, his younger sons (Joseph and Christian) were loading their guns. They had plenty of ammunition to make a good defense, but Jacob reached out. "No, boys. We cannot take life, not even in our own defense. Jesus taught us, 'Resist not evil; but whosoever shall smite thee on thy right cheek, turn to him the other also.'"

"But Father, they are liable to kill us. Look, we have enough guns. We're good shots. We could hit two or three in the first volley and easily reload before they could break in the cabin. We've got a chance if we fight, but who knows what will happen if we don't. Why, just last month, I heard Indians attacked a family over in . . ."

"Enough," said Jacob. "We will hide in the cellar and trust in God, no matter what happens."

Huddling in the dark cellar, they waited and prayed. All was quiet. Maybe the attackers had withdrawn. What could they want from their humble homestead?

The hours passed, and when the gray dawn first could be seen through the cracks in the cellar window, they started to breath easier. And then they smelled the smoke. It was not from their now-cool hearth. It was acrid and accompanied by the crackling of a growing inferno. Their attackers had torched their cabin.

There was nothing to do but escape. Jacob pushed his wounded son, his wife, and his daughter through the window. Screams greeted him from outside, but what else could he do? Out went Christian and Joseph, and then he climbed out himself.

The first three out of the cabin all lay dead on the ground, tomahawked as soon as they emerged. Indian braves held a struggling Christian and Joseph captive. Jacob fell down weeping as he was captured.

The following spring, Jacob escaped and after fifteen days made it back to the Shamokin, Pennsylvania, and eventually his Amish community. Several years later Christian and Joseph were released and reunited with their father.

Faithful to the End

Indians attacked and killed over two hundred settlers in this section of Berks County, burning almost every farm. Certainly, the politics of the war was a primary motive, but the background also included broken treaties and theft of Indian land as well as abuse. All in all, the Indians' attack on the Hochstetlers probably had nothing to do with their faith. However, it is likely that the Hochstetlers could have defended themselves had they not put their Christian convictions above self-preservation.

> If your faith remains strong after being tried by fiery trials, it will bring you much praise and glory and honor on the day when Jesus Christ is revealed to the whole world (1 Peter 1:7).

The Moravian Indian Massacre
Ohio—March 8, 1782

The Moravian Church traces its history back to John Hus. Like other Protestants, Hus's followers were severely persecuted and scattered, but a "hidden seed" continued in Moravia. In the early 1700s, Count Nicholas von Zinzendorf of Saxony (present-day Germany) allowed these oppressed Moravian Brethren to take refuge on his estate. Soon a Christian community named Herrnhut, meaning "under the Lord's watch," was thriving on Zinzendorf's land.

The vision at Herrnhut was not simply to establish Christian communities, but to train believers to spread the gospel, especially to oppressed peoples. The first two missionaries were sent to the black slaves of the West Indies in 1732. When Zinzendorf died in 1760, 226 missionaries had been sent all over the world. No other church has equaled the Moravian Brethren in commitment to missions. They have often succeeded where others failed because they represented only the gospel and not the interests of any government. They refused to use violence, even in their own defense, and remained neutral in wartime— often at risk to their own lives.

David Zeisberger, who grew up at Herrnhut, became a missionary to the Indian tribes in Pennsylvania, first living among the Mohawks and learning their language, and later preaching to the receptive and peace-loving Delaware tribes.

Thousands were converted to Christ and formed villages of "Christian Indians." The Moravian Indians were both admired and hated—admired because of their industriousness and prosperity; hated because they refused to be drawn into hostilities between Indians and whites. Time and time again, the little bands of Moravian Indians were driven from one place to another.

In 1776, the Americans declared their independence from Britain. The British tried to stir up the Indian tribes against the American settlers. When Zeisberger used his influence to keep the Delaware nation from being dragged into the war, the British were furious. In early October 1781, the missionaries were taken prisoner and moved to Detroit, and the rest of the Christian Indians were forced to abandon their thriving villages along the Muskingum River in Ohio before they could harvest their crops. They got as far as the Sandusky River and set up a temporary village they called "Captives Town."

Deception and Death

The winter of 1781–1782 in Captives Town was brutal. Discouraged by the absence of their Moravian pastors and on the verge of starvation, a large party of men, women, and children decided to return to their former villages and harvest the corn that still lay in their fields. Arriving in early March, they set to work filling baskets with the ears still hanging on the stalks. They worked joyfully, hope rising in their hearts.

Unknown to them, an Indian war party had recently massacred a white settler and his family. An angry mob of white militiamen heard that the Moravian Indians had returned and thought the murderers might be hiding among them. At first pretending to be friendly, the militia lured the harvesters to gather in the main meetinghouse at one of the three abandoned villages. Once gathered, the militiamen locked the door and clubbed them to death. On March 8, 1782, ninety unarmed men, women, and children were massacred at Gnadenhutten (Tents of Grace) and the village burned to the ground.

Several years later, a party of Moravian Indians returned to the site of the massacre. Setting fire to the grass which had overgrown the once thriving village of Gnadenhutten, they found the bones of their murdered brethren and gave them a Christian burial.

In His Own Words

"Where shall we find a retreat, if only a little spot of earth whither we may flee with our Indians? The world is not wide enough. From the whites who call themselves "Christians" we can hope for no protection; among the heathens we no longer have any friends. We are outlaws! But the Lord reigneth. He will not forsake us."

—David Zeisberger, on hearing the tragic news of the massacre

---

God has said, "I will never fail you. I will never forsake you." That is why we can say with confidence, "The Lord is my helper, so I will not be afraid. What can mere mortals do to me?" (Hebrews 13:5-6).

Gregory of Constantinople
Greece— April 10, 1821

The Ottoman Empire resulted from the conquests of the Turkish Muslim warrior Osman in the late thirteenth century in Asia Minor. It advanced until, in 1453, Muhammad I overthrew the Byzantine Empire with the conquest of Constantinople (now Istanbul). A dynastic succession of *sultans* (Muslim sovereigns) from the House of Osman ruled the Ottoman Empire, which, at its height in the mid-1500s, controlled a vast area extending from the Balkan Peninsula to the Middle East and North Africa.

Initially, the Ottomans followed the classical Islamic tradition of protecting non-Muslim religious communities that possessed an accepted, written holy book. In return, they were required to pay a special tax. On this basis, the Ottomans recognized the Jews, the Greek Orthodox Church, and the Armenian Church, allowing each religious community to make its own educational arrangements and administer internal legal matters such as marriage, divorce, and inheritance.

In 1770, the Ottomans crushed a Greek rebellion among peasants who desired to acquire land. Then came the American and French revolutions, international fuel for more independence. In 1804, the Serbians achieved a semisuccessful revolt against the Ottomans. When they again revolted in 1820, the Greeks felt inspired, as well.

Ecclesiastical Tightrope

In 1745, a son was born to John and Asimina Angelopoulos, a family who preferred the rugged hill country of the Peloponnesus mountain range that held little attraction for the oppressive Turks. As the boy grew, he proved to be a brilliant scholar, excelling in whatever studies the local schools offered as well as the secondary education he received in Athens, Smyrna, and Patmos. He then became a monk, adopting the name of Gregory.

His record came to the attention of Metropolitan Prokopios (archbishop) of Smyrna, who appointed him chancellor of the archdiocese of the area. In 1789, the Greek Orthodox Church called Gregory to Constantinople and made him the ecumenical patriarch (functional leader for the whole church). Throughout this period, Gregory chaffed under Turkish oppression and sympathized with those desiring to throw off the Ottoman yoke.

In 1798, he withdrew from his responsibilities and retreated to Mount Athos to refresh his spirit, but in 1806 the church recalled him to the duties of patriarch. But as soon as he returned, he was again caught up in the tightrope of leading a church and speaking for justice, while avoiding doing anything that might prove personally fatal or disastrous to the church. After two years, he retired from office a second time. Ten years later (1818), he was again recalled because of the mounting tensions between Christianity and Islam.

In March 1821, Prince Alexandros Ypsilantis, a Greek who served as foreign minister to the Russian emperor, led a short-lived uprising of Greeks in

Moldavia. This rebellion inspired Archbishop Germanos of Pátrai to initiate another Greek uprising near the end of the month at the monastery of Aghia Lavra in the Peloponnesus. He was more successful, and the Ottomans panicked. Sultan Mahmud II blamed Gregory. A gang of his henchmen raided the vicarage in Constantinople on April 10 and dragged Gregory out to the main entrance gate and hanged him on the spot. Two metropolitans (primates) and twelve bishops as well as several laymen were also hanged.

The Turkish mob later dragged Gregory's body through the streets and threw it into the Bosporus River, but sailors recovered it a few days later some miles down the coast. It was finally interred in the Cathedral Church of the Annunciation in Athens. Of the three gates to the vicarage, the center gate (the site of the hanging) has remained closed in honor of Gregory V.

The war for Greek independence dragged on until September 14, 1829, when, after considerable international intervention, the Ottomans agreed to give up control of Greece.

Well, how much more do I need to say? It would take too long to recount the stories of the faith of Gideon, Barak, Samson, Jephthah, David, Samuel, and all the prophets (Hebrews 11:32).

John Smith
Guyana—1824

The London Missionary Society began its activities in Demerara (now Guyana) shortly after the end of the slave trade in 1707. But plantation owners in the Caribbean and their political and financial backers in Britain were by no means ready to abolish slavery. To forestall the abolitionists, they accepted "Amelioration" to improve slave conditions.

Hermanus Post, the owner of Plantation Le Ressouvenir, thought religion might cause the slaves to be more manageable, so he invited the London Missionary Society to send him a missionary. John Wray arrived in 1808 and built Bethel Chapel. When he was transferred in 1813, Rev. John Smith filled his vacancy.

Government authorities, however, strictly regulated what missionaries could do. "If you teach any of these slaves to read," Governor Murray warned Smith, "I'll have you deported." The Society's task, he insisted, was to make slaves content, not educate them.

Smith's work thrived. His journal entry for December 26, 1822, states, "Yesterday evening, a great many people came from various parts with a view of attending chapel today. Till past 9 o'clock I was engaged in finally examining candidates for baptism, and again this morning till near 12." He goes on to say that the gathered congregation was more than twice the capacity of the six-hundred-seat chapel and that he married five couples and baptized seventy-four individuals, "A comfortable Christmas to me."

But Smith had not confined himself to baptizing, marrying, and pacifying slaves. He taught some to read. In fact, five soon read well enough to be ordained as deacons.

Such large gatherings at the missions made the slaveholders nervous. With only about five thousand free people living among seventy-seven thousand slaves, they feared what they didn't control. On the other hand, many began to believe that Christianity and slavery were not compatible. An article in the local *Royal Gazette* stated, "It is dangerous to make slaves Christians without giving them their liberty." Some tried to stop their slaves from attending; others disrupted services with loud disturbances.

Finally, the British government sent a letter to Governor Murray instructing him that slaves should be given passes *assuring* that they could attend services. Murray, however, reinterpreted the order instructing plantation owners *not* to allow their slaves to attend Sunday services without passes. Many owners simply refused to issue any passes.

Insurrection

In England in April 1823, the Anti-Slavery Society, supported in Parliament by William Wilberforce, Thomas Clarkson, and Fowell Buxton, introduced a motion requiring the gradual abolition of slavery in all British colonies, but the planters, fearing they would be left without a labor force, convinced the majority to defeat the measure. Instead, Parliament approved further amelioration measures prohibiting the whipping of female slaves and prohibiting overseers from carrying whips in the field.

But when Governor Murray received these orders, he delayed issuing them. Some house slaves overheard their masters discussing them and, knowing that the governor had previously misrepresented the law, thought the order was for immediate emancipation. Rumor quickly spread. Fearing that the governor was withholding their freedom, many slaves decided to rise up and carry out the king's orders on their own.

On August 18, some twelve thousand slaves surrounded plantation houses, smashing windows, menacing masters and overseers, and seizing weapons. In all, they killed three whites before soldiers killed more than 250 slaves to restore "order."

On Wednesday, August 20, John Smith was arrested and charged with encouraging the rebellion and failing to inform the governor of the planned uprising. Smith was tried and condemned to death. The British government ultimately commuted his sentence, but this news did not arrive until after he died in prison early in 1824.

Seed of the Church

The tragic events in Demerara spurred on the antislavery movement in England. On August 28, 1833, the House of Commons finally approved the

Emancipation Bill that Wilberforce, Clarkson, and Buxton had introduced earlier. Unfortunately, attached to it was a condition that bound most of the freed slaves to their former masters until 1840.

Ann and Adoniram Judson
Myanmar [formerly Burma]—October 24, 1826

Ann and Adoniram Judson were the first American foreign missionaries. Adoniram was born August 9, 1788, in Bradford, Massachusetts, the son of a Congregationalist minister. At the age of sixteen, he entered Brown University, graduating after only three years. Having become a confirmed deist, he had and set out to "see the world," but after the shocking death of the very friend who had convinced him of deism, Adoniram returned home and entered Andover Seminary at age twenty where he made a "solemn dedication" of himself to God.

Young Judson soon determined to be a missionary, a calling shared by his sweetheart, Ann Hasseltine, who was only a year younger. In February 1812, they were married and two weeks later set sail for India, accompanied by another young couple.

But the British East India Company was hostile to the young missionaries and threatened to deport them. Uncertain where to establish a mission work, the Judsons finally arrived in Rangoon, Burma (now Myanmar)—a year and a half after leaving America.

Unlike India, which had a large European population because of the East India Company, only a handful of white foreigners lived in Burma. Though the majority of the Burmese people lived in poverty under the thumb of a cruel and unpredictable monarchy, there was no caste system. The language was difficult, and the Judsons spent twelve hours a day in language study. An even greater barrier to sharing the gospel was the Buddhist religion, which had no concept of (or even words for) an eternal God or eternal life with God for human beings. Nonetheless, over a period of ten years, eighteen Burmese converts formed the nucleus of the first Christian church in Burma.

"Tropical fever" claimed the life of the Judsons' infant son, Roger, in 1815 (their first child had been stillborn on board ship). For months at a time, the dreaded fever also put both Ann and Adoniram in bed. Still, Adoniram struggled day after day to translate the Greek New Testament into the Burmese language, which he finally completed in July 1823, just before Ann returned from a two-year medical leave in America.

By this time, several other missionaries had come to Rangoon, among them George Hough, who printed Adoniram's translation work, and Dr. Jonathan Price, a medical doctor, who was soon ordered to come to Ava, the royal city, to attend the king himself.

With other missionaries to nurture the little Burmese church in Rangoon, Adoniram and Ann also went north to Ava to establish a mission there, along with two Burmese foster daughters. But when the Burmese-British war broke out in 1824, all foreigners were suspected of being British spies and the men were thrown into the dreaded Death Prison. Eight months after Adoniram was arrested, Ann gave birth to a baby girl, Maria.

Adoniram was condemned to die, but after a year and a half of prison confinement, he, as a "neutral American," was finally released to help negotiate peace with the British. But the years of hardship, sickness, and struggle took its toll on Ann, who died October 24, 1826, at the age of thirty-six. Two-year-old Maria died a few months later.

Restored from Grief

Adoniram tried to bury his grief in a frenzy of mission work, but later spent two years as a recluse in the jungle. When he finally pulled out of his depression, he married Sarah Boardman, a young missionary widow, who bore eight children (only five lived to adulthood) before she died after eleven years of marriage. On leave in America, Judson married young Emily Chubbock in 1846, and they returned to Burma where she became mother to Adoniram's children and their own infant daughter.

But Adoniram's own health broke, and he died April 12, 1850, at the age of sixty-one. His legacy included a translation of the whole Bible in the Burmese language, a Burmese church of sixty-three congregations with over seven thousand believers, as well as inspiration to other American young people to dedicate their lives to foreign missions.

[Paul] said, "Why all this weeping? You are breaking my heart! For I am ready not only to be jailed at Jerusalem but also to die for the sake of the Lord Jesus" (Acts 21:13).

John Williams
New Hebrides (now Vanuatu)—November 20, 1839

When the eighteen-year-old ironworker apprentice bowed his head in the City Road Tabernacle of London and said yes to Jesus, it changed his life. Two years later, in 1816, he volunteered as a missionary with the London Missionary Society (LMS) and, after ordination and marriage to Mary Chauner, went to Tahiti.

It didn't take him long become impatient with the LMS policies. In 1821, he bought the schooner *Endeavour,* and two years later "discovered" the island of Rarotonga. He applied himself to learning the native language and eventually translated the Bible and other books. Not content to remain "within the narrow limits of a single reef," he built a larger ship, the *Messenger of Peace,* and visited every significant island within a two-thousand-mile radius before he returned to England in 1834. He not only evangelized the native peoples but also trained new believers as pastors and installed them over local churches on many islands. Williams cultivated friendships with the leading chiefs on Rarotonga and Samoa, and his reputation spread throughout the Polynesian Islands.

Great Successes

Between 1834 and 1838 while in England overseeing the printing of the Rarotongan New Testament, Williams recruited new missionaries and raised funds so he was able to return to the South Pacific with sixteen missionaries in his newly equipped ship, the *Camden*. He established his headquarters at Upolu, Samoa. In 1839, Williams left his wife in their home on Samoa and sailed west for Melanesia with the idea that if he could establish a successful mission in the New Hebrides, he could work from there south into New Caledonia and north to the Solomon Islands and New Guinea.

On his way, Williams stopped at Rotuma, which at that time was a kind of crossroads among the island world where he hoped to find some natives from the New Hebrides who might be able to help him connect with their people. In spite of this precaution, when Williams arrived at Erromanga, an island in the southern region, on November 20, 1839, some of the natives apparently thought he was connected to some unscrupulous white traders that had previously cheated them, and they clubbed Williams and another missionary, James Harris, to death and ate them. Williams was only forty-three. Their bones were later recovered and now lie buried beneath the native church of the mission at Apia, Samoa.

Williams's family remained on Samoa, where his son, John C. Williams, became British consul in 1858, holding the office for many years.

The London Missionary Society missionaries from Fiji and Samoa supported a series of Samoan and Rarotongan Christians who moved to Erromanga as missionaries with the purpose of preaching the gospel and teaching the children of the island. These missionary ventures often ended in tragedy, as some of the missionaries were killed and others starved to death because no one on Erromanga would assist them with acquiring food. It is estimated that approximately forty Samoan and Rarotongan Christians, both adults and children, died seeking to proclaim the gospel to the people of Erromanga. By the early 1840s all missionary efforts to reach the people of this tiny island ceased.

New Efforts

In June 1857, George and Ellen Gordon arrived on Erromanga, setting up their mission station at Dillon's Bay. They purchased the land for the mission from Kowiowi, a chief on the island, who had been responsible for the murder of John Williams seventeen years earlier. (See George and Ellen Gordon's story.)

I live in eager expectation and hope that I will never do anything that causes me shame, but that I will always be bold for Christ, as I have been in the past, and that my life will always honor Christ, whether I live or I die (Philippians 1:20).

Pierre Louis Chanel
Futuna—April 28, 1841

Dutch navigators first sighted the central Pacific island they called Horn or Allofatu in 1617. The residents called it by its present name, Futuna. But not until 1837, when Catholic missionaries came to the island, did Europeans choose to live there.

The Ends of the Earth

Pierre Louis Chanel was born in Cuet, France, in 1803. He was ordained a priest at the age of twenty-four and worked in the perish ministry for a few years, but letters from missionaries in distant lands continually stirred an eagerness in his heart to take the gospel to the ends of the earth where people had not yet heard of Jesus. So he decided to become a missionary and joined the newly formed Society of Mary. In 1836, he sailed for Oceania with his bishop, Jean-Baptiste Pompallier, and six other Marist missionaries.

They wandered round in the central Pacific for several months and finally selected the islands of Wallis and Futuna as their bases. In November 1837, Chanel was put ashore on Futuna, where he established the first Catholic mission.

The worship of evil spirits held the island people in utter terror through cannibalism and constant warfare, which had reduced the population to a few thousand. Chanel set about learning the native language and preaching the gospel. In the midst of the hardships of isolation, deprivation, and fever, he attended the sick and served the people so faithfully that it was not long until the islanders began calling him "the man with the kind heart." At first, Niuliki, one of two warring local chiefs, appeared friendly toward Chanel and extended him the protection of declaring him "taboo" to attack.

But then Niuliki became jealous when he saw his subjects drawn away from the idols, over which he had much control, and into the white man's religion. At that very time, his son, Meitala, and daughter converted to Christianity. Also, his war with the island's rival chief was not going well. Fearing that the island gods were angry with him, Niuliki issued an edict against Chanel to avert the movement toward Christianity.

Illness that kept Chanel bedridden much of the time compounded his discouragement over the chief's new hostility. There had been some converts, but Chanel felt more like a failure.

Seeing his opportunity, Niuliki's prime minister, Musumusu, hatched a plot with some of the other leading men against the Christians. At dawn on April 28, 1841, they attacked and wounded many of the new converts while they were sleeping. Then they went on to Chanel's hut, where they attacked Chanel, breaking his arm, smashing his left temple with a war club, and bayoneting him. But Chanel clung to life, muttering in the native language, *Malie fuai* ("It is well for me"). Finally, Musumusu grabbed an adze and split open Chanel's skull. But before the missionary died, he prayed for his assassin and comforted some of his wounded converts who were trying to come to his aid.

The attackers hurriedly buried Chanel's body in a makeshift grave. Later, the commander of the French naval station of Tahiti claimed Chanel's body and returned it to France for interment.

Seed of the Church

Tragic as Chanel's death was, his martyrdom renewed interest in the missions of Oceania. In 1842, two more Marist missionaries volunteered to resume Chanel's work on Futuna. Within two more years, almost the entire population of the island became Christian.

The truth is, a kernel of wheat must be planted in the soil. Unless it dies it will be alone—a single seed. But its death will produce many new kernels—a plentiful harvest of new lives (John 12:24).

Marcus and Narcissa Whitman (and twelve others)
Oregon Territory—November 29, 1847

In 1835, Presbyterian lay physician Dr. Marcus Whitman joined Reverend Samuel Parker in a missionary survey trip to the Northwest where they attended the annual fur trappers' rendezvous in Wyoming. There they met four Nez Perce Indian braves from the Oregon Territory, asking for someone to come and tell them about God's black book.

Whitman returned to his home in Boston, seeking support, and after marrying Narcissa Prentiss, the couple set out under the auspices of the American Board of Commissioners for Foreign Missions. Henry and Eliza Spalding and a single man, William Gray, joined them. Never before had white women crossed the Rocky Mountains.

They reached the Walla Walla River (in what is now southeastern Washington State) on September 1, 1836. Possibly tensions between the couples (years earlier Narcissa had jilted Spalding) caused them to separate. And maybe in a spirit of generosity, Marcus sent the Spaldings northeast to Lapwai, in present-day Idaho, to work with the more responsive and peaceful Nez Perce people while he and Narcissa located at Waiilatpu on the Walla Walla to work among Cayuse, even though they had been warned not to begin among this unstable and hostile tribe.

Nevertheless, the Whitmans worked hard, preaching, starting a school, planting crops, practicing medicine, and constructing buildings. Their early enthusiasm faded, however, when their two-year-old daughter drowned in 1839 and Narcissa began losing her eyesight. Most discouraging, the Cayuse did not respond to the gospel, at least not the way the Whitmans presented it. Gift giving was essential to Cayuse social and political life, yet the Whitmans saw the practice as a form of extortion. The Cayuse considered religion and domestic life closely entwined, yet Narcissa did not want them in her house.

When the mission board decided to close the mission in 1842, Marcus made a trip east in the middle of winter to convince them otherwise. He succeeded. And on the way west in 1843, he helped lead the first "great migration," which had been encouraged by the missionary reports from the Whitmans that women could, indeed, survive such a trip.

The wagon train of one thousand pioneers traveled what became known as the Oregon Trail, arriving finally at the Whitman mission at Waiilatpu for a much-needed rest before dispersing. The United States and Canada were vying for control of the territory at this point, and new U.S. settlers were greatly coveted.

Discouragement over Cayuse indifference to the gospel, combined with the potential of securing the Oregon Territory for the United States and aiding tired and sick pioneers, caused the Whitmans to lose focus on their mission work among the Indians. They took in eleven children from deceased settlers and set up something of a boarding school for others. Year after year, they welcomed huge wagon trains of exhausted, starving, and sick people pouring into the valley. All of the Whitmans' time went to serving the settlers . . . to the point that Marcus didn't even respond when the Indians sent for his help as a doctor.

In 1847, the settlers brought measles that wiped out nearly half of the Cayuse tribe. Enraged, and believing it to have been intentional treachery (since white people usually recovered), the Cayuse attacked the mission on November 29, killing fourteen whites, including the Whitmans, and burning down all the buildings.

Later, when a white militia captured those involved in the raid, Chief Tiloukaikt of the Cayuse declared on the gallows, "Did not your missionaries teach us that Christ died to save his people? So we die to save our people!" But he did not succeed in saving them. A small remnant was absorbed into the Nez Perce and Yakima tribes, but most were wiped out as whites settled the region.

Martyrs for Christ?

Possibly Marcus and Narcissa Whitman were more martyrs for the cause of American expansion than for the gospel of Christ. Only God knows whether they might have survived had they paid more attention to their missionary calling.

Of course, you get no credit for being patient if you are beaten for doing wrong. But if you suffer for doing right and are patient beneath the blows, God is pleased with you (1 Peter 2:20).

Mary Ann Paton
Vanuatu—March 3, 1859

Mary Ann Robson grew up in a Christian home in Scotland, and even though girls did not go to school at that time, her parents gave her a good homeschool education. While growing up, Mary had always desired to be a missionary. And so on April 2, 1858, she married John G. Paton and sailed with him fourteen days later to the South Pacific.

On November 5, 1858, they arrived at the island of Anatom, a southern island in Vanuatu, a group of eighty islands about fifteen hundred miles northeast of Australia, then known as the New Hebrides. Other missionaries had established a solid work on Anatom, and several converts from there agreed to accompany the Patons north to the island of Tanna, where they built a small house on the low-lying land adjacent to Port Resolution, not realizing that it was an area infested with malaria-carrying mosquitoes.

The Tannese people worshiped and feared many idols and had no concept of a loving God. Witches and wizards in each village cast spells they claimed controlled life and death. They stirred up warfare between the people, hoping it would drive out the missionaries. At first, the Patons felt overwhelmed by these warring cannibals. Then they realized that the Christians from Anatom had been just as savage only a few years earlier.

However, warfare between tribes increased, with some of the worst fighting happening right outside the Patons' house.

Three months after arriving on Tanna, Mary Ann gave birth to their son, Peter, on February 12, 1859. What joy he represented! But in less than three weeks, Mary became sick with fever and died on March 3. Paton's grief was so great that all he could say was, "But for Jesus, and the fellowship He vouchsafed me there, I must have gone mad and died beside that lonely grave!" To add to his sorrows, the baby boy, Peter, was taken from him as well on March 20, after one week's sickness.

Disease has taken the life of so many missionaries that we usually don't count its victims as martyrs. However, in this case there was a more sinister component. One of the chiefs later confessed that they had sold the swampy bit of ground to the Patons precisely because they knew it was deadly and thereby hoped to rid themselves of the missionaries. Finally ready to befriend Paton, he added, "Missi, if you stay here, you will soon die! No Tanna-man sleeps so low down as you do, in this damp weather, or he, too, would die. We sleep on the high ground, and the trade wind keeps us well."

Not long after this, white traders—who also hated missionaries because they discouraged the natives from buying rum and muskets—deliberately sent three sick sailors among the people to spread measles, knowing that the witch doctors would blame Paton. The epidemic killed a third of the people, and the survivors sought revenge.

Two chiefs protected Paton for a time, but that only increased the intertribal warfare. Soon Paton was running for his life, protected for a while by one chief, only to be chased by the same tribe the next day. Had a passing ship not rescued him, he almost certainly would have been killed and eaten. He had been on Tanna less than four years.

A Second Try

John then spent nearly two years speaking to churches in Australia and Scotland, raising financial support and recruiting more missionaries. One of those recruits, Margaret Whitecross, married John and later returned with him to the islands.

John longed to settle again on Tanna, but the mission board assigned the Patons to Aniwa a few miles east. Superstitions on Aniwa were just as godless, but possibly because the island was smaller, there was less warfare and cannibalism. As the Patons learned the language, they slowly gained the people's confidence and were able to present the gospel until nearly everyone on the island became a Christian.

In his later years, Paton traveled widely on behalf of missions, but he always returned to his home on Aniwa until old age and failing health forced him to leave the island permanently in 1904. Though he was very sad to go, he rejoiced that the people now lived in peace and faithfully worshiped God. He died January 28, 1907.

[Jesus said,] "Teach these new disciples to obey all the commands I have given you. And be sure of this: I am with you always, even to the end of the age" (Matthew 28:20).

The Three Massabki Brothers
Syria—July 10, 1860

Even though Pope Gregory IX provided the Franciscans with a letter of recommendation when he sent them to Damascus in 1233, Melek el-Ashraf, the sultan of the city, refused to permit them to preach the gospel openly. So they confined themselves to serving the spiritual needs of the resident European traders.

Still, ministry in the city where Paul received the gospel was dangerous. In the years that followed, at least eight Franciscans were martyred. Not until 1620 were they allowed to have a public chapel. In 1668 they worshipped in a Maronite church. (Maronites are associated with the Eastern Orthodox Church.) Finally in 1719, they experienced increased liberty: They obtained a new church in Bab Tuma, the Christian quarter, and founded a college for missionaries. In 1820 they built a large church over the site of the house of Ananias where Paul got back his sight.

Life seemed to be improving in 1856 when the Turkish sultan granted full civil liberties to all Christians throughout the empire, but then the Druses, an

Islamic sect, went on a terrorist campaign against Christians. Nevertheless, the eight Franciscans living behind thick walls of the monastery at Bab Tuma believed they were safe.

Serving with them by 1860 were three Maronite brothers—actual siblings—who taught at the school. These brothers were Francis, Abdel-Mohti, and Raphael Massabki. The tall, handsome Francis was married with three boys and five girls. In addition to teaching at the monastery, he moved through Damascus as stylishly dressed silk salesman with a large black turban.

Abdel-Mohti lived with his family in Francis's house, but he was a more reserved man, full of deep faith and true piety.

Raphael was a simple-hearted bachelor, short and physically weak, but dedicated in his faith.

Rampage

During the night of July 9–10, 1860, Ahmed Pasha, a Druse governor of Syria, issued secret orders for his henchmen to draw crosses in the streets of Damascus and say that Christian children were to blame. Fear spread throughout the Christian community that reprisals would be taken.

At sundown, Ahmed ordered his agents to incite hoodlums to go out in the streets and start fires. At the Orthodox Church, they killed everyone in sight and then set the church ablaze. The fire spread from house to house and looting followed. On the morning of July 10, more Christians were massacred—thousands in the end—their homes destroyed and their goods stolen. Some compassionate Muslims, aided by the Emir Abdel-Kader of Algeria, took pity on the survivors and helped them hide in the citadel.

Having seen to the safety of their wives and children, Francis, Abdel-Mohti, and Raphael headed for the Franciscan convent where many other Christians had taken refuge. The Franciscans barred the doors and served communion to all present, but in the middle of the night, a traitor admitted Ahmed's agents through a secret backdoor.

While slaughtering the eight Franciscans—Fathers Ruiz, Colta, Escanio, Solar, Alberca, Binazo, Fernandez, and Colanda—one of Ahmed's agents recognized Francis and said: "The sheik has sent us to save you from death—you, your brothers, your families, and all those who depend upon you for protection—on the condition that you deny your faith and convert to Islam."

Francis said, "The sheik can take my money and my life, but my faith, no one can make me deny. I am a Christian and on the faith of Christ, I will die."

Given a similar opportunity to save their lives by denying their faith, the other two brothers refused, and all three accepted martyrdom.

In Their Own Words

"The Christian must always be ready to spill his blood for the love of Christ, and that man's greatest joy is to receive the grace of martyrdom."

—Counsel frequently given by Abdel-Mohti Massabki
to his students

You must worship Christ as Lord of your life. And if you are asked about your Christian hope, always be ready to explain it (1 Peter 3:15).

George and Ellen Gordon
Vanuatu—May 20, 1861

By June 1857 when George and Ellen Gordon arrived in Vanuatu, a group of eighty islands about fifteen hundred miles northeast of Australia, then known as the New Hebrides, over forty missionaries and their children had been killed or died from starvation trying to bring the gospel to the violent residents of Erromanga, one of the southernmost islands. These martyrs were primarily Christians from Samoa and Rarotonga, who came to share their new-found faith, but also included the first foreign missionaries to step on the island at Dillon's Bay, John Williams and James Harris, whom the Erromangans had eaten. By the early 1840s all missionary efforts to reach these people ceased.

Taking up the Challenge

George Gordon, the son of Scottish-born parents, was born near Alberton, Prince Edward Island, Canada, in 1822. In 1848, Gordon's life was turned upside down by a powerful conversion experience, and he intentionally began proclaiming the gospel to everyone he met. After receiving his theological training, he responded to the challenge of Canadian Presbyterians and volunteered as a missionary. While studying tropical medicine in England, he met Ellen Catherine Powell, who was also eager for mission work. After their marriage, they left for the South Pacific.

In the meantime, even though missionary efforts to reach the people of Erromanga had ceased, white traders still visited them to obtain the aromatic sandalwood that grew on the island. Some of the traders were brutal in their treatment of the native peoples, using their guns and cannons to impose their trade wishes. By the mid-1850s the appearance of white people filled the people of Erromanga with both fear and anger.

Nevertheless, in 1857, this is where the Gordons chose to minister in one more attempt to present the gospel of Christ. Surprisingly, the Gordons had remarkable success, and within four years there were about forty believers, three of whom had completed the catechism training and been baptized.

During this period, George had observed how unscrupulous white traders were with the island people and had often warned them of their treachery.

In January of 1861, a typhoon devastated the island. Then in March, a group of sandalwood traders brought two sailors ashore who had measles. They deliberately exposed as many islanders as possible to these infected people, hoping the Erromangans would die thereby making acquisition of the sandalwood easier.

The plot worked. Measles killed hundreds. In some villages half the people died. Gordon nursed as many as possible, and only two of his patients died. Unfortunately, they happened to be children of one of the island's chiefs, and he thought Gordon had cast a spell on them. Maybe the missionary had conjured up the typhoon, too. In his anger and grief, the chief gathered a group of warriors and killed George and Ellen on May 20, 1861.

Back in Canada, upon hearing of the death of his brother and sister-in-law, James Gordon volunteered to take their place. By the time he arrived in Erromanga, the sandalwood had played out—the trees being almost entirely removed—but the white traders had switched to providing slaves for plantations in New Caledonia, Fiji, and Queensland. Ostensibly, the natives signed on voluntarily for a three-year stint, but with no way to get home, they often died as slaves.

The church on Erromanga welcomed James Gordon, and he helped it grow into a truly indigenous congregation by discipling native believers into strong leaders. For reasons unknown, however, he was killed on March 7, 1872, while working on the translation of the book of Acts. He had just reached Stephen's words in Acts 7:60: "Lord, do not hold this sin against them" (NIV).

Seed of the Church

In 1880, the Christians of Erromanga dedicated a church building at Dillon's Bay named the Martyrs' Church. One of the native pastors predicted that within a generation the whole island would be Christian. His words were prophetic, for by 1900, 95 percent of the population identified itself as Christian. For this goal the Gordons gave their lives.

Jean Théophane Vénard

Indochina (now Vietnam)—February 2, 1861

The first Christian missionary arrived in Vietnam (formerly Indochina) in 1533, but because an imperial edict forbade Christianity, a permanent mission was not established until 1615. After baptizing 6,700 Vietnamese at a new mission in the north, Alexander de Rhodes, a Jesuit priest, was driven from the country in 1630. Persecution had begun as the first Christian was beheaded. More were martyred in 1644 and 1645.

Persecution and martyrdoms continued unabated until 1841, when the threat of French warships provided a brief reprieve. However, in 1848, the new emperor offered bounties for the surrender of Christian missionaries. Persecution ignited in 1855 like wildfire in a dry forest until Christians were being slaughtered indiscriminately.

Within seven years, 115 native priests, 100 Vietnamese nuns, and more than 5,000 believers were martyred in the northern part of the country. In the south, more than 8,500 died for their faith, while in the east the toll may have been as high as 24,000. Certainly that many people willing to give their life in loyalty to Jesus Christ demonstrates a level of commitment only possible through the Holy Spirit.

Into Trouble

Jean Théophane Vénard was born in Poitiers, France, in 1829 and raised in a pious family. Later he studied at the College of Doue-la-Fontaine and at the Paris Seminary for Foreign Missions, which he entered as a subdeacon. He then was ordained as a Catholic priest in June, 1852, and departed as a missionary to the Far East that September. After a period of orientation in Hong Kong, he was assigned to a mission in Tonkin.

The emperor, Tu-Doc, was very hostile to Christians and had ordered their eradication. He was afraid that Christian missionaries would pave the way for French colonization. The persecution was so severe, that even before Father Vénard arrived, the other priests and bishops had fled to the forest, where they hid in caves. The new missionary joined them in these harsh circumstances, but his fragile health suffered from the exposure and poor food. Still, he ministered to the people at night and sometimes during the day when it seemed safe.

In 1858–1859, the emperor's fears were partially realized when French forces overran Saigon and various regions to the south. French occupation temporarily subdued persecution, but it also justified the emperor's vendetta against Christian missionaries. Finally, one of Father Vénard's own parishioners betrayed him, and he was arrested on November 30, 1860, and brought to Saigon.

The emperor judged his case personally and again and again offered him his freedom if only he would denounce Christ, but Father Vénard remained faithful and was finally sentenced to death. During his wait for the date of his execution, he was kept in a bamboo cage, not unlike those that more than a few American POWs were held in over a hundred years later.

When he was finally marched to his execution, local Christians said that he chanted hymns and psalms as he was marched to his death. The executioner envied his habit and offered to be careful to decapitate him swiftly if he would surrender his robe to him. Father Vénard smiled and said, "The longer it lasts, the better it will be."

In His Own Words

During the next two months while he awaited his execution, Father Vénard wrote often to his family, assuring them of his peace with God and his anticipation of receiving a white robe in glory. In one poetic letter he said, "A slight saber cut will separate my head from my body, like the spring flower which the Master of the garden gathers for His pleasure. We are all flowers planted on this earth, which God plucks in His own good time: some a little sooner, some a little later. . . . Father and son may we meet in Paradise. I, poor little moth, go first. Adieu."

> Others were tortured, refusing to turn from God in order to be set free. They placed their hope in a better life after the resurrection. Some were jeered at, and their Backs were cut open with whips. Others were chained in prisons. Some died by stoning, some were sawed in half, and others were killed with the sword (Hebrews 11:35-37).

Robert Jermain Thomas
Korea—July 24, 1866

Born the son of a Welsh Independent minister in 1839, Thomas began preaching at age fifteen. Later, he taught school for a time before enrolling as a student at the University of London. He graduated from New College in 1863, was ordained, married Caroline Godfrey, and joined the London Missionary Society (LMS) headed for China.

Sadly, three months after arriving in Shanghai, Caroline died.

Thomas became impatient with the LMS because it wasn't giving sufficient priority to unreached peoples, and he actually resigned. He visited Korea for two and a half months in 1865, familiarizing himself with the language and customs. In 1866, another opportunity came for him to visit Korea, this time as an interpreter on the *General Sherman*, an armed U.S. merchant-marine ship. On behalf of the National Bible Society of Scotland, Thomas took along hundreds of Bibles to distribute.

Other missionaries strongly advised Thomas not to go. Korea's vigorous policy to eradicate all "foreign" religion from the land had resulted in severe persecution and even the execution of thousands of secret Catholic believers. This was not the time to distribute Bibles openly, they advised. Besides, Korea forbade all uninvited foreign trade.

A Rude Ship

The sight of the *General Sherman* sailing up the Taedong river into Korea must have been intimidating. It was a retired (after the Civil War) U.S. gunboat, the former USS *Princess Royal*, ironclad and painted black, powered by steam as well as sails and still armed with two twelve-pounders and three smaller cannons. The Korean government asked the ship to leave immediately, but Captain Page replied, using Thomas as his interpreter, that they were intent on trading their cotton, tin sheets, glass, and other goods. The *General Sherman* continued upriver until it was stopped by the Crow Rapids.

Here, the Korean governor Park sent another message, "You have reached the walls of our city when asked to stay put at Keupsa Gate. You insist on trading with us, which is forbidden. Your actions have created a grave situation, so much so that I must inform my King and then decide what to do with you people."

That night unusually high tides and torrential rains raised the river level sufficiently for the *General Sherman* to continue upriver to anchor at the city of Pyongyang. The king's response was, "Tell them to leave at once. If they do not obey, kill them." But by this time, the river level had gone back down and the *General Sherman* was trapped.

For some reason, the Korean emissary was detained on board the ship. Tensions rose and shooting broke out between the crew and Korean soldiers onshore. It escalated until the *General Sherman* was firing its cannons, killing several Koreans onshore.

Finally, the Korean soldiers launched some flaming boats loaded with wood, pitch, sulfur, and saltpeter against the ship. It's uncertain whether the ship caught fire, being ironclad, but the acrid smoke forced the crew to abandon ship.

Soldiers and the mob waiting onshore killed everyone. Reportedly, Thomas made it ashore, where he continued exclaiming, "Jesus! Jesus!" in Korean and offered his Korean Bible to the soldier who had grabbed him. The man rebuffed his offer. When Thomas knelt to pray, the man cut off Thomas's head and threw it into the river.

Seed of the Church

Thomas's role in assisting the belligerent merchants may not have been exemplary, but God still used the incident for good. Reportedly, the Korean who killed him wallpapered his guesthouse with the pages of Thomas's Bible. But later their words convicted him, and he realized that he killed a good man. In time, he became a Christian. Over the years, people came from everywhere to "read the walls." Ultimately, the killer's nephew graduated from Pyongyang's Union Christian College and served as part of a team that revised the Korean Bible. The Word had come to Korea at the price of martyr's blood.

Show proper respect to everyone: Love the brotherhood of believers, fear God, honor the king (1 Peter 2:17, NIV).

Chief Maskepetoon
Alberta, Canada—1869

Even though the great Cree warrior, Chief Maskepetoon, once declared to Wesleyan missionary, Reverend Robert Rundle, "I will never become a Christian as long as there are horses to steal and scalps to take!" he became friends with Rundle and also listened respectfully to the teachings of Jean-Baptiste Thibault, a Catholic missionary, and Khunter, an Anglican. Shaking his head at their disagreements, he said, "I will wait until you agree among yourselves before I accept this new religion."

Age-old grudges kept the Blackfeet and Cree at war with one another, and Maskepetoon's reputation as a fierce warrior grew large. But he could not forget his father's many warnings that such a life produced only death and destruction and never led to peace. Sitting down with a tribal elder one day, the chief asked, "What is best in life?"

Thoughtfully, the old man gathered eight sticks and grouped them by fours. He held one bunch of sticks in his left hand and named them: *falsehood, dishonesty, hatred,* and *war,* describing each vice. With his right hand he picked up the second bunch and named them: *truth, honesty, love,* and *peace,* also describing each in detail. Holding up his left hand, he asked, "What shall I do with these? Keep them or burn them?"

"Burn them!" said Maskepetoon.

"And these?" The tribal elder held up his right hand.

"Tie them together," Maskepetoon cried, "and give them to me as a remembrance of all that you have said."

Not long after that, Maskepetoon began to read the Cree New Testament given to him by a Christian missionary and decided to follow the way of Jesus.

Maskepetoon's "Revenge"

The wars with the Blackfeet created great hardship for the Cree people, and Maskepetoon decided to "risk peace." With a small party of Cree, he set out for the Blackfoot camp, but before they reached their destination, a war party attacked them. All the other Cree fled for their lives, but Maskepetoon stood his ground, reading from his New Testament. Puzzled, the Blackfeet stopped shooting and surrounded the man who made no effort to defend himself.

Recognizing Maskepetoon, one of the war party asked what he held in his hand. "The word of the Great Spirit," Masketoon replied. "It is his will that we meet as brothers today."

The Blackfeet willingly laid down their weapons. "Our hearts are glad to make peace with you." And that day a truce was declared between the two tribes.

Chief Maskepetoon's reputation as a peacemaker gained credibility among the Indian tribes in what is now Alberta, Canada. At another time, the Blackfeet came to the Cree camp to smoke the pipe of peace to seal a truce. One of the Blackfeet in the circle was known as the man who had murdered Maskepetoon's father. Maskepetoon called the man to stand before him. Trembling, sure that he would be punished or killed on the spot, the man approached the chief. Instead, Maskepetoon handed him a suit of beautiful buckskin trousers and shirt, and brought his own horse into the circle. "You killed my father," he said to the man. "You must now become father to me. Wear my clothes, ride my horse. Tell your people that this is the way Maskepetoon takes revenge."

But resentment was growing against the white man; trouble was brewing. Reverend George McDougall, a Methodist missionary and advocate for the Indians, asked Chief Maskepetoon to invite both Cree and Blackfeet to come to a "summer camp" to meet the missionaries, school teachers, and Hudson's Bay officials and discuss their grievances.

Carrying both a white flag and a Bible, Maskepetoon and his sons set out for the Blackfoot camp. But they never returned. When the Cree discovered their lifeless bodies, they wanted to take immediate revenge. But for the moment, at least, they chose "the bundle of sticks that lead to peace" out of respect for their great Chief Maskepetoon.

[Jesus said,] "If your enemies are hungry, feed them. If they are thirsty, give them something to drink, and they will be ashamed of what they have done to you." Don't let evil get the best of you, but conquer evil by doing good" (Romans 12:20-21).

David Livingstone
Africa—April 30, 1873

By moonlight, they pulled their small boat into the shore of Lake Myassa. Fiercely painted warriors leaped from the jungle onto the beach, waving their spears. David Livingstone's porters raised their guns in defense against the dreaded *Mazitu*.

"Wait!" Livingstone ordered. He stepped from the boat and opened his shirt, exposing the ghostly whiteness of his skin. Cautiously, one warrior moved forward, his spear extended. He brought the tip to Livingstone's chest and drew it slowly down across the skin. A tiny trickle of blood, looking black in the pale light, followed the sharp point.

Suddenly, the warriors let out a frightened cry, turned, and fled back into the jungle.

Missionary, Explorer, Antislavery Activist

David Livingstone was a curious combination of missionary, doctor, explorer, scientist, and antislavery activist. He spent thirty years in Africa, traveling 29,000 miles to explore almost a third of the continent, from its southern tip almost to the equator. He was the first white to see Victoria Falls and cross the entire continent, west to east.

Born March 19, 1813, on an island off the coast of Scotland, Livingstone grew up in a Christian home. After receiving a degree in medicine from Glasgow University in 1840, Livingstone joined the London Missionary Society. With the Society's support, he went to South Africa in 1841. He ventured north by lumbering ox-wagon on a ten-week trip. But what he saw troubled him. The mission stations he visited seemed more interested in creating comfortable British outposts than pressing on to reach the unreached peoples of the interior. He also discovered that some of the missionaries were racist, thinking the Africans were unsuited for much more than servants or field hands.

On one shorter foray into the bush, a lion attacked and mauled Livingstone. It took months for him to recover, and the injuries to his shoulder bothered him the rest of his life. Mary Moffat, the daughter of Dr. Robert Moffat, Bible translator and mission director, nursed him until he was back to health . . . and in love with her.

Shortly after they were married in 1844, the Livingstones set out to establish a new mission station on the frontier. From there it was Livingstone's intention to travel deep into Africa to reach people who had never heard the gospel before.

On his first journey, he became aware of the devastation of the slave trade. When he returned to England in 1856, the Royal Geographic Society honored him as a major explorer, and the government commissioned him to return to Africa as a British consul.

He went back to Africa on his second expedition and started up the Zambezi River by riverboat. There he intended to establish Christian mission stations in the hope of spreading the gospel and stopping the slave trade. It was while he was away exploring the Lake Nyassa that Bishop Mackenzie, who had come to Africa join the mission, made a canoe trip on which he foolishly carried all the mission's medicines. The canoe capsized, losing the medicines. By the time Livingstone got back, everyone was so sick with malaria that the bishop and all the women died—including Livingstone's wife, Mary.

Shortly after that, Livingstone came across an official dispatch that conclusively proved that the Portuguese were behind the current slave trade. He sent off this proof to England, thinking the government would put international pressure on Portugal. However England chose to maintain good relations with Portugal rather than to embarrass their ally by exposing Portugal's violation of the treaty against the slave trade. To avoid any further "incidents," England ordered Livingstone out of Africa.

Years later, Livingstone returned on his own and went deep into the interior out of contact with the outside world. Many thought him dead until the *New York Herald* sent reporter Henry Stanley on an expedition to find him or bring back conclusive news of his death. In March 1871, Stanley started his search from Zanzibar. In the fall, he finally located Livingstone. The doctor was sick and out of supplies, but in good spirits. Their meeting is remembered by Stanley's famous words: "Doctor Livingstone, I presume?"

Though grateful for the visit and the fresh medicines and supplies, Livingstone would not come out of Africa. Stanley, however, returned to worldwide fame.

When Livingstone died on April 30, 1873, faithful African converts buried his heart beneath a tree according to his request because "his heart was in Africa." Then they wrapped and embalmed his body and carried it a thousand miles to the coast for transport to England.

Bishop James Hannington
Uganda—October 29, 1885

James Hannington, an Anglican minister, was appointed to be the first bishop of eastern equatorial Africa in 1882. Following in the footsteps of English missionaries C. T. Wilson and George Shergold-Smith in 1877, Hannington set out to carry the gospel—but ended up having to be carried instead, a victim to fevers in the unfamiliar climate.

After recuperating in England, Hannington set out again in October 1885, determined to fulfill his commission to plant Christian churches in East Africa. As he studied a map of the area, he decided to take a shortcut through Busoga, entering Buganda from the northeast, rather than from the south of Lake Victoria, saving himself hundreds of miles.

But when Buganda's king, Kabaka Mwanga II, heard that a white man was approaching from the north—considered Buganda's "back door"—he assumed that he was up to no good and sent a thousand warriors to the Luba chief of Busoga, with orders to stop him—permanently.

Too Late

As his party made camp for the night, James Hannington opened his journal and wrote the date: October 20, 1885. Flipping back in his journal to his entries for 1882, Hannington chuckled at the humorous sketches he had made of himself having to be carried on his first trip to Africa. What a weakling he had been! But he had learned a lot from the experience and felt more confident that he would be able to complete his journey. At least he was walking on his own two feet this time as he and his party made their way toward Buganda. Hannington was sorry that King Mutesa had died in his absence—he had been looking forward to meeting the old king who had invited the missionaries to teach the Christian faith in Buganda. Well, he would just have to develop a relationship with his successor.

Without warning, twenty warriors with spears and bows and arrows surrounded Hannington's party—"ruffians," he described them in his journal a few days later. Hannington was thrown to the ground as the warriors searched his clothes and personal belongings for anything of value. Thinking they were common robbers, the bishop yelled for help. But he was jerked to his feet and alternately pushed and pulled along. Thinking the "robbers" were about to throw him over a cliff, Hannington cried out, "Lord, I put myself in Thy hands. I look to Thee alone!"

But his captors kept dragging him along until his clothes were wet and torn, and his limbs aching with agony. Expecting instant death, Hannington began to sing: "Safe in the Arms of Jesus," and even laughing at the absurdity of his situation. To his surprise, the "robbers" suddenly stopped and pushed him into a hut. For the next few days they dragged him out as a trophy, showing off their prisoner. With presence of mind, he continued to write in his journal about this alarming turn of events, as well as to recite Scripture and pray.

Back in King Mwanga's court, Yosefu (Joseph) Mukasa, the twenty-five-year-old chief attendant and a Christian, courageously rebuked Mwanga for sending warriors to kill the white man without giving him the customary opportunity to defend himself or state his purpose. Mwanga knew his father, King Mutesa, had thought highly of Mukasa, whom he called "Balikuddembe," meaning "they will have peace." The young king shrugged in agreement and sent a messenger to spare the man's life.

But the messenger arrived too late. On October 29, 1885, Bishop James Hannington had been speared to death. (One of the warriors found Hannington's journal and later sold it to another expedition.) Now that the Englishman was dead, King Mwanga didn't want to be reminded that he had made a bad decision—so he condemned Yosefu Mukasa for questioning his order and had him beheaded on November 15 that same year.

In His Own Words
> "Go tell your master that I have purchased the road to Uganda with my blood."
> —The last words of Bishop James Hannington

The Boy Martyrs of Uganda
Uganda—January 31, 1885

Before Uganda became a British "Protectorate" around 1895, Uganda was still ruled by the Kabaka tribal kings. In 1877, two Anglican missionaries—Wilson and Shergold-Smith—walked nine hundred miles from the Indian Ocean until they reached Lake Victoria. On the other side of Lake Victoria (after sailing another two hundred miles), they were welcomed with great ceremony by King Kabaka Mutesa I. Mutesa had already heard the gospel from Henry Stanley, the English journalist who had come to Africa looking for David Livingstone, but it was hard to tell whether he was truly interested in the Christian faith or learning how to make guns and gunpowder from these Englishmen. But King Mutesa generously allowed his subjects freedom to choose their religion, whether Christian, Muslim, or traditionalist, and the Christian faith spread rapidly.

This meeting between King Mutesa and the English missionaries is considered the beginning of the Christian church in Uganda, and its Centennial was commemorated in 1977 . . . but that's another story.

Following the death of King Mutesa in 1884, his son, Mwanga II, took the Kabaka throne. But young Mwanga was not pleased by the Christian influence pervading his court which consisted of about three thousand people—ministers, guards, king's wives, children, servants, young pages—living together in a vast enclosure of over six hundred huts. The believers (called *abasomi*, or "readers," because they were so eager to read the Scriptures) gave their primary allegiance to the King of kings, and Mwanga felt his power and authority were threatened.

The King's Pages

It was a great honor to be a page in the Kabaka court. Only the healthiest and handsomest boys, chosen at about age twelve, became pages until they reached the age of twenty, when they were promoted to guards or soldiers. It was unthinkable for simple pages to refuse the desires of a king, but that's exactly what three young Christian boys did when the king made homosexual advances to them.

Mwanga had been king barely a year when Yusufu (Joseph), Makko (Mark), and Muwa (Noah) rejected his advances. Mwanga was outraged! He would nip this defiance at the root before it spread.

A great fire was built at Busega Natete, and the boys—the youngest of whom was only eleven and the oldest fifteen—faced death by burning. All the people were weeping, and the boys' parents pled with them to give up their Christian faith. But the boys would not. They even began to sing: "O that I had wings like the angels. I would fly away and be with Jesus." (This song became known as the "Martyrs' Song" in all the Christian churches in Uganda.)

Angry because he couldn't frighten the boys into denying their faith, King Mwanga ordered his warriors to chop off their arms and throw them alive into the fire. Yusufu, the youngest, pleaded, "Please don't cut off my arms. I will not struggle in the fire that takes me to Jesus."

Shaken by the steadfast faith of such young boys, forty persons who watched them go to their deaths that day put their faith in Jesus. They knew what it might mean, and the persecution of Christians in Uganda had only begun.

In Their Own Words

"Tell the king that he has put our bodies in the fire, but we won't be long in the fire. Soon we shall be with Jesus, which is much better. But ask him to repent . . . or he will land in a place of eternal fire."

—Yusufu, Makko, and Nuwa on January 31, 1885,
just before being thrown into the fire

[Jesus said,] "Don't be afraid of those who want to kill you. They can only kill your body; they cannot touch your soul. Fear only God, who can destroy both soul and body in hell" (Matthew 10:28).

The Martyrs of Uganda

Uganda—June 3, 1886

King Mwanga II of Buganda was annoyed. He had tried to stamp out this pernicious Christian faith by killing three of his young pages who dared to defy his wishes. And he'd stopped James Hannington, the English missionary, by having him speared before he even reached Buganda's borders. But the Christians kept popping up everywhere, like a head full of lice—and just as hard to get rid of! Why couldn't they keep quiet about what they believed? He might leave them alone if they didn't keep trying to convert their families and all their fellows.

Mwanga was getting tired of killing a Christian here, another one there. Even Karoli (Charles) Lwanga, the overseer of all his pages, had that silly happy smile common to these Christians. He would settle this thing once and for all!

On a day late in May 1886, King Mwanga called for the chief of his pages. "Lwanga, I want you to assemble all the pages together first thing tomorrow morning!"

The Road to Namugongo

After passing word of the king's command among his charges, Charles Lwanga laid down in his hut with a heavy heart. He had known it was only a matter of time before he would lay down his life for his Savior. But he wished he could spare the young boys who had been entrusted into his care. He had trained them to be exemplary servants to the king—but he had also pointed many of them to Jesus Christ as their Lord and Savior.

"Lwanga! Lwanga!" Hearing his name in an urgent whisper, Charles sat bolt upright. Four of his pages crept into his hut—Mbaga, age 17; Gyavira, also 17; Mugagga, 16; and Kizito, only 14. "Please baptize us tonight," the boys begged. "If we are killed, we want to be sure that we will go to heaven to be with Jesus." Astounded at their faith, Charles Lwanga secretly baptized the four boys.

The next morning Lwanga gathered all his charges before the king. King Mwanga came right to the point: "All those who pray to Jesus, stand over there." Charles Lwanga strode to the designated spot. Within moments, more than thirty pages had joined him.

King Mwanga was furious! "Tie them up!" he roared to his guards. "Take them to Namugongo"—the place of execution, a seventeen hour walk—"and burn them alive!"

The head executioner was aghast. His own son, Mbaga, was among them! When did *he* become a Christian? "Please, my son," he pleaded as he tied the arms of the other boys, "it is not too late to reject this Jesus. Then I will not have to kill you!"

But Mbaga pointed bravely upward. "I want to die for the cause of God."

As the boys marched the many long miles toward Namugongo, Gyavira saw one of his friends with whom he had recently had a quarrel among the Christians. "Mukasa, my friend!" he cried. "How happy I am to see you again! Thank God for this reunion. Let us die together for Jesus Christ." The two boys shook hands as a token of their forgiveness.

The group had been whittled down to twenty-six still alive when they reached the place of execution. (Several had been speared or beheaded along the way—either because they could no longer walk, or because the executioners were afraid the king might relent and pardon his favorites.) But the stakes for burning were not ready, so the condemned had to wait seven days. They

191

spent their time singing and praising God, in spite of the cold and the cords that bound then tightly, cutting into their flesh.

On June 3, the young men were brought out in small groups. As each group appeared, the others welcomed them with joyful shouts. Little Kizito, the youngest, kept giggling as if it were a game. But he shouted to his companions: "Pray the Our Father [the Lord's Prayer] and suffer bravely!" And Mugagga called out just before being tied with two others thrown on the fire: "Good-bye, my friends. I am going to the good God!"

Seed of the Church
All twenty-six were burned that day at Namugongo . . . but the flames sparked a surge of conversions to Christianity. June 3 is commemorated each year as Martyrs Day in the Uganda Christian Church (both Catholics and Protestants were numbered among them), and many African youth groups, youth choirs, and children's magazines bear the name of youthful Kizito.

Chief Spokane Garry
Washington State—January 14, 1892

Before seeing a Bible, many Native American peoples knew God in the way Romans 1:19-20 describes: "The truth about God is known to them instinctively. God has put this knowledge in their hearts. From the time the world was created, people have seen the earth and sky and all that God made. They can clearly see his invisible qualities—his eternal power and divine nature." And God did not ignore those who responded faithfully.

Such was the case with some tribes of the western plateau encompassing parts of Montana, Wyoming, Idaho, Washington, and Oregon. In the latter part of the eighteenth century, shamans who variously worshiped God as Quilent-sat-men (He who made us) or Amotkan (He who lives on most high) communicated similar prophecies that men with white skins wearing strange clothes (or in one case, black shirts) would come bringing them a new moral law found written in leaves bound together. In the meantime, these prophets called their people to repent of past evil, live righteously, and pray daily.

So widespread was the spiritual hunger that during his first trip to the region, a dozen chiefs asked George Simpson of the Hudson's Bay Company to send black-book teachers to them. In 1825, chiefs from the Middle Spokane and Lower Kootenay tribes sent two of their own sons with some traders to the mission school at Red River in Manitoba.

New Life in Christ
The chosen boys were Kootenai Pelly (from the Nez Perce tribe) and Spokane Garry (about age fifteen). Four years later, they returned to their people able to read and write, having memorized many Scriptures, hymns, and the

catechism, and most important, committed to Jesus. Crowds gathered from hundreds of miles to hear about the Master of Life. Garry faithfully stressed the need for faith in Jesus Christ for salvation and forgiveness of sin.

It was apparently the preaching of these young believers that led the Nez Perce to send a delegation all the way to St. Louis in 1831 asking for missionaries to come to them. Of the Nez Perce, Captain Bonneville said, "Their honesty is immaculate and their purity of purpose are most remarkable, more like a nation of saints than a horde of savages."

Betrayal

But the prophecies of the old shamans had carried a somber warning as well. After the religious teachers there would come other white men who would overrun their country and make slaves of all the people. Resistance would be futile, causing needless bloodshed.

Even though missionaries like Marcus and Narcissa Whitman unwittingly facilitated this tragedy, Spokane Garry remained true to his Christian calling. By 1870, most tribes had lost their land, the white missionaries had taken over or abandoned the native church rather than build on indigenous leadership, and the most obvious legacy of association with whites was whiskey, disease, and moral decay.

Still, Chief Garry invited Henry Spalding (an associate of the Whitmans) to return and conduct revival meetings. In three trips, over six hundred people gave their lives to Christ, but the missionary society could not find the personnel to send a permanent teacher until 1884. Upon arrival in Spokane Falls, Reverend J. Compton Burnett bought a piece of land from the Northern Pacific Railroad that Indian people had cultivated for years with the permission of the Indian Service. The land dispute destroyed all hope of Burnett's ministry.

Garry, too, suffered when land grabbers stole his farm. The hearing dragged on, and he eventually lost his animals. too. The promised government annuity of one hundred dollars a year never arrived, and by 1891, Chief Garry was alone, sick, and destitute. When a con man offered to get his farm back for him for five dollars, Garry said, "I am dying, and all I am thinking of is God. Soon I'll have nothing more to do with this world." He died in his sleep on January 14, 1892.

In His Own Words

Spokane Garry copied this hymn by Philip P. Bliss into his private journal.

> I am so glad that our Father in heaven
> Tells of his love in the book He has given;
> Wonderful things in the Bible I see—
> This is the dearest, that Jesus loves me. . . .
> I am so glad that Jesus loves me,
> Jesus loves even me.

Samuel Morris

Indiana—May 12, 1893

Samuel Morris was born in 1872 in the West African country of Liberia as Prince Kaboo, son of a king (probably a regional chief) of the Kru tribe at a time of ongoing warfare with the neighboring Grebos. In the country at large, the Kru outnumbered the Grebos, but in Kaboo's region the Grebos repeatedly defeated his people.

When a defeated king could not pay the war taxes imposed by the victor, a "pawn" was often surrendered until the debt could be paid. Kaboo was first given as surety when he was a small child, but his father redeemed him rather quickly. However, when he was a young adolescent, war broke out again. His people were defeated, and he was surrendered a second time while his father attempted to raise his ransom from their war-ravaged villages. As time passed, the Grebos inflated the price, intent on crushing the Krus forever. They also increased the pressure by whipping Kaboo daily with a thorny, poisonous vine. Kaboo became so weak from loss of blood and fever from the poison that he had to be carried and draped over the X-shaped whipping post.

Then one day in front of a circle of bloodthirsty onlookers, as the whip was about to fall, a light flashed over him so brightly that it blinded everyone around him, and a voice commanded him to rise and run. With unexplained strength, Kaboo fled into the jungle, where he concealed himself in a hollow tree until night. He emerged to find a small light guiding him on. He hid by day and traveled at night until he came to the town of Monrovia, where some missionaries took him in. (Later, an independent Kru captive named Henry O'Neil confirmed Kaboo's story, attesting that he was an eyewitness to his escape.)

Following Kaboo's arrival at the mission station in Monrovia, he became a Christian and, while studying the Bible, noted that Saul's experience on the road to Damascus was very similar to what had happened to him. Kaboo—having adopted the name Samuel Morris—determined to go to America to study God's Word and learn more about the Holy Spirit. He talked his way onto a ship full of cutthroat sailors, who hated him as a black person and were just as eager kill each other. Sammy not only intervened—standing up to a cutlass-wielding murderer—he made peace among the crew and won their friendship. He prayed for healing from their diseases and led most of them to Christ.

In New York, Sammy brought revival to Stephen Merritt's street mission and to various local churches in which he preached. Stephen Merritt sent him on to Taylor University in Indiana, where Sammy did much the same. Soon the newspapers were carrying reports of this remarkable African young man who was instigating revival wherever he went, even at a local roller-skating rink.

In the winter of 1892–1893, however, Taylor University was nearly ready to close its doors for lack of funds. But Sammy's example of faith not only made him a leader among his fellow students; it also inspired a discouraged faculty and administration. The board of trustees created a Samuel Morris Faith Fund, which saved the university.

194

Sammy, however, became ill during that winter, complicated by the injuries he had suffered while in captivity. He had dreamed of returning to Africa to tell his people about Jesus, but he told a visitor, "I am so happy; I have seen the angels. They are coming for me soon. The light my Father in heaven sent to save me when I was hanging helpless on that cross in Africa was for a purpose. I was saved for a purpose. Now I have fulfilled that purpose. My work here on earth has been finished."

Seed of the Church

Samuel Morris died on May 12, 1893. God used his death to inspire a substantial number of Taylor students to go to the mission field, many to Africa in Sammy's stead. There was even a Taylor University Bible School established in Africa.

But perhaps the captain of the tramp ship on which Sammy came to New York paid him the most fitting tribute. When he learned that Sammy had died, he was so overcome that he at first could not speak. Then he said that most of the old crew were still on board and eager to find out about their beloved hero and minister. After all, he had changed life on that ship. Before he came aboard, no one had ever prayed out loud, but after Sammy shared the gospel, they became like one family—a family that could talk to their Father.

Bernard Mizeki
Zimbabwe—June 18, 1896

When Bernard Mizeki was born in about 1861, the colonial government called his homeland Portuguese East Africa. It is now known as Mozambique. At fourteen years of age, he left home to live in the slums of Cape Town, South Africa, and work for a butcher. The discouraging conditions in the slums led many to drown their misery in alcohol, but Bernard chose to spend his evenings in classes at the Anglican school.

Bernard was an excellent student, quickly learning English, French, and Dutch, as well as eight African languages, while mastering his other subjects. But it was the witness of the Cowley Fathers, his teachers from the Society of Saint John the Evangelist, that led him to Christ, and he was baptized on March 9, 1886.

Partially because he learned languages so easily, Bernard felt God call him to be a missionary. In 1891, Bishop Knight-Bruce assigned him to a post in southern Zimbabwe. In Nhowe, the village of Paramount Chief Mangwende, Bernard divided his time between prayer, studying the local language, making friends with the villagers, and tending his subsistence garden. He eventually built a mission complex and opened it for the children he loved dearly. He also helped translate the Scriptures and part of the *Book of Common Prayer* in the local Mashona language.

Bernard tried to follow the example of the apostle Paul in Athens by building on what truth the people already had, in this case their monotheistic faith in one God and their sensitivity to spirit life. He only opposed those pagan customs that were in conflict with the gospel, which he boldly proclaimed at every opportunity. As an additional example of identifying with the local people, Bernard married Mutwa, a young Mashona woman related to Chief Mangwende.

Opposition
Over the next five years (1891–1896), many local people came to faith in Christ at the Nhowe mission. But after relocating his mission complex near a grove of trees considered sacred to the Mashona ancestral sprits, Bernard cut down some of the trees and carved crosses into others, angering local religious leaders.

In 1896 when the behavior of many white settlers provoked the first great rebellion in what was then Rhodesia, anyone associated with the colonialists was in danger. Some of Bernard's friends warned him, "They will think you are a government agent because you are a missionary. Black or white doesn't matter. You should flee while you can!"

"But I don't work for any foreigners," he said. "I only work for Jesus Christ, and I will not abandon you converts or leave this post."

On June 18, 1896, as part of the uprising, two of Chief Mangwende's sons speared Bernard and left him for dead.

Seeing how grave his wounds were, his wife, Mutwa, who was pregnant at the time, and a helper bathed his wounds, then went to get food and blankets. Later they reported that as they were returning to the hillside, they saw a blinding light over where Bernard lay and heard a rushing sound, "Like the sound of many wings." But when they got there, Bernard's body was gone.

Seed of the Church
Bernard's life and death greatly encouraged the Anglican Church in Zimbabwe. His memory is preserved in books, in schools bearing his name, and through the Bernard Mizeki Men's Guild. A shrine, erected at the site of his martyrdom, draws a huge crowd for an open-air memorial service each year on the weekend nearest to June 18.

Lizzie Atwater
China — August 15, 1900
Shansi Province in northern China crouches between the Yellow River on the west and a rugged mountain range on the east. Of the 188 foreign missionaries—adults and children—killed in the Boxer Rebellion during its reign of terror at the turn of the century, 159 were killed in this one province alone.

Here the Boxers operated with impunity, with the belligerent blessing of Governor Yü Hsien, a noted Boxer sympathizer. But local officials were often more protective. In July, as mob violence escalated in Taiyuan, the capital city of Shansi Province, a small group of missionaries—seven adults and three children—took refuge in Fenchow, where the magistrate was known to treat foreigners kindly. They hoped for the best . . . but expected the worst. One of the missionaries, Lizzie Atwater, had recently married Ernest Atwater, a widower, who had been left with four young girls. Pregnant with her own child, Lizzie wrote to her sister from Fenchow: "They beheaded thirty-three of us last week in Taiyuan." Two who died in the massacre were her own step-daughters, Ernestine, age ten, and Mary, age eight, who were away at school.

Letter of Life

On August 3, 1900, Lizzie wrote what would be her last letter to her family:

Dear ones, I long for a sight of your dear faces, but I fear we shall not meet on earth. . . . I am preparing for the end very quietly and calmly. The Lord is wonderfully near, and He will not fail me. I was very restless and excited while there seemed a chance of life, but God has taken away that feeling, and now I just pray for grace to meet the terrible end bravely. The pain will soon be over, and oh the sweetness of the welcome above!

My little [unborn] baby will go with me. I think God will give it to me in Heaven, and my dear mother will be so glad to see us. I cannot imagine the Savior's welcome. Oh, that will compensate for all these days of suspense. Dear ones, live near to God and cling less closely to earth. There is no other way by which we can receive that peace from God which passeth understanding. . . . I must keep calm and still these hours. I do not regret coming to China, but am sorry I have done so little. My married life, two precious years, has been so very full of happiness. We will die together, my husband and I.

I used to dread separation. If we escape now it will be a miracle. I send my love to you all, and the dear friends who remember me.

Pretense of Protection

Hearing that several foreign missionaries had managed to survive under the protection of the local magistrate, the devious governor appointed another magistrate to Fenchow, who promptly ordered the foreigners out of the city under armed guard "for their protection." Snuggling her husband's surviving daughters, Celia and Bertha, close to her in the cart, Lizzie gave her letter to a Chinese believer and asked him to see that it got to her family.

On August 15, when the missionaries were well away from the relative safety of a friendly town, the soldiers turned on the missionaries, hacking them to death with their swords and tossing their bodies into a pit. Eleven precious lives, including the unborn infant, spilled their blood into China's soil that day and were reclaimed by heaven.

Seed of the Church
"We do not begrudge them—we gave them to that needy land. China will yet believe the truth."

—Lizzie Atwater's father in Oberlin, Ohio

Don't worry about anything; instead, pray about everything. Tell God what you need, and thank him for all he has done. If you do this, you will experience God's peace, which is far more wonderful than the human mind can understand. His peace will guard your hearts and minds as you live in Christ Jesus (Philippians 4:6-7).

Chang Shen
China—1900

In 1898, young Emperor Kuang Hsu of China was convinced that Christian moral and social reforms were the only hope of saving his chaotic country. But the secret Boxer Society, afraid that the emperor was about to sell out the country to foreign domination, staged a coup and installed his aunt, Tzu Hsi, as empress of China.

The Boxers had legitimate resentments. Foreign money funded the opium trade to millions of addicted Chinese; foreign-built railroads cost many jobs; foreign powers forced China to sign exploitive treaties. But to the Boxers, all foreigners, including Christian missionaries, were responsible for every evil China suffered, including drought and poor crops. They poured lies and distortions into the empress's ear: "Christian missionaries steal Chinese spirits." "Christians gouge out the eyes of our children to use in their medicines." "Foreign blood must be spilled before the gods will send rain."

As the twentieth century dawned, the empress finally issued the edict the Boxers had been waiting for: "By Imperial Command Exterminate the Christian Religion! Death to the Foreign Devils!" The edict unleashed a reign of terror and death known as the Boxer Rebellion. Hundreds of foreign missionaries, Protestant and Catholic and Orthodox, were murdered; others barely escaped with their lives. But Chinese Christians suffered even more. Thirty thousand Chinese Catholics endured mutilation, torture, and death. Two thousand Chinese Protestants suffered the same fate. But each tragedy had its own triumph.

"I Was Blind; Now I See"
His name was Chang Shen, but he was known as *"Wu so pu wei te"* to his fellow villagers in Manchuria: "One without a particle of good in him." His

wife was so fed up with his gambling, thieving, and chasing other women that she took their daughter and left. His failing eyesight soon earned him a new nickname: Blind Chang. "The judgment of the gods," his neighbors clucked.

In 1886, Chang heard about a mission hospital that helped people who had lost their sight. Unable to see, he nonetheless traveled hundreds of miles to get to the hospital—but every bed was taken. Crushed, Chang poured out his story. Moved to pity, the hospital evangelist gave up his own bed. With the help of the mission doctors, Chang's sight was partially restored. But even more, he believed the gospel and joyfully gave his heart to Christ.

"Can I be baptized?" he asked the medical missionary.

"Go home and tell your neighbors that you have changed. I will visit you later and if you are still following Jesus, then I will baptize you."

True to his word, the missionary visited Chang's village five months later—and found hundreds of people eager to hear the gospel after hearing Chang Shen's testimony. By now, nothing could stop Chang from his new calling as a Christian evangelist. Even though his eyesight once again failed, he had nearly memorized the New Testament and much of the Old. He traveled from village to village, preaching to anyone who would listen.

As the Boxer Rebellion spread its tentacles into Manchuria, they were told, "For every Christian you kill, ten will spring up while that man Chang Shen lives. Kill him and you will crush the foreign religion." Hearing that fifty Christians had been rounded up and would be executed if they didn't betray him, Chang boldly strode into the village. "I'll gladly die for them!" he cried.

Three days later he was driven to the local cemetery in an open cart, then forced to kneel. Witnesses heard him cry, "Heavenly Father, receive my spirit!" just before the heavy sword severed his head from his body.

A rumor spread throughout the countryside: "Blind Chang will rise from the dead!" Nervous, the Boxers insisted that the body be burned—then they fled the area. Even in death Chang Shen saved many lives by his powerful witness.

In His Own Words

> *Jesus loves me, he who died,*
> *heaven's gate to open wide;*
> *he will wash away my sin,*
> *Let his little child come in.*
>
> —Song sung by Chang Shen on his way to his execution

God so loved the world that he gave his only Son, so that everyone who believes in him will not perish but have eternal life (John 3:16).

Mitrophan Tsi-Chung
Beijing, China—June 11, 1900

Protestants and Catholics were not the only Christians to suffer during China's infamous Boxer Rebellion. Per capita, Orthodox Christians may have experienced the most martyrdoms. Of the 1,000 believers at the Russian Ecclesiastical Mission in Beijing (then called Peking), 222 died for Christ.

Afterward, Archimandrite Innocent, the senior priest at the mission filed this report:

> The day of reckoning for most Orthodox Chinese was June 11, 1900. On the eve of that day leaflets were posted in the streets, calling for the massacre of the Christians and threatening anyone who would dare to shelter them with certain death. In the middle of the night, gangs of Boxers with flaming torches spread over [Beijing], attacking Christian houses, seizing Christians and forcing them to deny Christ. Some, terrified by torture and death, indeed renounced the faith in exchange for life and burned incense before idols. Others, undaunted, confessed Christ. Their fate was horrible. They were ripped open, beheaded, burned alive. After that day, the search for Christians and killings continued: Christian houses were destroyed; people were brought out of town to where Boxers' temples had been set up; they were interrogated and burned at the stake.

The torture suffered by many was unbelievable. The report says that Ia Wang, a mission schoolteacher suffered martyrdom "twice." First, the Boxers slashed her with swords and then buried her half-dead. A non-Christian neighbor heard her groaning and carried her to his cabin. There the Boxers found her again, and this time they tortured her to death.

In both instances, she refused to throw incense on the censers of the idols that the Boxers brought with them. She would not deny Christ to save her own life.

No Refuge

Mitrophan Tsi-Chung was the first Chinese Orthodox priest. For fifteen years he served God tirelessly. After the Boxers swept through the city and burned the mission, said Archimandrite Innocent, about seventy Christians gathered at Mitrophan's house along with his wife, Tatiana, and two of his three sons: Serge and John. (Isaiah, his oldest son, had been beheaded a couple days earlier.) He welcomed and comforted everyone. At about ten in the evening on June 11, Boxers and soldiers surrounded the house. Mary, Isaiah's grief-stricken bride, was at the house, and she helped several people, including Tatiana, escape over the garden wall. Sadly, Tatiana was captured the next day and executed.

While Mary was helping others escape, the Boxers raided the house and captured her. They pierced her feet and hands in mockery of Christ's crucifixion, encouraging Mary all the while to renounce Christ, leave, and save her life. "I was born here at the church," she said. "I will die here, too." Then they executed her.

In an attempt to get Mitrophan to denounce Christ, the Boxers stood his youngest son, John (only eight) before him and proceeded to slash the boy's shoulders and then hack off his nose, ears, and toes. They taunted him, calling him a "child of demons." But John answered, "I believe in Christ, not in demons. It does not hurt to suffer for Christ."

Finally, unable to get Mitrophan to deny Christ, the Boxers dragged him into his yard and stabbed him to death.

Under military pressure from the occupying forces of Great Britain, Germany, Russia, France, the United States, Japan, Italy, and Austria, Chinese authorities finally agreed to abolish the Boxer Society on February 1, 1901. On September 7, China signed the Peace Protocol of Peking with the allied nations, officially ending the Boxer Rebellion.

Tertullian's comment "The blood of Christians is seed" proved accurate in China. The courage of the martyrs, both Chinese and missionary, inspired a threefold increase in Chinese Christians in the next decade.

James Chalmers and Oliver Tomkins
New Guinea—April 5, 1901

The boy was restless and loved excitement. He seemed to ignore the risks when adventure was afoot. He was an acknowledged leader among his peers, especially when fighting erupted between rival schools. Such a boy can drive a mother to distraction and cause his teachers to shake their heads and predict an early downfall.

But just such a boy (or girl, or man, or woman) God may need to take the gospel into remote areas of the world where danger lurks on every side. And just such a boy was James Chalmers, born to a stonemason's family in Scotland in 1841.

Despite his unruly spirit, James was in Sunday school every week. One Sunday his teacher read a letter from missionary to the Fiji Islands. Fixing the young teens with his eyes, the teacher said: "I wonder if there is a boy here this afternoon who will become a missionary, and by and by bring the gospel to cannibals like these?"

James's spirit rose to the challenge. *Yes,* he said in his heart, *God helping me, I will.*

More rebellious years would pass before James remembered his vow. But at the age of eighteen he heard an evangelist preach on Revelation 22:17: "The Spirit and the bride say, 'Come.' Let each one who hears them say, 'Come.' Let the thirsty ones come—anyone who wants to. Let them come and drink the water of life without charge." Convicted by his many sins, the "wild lad" felt the message was intended for him.

James Chalmers did not wait to go to the cannibals to become a missionary. Right away he began to challenge others to "Come!"—as a Sunday school teacher, working in the slums of Glasgow, and preparing for missionary service at Cheshunt College. As a candidate of the London Missionary Society, James and his new wife, Jane—a suitable mate with the same sense of mission and adventure—set sail on January 4, 1866, for Rarotonga, an island in the South Pacific.

Forever "Tamate"

By the time the Chalmers arrived on Rarotonga, they'd already been shipwrecked and had to finish their journey on a pirate ship with "the bully of the Pacific" for a captain. As the natives of Rarotonga welcomed the party, a greeter called out: "What fellow name belong you?" James called out, "Chalmers!" Misunderstanding the name, the greeter called out, "Tamate!" And Tamate he was called from that point onward.

Rarotonga, it turned out, had already been "Christianized," though the converts needed discipling. Once the work was stable, Tamate turned his restless spirit to the savage tribes of New Guinea. In 1877, instead of going back to Scotland on furlough, he and Jane made their home among the cannibals and called them friends. His fearlessness won their respect; his compassion won their loyalty and friendship. In 1878, tribal warfare and cannibalism were rampant; in 1882, there were "no cannibal ovens, no feasts, no human flesh, no desire for skulls." (Jane Chalmers, however, died in 1879, as did a second wife in 1900. James's response was to "bury my sorrow in work for Christ.")

In April 1901, James and a young missionary named Oliver Tomkins sailed for Goaribari Island to make friends with the wild tribes there. The captain and crew were uneasy about the unruly behavior of the well-armed natives when they met the boat on April 4. But Tamate and Tomkins went ashore early the next day, saying they would "be back by breakfast." But the two men did not return.

Alarmed, the ship's captain pulled anchor and went for help. Later, British investigators learned that the two men had been invited into a feast hall, supposedly in welcome. As they entered, they were clubbed from behind, then beheaded, and their torsos cut up and boiled, providing a "feast" for the islanders.

Seed of the Church

When the cablegram went around the world with the news that James Chalmers had been killed and eaten by cannibals, a colleague wrote: "His name shall kindle many a heart to equal flame." In Sunday schools across the world, teachers told their young charges the story of James Chalmers, many of whom vowed that one day they would take his place.

Let the thirsty ones come . . . and drink the water of life without charge (Revelation 22:17).

Eleanor Chestnut

China—October 28, 1905

Eleanor Chestnut was orphaned soon after her birth in 1868 in Waterloo, Iowa. Nevertheless, the impoverished aunt who raised her helped instill Christ's sacrificial love within her. After graduating from Park College in Missouri, Eleanor went to the Woman's Medical College in Chicago, where she earned her way through medical school by nursing the aged. (She nursed Dr. Oliver Wendell Holmes in his final illness.) However, she had only enough to afford an attic for accommodations and little more than oatmeal for food.

She continued her education at Moody Bible Institute and then volunteered as a medical missionary to China in 1893.

The American Presbyterian Mission Board assigned her to a remote mission station three hundred miles up the Bei Jiang River from Guangzhou. The need for medical services was so great that she lived on no more than $1.50 per month in order to pay for the bricks and mortar needed to build a hospital. While local laborers worked on the building, Dr. Chestnut used her own bathroom to perform essential surgery.

More than the Shirt off Her Back

On one occasion after Dr. Chestnut amputated the leg of an injured laborer, complications arose that required skin grafts in order for the wound to heal. Because the patient no relatives or friends who were willing to serve as donors for the graft, members of the staff wondered the next day how it was that Dr. Chestnut had managed to perform the needed surgery. When one of them noticed that Dr. Chestnut was limping and inquired about her, she answered curtly, "It's nothing."

Finally, a nurse revealed that Dr. Chestnut had taken skin from her own leg to save the life of the patient. On herself she had used only local anesthetic so she could complete the operation on the laborer.

With such a sacrificial heart, Dr. Chestnut traveled tirelessly on horseback to hold clinics in neighboring villages. Back at the mission station where the hospital had finally been completed, she lived without complaint in cramped, uncomfortable quarters on the second floor.

Thinking First of Others

During the Boxer Rebellion of 1900, Dr. Chestnut was one of the last missionaries to flee the region . . . and one of the first to return the following spring.

On October 28, 1905, Dr. Edward Machle—another doctor at the hospital—got into a dispute with some of the Buddhist priests from the adjacent temple over a temporary structure they wanted to build on mission property.

The doctor and the priests soon arrived at an agreement; however, some antiforeign agitators—probably left over from the Boxer Rebellion—stirred the gathered crowd into a mob that attacked the mission station. One of the Buddhist monks urged the missionaries to escape to a nearby grotto for refuge. But only three of the missionaries made it to safety.

When the riot was over, searchers discovered in the burnt rubble of the mission station the bodies of Rev. and Mrs. John Peale, Ella Machle and her ten-year-old daughter, and Dr. Eleanor Chestnut.

Witnesses to the riot claimed that rather than run for safety, Dr. Chestnut had gone back into the melee to use a torn strip of her own dress to bandage the forehead of a boy who had been hit by a flying stone.

Let this mind be in you, which was also in Christ Jesus: Who, being in the form of God, thought it not robbery to be equal with God: But made himself of no reputation, and took upon him the form of a servant, and was made in the likeness of men: And being found in fashion as a man, he humbled himself, and became obedient unto death, even the death of the cross. Wherefore God also hath highly exalted him, and given him a name which is above every name (Philippians 2:5-9, KJV).

John Harper
North Atlantic Ocean—April 15, 1912

Born to a godly Scottish family in 1872, saved at the age of eighteen, John Harper had a burden to tell people the Good News about Jesus. God had showed him in a vision that both "good" people and "bad" people were lost without Christ—indeed, *he* would be lost except for God's great love that had sent his own Son to die on the cross for his sins.

He started out a determined, young, street-corner evangelist, and ended up as pastor of the Paisley Road Baptist Church near Glasgow, which grew from twenty-five people to five hundred in thirteen years. In 1904, he married Annie Bell, and two years later the happy couple looked forward to the birth of their first child. But his utter joy was tested when Annie died in childbirth, leaving him with a motherless baby girl he called Nana.

But John Harper's faith was in God, and he still wanted to share the gospel. In 1910 he accepted a call to become the pastor of the Walworth Baptist Church in London. News of the many people being saved under his ministry spread, and in 1911 he was invited to Moody Church in Chicago to conduct special services. The special services became a revival, and he was invited back the next April of 1912.

Not wanting to leave five-year-old Nana again so soon, John Harper booked passage for himself and his daughter on *Titanic*.

The Titanic's *Last Hero*

John Harper walked around the decks of the massive ship, little Nana's hand tucked securely in his own. He was so glad he'd brought his motherless daughter along with him on his trip to Chicago. He couldn't bear to be parted from her for long. And the maiden voyage of *Titanic* was surely a trip to remember.

"Look, Papa!" Nana cried, pointing to the sunset. "The sky is so red!"

Harper grinned. "'Red sky at night, sailors delight,'" he teased. "It's going to be beautiful in the morning. But now . . . it's your bedtime!"

But during the night Harper sat up, startled, as the whole ship seemed to shudder. Then he heard urgent voices: "Everybody out! Everybody out!" He woke his little sleepyhead, bundled her in warm clothes, and carried her up on deck. People were starting to panic as word spread: an iceberg had torn a hole in the side of the ship!

Lifejackets were handed out. Harper put one on little Nana, then swung her into a lifeboat as people pushed and shoved. "Let the women and children and the unsaved into the boats!" Harper shouted, as he turned back to help others.

He spotted a man without a lifejacket. "Are you saved?" he asked. The man looked at him angrily and pushed him aside. "Here," Harper said, taking off his jacket. "You need this more than I do."

As the dark waters of the Atlantic crept higher and higher up the decks of the sinking ship, John Harper's voice could be heard again and again: "Brother . . . sister, are you saved? It's not too late! Ask God to forgive your sins and accept Jesus as your Lord and Savior. Be sure where you will spend eternity!"

At 2:20 A.M. of April 15, the stern of the great ship rose high in the air, then began its long, slow plunge toward the ocean bottom as people jumped or were thrown into the sea. As Harper struggled in the icy water, he saw a man float by clinging to a board. "Are you saved, brother?" he called. "No," the man gasped.

"Then believe on the Lord Jesus Christ, and you will be saved!"

The icy waters were taking their toll, and John Harper slipped beneath the surface. The man clinging to the board was later picked up by a rescue ship. Harper's words burned in his mind until, at last, he gave his life to Jesus. He was John Harper's last convert.

In His Own Words

"Are you saved? Believe on the Lord Jesus Christ, and you shall be saved!"

—John Harper's last words before he sank beneath the icy waters of the Atlantic

---

I command you to love each other in the same way that I love you. And here is how to measure it—the greatest love is shown when people lay down their lives for their friends (John 15:12-13).

Lottie Moon

China — December 24, 1912

She stood only four feet three inches, but Lottie Moon, Southern Baptist missionary to China for forty years, had stamina, a lively spirit, vision, and a passion to win souls for God. A spitfire of a girl, born to a wealthy family on a Virginia tobacco plantation in 1840, she rebelled against her Southern Baptist upbringing until a revival broke out at Albemarle Female Institute where she was studying to become a teacher. "I went to the service to scoff," she admitted, "and returned to my room to pray all night."

Opportunities for educated women were limited in the late 1800s, both in the South and on foreign mission fields. But hearing a pastor preach on the text "Lift up your eyes, and look on the fields; for they are white already to harvest" (John 4:35, KJV), Lottie resigned as associate principal of a girls' school she had founded in Georgia and headed for China in 1873.

Raised in a family "of culture and means," Lottie at first thought of the Chinese as an inferior people and insisted on wearing American clothes to maintain a degree of distance from these "heathen" people. But gradually she came to realize that the more she shed her Westernized trappings and identified with the Chinese people, the more their simple curiosity about foreigners (and sometimes rejection) turned into genuine interest in the gospel. She began wearing Chinese clothes, adopted Chinese customs, learned to be sensitive to Chinese traditions, and came to respect and admire Chinese culture and learning. In turn she was deeply loved and revered by the Chinese people.

Lottie began her tenure as a missionary by teaching in a girls school—but while accompanying some of the seasoned married women on "country visits" from village to village outside the bigger cities, she discovered her passion: direct evangelism. But there were so many hungry, lost souls, and so few missionaries!

She wrote constant letters and articles back home, encouraging Southern Baptist women to organize mission societies in the local churches to promote missions and collect funds to support missionaries—and to consider coming themselves. Catching her vision, Southern Baptist women organized Women's Missionary Unions (WMU) and even Sunbeam Bands for grammar-school children. The first Lottie Moon Christmas Offering for China in 1888 collected $3,315.26, enough to send three additional missionaries to assist Lottie.

Martyr to Hunger

The War with Japan (1894), the Boxer Rebellion (1900), and the Nationalist uprising that overthrew the Qing Dynasty in 1911 all profoundly affected mission work. Famine and disease took their toll as well. When Lottie returned from her second furlough in 1904, she agonized over the suffering of the people who were literally starving to death all around her. She pled for more money and more resources, but the mission board was heavily in debt and could send nothing. Even mission salaries were voluntarily cut.

Unknown to her fellow missionaries, Lottie Moon—the Southern belle who was once described as "overindulged and under-disciplined"—shared her own meager money and food with any and everyone around her, severely affecting both her physical and mental health. In 1912, she only weighed fifty pounds. Alarmed, fellow missionaries arranged for her to be sent back home to the United States with a missionary companion, but she died on Christmas Eve on board ship in Kobe Harbor, Japan. Her body was cremated and the remains returned to loved ones in Virginia for burial.

Since her sacrificial death at the age of seventy-two, Lottie Moon has come to personify the missionary spirit for Southern Baptists and many other Christians as well. The annual Lottie Moon Christmas Offering has raised a total of $1.5 billion for missions since 1888, and finances *half* the entire Southern Baptist missions' budget every year.

In Her Own Words
"I pray no missionary will ever be as lonely as I have been."
—Lottie Moon's notation in her bankbook
as she withdrew the last of her savings
to send to famine relief workers

Although you have been forsaken . . . I will make you the everlasting pride and the joy of all generations (Isaiah 60:15, NIV).

Harriet Tubman
New York—March 10, 1913

They called her Minty (short for Araminta) as a child and Moses as an adult for "conducting" over three hundred slaves north to freedom on the Underground Railroad. She had been born to Ben and "Old Rit" (Harriet) Ross in the slave quarters on the Edward Brodas tobacco plantation in the Tidewater Flats of Maryland around 1820. Before she was thirteen, she had shed the pet name of Minty and went by Harriet, after her mother.

That was the year she saw an older slave run for freedom. The overseer gave chase, and mischievous Harriet followed to see what would happen. The runaway tried to hide in a little country store, but the overseer went in after him. The slave was cornered, breathing heavily, while the overseer threatened to whip him then and there. "You, girl!" the angry overseer shouted at Harriet when she appeared in the doorway. "Help me tie this man up."

Harriet didn't move. Realizing she was giving him a chance, the slave darted past Harriet and started to run. In an effort to stop him, the overseer grabbed a two-pound weight and threw it at his prey. But in that same moment, Harriet stepped in the way.

The weight struck her full in the forehead, knocking her backward. She was unconscious for days; then she slipped in and out of a stupor for months. But as Harriet slowly recovered, a constant prayer was on her lips—for her master: "Change his heart, Lord; convert him." The wound finally healed . . . but for the rest of her life Harriet suffered severe headaches and bouts of narcolepsy.

As winter turned to spring, a rumor went around the slave quarters: the master was going to sell Harriet to the next slave trader who came along for her part in letting the slave escape. Rebellion surged in her heart, and her prayer changed. "Lord, if you're never going to change Massa Brodas's heart—then kill him, Lord! Take him out of the way."

Within weeks, Edward Brodas became ill and died even before the new tobacco crop had been planted. Conscience-stricken, Harriet thought she had killed him!

Edward Brodas had promised Harriet's parents their freedom when he died. But his will stated only that none of his slaves could be sold outside Maryland.

Even in the face of this betrayal, Harriet regretted that her master had died without "changing his heart." She often said, "I would give the world full of silver and gold to bring that poor soul back. . . . I would give myself. I would give everything!"

Underground Railroad

In 1844, at the age of about twenty-four, Harriet married a free Negro named John Tubman. When she talked to her husband about running away, he said he would tell her master if she tried it! But Harriet couldn't give up the hope of freedom. She had heard about an "underground railroad" that took slaves to freedom in the northern states. In 1849, she knew the time had come. She traveled only at night, using all the woodlore she knew to make her way north. At each friendly "station," she was told where to go next.

When she arrived in Pennsylvania, the taste of freedom was exhilarating! But instead of sitting back and enjoying freedom for herself, Harriet went back to lead other slaves to freedom, over three hundred during her lifetime without "losing a soul." By 1860, the reward for her capture had reached a staggering forty thousand dollars.

On these journeys, she often lay alone in the forests all night. Her whole soul filled with awe at the mystery of God's presence and thrilled her with such deep emotions that all other cares and fear vanished. Then she would talk with her Maker "as a man speaketh unto his friend," just like Moses of old (Exodus 33:11, KJV). And her childlike petitions received direct answers, beautiful visions that lifted her up above all doubt and anxiety into serene trust and faith.

During the Civil War, the Union Army recruited her as a "nurse" and a spy. But even though she was greatly respected, she never received any of the army pay due her.

After the war, when slavery was finally abolished, Harriet established a home for the sick, poor, and homeless in Auburn, New York, where she finally died in her nineties on March 10, 1913.

In Her Own Words
"I always tole God, I'm gwine to hole stiddy on to you, an' you've got to see me trou."

—Harriet Tubman

Armenian Teenager
Armenia—April 24, 1915

Caught between the Ottoman (Turkish) and Russian empires, Armenians long struggled to retain their national identity. Armenia was one of the first nations to accept Christianity in the fourth century; in the nineteenth century, evangelical missionaries brought renewal and fresh life to the ancient Armenian Church—though missions faced major obstacles both within and without the church. With old traditions threatened, the Church patriarch banned Bibles and other books brought by missionaries. At the same time, laws under the ruling Turkish Muslim government forbade the conversion of a Muslim to Christianity, under punishment of death.

In 1856, these laws were suddenly lifted, and for a few brief years Armenia enjoyed complete religious liberty. Even the secretary to the ruling sultan became a Christian. But the Ottoman Empire was in serious decline, losing all its conquests in Europe and Africa. In order to maintain control of its shrinking territory, the Ottoman government once again cracked down on its ethnic minorities, effectively shutting down the aspirations of Armenians for full political participation.

During the reign of Sultan Abdul Hamid II (1876–1909), systematic massacres of the Armenian population cost an estimated 300,000 lives. But even this was not good enough for a group known as the Young Turks, who seized power in a coup and set up the Committee of Union and Progress (CUP), advocating an exclusively Turkish state. As World War I loomed, the Young Turks found a perfect cover to implement a genocidal program, secretly adopted by CUP and aimed at the Armenian population. Their "justification": some Armenians had joined the Russian army as soon as it crossed the Ottoman frontier. Ethnic "removal" was necessary to suppress "revolutionary Armenians."

First, Armenian soldiers in the Turkish army were disarmed and assigned to labor battalions in order to prevent a coup or backlash; many were then killed. On April 24, 1915, a long list of Armenia's intellectual and business leaders were rounded up and executed. That date set in motion a widespread deportation of the remaining Armenian population. Women, children, and the elderly were driven from their homes with only the clothes they were wearing. Forced to march into the desert and denied food and water, many fell under the scorching sun. Others were attacked and butchered by local bands of Kurds. Some women were simply raped and killed; others were forcibly placed in harems and made to accept Islam—or be killed.

It is estimated that 600,000 died on April 24 alone. By the end of the ruthless massacres and death marches in the desert, one and a half million "Christian Armenians" had died—out of a total population of only two and a half million. In the midst of the slaughter, America's ambassador to the Ottoman empire, Henry Morgenthau, Sr., sent a desperate cable: "A campaign of race extermination is in progress under a pretext of reprisal against rebellion."

"Christ, Always Christ!"

A young Armenian dragged herself into an American relief camp just inside Russian territory and collapsed in relief. A nurse quickly brought her food and water and asked if she was in pain. The teenager shook her head. "But I have learned the meaning of the cross," she murmured. At the nurse's perplexed look, the girl exposed her shoulder. The shape of a cross had been burned deeply into her flesh. Then she told her story.

Rounded up with others in her village and separated from home and family, she was asked to choose: Muhammad or Christ? "Christ, always Christ!" she replied. Seven days in a row she was asked the same question, and her reply was always the same. And each time she answered, part of a cross was burned into her shoulder. Finally she was told that the next day would be her last chance. If she chose Muhammad, she would live; if she chose Christ, she would die. But that night, hearing rumors that Americans were close by, she escaped to safety. "That," she finished, "is how I learned the meaning of the cross."

"If any of you wants to be my follower," [Jesus] told them, "you must . . . shoulder your cross, and follow me. If you try to keep your life for yourself, you will lose it. But if you give up your life for my sake and for the sake of the Good News, you will find true life" (Mark 8:34-35).

Mary Slessor
Nigeria—January 13, 1915

"We don't want you here," snarled the leader of the gang blocking Mary Slessor from escorting the boys and girls to Sunday school at Wishart Church in Dundee, Scotland. "Go on—get out."

"No, I won't," said the twenty-year-old factory worker as she tossed her mane of red hair. "I'm going to teach Sunday school today. Why don't you come with us?"

The bully's eyes narrowed. "I'll make you leave!" he threatened. As he spoke, he pulled a cord from his pocket with a heavy lead weight tied on the end. When Mary didn't move, he began to swing the cord slowly around his head. Still Mary didn't budge. Several of the children screamed as the lead weight swung closer and closer to Mary's head. On the next round, the weight grazed her forehead, but Mary didn't flinch.

"The lassie's got game, boys!" the bully said as he stopped swinging the weight and stepped aside. Then he and his gang followed her into the basement Sunday school room.

Courage to Go ... Even Alone

Mary Slessor was born in Aberdeen, Scotland, in 1848, the daughter of a shoemaker. When David Livingstone died in 1874, his life inspired many—including this courageous Sunday school teacher. Two years later Mary arrived in Calabar (what we know today as southern Nigeria, Africa). She was twenty-seven.

Mary's first assignment was to a mission station along the coast. Uncomfortable with the difference in lifestyle between European missionaries and native peoples, Mary chose to live simply, African-style, enabling her to send her salary back to Scotland to support her family.

But Mary, like David Livingstone, was a pioneer, and she set her face toward the interior of Africa, which had never heard the gospel. Her goal was the Okoyong people. When she arrived, the only trade was in guns, gin, and chains, but Mary encouraged the people to grow more crops to sell—both to give them a better standard of living and to give them less time for drinking and fighting.

Mary also believed that school and the gospel went hand in hand. People had to learn to read so they could read the Bible for themselves. She also challenged pagan customs—such as witchcraft, twin murder, human sacrifice, polygamy, and slavery—that were contrary to the gospel. Her reputation as a peacemaker soon brought chiefs from other villages to seek her advice. In 1892, the British appointed her as official vice-consul (similar to a judge) for the area.

Seed of the Church

Many years later, in a mud house with a thatch roof along the Calabar River in West Africa, Mary received a package from Scotland. With a smile she unwrapped a framed picture of a handsome man with a pretty wife and several small children. "Who is it, Mama?" asked Janie, her adopted African daughter, examining the picture.

So Mary told Janie and her other adopted children about the bully who came to Sunday school. He was now grown up and had a respectable job.

"Look!" cried Janie. "Something's written on the back!"

It said: "To Mary Slessor, in grateful memory of the day that changed my life."

In 1902, after fifteen years among the Okoyong people, eleven young people were baptized, seven of whom were her own adopted children. But Mary was restless. There were still tribes who had never heard the gospel of Jesus Christ! She was due for a furlough in 1904. Instead, in spite of deteriorating health, Mary spent her own time and money to search out a new mission base in order to reach the fierce Aros and Ibibios tribes.

Finally, on January 13, 1915, at the age of sixty-six, she succumbed to fever and dysentery for the last time. But her spirit and influence lived on.

Be strong and courageous! Do not be afraid or discouraged. For the Lord your God is with you wherever you go (Joshua 1:9).

Grand Duchess Elizabeth
Russia—July 18, 1918

On the heels of the World War I, the tsarist regime in Russia—maintaining its grip on power through oppression of its own people but fatally weakened by the war with Germany—was overthrown by revolutionaries seething within its own borders. Rejecting religion as one of the pillars of the old regime, the Bolshevik Party also turned its fury on the Russian Orthodox Church.

Caught in this maelstrom was Grand Duchess Elizabeth, the German-born granddaughter of Queen Victoria of England, who married Grand Duke Sergei Alexandrovich, son of Tsar Alexander II of Russia. Nurtured in the Anglican Church, Elizabeth deeply embraced Orthodoxy after her marriage. In 1905, her husband was assassinated by a terrorist's bomb. A gentle woman with a compassionate heart, Elizabeth visited his murderer, a man named Kaliev, hoping to heal his heart by forgiveness.

The death of her husband was a turning point for Elizabeth. Rejecting the frivolous social life of the court and selling her jewels, she founded the Convent of Mary and Martha in 1909, a sisterhood dedicated to inner service to God *and* active service to one's neighbor in the name of Christ. The convent included a twenty-two-bed hospital, a dispensary, and an orphanage for abandoned children. Elizabeth and her sisters regularly visited Hitrovka, Moscow's notorious slum, to bring medical, material, and spiritual aid to the poor.

As the tide of revolution surged forward, Elizabeth rejected political involvement but would not speak against her family. And in the end, she suffered their fate.

The Assassin's Story

We knew that the fate of the tsar and his family in Ekaterinburg, and of other members of the imperial family in Alapaevsk, had already been decided in Moscow, and were only waiting for the order to carry out the sentence. . . . Upon receiving the news of the execution of the tsar and all his family from Ekaterinburg we immediately put our plan into action. . . . It was the night of the 17th to 18th July 1918. When we were sure the whole town was asleep, we quietly stole though the window into the school building. . . . We entered through the unlocked door into the building where the women were sleeping and woke them up, telling them . . . they were to be taken to a safe place because of the possibility of an armed attack. . . . After that, we went into the room occupied by the men. We told them the same thing as we had to the women. . . .

At last we arrived at the mine. The shaft was not very deep and, as it turned out, had a ledge on one side that was not covered by water. . . . After throwing [Elizabeth] down the shaft, we heard her struggling in the water for some time. We pushed the nun lay-sister Varvara down after her. We again heard the splashing of water and then the two women's voices.

It became clear that, having dragged herself out of the water, the grand duchess had also pulled her lay-sister out. But, having no other alternative, we had to throw in all the men also. . . . After a short time we were able to hear all their voices again. Then I threw in a grenade. It exploded and everything was quiet. But not for long. . . . After a short while we heard talking and a barely audible groan. I threw another grenade. And what do you think—from the ground we heard singing. I was seized with horror. They were singing the prayer: "Lord, save your people!" . . .

It was impossible to leave the deed unfinished. We decided to fill the shaft with dry brushwood and set it alight. Their hymns still rose up through the thick smoke for some time yet.

When the last signs of life beneath the earth had ceased . . . we returned to Alapaevsk by first light and . . . told everyone that the grand dukes had been taken away by unknown persons!

Elizabeth's body was recovered two years later, taken to Palestine, and buried in the Church of St. Mary Magdalene. In 1998, a statue of Elizabeth was included in those of ten twentieth-century martyrs erected in front of Westminster Abbey to commemorate all Christians who have died by persecution worldwide.

Even if you should suffer for what is right, you are blessed. Do not fear what they fear; do not be frightened. But in your hearts set apart Christ as Lord (1 Peter 3:14, NIV).

Mary McLeod Bethune
Florida—November 1, 1920

At the age of nine, Mary Jane could pick 250 pounds of cotton a day. Even though she had been born free on July 10, 1875, the fifteenth child of Sam and Patsy McLeod, life on a cotton plantation in Mayesville, South Carolina, was not that different for the McLeods than it had been during five generations of slavery.

But when a black missionary woman started a school that Mary could attend, she discovered that the main difference between the lot of white people and black people in this life was that white people could read. School became a burning passion.

Within a few years, the teacher recommended her for a scholarship to Scotia Seminary in Concord, North Carolina—a school for the daughters of "freedmen"—where Mary studied literature, Greek, Latin, the Bible, and American democracy. She soaked up knowledge like a thirsty sponge, but she also wanted to give back what she learned. Deciding to become a missionary to her own people back in Africa, she attended Moody Bible Institute in Chicago. But when she graduated and applied to the Presbyterian Mission Board, she was told: "We have no openings for a colored missionary in Africa."

It was the bitterest disappointment of Mary's life. But it was also a turning point. If she couldn't go to Africa, she would teach her people at home in the South. Years later when someone said to her, "What our people need is a few millionaires. Before I die, I'm going to make a million dollars," Mary responded, "I'd rather make a million readers." In her mind was a school where young girls and boys would learn not only useful trades but the arts and sciences and the rights and responsibilities of citizenship. "Greek and a toothbrush!" she'd say and laugh when someone asked her philosophy of education.

After marrying Albertus Bethune, she moved to Daytona, Florida, and started her "school-on-a-shoestring." She determined to build a school to teach the head (classical education), hands (practical education), and heart (spiritual education). In 1904 she started with five little girls . . . and by 1923, her vision had become Bethune-Cookman College.

Anchored in the Lord

Though her girls needed an education, even more they needed to know their worth before God after years—centuries—of living in a society that told them they were inferior.

"For God so loved the world," Mrs. Bethune often read in her rich contralto voice, "that He gave His only begotten Son, that whosoever believeth in Him should not perish, but have everlasting life." She looked up at the eager faces in front of her. "Did you hear that word, 'whosoever'? That whosoever means you! God loves you so much he sent his Son Jesus to die for you. Not just white people. Not just rich people. You!"

Mrs. Bethune was so convinced that true human dignity comes from God, our Creator and Savior, that in 1920 she launched a voter-registration drive in Daytona, Florida. Two nights before the election, while Mrs. Bethune was away, the Ku Klux Klan raided the school, burning a cross on the lawn. Many of the students were terrified.

"Maybe we shouldn't vote tomorrow," said some of the staff the next day when Mary returned. "Those Klansmen mean business!"

214

"That's the very reason we have to vote tomorrow," said Mary. "Tonight we are going to have choir practice in Faith Hall, and I want every light turned on."

"But why? They'll see us!"

"Exactly. Evil deeds love darkness rather than light. We will stand in the light."

When the Klan came again on Monday, November 1, 1920, Mary was standing outside the brightly lit hall with the strains of spirituals floating out into the air.

Lit by their torches, she saw the white-hooded horsemen. She heard the clank of a can and the bump of wooden beams. "This is a warning!" yelled one of the men. "Don't bring your people to vote tomorrow, or we'll burn your school to the ground!"

"Hear that song?" Mary called. It spoke of trust in Jesus. "If you burn this school to the ground, we'll build it up again. If you burn it a second time, we'll just build it again and again and again."

There was some mumbling from the dark, and then the cowardly specters galloped away with their torches. Behind on the lawn, they left some useful timbers and a can of kerosene.

The following day, over one hundred African-Americans voted in Daytona.

Miguel Pro
Mexico—November 23, 1927

The Mexican Revolution began in 1910 in an effort to overthrow the thirty-year dictatorship of Porfirio Díaz, during which power and wealth were concentrated in the hands of a select few. Though colorful figures like Emiliano Zapata and Francisco "Pancho" Villa fought battles in the countryside, it was an elite postrevolutionary congress that wrote the new constitution, one that claimed to redistribute property, but did little to consider the will of the people. In 1925 President Plutarco Elias Calles attempted to establish a national church and eradicate the Catholic Church. He placed all primary education under secular supervision; confiscated the property of all church-affiliated agencies such as schools, hospitals, and charitable institutions; required the registration of all priests—expelling all foreign-born priests—and closed seventy-three convents.

For a country that was 97 percent Catholic, these measures triggered a general strike in 1926. With the knowledge of the pope, the Mexican bishops closed the country's Catholic churches in protest against the government's repressive measures. The crisis escalated as the government announced that any priest who dared to perform the sacraments—communion, baptism, confession, confirmation, and marriage—risked arrest or even execution!

"Viva Cristo Rey!"

Miguel Pro had been born in Mexico on January 13, 1891, into a family of six brothers and sisters. Two of his sisters entered the religious life, and at age twenty, Miguel asked God what his will was for him. Subsequently, he joined the Jesuits at the Hacienda El Llano. However, after the government raided his monastery, Miguel's superiors ordered him and other novices to flee the country. Miguel spent time in the United States, Grenada, and Belgium where he was ordained a priest on August 21, 1925.

In 1926, during the height of the revolution, Father Pro returned to Mexico with the permission of his superiors. Often traveling by bicycle, he evaded the police in any way possible, sometimes disguised himself as a mechanic, a servant, or even a refined gentleman.

Once, according to biographer Ann Ball, as several police cars pursued Pro through the streets of Mexico City while he rode in a taxi, he told the driver to slow down as he rounded a corner. Father Pro rolled out, lit a cigar, and began strolling arm in arm with an attractive young woman. When the police roared by, they paid no attention to the romantic young couple on the sidewalk.

Ball also claims that disguised as a police officer, he slipped into the police headquarters on several occasions to bring the sacraments to prisoners before their executions.

And then in November 1927, government agents accused Father Pro and his brother Humberto of a bombing attempt on former president General Obregon. Even though the authorities knew the brothers were innocent, they were Catholic priests and therefore considered enemies of the corrupt regime, the perfect scapegoats. Without a trial, President Calles condemned the brothers to death.

On November 23, as Father Pro was led from his cell to the execution wall, a man arrived yelling that he had in his hand a stay of execution that would free the brothers, but the authorities—who could hear his announcement—would not admit him. One of the policemen asked Father Pro for his forgiveness, which he freely gave.

Father Pro was granted his last request to kneel and pray. When he rose to his feet, he spread his arms wide in the form of a cross and cried out, "May God have mercy on you! May God bless you! Lord, thou knowest that I am innocent! With all my heart I forgive my enemies!" Then, just before the hail of bullets riddled his body, he shouted, *"Viva Cristo Rey!"* (Long live Christ the King!)

At least ninety thousand Mexicans died before the summer of 1929, when the Mexican government finally relaxed its anticlerical legislation.

Now Jesus was standing before Pilate, the Roman governor. "Are you the King of the Jews?" the governor asked him. Jesus replied, "Yes, it is as you say" (Matthew 27:11).

Manche Masemola
South Africa — February 4, 1928

A statue of a virtually unknown teenage girl from South Africa joins other notable Christians—Dietrich Bonhoeffer, Dr. Martin Luther King Jr., Oscar Romero—in a memorial gracing the entrance to Westminster Abbey, representing the hundreds of thousands of Christian martyrs in the last century from all the major continents.

Her name: Manche Masemola, born around 1913 into the Pedi tribe in Sekkukhuneland, in the Transvaal. The Masemola family lived in Marishane, a small town near Pietersburg. Manche did not go to school but worked with her father and mother, two older brothers, and a younger sister, Mabule, to eke a living from the barren lands "reserved" for her tribe.

In 1919, when Manche was only five or six years old, Father Augustine Moeka, an Anglican priest, established a Christian mission in Marishane by permission of the Pedi chief, who welcomed missionaries from all churches. Manche's parents, however, followed the practices of the traditional animist religion and wanted nothing to do with the Christians. But as she reached her teen years, Manche was curious, and with her cousin, Lucia Masemola, stole away to the mission church to hear Moeka preach.

A Baptism of Blood

A heart-hunger to hear more about the Christian faith drew Manche and her cousin back to the mission again and again in spite of parental disapproval. In October 1927, Manche and Lucia began attending classes twice a week to prepare for baptism.

Manche's parents were upset. They cajoled; they threatened. But the girls continued their classes. Then the threats became real. "Manche's mother said she would force us to leave the church," said cousin Lucia. "She beat Manche every time she returned from church." One day the mother even tried to kill her daughter with a spear. But Manche endured the beatings and continued to prepare for baptism.

Convinced that her daughter had been bewitched by this foreign religion, Mrs. Masemola confiscated Manche's clothes so that she could not leave their hut. After all, it was February, the rainy season. But Manche simply ran away naked and hid in the bush.

When her parents found her on a remote hillside, they called a *sangoma*, or animist doctor, to give her a potion to drive away the evil spirit. Trapped, naked, unable to run, Manche refused to drink the potion. Taking turns, her father beat her, then her mother . . . until finally she drank and collapsed at their feet.

Sixteen-year-old Manche was dead.

The Masemolas buried their daughter on the hillside beside a large granite rock. Within a few days, their youngest daughter, Mabule, became very ill. The parents took her to the nearby mission hospital but it was too late; the girl died.

Now there were two graves side by side on the hillside. In a gesture that hinted at remorse, Mr. Masemola planted euphorbia trees beside their graves. The story of the young teenager who died for her faith before she could be baptized spread through the African Anglican community. In 1935, a small group of Christians made a pilgrimage to her gravesite. From time to time, other groups of Christians would visit her grave. Never punished for their crime, her parents must have been affected by their daughter's commitment to her new faith, even in death—because forty years later, in 1969, Mrs. Masemola became a Christian herself and was baptized.

In 1975, the Traditional Anglican Communion added Manche Masemola's name to the list of martyrs remembered throughout the church year, and hundreds now visit the young teenager's gravesite each August (during the dry season), honoring her single-minded desire to know God.

In Her Own Words
"I shall be baptized with my own blood."
—Manche Masemola, confiding to
Canon Moeka that she Might be killed before finishing
her preparation for baptism

[God said,] "I will give them singleness of heart and put a new spirit within them. I will take away their hearts of stone and give them tender hearts instead, so they will obey my laws and regulations. Then they will truly be my people, and I will be their God" (Ezekiel 11:19-20).

Part 4

Regions Beyond: Twentieth-Century Frontiers

In many ways, World War I interrupted the expansion of "Great Century" missions. Notable missionaries continued to go out—Albert Schweitzer to Africa, E. Stanley Jones to India, Gladys Aylward to China—but according to the Foreign Missionary Conference, the number of volunteers fell from 2,700 in 1920 to 250 in 1928. The Great Depression and World War II further preoccupied the church as well as the rest of society.

A new vision for Christian missions came in the form of a call to reach the small tribes and remote people groups tucked away in inaccessible regions, people cut off from the classic cultures, common trade routes, or literate education. If God was not willing for any to perish, they also needed the Good News. But how could they hear it?

The answers wed pioneering mission work with emerging technology.

- Clarence Jones founded HCJB radio in 1931, broadcasting from Quito, Ecuador, to a handful of listeners in the Andes. Within ten years, HCJB's Christian broadcasting reached around the world, twenty-four hours a day, in many languages. This powerful gospel station was followed by the Far East Broadcasting Company in 1948, Trans World Radio in 1954, and others.
- Joy Ridderhof founded Gospel Recordings in 1939. Using primitive portable recording devices, she found native people in remote tribes who could also speak the common trade language. Using a series of interpreters (English to trade language, trade language to native dialect) she recorded the basic gospel message in these unwritten languages, which could be played back on simple (e.g., hand-cranked) "record players."
- Confounded by the myriad of languages among the Indians in Central and South America, Cameron Townsend founded the Summer Institute of Linguistics in 1934 to train translators, as well as the Wycliffe Bible Translators to raise funds and accomplish the translation of the Scriptures in hundreds of languages.
- In 1945, Betty Greene, a former WASP (Woman's Air Force Service Pilot) became the first pilot for Christian Airmen's Missionary Fellowship, later to be known as Missionary Aviation Fellowship (MAF). She and her fellow pilots could support missionaries in remote areas with a forty-five

minute flight that would otherwise require a two-week trek through the jungle. Starting in 1948, similar support for Wycliffe Bible Translators was provided by Jungle Aviation and Radio Service (JAARS).

Such specialized efforts supported missions focused on the third world: New Tribes Missions, Artic Missions, Orinoco River Mission, Mission to Unreached Peoples, Latin American Mission, South American Indian Mission, Andes Evangelical Mission, and several others. Even in the States, "forgotten" people in remote logging towns were reached by Village Missions as well as the much older American Sunday School Union.

But once again, when the gospel encountered pagan and often hostile cultures, there was risk of persecution and in some cases martyrdom.

Bearing the Cross

In 1943, New Tribes Mission was launched in martyrdom as five of its founders—Dave Bacon, Cecile Dye, George Hosback, Bob Dye, and Eldon Hunter—marched off into a Bolivian jungle in 1943 to take the gospel to tribespeople who had long suffered inhuman abuse from traders, rubber hunters, and white adventurers. They never returned. In 1958, Cornelius Isaak, a Mennonite missionary, was speared to death attempting to reach the same tribe. In years since, NTM lost Mark Rich, Dave Mankins, and Rick Tenenoff from Panama; Tim Van Dyke and Steve Welsh in Colombia; and Martin Burnham in the Philippines.

Perhaps the martyrdom that most rocked the twentieth century was the massacre of Jim Elliot, Pete Fleming, Nate Saint, Roger Youderian, and Ed McCully in the jungles of Ecuador in 1956 by the Waorani ("Auca") Indians they were trying to reach. A joint effort by Wycliffe missionaries and MAF pilot Nate Saint, their loss was discovered by radio only hours after it occurred, and within a week, a *Life* magazine photographer arrived on the scene to report the event to a watching world. However, far from setting missions back, thousands of young people in Bible schools, Christian colleges, and seminaries stepped forward upon hearing this news to offer themselves as replacements for these courageous Christians.

The Reformation Feud Revisited

In Latin America, Roman Catholic opposition to Protestant missions had always been stiff. During the Mexican Revolution, liberals and Protestants who had suffered severely under the Diaz regime took out their fury on the property of the Catholic Church. Once the revolution was over, however, the Catholic hierarchy consolidated its power and issued a pastoral letter in 1944 to all priests, urging them to oppose "the Protestant campaign." While foreign missionaries were not martyred at this time, James and Marti Hefley claim in their book, *By Their Blood*, "Scores, perhaps hundreds, of evangelical pastors, evangelists, and lay leaders were murdered by Catholic fanatics."[1]

Even worse attacks took place in Colombia where the bishops ordered a letter read in every Catholic Church calling Protestants "false prophets" and "devouring wolves" and praising "Our Lady . . . who has always killed off all heresies."[2] Soon a Colombian priest published a book justifying the Spanish Inquisition and the St. Bartholomew's Day Massacre and encouraging "the final extirpation of Protestantism from our midst."[3]

The Hefleys go on to say, "From 1944 to 1958, 120 evangelicals or members of evangelical families were killed. . . . Eighty-five Protestant churches and chapels were destroyed by fire or dynamite. An additional 183 houses of worship and 206 Protestant primary schools were closed by official orders. Over fifteen thousand evangelicals were driven from their homes."[4] Specific, documented events in both Mexico and Colombia demonstrate a barbarity that had seldom been seen since the Inquisition. These events did not occur as a direct result of missionaries encountering wild tribal people who attacked them, even though missionaries did evangelize many previously unreached tribes in Latin America. Instead, persecution arose primarily from interfaith rivalry as Protestant missionaries evangelized vast numbers of *virtually* unreached people, that is, nominally Catholic, who knew almost nothing at that time of the gospel.

Modern Dangers

While missionary aviation shortened travel time and saved many lives by providing medicine and evacuation, it was not always safe. Most missionary pilots were highly trained and capable of navigation and flight under the most extreme conditions. But mechanical failures, unpredictable weather, and errors were inevitable. For instance,

* In 1955, pilot Al Lewis was killed instantly when his plane crashed into a mountain in New Guinea while he was trying to support C&MA missionaries Jerry and Darlene Rose.
* Jungle Aviation and Radio Service had flown thousands of hours over a twenty-five year span without one fatal accident until 1972, when a Piper Aztec, piloted by Doug Hunt, lost its right engine and crashed in Papua New Guinea, killing all seven persons aboard.
* Missionary pilots Job Orellana and Daniel Osterhus died instantly in 1997 when their Cessna 185 plane slammed into a ninety-five-hundred-foot mountain in Ecuador.
* Among the dozens of missionary aviation programs, a total of fifteen missionary planes crashed in 2000, resulting in sixteen deaths and six serious injuries.

Occasionally, missionary pilots doing relief or rescue work in regions near revolutions or war have encountered hostile gunfire. Though Missionary Aviation Fellowship operates more than seventy aircraft in remote regions of twenty-four countries, only six MAF planes have ever been hit by gunfire, and none of those crashed. However, other pilots have not been so fortunate. Perhaps one of the most bizarre and tragic incidents occurred on April 20, 2001.

Experienced pilot Kevin Donaldson was ferrying Jim and Roni Bowers and their two children, Cory and baby Charity, from Leticia on the border of Peru to their home in Iquitos, Peru, where they served as riverboat missionaries on the Amazon with the Association of Baptists for World Evangelism. An American CIA-operated reconnaissance plane watching for drug smugglers did not recognize the small Cessna 185 float plane that seemed to be coming from Brazil. Within minutes a Peruvian Air Force jet fighter—guided by an American reconnaissance plane—intercepted and shot down the missionaries' plane, killing Roni and Charity and severely wounding the pilot, Kevin Donaldson.

Specialty Missions and the Future

Perhaps the efforts to reach the "regions beyond" that spawned specialty missions such as aviation, communications (either print or radio), translation and literacy, medical and relief efforts provided a model for the next generations of missions. As nationalism expelled anyone identified (rightly or wrongly) with colonialism, and as Islam and other religions hostile to Christianity became more militant, evangelism and church planting needed to come under the control of indigenous leaders. But today, as never before, there is an open door for Christian service and the missionary support skills learned in the last half of the twentieth century.

Notes

1. James and Marti Hefley, *By Their Blood* (Grand Rapids: Baker, 1979, 1996), 562.
2. Ibid., 624.
3. Ibid.
4. Ibid., 625.

The Witnesses

Barbrooke Grubb

Paraguay—May 28, 1930

Ultimately heralded as the "Livingstone of South America," Barbrooke Grubb was born on August 11, 1865, at Liberton in Midlothian, Scotland. As a boy, he delighted in wrestling and feats of strength and was filled with mischief. He completed his education at George Watson's College in Edinburgh, where he studied primitive peoples.

In 1884 he met Dwight Moody and Ira Sankey, the dynamic evangelists from the United States, and ended up devoting his life to missions. On his nineteenth birthday, Grubb decided to join the South American Missionary Society and two years later went to the Falkland Islands, where he spent four years. But he always felt called to the Indian tribes of the northern interior of South America.

Nothing pleased him more than his assignment in 1890 to the unexplored interior of Paraguay, known as the Chaco, and the wild tribes of Indians who lived there. Initially, Grubb employed the unusual (at that time) tactic of going right into the interior, first to explore the territory and make friends, and then to live right with the Indians rather than build a large station on the perimeter of the field to which the Indians came. Though later he did set up mission stations, they were in the heart of the Chaco and designed for the sake of the Lengua people rather than the convenience of the missionaries. At these stations, the Indians learned better agricultural techniques, industry, and the gospel.

Some of his greatest challenges came from the oppressive superstitions among the Lenguas promoted by witch doctors, who lived off their fears. Grubb readily confronted the witch doctors, studying their mysteries and learning secrets otherwise hidden from all those outside their guild. With this knowledge he contemptuously exposed them publicly, a tactic he concluded was the most effective way to undermine their power among the people.

Attacked in the Swamp

Every aspect of life in the Chaco was threatening, from the heat that frequently exceeded 110 degrees in the shade to the drought in the dry season and floods in the rainy season. Jaguars, poisonous snakes, and fifteen-foot alligators waited in the swamps. One day the adventurous Grubb killed an attacking alligator by ramming a sharpened pole into its mouth and than hammering it home with an axe.

But it was an attack from a two-legged "friend" that came closest to taking his life.

Grubb arranged for Poit, an Indian from a western village, to keep some cattle while Grub returned to England on furlough. The idea was to show the villagers how agriculture could free them from dependency on the fickle fortunes of hunting and gathering.

When Grubb was gone, however, Poit slaughtered several of the cows and threw feasts to impress his friends. When Grubb returned—which Poit had not expected would happen—Poit feared having to account for the missing cattle. On their way to Poit's village, Poit shot Grubb in the back with an arrow with a seven-inch iron tip.

Poit fled, first reporting that a jaguar had attacked them both, and only he had escaped alive. Then he amended his story to say that while trying to shoot the jaguar, he had accidentally missed and hit Grubb.

In the meantime, Grubb wedged the arrow that threatened to pierce his lungs into the fork of a sapling and pulled it out. He then crawled miles through the swamp and brush until he collapsed on a trail where another Indian found him. He then survived a hundred-mile trek through searing heat to the mission station where he finally recovered.

Seed of the Church

The mission to the Lenguas started in 1890 was fully established by 1910, and Grubb was already working with the Toothli and Suhin tribes of the west and the Sanapana in the north. He then moved to Argentina and Bolivia and established a strong mission among the Matacos and a prosperous beginning among the people of the Pilcomayo. He also worked among the Tobas and converted many of the Tapui Indians of Bolivia. Grubb accomplished all this before he died on May 28, 1930.

> Since we are surrounded by such a huge crowd of witnesses to the life of faith, let us strip off every weight that slows us down, especially the sin that so easily hinders our progress. And let us run with endurance the race that God has set before us (Hebrews 12:1).

Jack Vinson

China—1931

After the fierce but short-lived Boxer Rebellion in 1900, and with the rise of President Chiang Kai-shek and his Nationalist government, missionaries poured back into China. Many dedicated their lives to China, inspired by those who had courageously faced death for the sake of the gospel.

But China could not be called a peaceful country—or safe. The Communists resisted Chiang Kai-shek's Nationalist government and continued to direct hostility at missionaries, churches, and Chinese believers. Plagues and famines decimated the countryside, which got blamed on foreigners and their "foreign god." Muslim rebellions sprang up. And if political civil war and harsh conditions weren't enough, there were always bandits.

In 1931, Rev. John Vinson, a Southern Presbyterian missionary in Kiangsu Province, had already survived the loss of his dear wife and a recent operation. The younger missionaries—who affectionately called him "Uncle Jack"—tried to get him to slow down and stay put in Haizhou, but he was eager to visit various villages in the country and encourage the Christians there. "I must witness for the Lord while I can."

In the marketplace of one of the small rural towns, he was joyfully greeted by the Christian believers, some of whom he had baptized. During the night, which he spent in the town's small church, a swarm of bandits raided the town, terrorizing the people, burning, looting, and killing anyone who resisted. Before leaving they rounded up 150 hostages, including Reverend Vinson, for whose release they expected the largest ransom.

Immediately the Nationalist Army pursued the bandits and surrounded them in another small village. The bandit chief was shrewd. "Write a letter to the army's commanding officer persuading them to withdraw," he told Vinson, "and we'll let you go free."

"Will you also free these other prisoners?" Vinson asked.

The bandit looked at him ludicrously. "Of course not!"

"Then I, too, refuse to go free," said the missionary.

Angry that Vinson wouldn't cooperate, the bandits tried to shoot their way out that night. In the confusion, 125 of the captives managed to escape, while many of the bandits were killed. But the bandit chief still had his prize hostage.

But Vinson, still recovering from an operation, couldn't keep up with the fleeing bandits, even though his captor threatened him with a gun. "I'm going to kill you," screamed the man. "Aren't you afraid?"

"No." Jack Vinson was calm. "If you kill me I will go right to God."

In fury, the bandit shot Vinson, then grabbed a sword and beheaded him.

Afraid? Of What?

A fellow Southern Presbyterian missionary, E. H. Hamilton, was also traveling from village to village in Kiangsu Province when he heard the tragic news. As witnesses told how Jack Vinson had refused to save himself unless all could be saved, Hamilton's feelings erupted into a poem that spoke to the hearts of all missionaries in China, the last verse of which reads:

> *Afraid? Of what?*
> *To do by death what life could not—*
> *Baptize with blood a stony plot,*
> *Till souls shall blossom from the spot?*
> *Afraid—of that?*

Johan and Susanna Kroeker
Siberia—post-1932

They arrived by ship in Bombay, India, on December 9, 1900—two of the first General Conference Mennonite Church overseas missionaries. Johan and Susanna Kroeker and P. A. and Elizabeth Penner, both newly married, went through customs quickly because they had almost nothing with them. The two couples formed a close bond as they struggled to learn the Hindi language and the strange customs of their new country. Johan and P. A. took "seven, long tedious trips" surveying the state of Madhya Pradesh for a good place to establish a mission, while their brides kept each other company. The Penners finally settled in Champa, and the Kroekers in Janjgir, seven miles away. Johan and P. A. often preached together in the local markets. Their focus: to establish a church and work with orphans. By 1903, the Kroekers had seventeen orphans living with them.

Johan Kroeker, a big man with a long bushy beard, looked intimidating, but he soon won coworkers and the Indian people alike with his gentle spirit. Children were born, and the two families spent many Sunday afternoons together, the two men giving each other haircuts as their wives drew encouragement from one another.

But the Indian climate took its toll. P. A. buried his wife and a daughter. Johan suffered many bouts of eczema, which became so debilitating that in 1909, he and Susanna and their five children who had been born in India returned to their native Russia.

Resigning from the mission board, the Kroekers disappeared from the pages of Mennonite history . . . until recently.

"Plead My Case"

In 2000, as the centennial of "overseas missions" in the General Conference Mennonite Church drew near, Canadian historians wanted to highlight these "first" missionaries. Plenty was known about the Penners and their descendents. But whatever happened to the Kroekers when they returned to Russia? In the search for information, the Commission on Overseas Mission made several amazing discoveries: the sole surviving daughter of the Kroekers, age ninety, lived in Germany; and a grandson of Johan and Susanna was living right there in Manitoba—and he had his grandparents' photo album and a diary kept by Susanna Kroeker, written in gothic German script.

As the diary was translated, the faithful journey of Johan and Susanna was revealed. After returning to Russia, they settled in Pavlodar, Siberia (now Kazakhstan), where Johan preached, delivered babies (three more of his own), and was the local dentist. But life was dogged by hardship. In 1921, three of the Kroeker children died by accident and illness within eight days. As the Bolshevik Revolution gained momentum, the family kept trying to immigrate to the United States. To raise the needed money, Susanna sold her dentures for 35 rubles, Johan sold his books, and their oldest daughter took in sewing.

The last entry referring to emigration was dated 1925: "There has come good news from America."

But the Kroekers never made it to America. To escape the Revolution, they headed for northeastern Russia and tried to cross the frozen Amur River into China, along with other Mennonite refugees. But for reasons unknown, their guide—a fellow Mennonite whom they thought they could trust—notified the authorities, and they were arrested.

Susanna was sent to a collective farm to work; Johan was sent to a Siberian prison. A letter smuggled out of the prison in 1932 brought words of encouragement and faith from a loving husband and father, even though his health had been "shattered by malnutrition." Susanna—who later died of starvation herself—never saw Johan again.

In Their Own Words

"Dear children, honor your mother and help her in her old age without murmuring. . . . Ingratitude is the world's reward as you too will experience, but in spite of that, do not be weary of well-doing. There is a God and a Savior and the Holy Spirit. . . . Hold fast to your faith and we will be united after this short life on earth is done."

—From the last letter of Johan Kroeker to his wife
and children from a Siberian prison

"Plead my cause and give me judgment against an impious race; save me from malignant men and liars, O God. . . . How deep am I sunk in misery, groaning in my distress; yet I will wait for God" (From Psalm 43, quoted in Johan's letter).

John and Betty Stam
China—December 8, 1934

When John Stam finally learned that he had been accepted by China Inland Mission (CIM) and would sail for China on the *Empress of Japan* in late summer of 1932, he wrote Betty Scott the letter he had written a thousand times in his mind: "Would you marry me so together we can serve God as husband- and-wife in China?" He had met the girl of his dreams two years earlier at Moody Bible Institute in Chicago but had forestalled proposing to her until God confirmed that he wanted them both to serve on the same mission field.

Betty, the daughter of missionaries still in China, was a year ahead of John in school and had returned to China herself with CIM the year before. She welcomed him at the dock.

After their wedding and a short honeymoon, the couple spent a year in language study under the tutelage of a veteran missionary couple and then was assigned to the city of Tsingteh in the southeast corner of Anhwei Province. It was scary to be in such a remote place, especially when, on September 11, 1934, their daughter, Helen Priscilla Stam, was born. But in spite of rumors of communist aggression, in spite of the fact that twenty-seven Protestant missionaries had been killed in China in the past ten years (1924–1934), in spite of isolation (no cars, no telephones), John wrote to his parents, "We do praise the Lord for the privilege of being here." And on December 5, 1934: "Things are always happening otherwise than one expects . . . [but] the Lord helps us to be quite satisfied, whatever He sends our way."

The Knock at the Door

Two days later, loud knocking interrupted the Stams' early morning bath time. Betty heard her husband go to the door, followed by a babble of high-pitched voices in Chinese as their neighbors said, "Hide! Hide! Communist soldiers . . . they've captured the city. All means of escape have been cut off."

Clutching their baby to her chest, Betty said, "We must pray—it is our only hope." But while they were praying, soldiers in the uniforms of the Red Army burst into the house demanding money and jewelry. When the Stams couldn't satisfy their demands, the soldiers allowed John to write a letter to China Inland Mission with a demand for twenty thousand dollars in ransom. The letter was dated December 6, 1934, and ended with the words, "As for us, may God be glorified whether by life or by death."

As the soldiers marched the Stams out of town, John smiled and called to a local postmaster, "I don't know where they're going, but we're going to heaven!"

The second night of the Stams' captivity, the Communists locked the missionary family in a bedroom of the abandoned house of a rich man. At dawn the next morning, the soldiers rousted John and Betty out of the house, ordering them to leave the baby behind. With a last tender look, Betty left little Helen bundled in the middle of the big bed.

On a hillside outside of town, John was pushed to his knees; a sword flashed. Betty fell to her knees beside him. The sword again whistled through the air.

Seed of the Church

That night when the Red Army pulled out of town, a small group of frightened Chinese Christians crept back into town. Finally, drawn by the sounds of an infant crying, they found little Helen, safe on the bed where her mother had left her. In a bag beside her was evidence of a mother's loving care: a clean gown, several clean diapers, and two five-dollar bills pinned to the clothes.

Using the money Betty left behind, Helen Priscilla Stam was smuggled out of communist territory and taken to a hospital, where she was pronounced in perfect health, then delivered safely to her missionary grandparents, Dr. and Mrs. C. E. Scott.

Hearing about the martyrdom of John and Betty Stam during a memorial service at Moody Bible Institute, seven hundred young people stood to their feet to dedicate their lives to missionary service.

I trust in God, so why should I be afraid? What can mere mortals do to me? (Psalm 56:11).

Mitsuo Fuchida

Japan—December 7, 1941

As 360 Japanese fighter planes mounted into the early dawn, Captain Mitsuo Fuchida tried to control his rising excitement. He was born for this day. He would lead the surprise attack on Pearl Harbor, Hawaii. His objective: to cripple the American naval force in the Pacific. He gave little thought to the possible consequences of pitting Japan against the United States—only that striking a blow for Japan against the Americans satisfied a deep hatred within him. Hadn't Asian immigrants to America been harshly treated? taken advantage of? Whatever happened this day, the Americans deserved it.

At 7:49 A.M., Fuchida picked up his radio mike. "All squadrons . . . attack!" The torpedo planes, dive bombers, and fighters dropped from the sky. For the next few hours, death and destruction rained from the sky, filling the harbor with explosions and twisted metal, raging fires and smoke, sinking ships and leaking fuel, the cries of the wounded and dying, and youthful bodies sinking beneath the dark water.

Finally, Mitsuo Fuchida picked up his mike for one last call: *Tora! Tora! Tora!* ("Tiger! Tiger! Tiger!"), the code to his superiors for "Success!" His chest went out when he heard the American president call it "a day that will live in infamy!"

As the most experienced pilot in the Japanese Navy, Fuchida saw action in the Solomon Islands, Java, and the Indian Ocean. But a severe bout of appendicitis took him out of action just before the Battle of Midway. Japan's defeat that day only fueled his determination to seek "revenge" on America. He attended a military conference in Hiroshima but was recalled to Tokyo—the day before America dropped its atom bomb. When Fuchida saw the devastation, he knew the inevitable: Japan would surrender.

After the war, the Japanese military was disbanded. Captain Mitsuo Fuchida returned to his rural village—but his bitter arrogance drove him on a new mission: to collect evidence on how Americans had treated their Japanese prisoners of war.

A Second "Day to Remember"

As Japanese POWs returned, Fuchida interviewed each one. To his discomfort, a strange story began to emerge as prisoner after prisoner told him about an American woman who had come to the camps bringing blankets, clothing, food, and doing many acts of kindness. Stranger still was the reason she gave when asked why. The Japanese army, she told them, had killed her missionary parents in the Philippines. "I knew what their last prayer had been before they were executed," she said, "and because of that prayer I knew I needed to befriend any Japanese person in need."

What prayer? How could she know what her parents' last prayer had been? Fuchida was puzzled and strangely driven to discover what could make this woman act this way. As he got off the train one day in Tokyo's Shibuya Station, someone handed him a tract, "I Was a Prisoner of Japan," written by an American named Jacob DeShazer. This man, too, claimed he had become a Christian from reading the Bible in prison, and God had taken away his hatred for his former enemies. The Bible . . . maybe that would have the answers to these strange testimonies.

Obtaining a New Testament, Fuchida began reading the life of Jesus. Matthew, Mark, Luke . . . and suddenly there was his answer to the mysterious prayer. As Jesus was being cruelly tortured and killed by his enemies, he prayed, "Father! Forgive them! They don't know what they're doing!" So *that* was the prayer Christians prayed. Suddenly he felt the conviction of his sins. Jesus' prayer meant, "Father, forgive Mitsuo Fuchida, too."

That day, April 18, 1950, became the second "day to remember" in Fuchida's life.

Seed of the Church

I would give anything to retract my actions . . . at Pearl Harbor, but it is impossible. Instead, I now work at striking the death-blow to the basic hatred which infests the human heart and causes such tragedies. And that hatred cannot be uprooted without assistance from Jesus Christ.

—Mitsuo Fuchida, commander of the attack on Pearl Harbor

Jesus said, "Father, forgive them, for they do not know what they are doing" (Luke 23:34, NIV).

Maximilian Kolbe
Poland—August 14, 1941

He was born Raymond Kolbe on January 8, 1894, into a devoted Catholic family in Russian-occupied Poland. His father, Julius, was a weaver by trade, but later enlisted in Pilsudski's army to fight for Poland's independence. When Julius was hanged by the Russians in 1914 as a traitor, his wife, Marianne Kolbe, entered religious life as a Benedictine nun.

Raymond burned with the same patriotic zeal as his father. He was fascinated by the military and excelled at mathematics and physics, but a vision he

230

had at age twelve shaped the course of his life. He said of the vision, "I asked the Mother of God what was to become of me. Then she came to me holding two crowns, one white, the other red. She asked if I was willing to accept either of these crowns. The white one meant that I should persevere in purity, and the red that I should become a martyr. I said that I would accept them both."

Raymond became a novice in the Conventual Franciscan Order at age sixteen, taking a new name—Maximilian—along with the habit. He was ordained a Franciscan priest in Rome in 1918, and eventually earned his doctorate in theology.

During this time, Maximilian contracted tuberculosis. Though he recovered, he struggled with weak health the rest of his life. But Maximilian's active mind and heart burned with spiritual energy. In between medical leaves to treat his tuberculosis, he began publishing a magazine, *Knight of the Immaculate*, for the purpose of "fighting apathy" and "illuminating the truth." At its peak, the magazine had a circulation of 750,000 copies a month. Later he also began printing a Catholic daily newspaper, *The Little Daily*, which had a weekday press run of 137,000 with 225,000 on Sundays.

In 1927, he established the "City of the Immaculate" monastery in Niepokalanow. Within ten years, the monastery became one of the largest self-supporting friaries in the world, with almost 800 inhabitants. While his monastery was growing, Maximilian traveled to Japan, where he began to publish *Knight of the Immaculate* in Japanese, and established a second monastery in Nagasaki, which survived the nuclear bombing and has been a center for Franciscan work in Japan to this day.

When the Nazis invaded Poland in 1939, Maximilian—who had returned from Japan because of poor health—was arrested, along with several brothers, by the Gestapo. Freed after a few months, Maximilian turned the monastery into a home for three thousand refugees, two-thirds of whom were Jews, and spoke out against Nazism through his press. He was rewarded by arrest and confinement in Pawiak prison in Warsaw on February 17, 1941.

Number 16670

In May, Maximilian Kolbe was transferred to Auschwitz and branded with the number 16670. "Courage, my sons," he told his fellow brothers and priests, "don't you see that we are leaving on a mission? They pay our fare in the bargain. What a piece of good luck! The thing to do now is to pray well in order to win as many souls as possible."

On the last day of July 1941, the camp siren announced an escape from block 14A. At evening roll-call, Camp Commandant "Butcher" Fritzsch called the names of ten prisoners at random to die in retribution. As the name of a Sergeant Francis Gajowniczek was called, the man cried out, "My wife! My children! I shall never see them again!"

At that moment, Maximilian Kolbe stepped forward. "I wish to die for that man. I am old." (He was forty-seven.) "He has a wife and children." Fritzsch shrugged. He didn't care who died. Maximilian marched with the other nine doomed men to cell 18, where they were left to starve to death. An SS guard testified later that he could hear "Father Max" encouraging the others with songs and prayers until he was too weak to speak.

Sgt. Gajowniczek survived the war and returned to his wife and family. In 1971, Gajowniczek attended the beatification ceremony of the man who gave up his life for him—Saint Maximilian. Gajowniczek died of old age in 1995.

In His Own Words

"The real conflict is the inner conflict. Beyond armies of occupation and the hecatombs of extermination camps, there are two irreconcilable enemies in the depth of every soul: good and evil, sin and love. And what use are the victories on the battlefield if we ourselves are defeated in our innermost personal selves?"

—Maximilian Kolbe

Do not be overcome by evil, but overcome evil with good. (Romans 12:21, NIV).

Jacob DeShazer

Japan—April 18, 1942

Sergeant Jacob "Jake" DeShazer was on KP duty December 7, 1941, when he heard the news that stunned the world: a sneak attack by Japanese bombers had destroyed the entire United States navy fleet stationed at Pearl Harbor, Hawaii. Hurling a potato at the kitchen wall, DeShazer screamed, "Jap, just wait and see what we'll do to you!"

A month later, when Lt. Col. Jimmie Doolittle wanted volunteers for a secret—and dangerous—mission against the Japanese, DeShazer was among the first to step forward. And on April 18, 1942, Doolittle's Raiders took off in sixteen B-25s from the deck of the USS *Hornet*. No sooner had the B-25s cleared the deck than the *Hornet* and its support ships changed course. In 1942, aircraft carriers could launch planes but not land them again. Doolittle's Raiders were on their own.

Bombardier Jake DeShazer felt elated as he sent his payload hurtling out of the sky on Tokyo and other cities on Japan's mainland. But when the fuel tanks ran dry on two of the B-25s, the crews had to bail out, hoping for friendly rescuers.

They were anything but. Eight out of eighty of Doolittle's Raiders became prisoners of the Japanese. Two pilots and a gunner were executed; the remaining five were interrogated, beaten, fed potato peel soup, and kept in isolated cells 5 feet by 8 feet with no books, no pen and paper, no human companionship. DeShazer's body shivered in winter and poured sweat in summer. For forty long months—thirty-four of those in solitary confinement—DeShazer's body weakened; at times he thought he might go crazy. But his bitter hatred of the Japanese remained robustly healthy. He wanted revenge.

The Best Revenge

After twenty-five months in confinement, the American POWs were finally given a Bible. As the lowest ranking prisoner, DeShazer had to wait until the other officers were done; then he had three weeks to devour the precious words. He had a praying mother; he'd often heard that "Jesus was the answer." What did that mean?

He found out. After reading through the Bible not once, but again and again, DeShazer was amazed at God's faithfulness to his people; at the Old Testament prophecies that were accomplished in the New; at Christ's willingness to die for *his* sins. How could he change from the revengeful creature he had become? As he read Romans 10:9, he discovered the answer. "Boy, that hit me!" he later wrote in a pamphlet, *I Was a Prisoner of the Japanese*. "It was the best news I'd ever heard in my life. There are just two things: you confess with your mouth and believe in your heart. And I did! . . . I believe heaven came down there in that prison cell."

Right away, Jake DeShazer had opportunities to put his newfound faith into practice—responding to his cruel prison guards with words of kindness. And in early August 1945, DeShazer felt compelled to fall to his knees in his cell and pray for peace, groaning in his spirit. Only later did he learn that the atomic bomb had been dropped on Hiroshima on August 4. Japan had surrendered.

When Doolittle's Raiders were finally released, DeShazer determined to return to Japan—only this time, instead of bombs, he would be armed with the Word of God. On December 28, 1948, Jake and his wife, Florence, landed in Yokohama as Free Methodist missionaries, and for the next thirty years shared the love of Christ with the very people he had hated. Thousands of Japanese read his testimony, *I Was a Prisoner of the Japanese*, and believed in the God who could change hatred to love—including Mitsuo Fuchida, the commander of the surprise attack on Pearl Harbor. For many years the two men— one American, one Japanese—worked together, witnessing to the power of God to reconcile enemies into Christian brothers.

Seed of the Church

"You destroy your enemy when you make him your friend." Abraham Lincoln

---

[Jesus said,] "You have heard that the law of Moses says, 'Love your neighbor' and hate your enemy. But I say, love your enemies! Pray for those who persecute you! In that way, you will be acting as true children of your Father in heaven" (Matthew 5:43-45).

May Hayman and Mavis Parkinson

Papua New Guinea—September 2, 1942

We know it now as the Republic of Indonesia, but in the first half of the twentieth century, this string of tropical islands bore colonial names: the Dutch East Indies, Dutch New Guinea, and Papua New Guinea (an Australian colony). New Guinea, one of the world's largest islands, is a land of forbidding jungles and perilous mountain ranges, making travel difficult and isolating the numerous tribes. The language barrier alone (at least five hundred separate languages) made it a difficult mission field.

The good news about colonialism was that the Dutch and Australians opened the doors wide to Christian missionaries, both Protestant and Roman Catholic. The bad news about colonialism was that Christianity was seen as the religion of the foreign intruders. Opposition among the Muslim population generated a groundswell of independence movements in the 1920s and 1930s.

The Australian Anglican Church had sent the first missionaries—Samuel and Elizabeth Tomlinson—to its new colony (Papua) in 1891, where they labored long and fruitfully. Hospitals and schools were built, more missionaries came, both clergy and laypeople. Among them, two single women—one a nurse, the other a teacher—left their home in Epping, New South Wales, in Australia to join the band of Anglican missionaries in Papua New Guinea.

The Japanese Invasion

As World War II loomed over the Pacific, a Japanese invasion seemed imminent. Advisors encouraged the expatriate missionaries to get out while they could, but most were reluctant to abandon their posts and their people. The Anglican bishop of Papua, Philip Strong, wrote to his clergy: "We must endeavor to carry on our work. God expects this of us. The church at home, which sent us out, will surely expect it of us. The universal church expects it of us. The people whom we serve expect it of us. We could never hold up our faces again if, for our own safety, we all forsook Him and fled, when the shadows of the Passion began to gather around Him in His spiritual and mystical body, the Church of Papua."

These were no idle words. On July 21, 1942, the Japanese invaded the island along the northern coast near Gona. As they advanced, missionaries and converts were pushed into hiding. Concerned for the safety of the young single women under his care, Bishop Strong urged nurse May Hayman and teacher Mavis Parkinson to leave the Gona mission and move farther inland. Their reply: "Don't move us from here, let us stay."

With gentleness and firmness, Bishop Strong told them that terrible things might happen, "worse than death." Still the two young women resisted. "What would the sick people do in the hospital if I go?" May asked. Mavis added, "What will the children do if their teacher leaves?"

The net and the noose tightened. Rounded up with several other missionaries and Papuan lay evangelists, May and Mavis were taken to the beach and forced to kneel. In Japanese fashion, a razor sharp sword flashed, and the two women were beheaded.

The Anglican Church honors twelve New Guinea martyrs—including May and Mavis—on September 2. They include five priests, two nurses, two teachers, a builder, and two Papuan evangelists. But during World War II, over three hundred Christians lost their lives in Papua New Guinea. The largest majority—almost two hundred—were Roman Catholics. But Christian martyrdom knew no denomination as Methodists, Salvationists, Lutherans, Anglicans, members of the Evangelical Church of Manus, and Seventh-day Adventists also laid down their lives. And Christian martyrdom bonded Australian and Papuan, men and women, young and old, married and single, with heaven as their country.

In Their Own Words

"We are in God's hands. If He calls us to suffer, we are ready to suffer. We must do this work."

—Mavis and May, refusing to leave their posts in Papua New Guinea

---

Use every piece of God's armor to resist the enemy in the time of evil, so that after the battle you will still be standing firm (Ephesians 6:13).

John Hewitt

Japan—ca. January 15, 1942

For centuries, Japan—that small cluster of islands in the Pacific able to wield so much terror and might against its bigger neighbors—was closed to the gospel of Jesus. Each reigning emperor was reverenced as the incarnation of the Sun Goddess, the primary deity of the Shinto religion, so to worship any other "god" was a traitorous act.

But in spite of being Japan's "national religion," Shintoism has waxed and waned. In the sixteenth century, Roman Catholic missionaries brought the gospel of Jesus to the island and at first enjoyed huge success, baptizing 150,000 converts in thirty years. Alarmed, Shinto devotees stirred up the people, raised an army, and in 1638 massacred thirty-seven thousand Japanese Catholics in one city alone.

In the second half of the nineteenth century, a trade treaty with the United States opened Japan's doors to Protestant missionaries for the first time. Again, the missionaries baptized many new believers. Again, Shintoists, threatened by this "foreign religion," cracked down, throwing Christian believers into prison by the thousands. Between 1868 and 1873, at least two thousand Christians died in Japan's prisons. This time, however, the Christian church continued to thrive under the leadership of Japanese Christians.

In 1929, however, Prime Minister Baron Tanaka vowed to bring "the whole world under the Shinto roof." With the backing of the military, Shintoists once again stepped up their battle against Japanese Christians.

From Ireland to Insane Asylum

We know very little about John Hewitt except that he grew up in Ireland and was sent by the Plymouth Brethren as a missionary to Japan, joining a fellow Irish missionary, Robert Wright, in the 1930s. Robert Wright had tried his own version of "tent making" in Kobe, Japan, working in a foreign-owned drugstore. But Wright soon realized that full-time employment left precious little time for language study or sharing the gospel. Moving to Tokyo, he joined himself to an assembly of Christians that had been started by a Japanese eye doctor. When John Hewitt joined him, the two Irishmen devoted themselves to language study and sharing the Good News in a land that seemed particularly unresponsive to the gospel message.

As the world tottered toward World War II, anti-foreigner and anti-Christian attitudes were at an all-time high. For the first time, foreign missionaries were among those rounded up and jailed. John Hewitt and Robert Wright were arrested in October 1941 and held in separate cells with street thieves. (Wright reported that he could hear Hewitt preaching to his cell mates.) After five days of interrogation ("Do you believe in the deity of the emperor?" "Do Christians bow before our sacred shrines?"), the two men were released. Wright boarded an ocean liner heading across the Pacific, but a few days out to sea the ship turned back: The Japanese had attacked Pearl Harbor. Now the Pacific Ocean was a war zone.

Back in Japan, John Hewitt had been rearrested and locked in Sugamo Prison. On or about January 15, 1942, unknown to his fellow missionaries or Japanese Christian friends, he was committed to an asylum for the insane. Months later, his Buddhist neighbor received a notice from the government: Prepare for John Hewitt's funeral. Somehow word reached two women missionaries who had not been imprisoned, and they hastened to the asylum. They found their brother missionary lying on the floor, so weak from malnutrition that he couldn't even stand.

"Praise the Lord!" he whispered when he saw their concerned faces. How comforting it must have been to know that he didn't die alone and unknown—for later that night John Hewitt died. His Buddhist neighbor gave him a Buddhist funeral, but the two missionaries talked the local police into letting them give him a Christian funeral as well.

Even though John Hewitt was the only Protestant missionary to die in Japan during World War II, many Japanese pastors were jailed for teaching "the religion of the enemy."

In His Own Words
"Have no fellowship with the unfruitful works of darkness, but rather reprove them. For it is a shame even to speak of those things which are done of them in secret."
—Ephesians 5:11, scrawled in Hewitt's handwriting and found after his death in the insane asylum

Lucian Tapiedi

Papua New Guinea — July 21, 1942

Born in 1921, the son of a sorcerer in the village of Taupota on the north coast of Papua New Guinea, Lucian Tapiedi's early childhood was rooted in the traditional spells and superstitions of Papuan village life. But his father died while Lucian and his siblings were still quite young, a fork in the road that landed Lucian in mission schools for the remainder of his education. An athletic and handsome young man with a sturdy build, Lucian decided not only to embrace the Christian faith but also to study to become a teacher.

At St. Aidan's Teacher Training College, which he entered at the age of eighteen, the diligent and cheerful Lucian became known not only for his love of physical recreation but also for his musical talents. After his graduation in 1941, Lucian joined the staff of the Sangara Anglican Mission as a teacher and an evangelist.

But in December of that same year, the Japanese bombed Pearl Harbor, plunging the Pacific into World War II. In Papua New Guinea, mission staff anxiously followed events by radio broadcast. "Japan invades Malaya [now Peninsular Malaysia]!" . . . "Guam and Wake Island fall to the Japanese!" . . . "British surrender in Hong Kong!" . . . "Manila falls to Japanese!" . . . "Japan invades Burma!" . . . "Solomon Islands fall!" . . . "British surrender Singapore!" . . . "Japan overruns Dutch East Indies!" . . . "Japanese invades Dutch New Guinea" . . . "American and Filipino forces surrender on Corregidor!"

On July 21, 1942, Japanese forces landed on the northern coast of Papua New Guinea near the mission station at Gona. As the invaders rounded up foreign teachers, nurses, and evangelists in the immediate area, another small group of mission workers, hearing of the invasion, headed inland, hoping to avoid capture. Though Lucian Tapiedi could have melted into the local population, the twenty-one-year-old teacher would not abandon his fellow workers. Along the way, other fleeing missionaries joined them until the group numbered ten persons.

Coming upon a village among the Orokaiva people, the group asked for shelter. Instead, the group was divided, and each one put under guard by different men of the tribe. Lucian's guard, a man named Hivijapa, took his prisoner away from the village to a nearby stream and killed him there. At least six of the prisoners were handed over to the invaders, who beheaded them in Japanese custom on Buna Beach. All ten lost their lives.

In Memory of Lucian

What transpired between Lucian and his murderer alongside that stream? How did he die? Only heaven knows. But later Lucian's killer came under great conviction, converted to Christianity, and took the name Hivijapa Lucian to honor the young man he had persecuted. A shrine marks the place along the stream where Lucian Tapiedi died, but that was not enough for Hivijapa Lucian, who built a church at Embi dedicated to Lucian Tapiedi's memory.

A visitor to the Sangara mission station in Papua New Guinea today might be shown three gravestones. Two bear the names of Australian missionaries Mavis Parkinson and May Hayman, also killed during the Japanese invasion in 1942. Etched on the third is the name of a beloved Papuan coworker, Lucian Tapiedi.

Fifty-plus years later, on July 9, 1998, at Westminster Abbey, ten limestone statues were unveiled commemorating a sampling of twentieth-century Christian martyrs "willing to die for what they believed," representing every continent and a wide variety of Christian denominations. The statues honor notable persons such as Franciscan Maximilian Kolbe of Poland; Baptist pastor Martin Luther King Jr. of the United States; Catholic bishop Oscar Romero of El Salvador; Lutheran pastor Dietrich Bonhoeffer of Germany; Elizabeth, an Orthodox nun martyred during the Bolshevik Revolution; Anglican archbishop Janani Luwum of Uganda; Manche Masemola of South Africa (a Christian teen slain by her animist parents); Presbyterian evangelist Esther John in Pakistan; Pastor Wang Zhiming of China . . . and Lucian Tapiedi of Papua New Guinea.

In His Own Words

"I will stay with the Fathers and Sisters."

—Lucian Tapiedi, choosing to live or die
with his missionary brothers and sisters

Five New Tribes Martyrs
Bolivia—1943

God seems to have a special place in his heart for impetuous saints. Remember the apostle Peter, eager to walk on water, wanting to build memorials on the mount of transfiguration, and claiming that *he* would never forsake Jesus even if others did?

Well, this—*hmm*—"spontaneity" might describe the first New Tribes Mission volunteers who in 1942 headed into the Bolivian jungle searching for a ferocious tribe whose language, customs, location, and even correct name they didn't know. They believed "God had called them reach this so-called 'hardest tribe' first."

The party of sixteen (including women and children) were emboldened by the conversion of a hundred Bolivians before they reached their base camp in the jungle, leaving them eager to meet the dreaded the *bárbaro* (who turned out to be the *Ayorés*). Learning basic jungle survival, fighting malaria, and blazing trails deeper into the unknown green occupied them for over eight months before five men—Dave Bacon, Cecil Dye, George Hosback, Bob Dye, and Eldon Hunter—were ready to attempt "first contact."

These fierce Indians frightened all their neighbors with their deadly short arrows. They attacked any outsider that came near, and they especially hated white men. But George Hosback, the youngest of the five, spoke for the others: "Of course it is risky going to [the Ayorés], but didn't God stop the mouths of lions by His angels, and 'quench the violence of fire by his presence? And is He not 'the same yesterday, today and forever'?"

So, on November 10, 1943, the five men marched off with high hopes.

Silence

The wives and children and two remaining men waited for a month with no word from the advance party. Finally, the two men aided by four Bolivians went into the jungle searching for them. In early January the search team sent back word that they had found evidence of a camp . . . with broken items belonging to the missionaries. Not good.

Then one of the search team was wounded by an arrow, and they had to retreat.

A larger team made up of Bolivians was sent out. They were well armed and ended up shooting and killing an Ayoré who threatened them. That team gave up and returned.

For years the wives prayed and clung to the possibility that their husbands would escape and one day walk out of the jungle, but first contact without bloodshed came a completely different way. Joe Moreno had worked for Cecil Dye. Though he only had a sixth grade education, he set about learning the known bits of the Ayoré language. He tracked them from a distance through the jungle, discovering their habits. He left knives, wire, and pieces of metal for them as gifts. A break came when the Indians left gifts of their own for Joe in exchange. His tedious efforts finally convinced the Ayorés that the *cojñone* (the civilized ones) were not intent on killing them—their only experience in the past—and on August 12, 1947, several of the Indians came to Joe wanting to be friends.

Within a year, extensive interaction was occurring. Cecil Dye's wife, Jean, even went back into the jungle to live with one group. Slowly she and other missionaries learned the language and began preaching the gospel. Finally, in 1949 an Ayoré man who was from the region where the five missionaries had

239

disappeared, reported that he had been present when they were killed. The silence was over, but many Ayorés were coming to Christ.

Seed of the Church

Although experience has not dimmed the mission's dedication to take the message of Christ "where no witness of the gospel has yet reached," methods have changed. And now more than three thousand missionaries from thirty-nine countries serve with NTM. Bruce Porterfield is one missionary who, specifically because of the death of the five in Bolivia, volunteered to take their place. He, too, has faced Indians intent on killing him, once being surrounded by many with drawn arrows. Later when they had come to Christ, they reported that they couldn't shoot because someone unseen had pinned their arms. But Bruce can't answer why the Lord spared his life dozens of times while allowing others to die. "Perhaps," says Bruce, "He chose to multiply their lives more through death than through an extended existence. We have lots of evidence that there are thousands serving the Lord that began like me with the conviction, 'Lord, I'll take their place.'"

Franz Jägerstätter
Germany—August 9, 1943

When Rosalia Huber had a baby in 1907 in the village of St. Radegund, Austria, she named him Franz even though she and the boy's father, Franz Bachmeier, were too poor to marry. Several years later, however, after Bachmeier was killed in World War I, Rosalia married Heinrich Jägerstätter, a local farmer, who adopted young Franz. The boy gained more than a legitimate name: His stepfather's library was full of books that captured his imagination . . . at least when he wasn't getting into trouble.

Some suggested that he may have fathered an illegitimate child, himself, as a young man, but in 1936 he settled down and married Franziska.

It was also about this time that his Christian faith coalesced and demonstrated itself not only in serving as the sexton in his local church but also in encouraging others. He wrote to his godchild, "I can say from my own experience how painful life often is when one lives as a halfway Christian; it is more like vegetating than living."

Two years later, Franz's faith was tested as many Austrians became enamored with Nazism. He was well-enough read to understand how anti-Christian its racial hatred was. His convictions became so outspoken that he stopped frequenting taverns, not to abstain from all drink, but to avoid getting into fights over Nazism. In the referendum on the *Anschluss* (the annexation of Austria by Germany) in March 1938, Franz cast the only dissenting local vote.

Resisting Evil

Once the Nazis were in power, he refused to collaborate, even to the point of rejecting the family and farm subsidies from them to which he was entitled. When the Germans began drafting Austrians, even Franz's spiritual advisors (at least three priests and the bishop of Linz) recommended cooperation "for the sake of the family" (he had three small children by then) and because "You won't be responsible for the government's wrong-doing since all God requires of you is to obey the authorities."

In the summer of 1940, Franz Jägerstätter was first called up for military service. He reported for induction, but subsequently the mayor of his town arranged for him to return to his farm after a few days. In February 1943, he was called up again for active service with motorized replacement unit 17. "At first, he ignored the call-up because he rejected National Socialism and therefore refused military service on its behalf," claim Nazi records, still available for inspection in Prague.

"Everyone tells me," Franz wrote, "that I should not do what I am doing because of the danger of death. I believe it is better to sacrifice one's life right away than to place oneself in the grave danger of committing sin and then dying."

On March 1, 1943, he yielded to pressure from relatives and his local priest and reported for duty but immediately announced that because of God's command to "love thy neighbor as thy self" he could not fight with weapons but was willing to serve as a medical orderly.

That was not acceptable to the Third Reich. In May, the government transferred Franz Jägerstätter to a prison in Berlin. His lawyer, wife, and parish priest all tried to change his mind, but he refused even though he knew his resistance could not stop the Nazi death machine. He was executed on August 9, 1943.

In His Own Words

Since the death of Christ, almost every century has seen the persecution of Christians; there have always been heroes and martyrs who gave their lives—often in horrible ways—for Christ and their faith. If we hope to reach our goal some day, then we, too, must become heroes of the faith.

—Franz Jägerstätter, in a letter circa 1936

[Jesus said,] "I say, love your enemies! Pray for those who persecute you! In that way, you will be acting as true children of your Father in heaven. For he gives his sunlight to both the evil and the good, and he sends rain on the just and on the unjust, too. If you love only those who love you, what good is that? Even corrupt tax collectors do that much. If you are kind only to your friends, how are you different from anyone else? Even pagans do that" (Matthew 5:44-47).

Corrie and Betsie ten Boom
Germany — ca. December 20, 1944

Out of simple Christian charity, the ten Boom family began receiving refugee children, missionary kids, and orphans into their home in Haarlem, Holland, in the 1920s. They called their often-crowded combination home and watchmaker shop the Beje (pronounced *bay-yay*).

In 1940, the German army invaded Holland, and Nazi forces occupied the country for the next five years. Because of the ten Booms' reputation, people came to them for help, and in 1943, the family began hiding people in danger of arrest by the gestapo, many of them Jews, fleeing Nazi racial laws.

The gestapo raided the Beje on February 28, 1944. The ten Boom family and twenty-nine other people were arrested, but the Jewish people in "the hiding place," the secret room in the attic, escaped detection. Father Casper ten Boom died in captivity on March 9, 1944. Son Willem and married daughter Nollie (and her son), who happened to be present, were later released. But Betsie, the oldest daughter at fifty-nine, and Corrie (fifty-two) were ultimately assigned to the German concentration camp at Ravensbruck.

While imprisoned together, Betsie ten Boom said to her sister Corrie, "The most important part of our task will be to tell everyone who will listen that Jesus is the only answer to the problems that are disturbing the hearts of men and nations. We will have the right to speak because we can tell from our experience that his light is more powerful than the deepest darkness. How wonderful that the reality of his presence is greater than the reality of the hell about us."

Conditions went from bad to worse until they were put in a barracks crawling with fleas that was cold, smelly, and lacking in proper ventilation. But as Betsie and Corrie fought the fleas and studied their Bible together, they came across 1 Thessalonians 5:16-18, encouraging believers to rejoice in all things. Betsie said, "That's it, Corrie! That's his answer. Give thanks in all circumstances!" Corrie tried hard: Yes, they were together rather than separated. Yes, the guards had overlooked their Bible when they were inspected. And possibly it was good that so many were crowded into their cramped quarters . . . so that more could hear the gospel. But when Betsie thanked God for the fleas, Corrie stopped her. "Betsie, there's no way even God can make me grateful for a flea."

Weeks later after enjoying Bible study and praise with other prisoners, Betsie offered a reason to be grateful: "You know we've never understood why we had so much freedom in the big room. Well, I've found out. The guards won't come into this room because of the fleas."

Shortly before Christmas, Betsie died of starvation, exposure, and ill treatment. Possibly due to an administrative error, Corrie was released a few days later on January 1, 1945. After the war ended and Corrie took a season to recover, she established a home for disabled people and ex-prisoners from the concentration camps—a ministry for which Betsie had had a strong vision and spoke of often.

Corrie ten Boom went on to be a worldwide evangelistic speaker and writer, often emphasizing the themes of forgiving one's enemies, how God works through weakness, getting along with less, and what to do when evil seems to win. Certainly most well-known is her book *The Hiding Place* (also made into a movie), written with John and Elizabeth Sherrill.

In Her Own Words
"We must tell people what we have learned here. We must tell them that there is no pit so deep that He is not deeper still. They will listen to us, Corrie, because we have been here."
—The dying words of Betsie ten Boom

Always be joyful. Keep on praying. No matter what happens, always be thankful, for this is God's will for you who belong to Christ Jesus (1 Thessalonians 5:16-18).

Casper ten Boom
Germany—March 9, 1944

Casper ten Boom was a watchmaker in Haarlem, Holland. His business and three-story combined store, workshop, and home had been in the family for over one hundred years when the German army invaded Holland in 1940. But the eighty-year-old Casper had not waited for trouble to teach his family how to respond. Biblical instruction and practical application had been a part of the family experience long before.

He and his wife, Cor, had three grown daughters—Betsie, Nollie, and Corrie—and one son, Willem. Nollie and Willem were married and lived in less-crowded parts of the city. Betsie and Corrie were seemingly content with their spinsterhood and lived at home. Corrie, especially, was extensively involved in leading Bible clubs for girls.

Since 1920 the ten Booms had regularly received refugee children, missionary kids, and orphans into their home, so it was natural for people to seek their help as the Nazis occupied their country. The ten Booms even created a secret room at the back of the third floor of their house in which to hide Jews fleeing Nazi racial laws. It became known as "the hiding place."

When the gestapo began requiring Jewish people to wear the Star of David, Casper lined up and wore one too, much to the disapproval of a pastor friend from the country. Then on June 1, 1943, a young Jewish woman with her newborn baby came to them for protection. There seemed no way to keep a young infant silent should the Nazis inspect the house, as they often did, so when their pastor friend showed up again, he seemed like the perfect solution. But when Corrie asked him if he would take the baby to his home in the country, he replied, "Miss ten Boom, I hope you are not getting involved with

243

any of this illegal concealment and undercover business. It is not safe! Think of your father and your sister. She has never been very strong." He looked at the baby for just one moment, compassion fighting with his fear. Then he declared, "No. Definitely not. We could lose our lives for that Jewish child!"

Casper had entered the room by then. "Give the child to me, Corrie," he said, then looked at the pastor. "You protested about me wearing this Star of David. That I will remove, but we'll keep the baby! Should we end up losing our lives for this child, I would consider it the greatest honor that could come to my family."

The pastor left abruptly without a word.

On February 28, 1944, the gestapo raided the ten Boom dwelling. The family and twenty-nine other people were arrested, but the Jewish people in the hiding place escaped detection.

As Casper ten Boom was brought to the interrogation room, a gestapo officer said, "I'd like to send you home, old fellow. I'll take your word that you will behave yourself, and then you can die in your own bed where you belong. There's no need for this."

"If I go home today," Casper replied, "tomorrow I will open my door to anyone who knocks for help."

Less than two weeks later, on March 9, 1944, Casper ten Boom died while still under arrest, lying ill on a stretcher in a cold hospital corridor, age eighty-four. Son Willem and married daughter Nollie (and her son), who happened to be present at the time of the raid, were later released. But Betsie, the oldest daughter at fifty-nine, and Corrie (fifty-two) were ultimately assigned to the German concentration camp at Ravensbruck. There they lived under such harsh treatment and in such foul conditions that Betsie died shortly before Christmas. Miraculously, Corrie was released January 1, 1945.

In His Own Words

"Thou art my hiding place and my shield: I hope in thy word. Depart from me, ye evildoers: for I will keep the commandments of my God. Uphold me according unto thy word, that I may live: and let me not be ashamed of my hope. Hold thou me up, and I shall be safe (Psalm 119:114-117, KJV)", quoted by Casper ten Boomon the night of his arrest

Dietrich Bonhoeffer
Germany—April 9, 1945

At the age of fourteen, Dietrich Bonhoeffer said, "I want to be a theologian." This surprised his family. His father, Karl, was a famous psychiatrist and neurologist in Berlin, and although the family of ten was Lutheran, they rarely went to church. But Dietrich was quite serious and pursued theological studies at the University of Berlin, and later at Union Theological Seminary in New York.

While studying in New York in 1931, Dietrich asked Frank Fisher, a fellow student and committed black Christian from Alabama, if he could visit his church, the Abyssinian Baptist Church of Harlem. "I've never been to a black church before," Dietrich Bonhoeffer admitted. Frank shrugged, wondering how long this blond-haired, ruddy-faced seminarian with a thick German accent would last when he saw the *real* Harlem. But Dietrich came back week after week, volunteering to teach Sunday school and visiting in various homes around Harlem.

Friendship grew between the black American and the white German until one day when they went with some other seminarians to eat in a restaurant. The waiter took orders from the white men but ignored Frank. After realizing what was happening, Dietrich stood up. "If Frank cannot get service here, none of us will eat here." And he led the group out of the restaurant in protest.

Years later, back in Germany, Dietrich still held his friendship with Frank and his experiences in Harlem in high regard. He had recorded some of the music he'd learned at Abyssinian Baptist Church and played this music for his students and talked about the racial injustice he had seen in America, even among believers who worshipped the same Jesus. "Racism," he predicted, "will become one of the most critical future problems for the white church."

As Bonhoeffer watched the rise of Nazism under Hitler, he realized the danger of its racist philosophy. Saddened by how the German people—even many Christians—unquestioningly embraced Nazism, he helped form the Confessing Church. It proclaimed that Jesus alone is Lord and allegiance to Hitler was idolatry. Along with six thousand other pastors, he refused to accept the Aryan Clause that discriminated against anyone of Jewish descent.

Ultimately he became involved in a resistance movement to overthrow Hitler. His activities led to his arrest by the Gestapo in 1943 for involvement in Operation Seven, a rescue mission helping a group of Jews over the German border and into Switzerland.

One Sunday, as Bonhoeffer had just finished conducting a worship service where he was held in Schoenberg Prison, two soldiers came in and pronounced the fateful words for condemned prisoners: "Prisoner Bonhoeffer, make ready and come with us." Bonhoeffer turned to a fellow prisoner and said, "This is the end—but for me, the beginning of life." He was hanged along with several other resisters the next day, April 9, 1945, just a month before Hitler committed suicide and Germany surrendered.

In His Own Words

"To do and dare—not what you would, but what is right. Never to hesitate over what is within your power, but boldly to grasp what lies before you. Not in the flight of fancy, but only in the deed there is freedom. Away with timidity and reluctance! Out into the storm of event, sustained only by the commandment of God and your faith, and freedom will receive your spirit with exultation."

—Dietrich Bonhoeffer, 1944,
"Action" in "Stations on the Road to Freedom"
from *Letters and Papers from Prison*

[God said to Joshua,] "Have I not commanded you? Be strong and of good courage; do not be afraid, nor be dismayed, for the Lord your God is with you wherever you go" (Joshua 1:9, NKJV).

Eric Liddell
China—February 21, 1945

Known as "The Flying Scotsman" for winning the gold medal in record time in the 400 meter 1924 Olympic games in Paris, Eric Liddell inspired millions in more recent years through the movie *Chariots of Fire.*

Born January 16, 1902, to missionary parents in Tientsin, China, his parents intended to call him Henry Eric Liddell until a friend pointed out that a missionary's son might have a problem with those initials. So they named him Eric Henry.

When Eric was five, his family returned to Scotland for their first furlough. When the year's rest was over, and first his father and then his mother returned to China, Eric and his older brother and younger sister enrolled in boarding schools for missionary children. They spent the holidays with their relatives in Scotland.

By the time Eric was sixteen, running was his favorite sport, and he and his brother took either first or second place in six school track events. Eric's time of 10.2 seconds for the hundred-yard dash set a school record that remained unbroken for over seventy years.

By 1923, when his fame as a runner had become international, Eric spoke publicly for the first time of his faith in Christ to eighty people who gathered in the small town hall of Armadale, Scotland. He told of how he never questioned anything that happened to him. He didn't need explanations from God. He simply believed in God and accepted what came. Every newspaper in Scotland reported his testimony the next day.

Olympics

After winning several championships in the 100- and 220-yard dashes, Eric was the favorite for the 100-meter and the 4 x 100 and 4 x 400 relays. However, he was shocked to discover that the qualifying heats for those races were scheduled for Sunday, a day Eric held sacred and set apart for worshipping the Lord.

Without complaint, Eric resigned himself to run the longer races in which he didn't usually excel. But to the surprise of all—including himself—he finished third in the two-hundred-meter sprint, taking an unexpected bronze medal. Then he blew out the field in the four-hundred-meter race, coming in five meters ahead of the silver medalist and setting a world record of 47.6 seconds.

Back to China

The next year he returned to China as a missionary teacher. He was ordained in 1932 and married Florence McKenzie in 1933. As the Japanese invaded China, danger for foreign missionaries increased, and yet Eric continued to travel—usually by bicycle—to remote villages to share the gospel. His motto was "complete surrender." Threats from the Japanese became so severe that Florence and the children returned to Canada in 1941. But Eric remained in China, ministering under ruthless conditions. The Japanese required all missionaries to wear armbands and prohibited church services. But the Christians met in house churches anyway.

In March of 1943, the Japanese put Eric, along with other Americans and British, in an internment camp. There he taught math and Bible classes and organized sports activities and volunteered for every exhausting task . . . until he wore himself out.

Annie, the camp nurse, tried to get him to slow down, especially because of the intense headaches he was experiencing. At first, she thought it was the flu and sinusitis, but ultimately everyone realized he had a brain tumor. On February 21, 1945, he collapsed and said to the nurse, "Annie, it's complete surrender." Then he managed to scribble something on a scrap of paper. Within minutes, he died.

All eighteen hundred people in the camp attended his funeral.

On the scrap of paper was the name of his favorite hymn, "Be Still My Soul" (Katharina von Schlegel, born 1697), that he earlier had requested be sung at his funeral.

> *Be still, my soul—the Lord is on thy side!*
> *Bear patiently the cross of grief or pain;*
> *Leave to thy God to order and provide—*
> *In every change He faithful will remain.*
> *Be still, my soul—thy best, thy heavenly Friend*
> *Through thorny ways leads to a joyful end.*

Richard and Sabina Wurmbrand
Romania—February 29, 1948

Richard and Sabina Wurmbrand faced more than their share of crises and persecution during their lifetime—and never failed to use these dangerous situations as opportunities to share the gospel of Christ. Let's take a walk with the Wurmbrands through a life of danger and opportunity.

Prior to 1937: In a village in Romania, a godly old carpenter named Christian Wölfkes prays for years to win a Jew for Christ. A young Jewish man and his wife arrive in the village. For hours the old carpenter prays for these Jewish strangers. He gives them a Bible and encourages them to read the story of "the most well-known Jew of all time," Jesus Christ.

1938: The Jewish strangers, Richard and Sabina Wurmbrand, dedicate their lives to Christ.

1941: Romania supports Germany in the war against the USSR and is host to German forces. Richard Wurmbrand, now a pastor, engages in evangelistic activities with the occupying soldiers. During the Nazi terror, Richard and Sabina are repeatedly beaten and arrested. Sabina's family perishes in the mass extermination of Jews in concentration camps.

1944: Communists seize power in Romania, and Russian troops pour into the country. Pastor Wurmbrand ministers to his own oppressed compatriots and to the Russians.

1945: Richard and Sabina attend the Congress of the Cults. As many religious leaders come forward to swear loyalty to the new communist regime, Sabina tells her husband, "Richard, stand up and wipe the shame from the face of Jesus." Richard, knowing the cost, steps forward and tells the four thousand delegates that their duty as Christians is to glorify God alone. The mood of the crowd changes; the religious leaders begin to applaud. But from that day, Richard is a marked man.

1948: On February 29, as Pastor Wurmbrand leaves for church, secret police kidnap Richard and lock him in a solitary cell, designating him "Prisoner Number 1."

1950: The Communists arrest Sabina and assign her to forced labor on the Danube Canal. The Wurmbrands' nine-year-old son, Mihai, is left alone. During her three years of imprisonment, Sabina only saw her son for a few minutes.

1953: Sabina is released and continues her work in the underground church. She is told that her husband died in prison. Sabina refuses to believe the report and holds on to her hope of one day seeing Richard again.

1956: Richard is released after eight and a half years in prison. He was tortured and warned to never preach again. The bottoms of his feet had been beaten so often that he could barely walk. Throughout the rest of his life, he could only wear shoes for short periods of time. But once released he immediately resumes his ministry.

1959: Richard is betrayed to the authorities by an associate pastor in the underground church. He is rearrested and sentenced to twenty-five years. As he is hauled off in the police van, his last words to Sabina are: "Give all my love to Mihai and to the pastor who betrayed me."

1964: Richard is released from prison and resumes his work. Two Westerners cautiously make their way to the little attic home of the Wurmbrands. This is the first contact the Wurmbrands have with outside missionaries since their arrests.

1965: The Wurmbrand family is ransomed from Romania for ten thousand dollars, and Richard is again warned by the secret police to remain silent. In May, he testifies in Washington, D.C. before the U.S. Senate's Internal Security Subcommittee. As his story spreads rapidly across the country, he receives hundreds of speaking requests. The man who can barely walk continues to carry the gospel of peace. . . .

In Her Own Words
"A martyr does not make the truth. The truth makes a martyr."
—Sabina Wurmbrand

How shall they preach unless they are sent? As it is written: "How beautiful are the feet of those who preach the gospel of peace, Who bring glad tidings of good things!" (Romans 10:15, NKJV).

Richard and Sabina Wurmbrand (cont'd.)
Romania—February 17, 2001

Pastor Richard Wurmbrand, a Jewish Christian, suffered years of imprisonment and torture in communist Romania simply because he would not quit preaching about Jesus Christ. His wife, Sabina, also did three years hard labor, separated from her husband and child. By God's grace, the Wurmbrands were reunited and allowed to leave Romania—but it was only the beginning of *another* lifetime of turning crises into opportunities to share the love of God with a hurting world.

Let's continue our walk along the time line of a life well lived.

1966: Richard and Sabina begin their international speaking tour, revealing the atrocities committed against their brothers and sisters in communist countries. Pastor Wurmbrand learns that the Romanian secret police are plotting his death, but he continues to speak out.

1967: The Wurmbrands officially begin a ministry committed to serving the persecuted church, eventually called The Voice of the Martyrs. Pastor Wurmbrand's testimony, Tortured for Christ, is published.

1970s–1990s: Cold War tensions increase until Communism collapses in the Soviet Union and Eastern Europe, but oppression of Christians escalates in Asia, Eastern Europe, and the Middle East. The Wurmbrands' ministry to the persecuted church spans eighty countries, providing Bibles and literature, giving relief to families of Christian martyrs, supplying humanitarian aid to war-torn countries, equipping local Christians to win their persecutors to Christ, helping believers rebuild their lives and witness in former communist countries, informing the church worldwide of atrocities committed against Christians, and encouraging the worldwide church to minister to their persecuted brothers and sisters. In all these things, the staff draws encouragement and steadfastness from the lives and the words of the Wurmbrands.

1989: In Romania, thousands gather in a square protesting the oppressive regime of Nicolae Ceausescu. Many soldiers turn on the secret police and thousands are killed. Finally, on December 25, peace comes to Romania.

1990: Richard and Sabina return to Romania after twenty-five years of exile. Richard regrets the execution of the Ceausescus and preaches a message of love and forgiveness.

1994: Richard and Sabina return to Romania to officiate at the opening of the Agape Children's Home. The Voice of the Martyrs increases Scripture distribution in China even as the Public Security Bureau cracks down on "unregistered" churches.

1995: As the twentieth century draws to a close, persecution of Christians increases around the globe: Iranian Christian leaders Mehdi Dibaj and Pastor Haik are targeted and killed; the Islamic government of Sudan wages war against Christians and other non-Muslims; churches are burned in Indonesia; Australian missionary to India, Graham Staines, is burned to death in his car along with his two sons by a radical Hindu sect; Christians are imprisoned and even executed in Islamic countries for "blaspheming Muhammad"; two students in Littleton, Colorado, shoot and kill several classmates, including two who would not deny their faith in Jesus; another gunman sprays a youth group meeting at Wedgwood Baptist Church in Texas, killing several; Pastor Li De Xian of China is arrested numerous times for refusing to quit preaching the gospel. . . .

2000: Sabina Wurmbrand is diagnosed with cancer. She goes home to glory, leaving behind a legacy of love and compassion, and a fire for the work and Word of God.

2001: Richard Wurmbrand joins his wife in heaven on February 17, shortly before his ninety-second birthday.

In Her Own Words

"Your mission is to build the house of God. Build it with living stones, build it with souls."

—Sabina Wurmbrand, a few months before she died of cancer

Now God is building you, as living stones, into his spiritual temple. What's more, you are God's holy priests, who offer the spiritual sacrifices that please him because of Jesus Christ (1 Peter 2:5).

Bev and Helen Jackson
Idaho—March 26, 1950

In 1914, a church was built in a small frontier town in northern Idaho. That same year, Louis Beverley (Bev) Jackson was born in Long Beach, California, the first of four children to James Warren and Josie Gertrude Jackson. The church closed after two years and waited thirty-three years before Bev

250

and Helen Jackson found their way north to ring its bell on a snowy Sunday morning, March 26, 1950, announcing the resumption of regular services. Fernwood Community Church has proclaimed the gospel ever since.

Bev grew up in Southern California, joining a church as a teenager. But it wasn't until he was teaching Sunday school a few years later he realized that salvation comes from submission to a Person, and he accepted Jesus Christ as his Savior.

His administrative skills led to rapid career advancement in Lockheed Aircraft Corporation during World War II until he supervised three thousand employees. After the war, he and his wife, Helen, responded to a call to Christian service and after a period of training and ministerial ordination went out as "home missionaries" under Village Missions.

In true pioneering spirit, they took their five-year-old son, Dave, and six- month-old daughter, Jeannine, to northern Idaho. Fernwood retained its frontier flavor. On one side of the street stood a combined general store, post office, and hand-operated gas pump, on the other a saloon with a barber chair and pool table. A train station sat at one end of the town, the schoolhouse at the other end. Logs were sometimes still skidded out of the mountains by mules. Cattle roamed freely. And a herd of wild horses occasionally thundered through town trampling any unfenced gardens the deer hadn't eaten.

After checking out one of the first church services, some of the local lumberjacks gathered in the saloon to evaluate. "That kind of stuff ain't a-gonna hurt nobody," said one. Later the tough lumberjack came by the Jacksons' small trailer house at night. "I've come to have you pray for me. You're the only one around who can help."

Bev and Helen "worked the field" like the old circuit-riding preachers, living in Fernwood but also holding services in the nearby towns of Clarkia, Emida, and Santa.

Just a Hunting Trip?

Townspeople warned Bev not to bother an old hermit who lived up in the hills.

"Why not?" He and Helen had been visiting *everyone*, inviting them to church.

"Ol' codger comes into town once in a while, but anyone who disturbs him seems to disappear . . . or dies in a strange hunting accident!"

Bev nodded but got that steely glint in his eye, like when kids had teased him as a child about his having a girl's name. A few days later, he drove up the rutted path to the hermit's house. The man greeted him with reserve and listened while Bev explained why he'd come to town and invited him to church. Then the man nodded and said, "Want to go hunting?"

Bev recalled the warnings: unsolved disappearances, strange hunting accidents. "Well, thanks, but . . ." He looked back at his vehicle. "I don't have a rifle, and—"

"Got several. I'll give you one." He slapped Bev on the shoulder. "Picked up this old Japanese gun. Had it rebored just like a .300 Savage, lengthened the stock myself."

If he left now, Bev realized he might get no other chance to tell this lonely man about Jesus, so he let himself be guided into the shack.

That evening, Bev drove back to town with a rifle and two deer in the back of his suburban—meat enough to last several months—and a new friend on the mountain.

Seed of the Church

Over the years, Bev and Helen served several other small, rural churches. Their courage and love touched the hearts of thousands of men and women for Christ, some of whom also went into full-time Christian service. John Faughn was one of those who gave his life to Christ on that first Sunday morning in Idaho. Ike Badgett was an Idaho convert who became a missionary. He felt such gratitude for Bev and Helen that fifty years later he helped them settle in a retirement home and lived nearby to assist them until they died at age eighty-seven— Helen on November 3, 2000, and Bev on October 5, 2001.

> To me, to live is Christ and to die is gain. If I am to go on living in the body, this will mean fruitful labor for me. Yet what shall I choose? (Philippians 1:21-22, NIV).

Bill Wallace
China—February 1951

The young Southern Baptist surgeon from Knoxville, Tennessee, who had just been assigned to Stout Memorial Hospital in Wuzhou, China, in 1935, was an exceptionally eligible bachelor—tall, handsome, skilled, dedicated. *Too* dedicated in the opinion of some young women missionaries who entertained hope that Bill Wallace might change their single status. "Marriage to Bill would be bigamy," said one. "He's married to his work."

Even war couldn't shake the young doctor from his commitment to his patients. While he was away from the hospital at language school, the missionary staff left Wuzhou to escape rampaging bandits. But Bill did not follow. Instead, he reorganized the Chinese staff into his medical team. The captain of an American ship anchored nearby sent word that he couldn't be responsible for Bill's safety if he stayed even one more night. The doctor shrugged. "Tell your captain that he was not responsible for my coming here in the first place and he doesn't need to be responsible for my staying here."

Bill Wallace was stubborn—in all the right ways. He didn't budge when the Japanese sent their planes and bombs, even when the hospital took a direct hit. He kept on working at Stout Memorial during all the uncertainties of World War II—until Wuzhou officials evacuated the whole city just ahead of the advancing Japanese troops. Bill loaded his staff and equipment onto a large barge on the nearby river, creating a floating hospital that headed hundreds of miles upriver.

At the end of the war, Bill and his staff returned to the war-damaged hospital in Wuzhou. In a note to his sister, all he said was, "Dear Sis: Wuzhou. Love, Bill." And he was again tending patients. But the rise of Communism in China and the Korean War heightened anti-American feelings. Finally Bill Wallace and a nurse, Everley Hayes, were the only American missionaries who remained in the city.

The Knock on the Door

Loud banging outside the hospital compound one early December morning in 1950 and cries of "Let us in! We have a sick man!" sent a Chinese staffer scurrying to open the gates. About twenty communist soldiers rushed in and ransacked Bill Wallace's home. "We hide nothing," he insisted. "Our only work is healing the suffering and sick in the name of Jesus Christ."

But the soldiers "found" a gun under the doctor's mattress and promptly arrested him as a spy. And then the nightmare began. For endless days Bill Wallace was interrogated and brutally beaten, accused of everything from murdering and maiming Chinese citizens in his operating room to immorality with the nurses. No one could get in to see him, and he sat alone in a cold jail cell for two months. To keep from sliding into hopelessness and despair, Bill wrote Scripture verses on scraps of paper and stuck them into cracks in the wall.

But the pressure was relentless. Other prisoners—Catholic missionaries—heard him crying from pain and agony. And then one day the Catholic missionaries were told, "Bill Wallace has hung himself in his cell." They were asked to sign statements that the American doctor had committed suicide—but the Catholic missionaries would only state that they found him hanging in his cell.

Workers from Stout Memorial Hospital, who had been held under house arrest, were allowed to claim Wallace's body. Later nurse Hayes testified that Bill's body showed no evidence of hanging—no swollen tongue or bulging eyes from asphyxiation—but his upper body was a mass of bruises. No graveside service was allowed—only a quick burial in a cheap wooden coffin. But the Chinese Christians, risking their own lives, returned to erect a marker over his grave that simply said, "For To Me To Live Is Christ."

Seed of the Church

[Bill Wallace] was a martyr not because he died but because he so identified with the Chinese that they considered him one of them.

—Everley Hayes, missionary nurse
at Stout Memorial Hospital in Wuzhou, China

For to me, living is for Christ, and dying is even better (Philippians 1:21).

253

Francis Xavier Ford

China—February 21, 1952

Born in Brooklyn, New York, in 1892, Francis Ford was twenty years old when he learned that two American priests—Thomas Frederick Price and James Anthony Walsh—were recruiting missionaries for the newly organized Maryknoll mission. He applied and became the first student at the seminary. Ordained in 1918, he was one of the first four missionaries to leave for China.

In 1925, Ford was asked to direct the newly created Maryknoll mission territory of Kaying (now called Meizhou) in the northeastern corner of Guangdong Province. In 1935 he was ordained bishop of Kaying and chose as his motto the Latin verb *condolere*—"to feel compassion, to share with"—from Hebrews 5, which describes Christ as a high priest who because of having become human, is able to deal gently with us.

The motto summed up Ford's simple approach to mission work with an emphasis on person-to-person contact, visiting towns and villages, and inviting people to become Christians. "When you introduce people to Christianity," he told his fellow missionaries, "go back to the time when the church was a fishing vessel along the Sea of Galilee."

This dedication to being with the people led Bishop Ford to remain in China when the Japanese rolled across Asia, killing millions and driving even more from their homes. He even refused to leave the war-torn country when the Japanese attacked Pearl Harbor and brought the United States into the war.

Afterward, during the costly civil war, he distinguished himself by the way he cared for refugees and all those who suffered.

Bishop Ford also believed that the church of China had no real future unless it was set free from the methods, civilization, and control of the West, so he worked to build up a truly indigenous church with a well-trained local clergy and sisterhood as well as an educated lay leadership that would evangelize their own people.

Realizing that Chinese culture—which maintained considerable separation between the sexes—did not allow males to freely evangelize women, Ford saw the benefits of having religious sisters participate as full-fledged missionaries. Sisters were taken out of the mission compound and assigned roles that were until then considered inappropriate. They were able to mingle with the Chinese women in their own environment, speak their language, talk from a woman's point of view, and gear their instructions to the concrete daily lives of Chinese peasant women.

His small experiment in this regard in 1934 did much to enhance the role of women within the Catholic Church, especially in missions.

Spying Charges

In April 1951, after the Communists had taken control of Kaying, Ford was accused of spying. He and five nuns were placed under arrest for being enemies of the government. While declaring his innocence and his love for the Chinese people, Bishop Ford was beaten and dragged through the streets and then sent to a Communist prison in Canton where he died from injuries on February 21, 1952.

The nuns arrested with him were held under house arrest for six months and then deported from the country.

Seed of the Church

Today, there are estimated to be about twelve million Catholics in China in both the state approved "Chinese Catholic Patriotic Society" and the underground Catholic Church.

Because [a high priest] is human, he is able to deal gently with the people, though they are ignorant and wayward. For he is subject to the same weaknesses they have (Hebrews 5:2).

The Perez Family
Colombia — May 19, 1954

Throughout history, political power and national unity have often been tied to keeping one national religion. This is still true in many countries around the world today. But this reality was personified in Colombia, South America, in the 1940s and 1950s.

Colonized by Spain in the sixteenth century, Colombia was unquestionably Roman Catholic until the Liberal Party, which stood for a decentralized federal government, separation of church and state, and religious freedom, challenged the Conservative Party, which embodied a central church state and state church. The two parties battled back and forth for the presidency, plunging Colombia into a hundred years of civil war in the 1800s—and undeclared civil war in the first half of the twentieth century.

Even when the Liberal Party had been "duly elected," the Catholic Church went on the offensive. Protestants were denounced from the pulpit as "false prophets" and "devouring wolves." Protestants, said the bishops, "come not only to steal our faith . . . but to ruin our national and social structure." Open opposition to Protestants and evangelicals became both a religious and patriotic duty. According to James and Marti Hefley, "From 1944 to 1958 at least 120 evangelicals or members of evangelical families were killed. . . . Eighty-eight Protestant churches and chapels were destroyed by fire or dynamite. An additional 183 houses of worship and 206 Protestant primary schools were closed by official orders. Over fifteen thousand evangelicals were driven from their homes. Protestant children were shut out of public schools."

No foreign Protestant missionaries died during this time. All of the martyrs were Columbian evangelical Christians, ordinary families who simply wanted the freedom to preach the gospel and worship God in peace and safety. Like the Perez family.

From Persecution to Pastor

He was simply known as Pastor Perez. He and his wife pastored an evangelical church in the state of Huila, where they were raising their family of seven children. But mobs and vigilantes were attacking Protestant churches and families at will while local government officials looked the other way. And one day they came for Pastor Perez, taking his twelve-year-old son, Bernardo, as well.

Hanging the boy by his thumb, the police accused them of being bandits and wanted a confession. In agony, the boy denied it. The persecutors turned on the father and asked how many people he had killed. "I have killed no one!" said the desperate pastor. "I follow God's Word which does not permit us to kill or do evil against anyone."

With no witnesses to back up their accusations, the police let them go. But six months later, during the night of May 19, a mob of armed vigilantes broke into the Perez home, shot Pastor Perez and his wife, and hacked at the children with machetes. David Perez, a young teenager, grabbed the hand of one of his little sisters and ran across the yard, trying to escape. But one of their attackers chased them with a machete and literally cut her hand from his grasp.

David was the only member of the Perez family who survived that terrible night. He was taken into the home of Christian and Missionary Alliance missionaries Lee and Ruth Tennies, who raised him as their own son.

If you were young David, what would *you* do with your life? Think about it.

A few short years later, David Perez enrolled in the Alliance Bible Institute in Armenia, Colombia, to prepare to become a pastor . . . like his father.

Seed of the Church

"The road to evangelization of our nation is paved with the blood of our martyrs."

—a Colombian pastor, imprisoned
during the Great Persecution, sitting on a platform
twenty years later with leaders of both political parties and
evangelist Luis Palau at a Banquet of Hope

We are . . . persecuted, but not abandoned; struck down, but not destroyed (2 Corinthians 4:8-9, NIV).

Brother Andrew
World—1955—present

He has a last name—a good, Dutch family name. But when he began visiting Christians in Communist countries, where for safety's sake most believers called each other by their first names only, he too began referring to himself simply as "Brother Andrew."

Born as Andrew van der Bijl on May 11, 1928, in Alkmaar, a town in northwest Netherlands, Andrew grew up in the years between the two world wars. The sleepy village where his father was the blacksmith didn't provide much adventure for this imaginative boy, so he often created his own "adventure"—or mischief. But when the German soldiers rolled into town in 1940, his mischief now had the thrill of patriotic resistance: sugar in the soldiers' gas tanks, firecrackers outside their headquarters.

Andrew was sixteen when the Netherlands was liberated from the Germans in 1944. Most people were sick of war, but Andrew joined the Dutch army and was shipped to the East Indies to put down the rebellion against Dutch colonization. This would certainly provide the adventure he longed for!

But war was not glorious, as he'd imagined. These were real people he was being trained to kill—people who wanted to rule their own country just as the Netherlands wanted to be independent. When he wasn't fighting, he got drunk so he wouldn't have to think, and when he was fighting, he wore a bright yellow straw hat, daring the "enemy" to shoot him and end his misery.

He did get shot—in the ankle. Recuperating in a hospital bed, he began to read the Bible from cover to cover. Crippled and confused about life, he attended a tent revival, then found a church to attend every night of the week. Finally, one night he prayed, "Lord, if you will show me the way, I will follow you."

Open Doors

Following Jesus soon came to mean one thing for Andrew: God wanted him to be a missionary. But he needed training. While taking a two-year course with the Worldwide Evangelization Crusade (WEC) in Glasgow, Scotland, he came face-to-face with his destiny: In the year 1955, as atheistic communism was closing country after country to religious freedom, God spoke to Andrew with the words, "Strengthen what little remains, for even what is left is at the point of death" (Revelation 3:2). From that day on, Andrew believed that no doors could be closed. No borders, no barriers, no armies could withstand the power of prayer . . . and no power on earth could ever chain God's Word. He would travel to the countries behind the Iron Curtain to encourage and help the believers.

What he found on his visits astounded him: Even pastors of churches often did not have Bibles. Andrew began smuggling Bibles past the border checkpoints and giving them to the struggling churches. It is not uncommon for Brother Andrew to experience God's supernatural protection and direction during his trips. Once, as Andrew waited while a border guard searched

257

his car, full of boxes of Bibles, he prayed, "Father, You have made blind eyes to see—now I ask you to make seeing eyes blind." The guard, apparently seeing nothing of consequence, waved Andrew through!

Facing potential death, he admits, "I'm not brave. I'm often scared stiff. I drive my car to the Iron Curtain border [but] have not the guts to go on. So I pull back ten miles and find a small hotel. I begin to pray and fast until I have the courage or the liberty or the boldness to go in, and that always works. But I would not go if my heart is beating with fear."

Seed of the Church

At first, Brother Andrew worked alone. Then God gave him a wife, and now over three hundred partners in ministry. The work—now known as Open Doors—expanded from Europe to include China, Cuba, Africa, . . . and now to forty-five countries. In 2000, Open Doors distributed 738,535 Bibles; 170,009 Testaments; 91,615 Gospels; 1,608,333 discipleship books; 561,695 other forms of Christian literature.

Faith comes by hearing, and hearing by the word of God (Romans 10:17, NKJV).

Jim Elliot

Ecuador—January 8, 1956

By all accounts, Jim Elliot, born in Portland, Oregon, in 1927, was a candidate for the American dream. He was good looking, had an engaging personality, knew how to work hard, played sports, got good grades, and graduated in 1949 with highest honors from Wheaton College. But Jim Elliot's dream was to know God and to serve him on the mission field, sacrificially if need be. Jim wrote in his journal: "He is no fool who gives what he cannot keep to gain what he cannot lose."

At Wheaton College, Jim fell in love with Elisabeth Howard, but hesitated to ask her to marry him until God gave him a direction for his life. In 1952 that direction was clear: God was calling him to Ecuador, to bring the gospel to Indian tribes who had never heard of Jesus. Elisabeth joined him a year later, and they were married in Quito.

The courtship of Jim Elliot and Elisabeth Howard was frustrating by most standards. Although strongly attracted to one another in college, Jim did not want a love relationship to distract him from being single-minded about serving the Lord. After graduation, their relationship was put on "hold" for two years while Jim sought a clear direction from God. Even after Elisabeth joined him in Ecuador and they were engaged, Jim warned that it might be another five years of language study and exploration before they could settle down to serve as a married couple.

But during this time of waiting, Jim wrote in his journal: "I have not lost one nameable thing by putting [Betty] and our whole relationship . . . into His hands." And, "I wonder sometimes if it is right to be so happy. Day follows day in an easy succession of wonders and joys—simple good things like food well-prepared, or play with children . . . or supply of money for rent or board within hours of its being due."

By God's grace, the wait was shortened. A couple was needed to open a new school in Puyupungu, and Jim and "Betty," as he called her, were married in Quito on October 8, 1953 before heading for their new village. Now, truly, Jim's "cup was running over."

A few years later, the Elliots teamed with four other missionary couples— Pete and Olive Fleming, Nate and Marj Saint, Roger and Barbara Youderian, and Ed and Marilou McCully—in a daring, secret plan to make contact with the fierce Waorani tribe (sometimes called the Aucas). "Daring" because the Waorani had a reputation for killing outsiders. "Secret" because the missionaries did not want any publicity to ruin their chances of making contact.

After months of locating a village by plane and air-dropping gifts, the five men decided to make contact. Pilot Nate Saint flew them to a sandy beach on the banks of a nearby river on Tuesday, January 3, 1956. They waited. On Friday a Waorani man and two women appeared at their camp for a friendly exchange. The men were excited. But on Sunday, their wives waited in vain for the daily radio contact. A search party discovered their husband's bodies, pierced by Wuaorani spears, floating in the river.

A tragedy? Yes. A tragic waste of young lives? No. Because several years later Jim's wife, Elisabeth, and Nate's sister, Rachel, were invited to live in that same Waorani village, translate the Scriptures, and share the gospel. Many of the Waorani murderers gave their lives to Christ.

In His Own Words

"The sheer joy of being in the will of God and the knowledge of His direction is my general experience."

—Jim Elliot in a letter to his parents as he sailed
to Ecuador in February 1952

You have made known to me the path of life; you will fill me with joy in your presence (Psalm 16:11, NIV).

Nate Saint
Ecuador—January 8, 1956

Born in 1923, Nate Saint grew up in Philadelphia, inventive by nature and eager to fly airplanes. He took flying lessons in high school and served in the U.S. Army Air Corps during World War II. After the war, he enrolled in

Wheaton College to prepare for foreign mission work and married Marjorie Farris. But in 1948 he and Marj dropped out to join the Missionary Aviation Fellowship and established a base at Shell Mera, an abandoned oil exploration camp on the edge of the eastern jungles in Ecuador. From there he flew short hops to keep missionaries supplied with mail, medicines, and other supplies.

Shortly after arriving in Ecuador, Nate began hearing stories of the fierce and reclusive Waorani Indians in the neighboring jungle. Stories had circulated for centuries about their spearing any intruders, from the Spanish conquistadors and Catholic priests to eight Shell employees killed just five years earlier.

Some anthropologists criticize missionaries for "disrupting" indigenous cultures. But the Waorani's blood culture threatened their tribal life with unending feuds and wanton killing, even the practice of burying a living child with its dead parent.

They enjoyed no organized sports, festivals, or religion (other than a general fear of the jungle spirits). There was no civic law or respect for elders or leaders; raw power controlled everything. There was no neighborly cooperation or organization (except in the hunt). Though they observed many taboos, they had no written language and only a limited oral history. Indeed, they were so savage and so lacking in the social restraints commonly known as civilization that they were a dying people.

Paying the Price

Despite the stories of the brutality of the Waorani, Nate Saint felt a strong desire to share the gospel with these people. He and four other missionaries decided to fly into the jungle in order to meet the Waorani. Saint was speared to death on the beach along the Curaray River along with the other four missionaries who tried to bring the gospel to the Waorani. The missionaries left behind five widows and nine fatherless children. One of those children was Steve Saint, who, as a small boy, had often stood by the Shell Mera runway waving to his dad as the small, yellow plane rose into the humid jungle air.

A little over two years after the massacre, Rachel Saint (Nate's sister) and Elisabeth Elliot (the widow of Jim Elliot, another of the missionaries killed) reestablished contact with the tribe and went to live with them. Elizabeth stayed a little over two years helping to translate the Scriptures into their language. Rachel remained among them for thirty-four years, sharing the gospel. Steve Saint grew up in Quito, Ecuador, often spending vacations in the jungle with his Aunt Rachel. In fact, he was baptized at age fourteen in the Curaray River, very near the site of the massacre by Kimo, one of the men who had helped kill his father but who by then was a caring pastor.

Seed of the Church

Some forty years after his father's death, Steve was present when a group of thirty-four university students from the States visited the Huaorani. "Where are the savages?" one of them asked him.

"You are among them," Steve answered. Seeing that the guests could hardly believe the answer, he suggested that they ask the Indians.

Dawa, one of the women responded, pointing to her aging and gentle husband who sat next to Steve. "Hating us, he speared my father, my brothers, and my mother and baby sister whom my mother was nursing in her hammock. [Then] he took me and made me his wife."

Putting his arm around the old man, Steve Saint added, "He killed my father, too."

Dawa explained to stunned visitors. "Badly we lived back then. But now, walking God's trail, which he has marked for us on paper [the Bible], we live well."

Don't you know that those who do wrong will have no share in the Kingdom of God? . . . There was a time when some of you were just like that, but now your sins have been washed away, and you have been set apart for God. You have been made right with God because of what the Lord Jesus Christ and the Spirit of our God have done for you (1 Corinthians 6:9-11).

Esther John
Pakistan—February 2, 1960

She was born in 1929, one of seven children in a Muslim family, and named Qamar Zia. At that time India was still the "jewel" of the British Empire, even as the demand for independence was growing louder and stronger. The idea of a separate homeland for the Muslim provinces in the northwest was also gathering momentum.

Qamar Zia began her education in a government school, but in her teens attended a Christian school. The deep faith of her teachers touched the sensitive spirit of the young woman and she eagerly read the Bible to learn what was at the core of this Christian faith. One day her reading took her to the book of Isaiah, chapter 53:

Who has believed our message? To whom will the Lord reveal his saving power? . . . He was despised and rejected—a man of sorrows, acquainted with bitterest grief. We turned our backs on him and looked the other way when he went by. He was despised, and we did not care. Yet it was our weaknesses he carried; it was our sorrows that weighed him down. . . . He was wounded and crushed for our sins. He was beaten that we might have peace. He was whipped, and we were healed! All of us have strayed away like sheep. We have left God's paths to follow our own. Yet the Lord laid on him the guilt and sins of us all.

261

Without understanding all that conversion meant, Qamar Zia felt herself drawn to this Savior who died for her sins.

In 1947, India gained independence from Great Britain. Shortly thereafter, the Indian subcontinent was partitioned into Hindu dominated but largely secular India and the newly created Muslim state of Pakistan. Immediately the region was plunged into rioting and chaos as Muslims, Sikhs, and Hindus found themselves on the wrong side of the partitioned provinces, Punjab and Bengal.

Qamar Zia was only eighteen years old when her family became part of the population upheaval and moved to Pakistan. But in the coastal city of Karachi, she met a Christian missionary named Marian Laugesen, who gave her a New Testament. As she devoured the Word, Qamar Zia's secret faith began to grow.

A Family Matter

But the young woman faced increasing pressure to marry a Muslim husband. At age twenty-five, she ran away from home, once again found Laugesen in Karachi, and worked in an orphanage there. At this time Qamar Zia changed her name to Esther John. Under pressure from her family to return home and marry, Esther took a train to the central city of Sahiwal in the Punjab, where she got a job working in a Christian mission hospital. Eager to become a teacher, she enrolled in a Bible training school.

After completing her studies, Esther made her home with American Presbyterian missionaries and began to evangelize in the villages. Making her rounds from one village to the next by bicycle, Esther taught the women to read after earning their trust and respect by working side by side with them in the fields.

Her family was perplexed and upset at Esther's refusal to marry a Muslim. Sometimes her relationship with her family seemed peaceful, but then old tensions flared up over her conversion to Christianity. On the morning of February 2, 1960, Esther was discovered lifeless in her bed, viciously murdered during the night.

Esther's death remained a mystery . . . but most who knew her believe that her conversion from Islam to Christianity provoked fear and hatred for her "betrayal." She was buried in the Christian cemetery in Sahiwal, and a chapel to her memory was built at the hospital where she had worked. And in 1998, her statue joined nine others at Westminster Abbey in London, commemorating Christian martyrs around the world.

[Jesus said,] "Don't imagine that I came to bring peace to the earth! No, I came to bring a sword. I have come to set a man against his father, and a daughter against her mother, and a daughter-in-law against her mother- in-law. Your enemies will be right in your own household! If you love your father or mother more than you love me, you are not worthy of being mine. . . . If you refuse to take up your cross and follow me, you are not worthy of being mine. If you cling to your life, you will lose it; but if you give it up for me, you will find it" (Matthew 10:34-39).

Dag Hammarskjöld

Congo—September 17, 1961

Dag Hammarskjöld was born in Sweden in 1905 and educated in the universities of Uppsala and Stockholm. Concerning his upbringing, he said, "From generations of soldiers and government officials on my father's side I inherited a belief that no life was more satisfactory than one of selfless service to your country—or humanity. This service required a sacrifice of all personal interests, but likewise the courage to stand up unflinchingly for your convictions. From scholars and clergymen on my mother's side, I inherited a belief that, in the very radical sense of the gospels, all men were equals as children of God, and should be met and treated by us as our masters in God."

And yet after years of government and diplomatic service in which he even became the chief of the Swedish delegation to the United Nations, he confided in his personal journal: "I demand what is unreasonable: that life should have meaning. I struggle for what is impossible: that my life shall acquire meaning. I dare not believe, I do not see how I shall ever be able to believe: that I am not alone."

Then, in 1953, he experienced a spiritual awakening that salvation could not be earned. "Not I," he wrote, "but God in me."

On April 1, the UN elected him secretary-general (a post to which he was reelected in 1957), and six days later he entered in his journal the following quotation from Thomas à Kempis's *Imitation of Christ:* "Being grounded and strengthened in God, they are incapable of any kind of pride; and since they return to God all the gifts with which he has blessed them, they do not at all receive glory from each other; but they seek only the glory of God alone." In spite of the honor of such a high office, he felt the sacrificial life of Jesus brood over his destiny: "That the way defined by one's calling ends on the cross, the one who had accepted his destiny knows—even when it leads him through the jubilation around Gennesareth or the triumphal entry into Jerusalem."

His accomplishments in the UN were substantial: In 1954–1955, he personally negotiated the release of American soldiers captured by the Chinese in the Korean War. During the Suez Canal crisis of 1956, he eased tensions (and possibly deflected war) by sending in the first-ever international peacekeeping force. In 1958, he suggested to the General Assembly a solution for the crises in Lebanon and Jordan. In 1959, he sent a personal representative to Southeast Asia when Cambodia and Thailand broke off diplomatic relations and another to Laos when problems arose there.

When the newly liberated Congo faced mutiny in its army, the secession of its province of Katanga, and the threat of intervention by Belgian troops in July 1960, the UN responded by sending a peacekeeping force, with Hammarskjöld in charge of operations.

Unfortunately, in the year that followed, the crisis in the Congo worsened. Hammarskjöld arrived in Leopoldville in September 1961, only to learn that fighting had erupted between Katanga troops and the noncombatant forces of the UN. A few days later, in an effort to secure a cease-fire, he left by air for a personal conference with President Tshombe of Katanga. Around midnight on September 17, he and fifteen others aboard his plane perished when it crashed near the border between Katanga and North Rhodesia (now Zambia).

After the crash, there were charges and denials of sabotage. Two commissions officially rejected theories of sabotage. Then in 1998, Archbishop Desmond Tutu, chairperson of South Africa's Truth and Reconciliation Commission, released documents on South Africa Institute for Maritime Research (SAIMR) letterhead that implicate the CIA and MI5 (England's security service), and a Belgian mining conglomerate, in "Operation Celeste" to get rid of the "troublesome" Hammarskjöld. The alleged motive was to prevent Katanga's mineral wealth from falling under communist control. These letters have also been denounced.

Faith Exposed

Whether or not Dag Hammarskjöld died from pilot error or foul play, his death made public (at his request) his private journal of faith (since translated and published in English as *Markings*) in which he prayed:

> Give me a pure heart—that I may see you,
> A humble heart—that I may hear you,
> A loving heart—that I may serve you,
> A believing heart—that I may remain in you.

Dr. Paul Carlson

Congo—November 24, 1964

It was meant to be only a short-term mission assignment. Paul Carlson, a promising young doctor just completing his residency in California in 1961, received a letter from the Christian Medical Society about the urgent need for medical doctors in the Congo. Even a "four-month term" would be welcome, the letter said. Paul had once considered medical missions, but his resolve had gotten lost in the demands of med school. Here was an opportunity to revive that inner urge—without having to make a major commitment.

Leaving his wife, Lois, and two young children in the States, Paul flew to the Congo and landed . . . in chaos. Belgium had granted independence to the large African nation barely a year earlier and abruptly withdrawn, without the crucial transition needed to establish a healthy new government. But for Paul, his five months of service in Ubangi Province was life changing. How could he settle into a medical practice in the United States, with its bulging churches and long lists of physicians in the phone book, when only three doctors could be found in the whole of Ubangi Province?

It wasn't easy leaving behind the security of a doctor's salary and the normal longing to raise one's children in a comfortable environment near family and friends. But Paul and Lois Carlson applied to the Evangelical Covenant Church of America as missionaries and arrived back in the Congo the summer of 1963 for a lifetime of service.

For Paul, that "lifetime" proved to be less than two years.

Over the Wall

Even though much of the Congo was in turmoil, medical work at the remote Wasolo mission hospital fell into a normal routine that first year. But aware of what was happening to believers in other parts of the country, "Dr. Paul" encouraged the Congolese Christians to faithfulness: "We do not know if we will have to suffer or die during this year because we are Christians. But it does not matter. Our job is to follow Jesus."

By August 1964, the Simba rebels were pushing toward Wasolo in "the forgotten corner" of northern Congo. Concerned for his family, Paul took his wife and children across the Ubangi River into the Central African Republic and then returned to his patients. Several times during the month of September, Lois made brief contacts with her husband via radio—then she heard dreaded news: Paul and three Catholic priests had been taken captive by the rebels. News of the American doctor's captivity filled newspaper headlines across the world. Unwilling to have their captive portrayed as a martyr, the rebels released a report that a "Major Carlson" had been arrested and would be tried as a spy.

For three tense months, threats of a "rescue invasion" kept the Simba rebels on edge. In Stanleyville, Paul Carlson was marched to a public square day after day and threatened with execution . . . then returned to the hotel that had been turned into a jail. His fellow prisoners included another American missionary, Charles Davis, five U.S. diplomats, and two American relief workers, as well as other foreign captives.

On Tuesday, November 24, prisoners and rebels alike were awakened by the roar of plane engines. The rescue invasion had begun! "Outside! Outside!" screamed the rebels, herding their hostages into the street, hoping to use the prisoners as a shield. Hearing machine gun and rifle fire, Paul and his fellow captives dropped to the ground. Then suddenly the gunfire stopped. "Run for it!" someone yelled. Paul and Charles scrambled to their feet and ran toward a nearby house surrounded by a stone wall. Paul motioned for Charles to go over the wall first—but as Charles reached back to help the doctor climb over, machine-gun fire split the air once more. Paul's bullet-riddled body fell into the street.

Grief-stricken, Charles Davis later said: "By letting me go first, Paul died that I might live."

In His Own Words
"My friends, if today you are not willing to suffer for Jesus, do not partake of the elements. . . . To follow Jesus means to be willing to suffer for Him."
—Paul Carlson to Congolese Christians gathered for communion at the annual church conference in early 1964

The greatest love is shown when people lay down their lives for their friends (John 15:13, written in the Lingala language on Paul Carlson's tombstone).

Irene Ferrel and Ruth Hege
Congo—January 24, 1964
Unlike some African countries coming out from under the rule of European colonialism, Belgian Congo (Zaire) did not prepare its conquered population for independence. "Christian" Belgium opened the door to Catholic (and later Protestant) missions from both Europe and America, built schools, and offered paternalistic benefits to its African "children." But the vast majority of military, political, and civilian posts of authority were filled by Belgians. Meanwhile, Leopold II, the playboy king of Belgium in the late 1800s, milked the Congo's vast riches for his own personal treasury. Capitalists from both Europe and America also lined their pockets (and the pockets of local chiefs), while the common people worked in conditions that rivaled slavery.

In 1959 a young Congolese named Patrice Lumumba made a visit to an All-African People's Conference in Ghana and returned with assurances that other Third World countries would support independence for Congo. Under pressure, Belgium granted full independence in June 1960—knowing full well that the Congolese had not been trained, educated, or given the experience to govern a nation during a century of colonialism. Installed as premier, Lumumba immediately ordered the Belgians to get out.

What happened next in Congo is a tangled web of military mutiny, mercenaries, and murder; UN technicians and troops trying to prop up a weak government; and communist willingness to train rebel leaders in guerrilla warfare. Rebels, plotting to overthrow the new Congolese government, recruited Simbali youth and promised them rewards if they exacted revenge for all that their ancestors had suffered under white rule.

In the midst of this "Simba uprising," many Christian missionaries, teachers, and medical personnel who stayed in the Congo after the Belgians left became targets for youthful guerrillas needing someone to blame for past injustices.

Women in the Bush

Barely four years into independence, rumors were flying as Simba rebels looted and burned villages and attacked government posts in the province of Kwilu, targeting a list of "undesirables." Missionaries were urged to "get out."

Irene Ferrel wasn't too worried. So far, the rebels had targeted only men. A graduate of the Bible Institute of Los Angeles (BIOLA), Irene had arrived in the Congo ten years earlier as a missionary with Baptist Mid-Missions. She put her passion for teaching to work at the Kwilu mission school and dispensary, which had been established to aid isolated villagers in the bush. But as reports of atrocities increased, even the local Congolese urged Irene and her coworker, Ruth Hege, to leave the mission. Reluctantly they agreed. On January 24, 1964, Irene and Ruth held a final worship service with their African Christian friends and coworkers. It was so hard to say good-bye! But they had to get to bed—a helicopter would land at the mission the next morning to pick them up.

In the middle of the night, Irene and Ruth were jolted from slumber as rocks crashed through their windows. A gang of young Simbali rebels, doped up on hemp and alcohol, dragged the two women from their beds and out into the bush. *Some of these boys can't be more than fourteen!* Irene thought. *Maybe I can talk to them.* But the young rebels were beyond any reason. They danced around the women in the bright moonlight, taunting and screaming. Then one of them fitted an arrow in his bow and let it fly.

The arrow pierced Irene's neck. Grasping it by its feathered end, she pulled it out, took a few steps, and then fell forward on her face. More arrows flew, striking Ruth as well. She fell in a heap beside Irene and pretended to be dead—even when one of the rebels jerked her head up so hard that her hair came out in his hand. Gloating at their "revenge," the Simbas left. Irene was dead, but Ruth crawled away to safety in the bush.

In the next two years, many more Christian missionaries and Congolese believers would be caught in the cross fire as the legacy of colonialism, racism, tribalism, and greed for power fought for the heart and soul of the Congo. The Congolese church was wounded, but—like Ruth Hege—survived to come back, even stronger than before. In 1968, there were fewer than one million Protestant Christians; by 1978, there were more than six million.

The Lord blessed Job in the second half of his life even more than in the beginning (Job 42:12).

Hector MacMillan

Congo—November 24, 1964

Dr. Paul Carlson was only one of hundreds of missionaries, Protestant and Catholic, from different countries and representing various mission boards who were captured and held hostage during the height of the "Simba rebellion" in the Congo in 1964 and 1965. Young Simbali youth, whipped into a frenzy by rebel leaders with a thirst for revenge for injustices suffered under European colonialism, made little distinction between government agents and missionaries who had come to the Congo to serve the people. Simply to be "white" or "foreign" was to be the enemy.

Most of the hostages were held in fairly large groups—men and women, families and singles, and children of every age. When Stanleyville, the second largest city in the Congo, fell to the Simba rebels in early August 1964, the missionaries at the Unevangelized Fields Mission (UFM) station known as "Kilometer Eight"—because of its distance outside of Stanleyville—were put under house arrest, including Hector MacMillan, a Canadian, his American wife, Ione, and their six sons.

House of Clay

Three decades earlier, Ione heard about John and Betty Stam's martyrdom in China and offered her life to God for missionary service. Graduating from Moody Bible Institute, the resolute young woman headed for Belgian Congo, where she met the boyish Scotch Canadian with the booming voice from Prairie Bible Institute (Alberta). Ione and Hector married in the Congo and spent the next twenty-three years as missionaries in their adopted country, during which they raised a family of six boys.

The missionaries tried to keep a normal routine going at Kilometer Eight during the four months of their captivity. But no one was fooled. Reports of a "rescue invasion" by Belgian mercenaries and American and British troops had their young, skittish captors on edge, and they knew they could be killed at any time. As tensions mounted, Hector talked with Ione about raising their sons "in the Lord," as though handing her the family reins. He also emphasized to his family that after death, the body is unimportant because the believer goes to be with the Lord. This spoke to Ione. She had recently read a biography of Adoniram Judson, missionary to Burma, who had nearly gone crazy with grief after his young wife died and he had to bury her in the raw dirt. She vowed, "If a member of my family is ever taken in death, by God's help I am not going to waste time and the energies he gave me worrying over a body of clay."

The next morning, the missionaries at Kilometer Eight heard the drone of planes overhead. They ran outside to gawk, then went back to their devotions and breakfast as usual. But as they sat down, Simba rebels burst into the room. "Outside! Everybody out!"

Once outside, the women and children were separated from the men and herded back inside one of the mission houses. Fearing for the men out in the yard, the women and children immediately began to pray. At that moment, the young soldier who had escorted them inside turned at the door and sprayed the room with machine-gun fire. Children screamed. Two of the MacMillan boys had been hit (but survived).

Almost simultaneously, they heard gunfire in the yard, then one of the men yelled, "You shot my friend!" More gunfire. Then silence.

Heart in her throat, Ione dared to look out. The rebels had fled; Hector lay crumpled on the ground. But the "body" lying beside him stirred and pushed himself to his feet. Only wounded, the missionary helped Ione and the other women carry Hector's body inside. "Your daddy has gone to be with Jesus," Ione comforted her crying sons.

Soon after the attack, mercenary soldiers and a senior UFM missionary arrived with trucks. "You must leave immediately! There is no room for baggage—just yourselves." The rescue team saw the bullet-riddled body of Hector MacMillan. "I'm sorry, ma'am, but . . . there is only room for the living. We cannot take your husband's body."

Ione, her two wounded sons, and the rest of the women and children climbed onto the crowded trucks. Ione realized God had prepared her for this moment. Hector was "away from [his] body" and "at home with the Lord."

Yes, we are fully confident, and we would rather be away from these bodies, for then we will be at home with the Lord (2 Corinthians 5:8).

Dr. Helen Roseveare
Congo/Zaire—October 1964

Becoming a doctor had been her daddy's idea. But while at Cambridge University studying medicine in 1945, Helen Roseveare fell in love with Jesus. From that moment on, she wanted to tell others about God's great love. Two years after she graduated with a medical degree, Heart of Africa Mission (later known as Worldwide Evangelization Crusade) assigned her to Ibambi, Congo, as a medical missionary.

Helen could never have anticipated the overwhelming medical needs in the Congo in 1953. "The ink was hardly dry on my medical diploma and overnight I became the Senior Chief Consultant of everything from pediatrics to geriatrics." From sunup till sundown, Helen was swamped with medical situations for which she rarely had the proper medicine or the right equipment—much less any time left over for evangelism. One day she looked up from her work to see a young African Christian—John Mangadima, sixteen years old—waiting to speak to her. "Dr. Helen, would you teach *me* to be a doctor?"

Helen was startled—but intrigued. As she taught the bright young man medicine, and he taught her Swahili, a vision began to grow: a training school for nurses. There would never be enough medical missionaries to meet the need. But if the Congolese themselves were trained and sent out to their home villages . . .

Energized by this vision, Helen oversaw the building of a thirty-two-bed training hospital. Four of her first five students passed the government exam for the nurse's aid diploma. But to her shock, other missionaries were critical. Training Africans to practice medicine wasn't *real* missionary work—especially for a woman. And the mission leaders, instead of lending support, reassigned her to Nebobongo. Helen channeled her frustration into building a new hospital and training African nurses. But when another missionary doctor—male—was assigned to Nebobongo as her "superior," basically demoting her after all her hard work, she felt demoralized. Plagued by self-doubts, strained relationships, and ill health, Helen took an early furlough, unsure whether she would return.

Living Sacrifice

But in 1960 her heart led her back to the Congo—just as the country won its bid for independence from Belgium and found itself plunged into a bloody civil war for power. Some missionaries were getting out, but Helen refused to leave. Now that she was back, she intended to stay. But her tenacity turned into a nightmare. In mid-August 1964, Simba rebels took over the mission at Nebobongo, holding Helen and other African Christian staff captive, even as they continued their work.

Late in October, the unthinkable happened: a rebel soldier invaded her bungalow during the night, brutally beating and raping her. Traumatized, Helen had to reach deep for spiritual assurance that God still loved her, that she wasn't abandoned—and to her surprise, found that God used her terrible experience to counsel and comfort other women who also had been violated during their captivity.

When mercenary soldiers freed the captives on the last day of 1964, Helen flew home to England, vowing never to return . . . until a letter arrived from John Mangadima the following August, describing the tragic neglect of the hospital at Nebobongo. "The condition of our country is no better than before the first missionaries came," he lamented.

The letter was a turning point for Helen. In 1966, sober but determined, her faith tested but unshaken, she returned to the Congo. With John Mangadima in charge of the Nebobongo hospital, she turned her energies to coordinating medical personnel and resources from various mission agencies. Within a decade, her vision for a network of clinics in various towns and villages, staffed by trained nationals, became a reality.

A student strike at the school where she had been a director for twenty years ended Dr. Helen Roseveare's term on the mission field in deep disappointment. Yet once again, Helen overcame disappointment by channeling her passion for missions into recruiting missionaries to reach those around the world who are still lost.

In Her Own Words
"I want people to be passionately in love with Jesus, so that nothing else counts . . . except knowing your sins have been forgiven by the blood of Jesus. We've only got this short life to get others to know the same truth."

—Dr. Helen Roseveare

Stanley Albert Dale
Indonesia—1968

He was "undersized" even as a young boy. But Stanley Albert Dale, born in 1916 in Australia, made up for his lack of brawn with a grit and determination that earned him a tough-as-nails reputation. At a revival tent meeting when he was seventeen, however, Stan met the biggest challenge of his life: committing his entire life to following Christ.

Serving with an elite group of Australian commandos during World War II, Stan was sent to New Guinea (now Irian Jaya, Indonesia). When his military service came to an end, Stanley Dale determined to get Bible training and go back—to bring the gospel to headhunters and cannibals who had never heard the saving name of Jesus. Several mission stations had already been established in parts of New Guinea, but Stanley's passion was to plow up new fields, so the seed of the gospel could be planted in pagan strongholds.

The Heluk River Valley

Stan Dale found his mission field among the Yali tribe in the easternmost part of what is now Indonesia. In 1961, accompanied by Bruno de Leeuw (a fellow missionary from the Regions Beyond Missionary Union), Stan hiked into the Heluk River Valley and set up camp between two warring villages— Yabi and Balinggama. Using a combination of sign language and the help of Dani porters, Stan and Bruno tried to communicate that they would like something to eat. The Yali tribespeople interpreted the request for food as a command to make peace, which was traditionally celebrated with the exchange of *anggerang owam*, or "kidney pigs." The peace that was established in May 1961 between the warring Yali, Dani, and Lani tribes in the Heluk River Valley was never broken and eventually spread throughout the entire Southern Yali territory.

Stan and Bruno began to construct an airstrip so their families and supplies could be flown in. When the airstrip was completed in March 1962, Dale's wife and five children joined him. Eager to share the gospel, Stan buckled down to learn the language. His first project was to translate the Gospel of Mark into the Yali language. Then he began the long, tedious work on the New Testament.

While still working on Bible translation, Stan was seriously wounded by five arrows in 1966 while trying unsuccessfully to protect two young men, new believers, who were attacked and killed while preaching the gospel in another village downriver. Many missionaries would have taken this as reason enough to move to a safer area, but not Stanley Dale. When his wounds healed, the tough Aussie came right back, confronting the pagan strongholds that still gripped many of the people.

The pagan priests were angry that Stanley Dale preached against the traditional superstitions and curses that kept the tribespeople in their power. One such superstition involved plots of "sacred ground" which could not be walked on or the entire village would be cursed. In September 1968, the missionary deliberately walked on the ground to show that the curse had no power—but he paid the ultimate price for his object lesson.

While Stanley Dale stood on the rocky banks of the Seng River with Phil Masters, a missionary colleague, an angry priest ambushed him and shot him point-blank with a bamboo arrow. Another priest, named Banu, also shot him in the back between his shoulder blades. With supernatural calm, Stanley Dale pulled out the arrows and broke them in half. With a cry, the Yali priests and warriors let fly a flurry of arrows. Ten, twenty, thirty . . . Stanley pulled them out, one by one, and broke them in half. The priests and warriors were dumbfounded. "Die! Die!" they screamed. Streams of blood poured from the wounds, but still he stood his ground.

When fifty to sixty arrows had pierced his body, Stanley Dale's life was finally spent—but the grip of the pagan curse had begun to crumble. By the end of that same year, almost twenty thousand believers among the Yali tribe had asked for baptism.

Fast forward to the year 2000. Others picked up Stanley Dale's translation work. On May 15 and 16 of the new millennium, three thousand people came together to celebrate a remarkable milestone—the entire Bible in the Southern Yali language.

Seed of the Church

"We are ready to be killed for you; to drown or be crushed in a landslide for your service. You died for us. . . . We are ready to suffer for you."

—Chant of former Yali warriors

Martin Luther King Jr.
Tennessee—April 4, 1968

Before he was known as a civil rights leader or a nonviolent activist, Dr. Martin Luther King Jr. was a preacher from Dexter Avenue Baptist Church in Montgomery, Alabama. He had trained at Morehouse College in Atlanta, Crozer Theological Seminary in Chester, Pennsylvania, and received his PhD in systematic theology from Boston University in 1955.

In December of that year, five days after Montgomery civil rights activist Rosa Parks refused to obey the city's rules mandating segregation on buses, black residents formed the Montgomery Improvement Association, elected King its president, and launched a bus boycott. King's home was bombed, and he was convicted along with other boycott leaders on charges of conspiring to interfere with the bus company's operations. Despite these attempts to suppress the movement, Montgomery buses were desegregated in December 1956, after the United States Supreme Court declared Alabama's segregation laws unconstitutional.

For King, faith and practice had always been inseparable. His grandfather, the Reverend A. D. Williams, and father, Martin Luther King Sr., were successive pastors of Atlanta's Ebenezer Baptist church. But both men were also civil rights leaders, with Williams having founded Atlanta's NAACP chapter. Nevertheless, it was Dr. King's exceptional oratorical skills as a preacher and his God-given courage that gained him national prominence until on the August 28, 1963, 250,000 people soared with hope as he delivered his famous "I Have a Dream" speech from the steps of the Lincoln Memorial. It concluded with the plaintive words of the old Negro spiritual, "Free at last! Free at last! Thank God Almighty, we are free at last!"

In 1958 a demented woman had stabbed Dr. King while he was signing autographs. The blade went in so far that the tip was on the edge of his aorta. After the surgery, the doctors said that if Dr. King had merely sneezed he would have died. But he hadn't sneezed, and God restored him to full health so he could complete his mission.

Ten years later, while giving a speech in Memphis, Tennessee, Dr. King said, "I am happy that I didn't sneeze. Because if I had sneezed, I wouldn't have been around" to take a part in several improvements that moved America a few steps closer to the dream he had portrayed in Washington. In legal terms, the most notable changes were desegregation and the Civil Rights Bill. But in moral terms, though many Americans came with great reluctance, we as a country moved toward more fair treatment of people of color. And as the biblical prophet Amos makes so very clear, God cares deeply about how we treat those who are oppressed (see Amos 2:6-7).

But in that same Memphis speech, Dr. King also spoke as though God had given him prophetic insight into what was to come his way from "from some sick white brothers." Nevertheless, he added, "It really doesn't matter what happens now." He knew he had completed his part, the assignment God had given him.

In His Own Words

"Well, I don't know what will happen now. We've got some difficult days ahead. But it doesn't matter with me now. Because I've been to the mountaintop. And I don't mind. Like anybody, I would like to live a long life. Longevity has its place. But I'm not concerned about that now. I just want to do God's will. And He's allowed me to go up to the mountain. And I've looked over. And I've seen the promised land. I may not get there with you. But I want you to know tonight, that we, as a people, will get to the promised land. And

I'm happy, tonight. I'm not worried about anything. I'm not fearing any man. Mine eyes have seen the glory of the coming of the Lord."
—Martin Luther King Jr., April 3, 1968

The next day, while standing on the balcony outside his motel room, he was assassinated by a hidden gunman.

[Mordecai told Esther,] "If you keep quiet at a time like this, deliverance . . . will arise from some other place, but . . . who can say but that you have been elevated . . . for just such a time as this?" (Esther 4:14).

Phillip Masters
New Guinea—1968

Phyliss and Phillip. No doubt the young couple got plenty of ribbing about their matching names. But when Phyliss and Phillip Masters, who both grew up in farm families near Sioux City, Iowa, got married in 1953, any potential mix-up of their names was not a major concern. Phyliss completed her education and taught two years of elementary school as the couple prayed for direction for their lives.

While attending Prairie Bible College in Alberta, Canada, Phyliss and Phil felt the call of God to go to Dutch New Guinea (now Irian Jaya, Indonesia) as missionaries. In 1961 the Masters family—including their children Crissie, Curtis, and Becky—exchanged the familiar comforts of Middle America to be missionaries with the Regions Beyond Missionary Union (now World Team). Two more sons were born in New Guinea.

Phil and Phyliss initially began work among the Dani tribespeople in the Toli Valley who had already begun to respond to the gospel. A teacher at heart, Phyliss was eager to help start literacy schools. Within two years, the Masters were working among the Kimyal tribe in the Eastern Highlands, learning the language, sharing the gospel message, baptizing believers, and setting up schools.

A Life Cut Short

Phil Masters was intrigued by the pioneer mission work of Australian Stanley Dale and Dutch Canadian Bruno deLeeuw among the fierce Yali tribe further inland along the eastern border. (See Stanley Albert Dale.) By 1968, Phil and his family had joined Stan Dale in the Heluk River Valley. With five children each in both families, the Masters and the Dales no doubt had a lot in common—not the least of which was to share the transforming power of Jesus Christ with these lost souls, caught up in the darkness of cannibalism and spiritism.

But even as some of the Yali people began turning toward the light of Christ, the pagan priests grew more hateful and resentful. Plotting an ambush, the priests attacked the two missionaries and several Christians along the rocky banks of the Seng River, cutting off one avenue of escape. As the others fled, Stanley Dale and a helper named Yemu turned to face the attackers, hoping to give the others time to get away. The attackers focused on Stanley Dale first. As arrows began to fly, Yemu ran toward Phil Masters, who urged him to keep going and get away. Phil, however, still stood his ground, knowing he could not help his friend, even as he saw Stan's body riddled with more than fifty bamboo arrows.

When Stanley Dale finally fell to the rocky ground, blood pouring from his extensive wounds, the warrior priests turned their fury on Phil Masters. Following his friend's example, Phil too stood his ground as scores of arrows pierced his body.

When both missionaries had finally fallen, the priests looked at each other in fear. Who had ever seen such courage? Why didn't they run? Why didn't they die right away? The normal course of events when an enemy had been killed was to cook him and eat him. But the priests were afraid to ingest this strange spirit. Dragging the bodies away from the river bank, they hid them in the tall grass. Later, a priest named Banu, afraid the two missionaries might resurrect from the dead, went back and beheaded the bodies.

Left alone to raise five children each, the two widows moved back to more established mission stations. Phyliss Masters, however, continued to work among the Dani people for another nineteen years—training literacy teachers, teaching children's classes, training Sunday school teachers at the different mission stations, and beginning a Women's Bible Class Ministry, just to name a few of the jobs she tackled.

Today, Phil and Phyliss's oldest daughter, Chrissie, and her husband, Dave, a pilot with MAF, continue doing mission work in what is now Irian Jaya, even as Phyliss, supposedly "retired," represents World Team at mission conferences, schools, women's retreats, and colleges, calling out and training a new generation of mission workers.

These trials are only to test your faith, to show that it is strong and pure. It is being tested as fire tests and purifies gold—and your faith is far more precious to God than mere gold. So if your faith remains strong after being tried by fiery trials, it will bring you much praise and glory and honor on the day when Jesus Christ is revealed to the whole world (1 Peter 1:7).

Betty Olsen
Vietnam—January 30, 1968

She was an unlikely heroine. Raised a "missionary kid" in Africa, Betty Olsen spent eight months each year away from her parents at boarding school. Homesick and resentful, redheaded Betty developed an attitude at school, rebelling against the school rules and keeping herself aloof from making close friends. Her sense of loss only deepened when her mother died of cancer when Betty was seventeen.

When her father remarried, Betty returned to the States to get her nursing degree, followed by graduation from Nyack Missionary College in 1962. Struggling with insecurities, Betty longed to get married and have her own family, but Mr. Right did not materialize. Unsure whether a mission board would accept her, she returned to Africa to work with her father and stepmother. But her obvious resentments and insecurities made her difficult to work with, and other missionaries requested that she be sent home.

Depressed and full of self-doubt, Betty could find no joy in her work as a nurse in Chicago. Contemplating suicide, she made an appointment with a youth counselor at her church. Why had God made her the way she was? Why didn't God answer her prayers for a husband and family? Why didn't people like her? She'd wanted to be a missionary—what was she supposed to do with her life now?

The counselor asked Betty, "How can you serve God if you aren't satisfied with the way he made you?" As they talked, she realized that in rejecting herself, she was rejecting God's design for the way he had made *her*. Whatever imperfections she had gave room for God's strength and grace to be revealed in her. She realized that her bitterness had driven her away from God—and had driven others away from her. The counselor pointed her to Scriptures showing that God wanted to develop her inner qualities to reflect "the beauty of Christ."

Counseling with young Bill Gothard—who later developed the famous Institute in Basic Youth Conflicts—gave Betty a whole new attitude and perspective on her life. Within a few years she had been accepted by the Christian and Missionary Alliance (C&MA) for medical work in Vietnam.

From Bitterness to Beauty

Vietnam in the 1960s was a dangerous place for foreign missionaries. Yet hundreds of Christian and Missionary Alliance missionaries stayed at their posts—hospitals, leprosariums, schools, churches—as the Viet Cong advanced into South Vietnam. On January 30, 1968, during the Vietnamese New Year, Tet, the Viet Cong and South Vietnamese soldiers clashed at Ban Me Thuot in what would later be called the Tet Offensive. Missionaries at the Christian and Missionary Alliance Bible School grounds were caught in the middle.

That one terrible week, the Viet Cong blew up two of the mission houses and mowed down several missionaries who were hiding in a garbage pit. In all, six American missionaries were killed, including a teenage girl whom Betty tried in vain to save with gunfire whizzing overhead. Three were captured and taken prisoner: Mike Benge, an American AID worker; Hank Blood, one of the C&MA missionaries; and Betty.

Months passed, and the surviving missionaries didn't know whether the captives were alive or dead. Months turned into years as the war raged, and hope faded. Then came the cease-fire agreement in 1973. The Americans agreed to leave if North Vietnam would release all their prisoners. The missionaries still in Vietnam eagerly scanned the lists of prisoners being released. Only one familiar name stood out: Mike Benge, the AID worker.

Mike had barely survived the long grueling marches in the jungles; Hank and Betty did not. After their deaths, he had endured confinement and beatings at the infamous "Hanoi Hilton" for five long years. But after his release, Mike made a point of meeting with the family members of his two fellow captives. Betty, he said, had suffered terribly in the jungle from malnutrition, dysentery, and exhaustion, which took their toll just two days after her thirty-fifth birthday. But in spite of her suffering, he said, "she never showed any bitterness or resentment. To the end she loved the ones who mistreated her."

Get rid of all bitterness, rage, anger, harsh words, and slander, as well as all types of malicious behavior. Instead, be kind to each other, tenderhearted, forgiving one another, just as God through Christ has forgiven you (Ephesians 4:31-32).

Gladys Aylward
China—January 3, 1970

Gladys Aylward, who had been born in London to a working-class family in 1902, could not give up the conviction that God had called her to China, not even when the China Inland Mission said she was unqualified. So when she heard that an elderly missionary in China wanted an assistant, Gladys saved the money she had earned as a parlor maid and bought a one-way train ticket. She arrived in Yangcheng, China, in November 1932.

The seventy-three-year-old missionary, Jennie Lawson, managed the Inn of Eight Happinesses for muleteers driving mule trains across the mountains. It offered not only food and a place to sleep but also Bible stories told by the two "foreign devils." Jennie Lawson, however, died a few months after Gladys's arrival, and she had to continue the work alone.

Prison Riot

About two years later, the mandarin of Yangcheng sent for Gladys. "Thank goodness you have come!" said the mandarin who was standing outside the local prison with the warden. From inside came bloodcurdling screams. Confused, the small Englishwoman bowed respectfully.

Wringing his hands, the warden said, "You must go in and stop the riot!"

"*Me*? Why don't you send in your soldiers?"

"Impossible!" the man cried. "They would all be killed!"

"But," Gladys protested, "if *I* went in there, they would kill *me*."

"Oh no," injected the mandarin. "You tell our people that God lives inside you. If what you say is true, surely he will protect you when you go inside the prison."

Gladys stared at the two men and swallowed hard. "All right, open the gate."

Inside the prison courtyard, prisoners were chasing each other with knives, screaming like madmen. Dead and wounded prisoners were lying everywhere. And running straight toward her was a huge man swinging a bloody ax over his head!

Gladys was so terrified she couldn't move. But when the man was only a few feet away, he suddenly stopped. One by one the other prisoners stopped yelling and running and just looked at her. Who was this short, little woman? What was she doing here?

Suddenly, Gladys got mad. "Give me that ax!" she demanded, holding out her hand. Wordlessly, the man handed her the bloody axe. Gladys looked at the prisoners. They were dressed in dirty rags. They were so thin their ribs showed. They looked cold and miserable. Suddenly, instead of being afraid of them, she felt sorry for them. "I have been sent by the warden to find out why you are fighting."

After several tense moments, a young prisoner stepped forward. "We don't know why we are fighting . . . but we are hungry and have nothing to do day after day."

Gladys frowned. "If you will promise to stop fighting and will bury the dead and take care of the wounded, I will speak to the warden on your behalf."

The prisoners agreed. As Gladys stepped outside, the city officials bowed to her with respect. She told the warden that the men must have work to do so they could earn money, buy food, and have self-respect—and she would return to inspect every day!

Flight of the Orphans

In 1938, the Japanese bombed Yangcheng. Already Gladys had adopted several orphans; now there were many more orphans who came to live at the Inn of Eight Happinesses. But the Japanese suspected that she was a spy, and it was no longer safe in Yangcheng. So in March 1940, Gladys fled over the mountains to the next province with a hundred children. A month later, she arrived safely without losing one child!

But Gladys was weak and ill. In 1942 an American friend helped her go back to England to see her family. Meanwhile, the Communists closed China to all foreigners.

In 1957, Gladys once again sailed for China, this time to Formosa. She started the Gladys Aylward Orphanage and soon had a hundred children. There, this small "unqualified" missionary served until her death on January 3, 1970.

Speak, and exhort, and rebuke with all authority. Let no man despise thee (Titus 2:15, KJV).

Nikolai Khamara
Soviet Union—1970s

Nikolai Khamara was a criminal. Having been arrested and convicted for robbery, he was sentenced to prison for ten years in the former Soviet Union. There he shared the same jail cell with some Christians. They intrigued Nikolai because they were able to be joyful even in the midst of great suffering, even when everything seemed hopeless.

He noticed that when they had a crust of bread, they shared it with someone who had none. Mornings and evening they folded their hands and spoke softly—though Nikolai could not tell to whom—until a peaceful expression appeared on their faces.

One day as he sat with two of them, one asked Nikolai, "What brought you here?"

"Ah," Nikolai waved his hand, "it was just my bad luck." Then he stopped. "No. It wasn't luck. It was because I am a man without a conscience. I did not care who I hurt." He then related his life of crime and turned aside with a shrug. "I am a lost man."

But before he could rise and walk away, a gnarled hand gripped his shoulder. "Wait friend," one of the Christians said. "Let me ask you a question. What is the value of a ten-ruble note if you lose it somewhere?"

Nikolai turned back, a frown wrinkling his brow. "What do you mean? Ten rubles are ten rubles. If I lose them"—he shrugged—"I'm out." Then he grinned. "But whoever finds them would be very happy."

"Exactly," said the Christian. "One more question. Suppose someone loses a gold ring. Would its value change?"

"What a foolish question! A gold ring is a gold ring. If you have lost it, somebody else will gain when he finds it. But its value doesn't change."

"Well, then," said the Christian, "what is the value of a lost man? Even if he is an adulterer or murderer, he is still a man, and doesn't his value remain the same?"

Nikolai nodded slowly.

"Every person is of such value that the Son of God forsook heaven and died on the cross to save him. God loves you, Nikolai. Nowhere in the Bible will you find Jesus asking someone what kind or how many sins he has committed. When he met men who had committed great sins, he said, 'Be of good cheer. Your sins are forgiven.' I also tell you that your sins are forgiven because Jesus died for you. All you have to do is believe."

The Faithful Believer

Nikolai did believe, and when he was released, he joined the underground church. Then one day, his pastor was arrested by the Communists, who tortured him to get him to reveal how the Christians printed and distributed gospel tracks. But the pastor did not crack.

279

Finally, the interrogator said, "Enough. We have a better way." And he brought in Nikolai Khamara, who had also been arrested. "If you do not tell all the secrets, we will torture one of your members in front of you."

"Oh, no. Nikolai, what should I do?" wailed Nikolai's pastor.

"Don't worry," said Nikolai. "Just be faithful to Christ and do not betray him. I am happy to suffer for the name of Christ."

But when the Communists prepared to gouge out Nikolai's eyes, the pastor withered until Nikolai said, "When my eyes are taken away, I will see more beauty than I see with these eyes. I will see the Savior. You just remain faithful to Christ to the end."

When they moved to cut out his tongue, Nikolai calmed his frantic pastor by shouting, "*Praise the Lord Jesus Christ!* There, I have said the highest words anyone can say. What does it matter now if they cut out my tongue?"

In this way, the communists martyred Nikolai for the sake of Christ, even while he encouraged his pastor not betray the church.

[Jesus said,] "If anyone acknowledges me publicly here on earth, I will openly acknowledge that person before my Father in heaven. But if anyone denies me here on earth, I will deny that person before my Father in heaven" (Matthew 10:32-33).

John Perkins
United States — February 7, 1970

"The highway police arrested Doug and the students and took them to the Brandon jail!" came the frantic voice over the telephone. Reverend John Perkins put down the receiver and looked at his wife, Vera Mae. "I've got to go to Brandon and do something," he said.

Perkins had already been in jail once—just before Christmas—when he and other folks from Voice of Calvary Ministries in Mendenhall, Mississippi, went to see a black teenager in jail. They'd heard he'd been beaten. The whole group had been "arrested"—including children—but never told what the charges were. Vera Mae and others from the community gathered at the jail, but they felt helpless and didn't know what to do. In 1969, black folks in Mississippi felt powerless against the whites who controlled everything.

That's when John Perkins got the idea for a boycott in Mendenhall. Whites owned everything, but they depended on blacks to buy from their stores. If blacks refused to buy, maybe the white folks would listen to what blacks wanted: justice, fairness, jobs.

The boycott started at Christmas and continued for several weeks. It got the attention of the store owners all right; it also angered many whites.

Now it was February 7, 1970. With two friends, Reverend Perkins drove to Brandon to see if they could post bond for Doug and the students. But when they got out of the car, sheriff deputies and highwaypatrol officers arrested them and threw them in jail.

Then the kicking and beating began. . . .

Let Justice Roll Down

John Perkins's mother had died in 1930 when John was only seven months old, and his daddy took off, leaving the kids in the care of John's sharecropping grandmother in Mississippi. John didn't grow up "religious," but he hung around the country church because that was the only place black folks could get together and socialize.

When John was sixteen, a white deputy shot and killed his brother Clyde while he was standing outside a movie theater. The family sent John to California for his own safety. After having dropped out of school, California was a chance to start over away from the overt racism of the South. He knew how to work hard, and soon he was experiencing a new feeling—success. Eventually, John married his sweetheart from back home, brought her to California, and started a family. This Perkins was going to be somebody!

But God interrupted John's plans. Visiting the church his young son attended, John accepted Jesus Christ, the living God who changes lives. He began reading the Bible for the first time. Discipled by others, he began speaking in both black and white churches. Then God told him to go back to Mississippi to help young people, who like he'd been, were going nowhere. But it wasn't easy going back during the civil rights movement. In the years that followed, John helped start a day-care center, youth program, church, adult education program, cooperative farm, thrift store, health center, leadership-development program, low-income housing development, and a training center.

But it was when he insisted on justice for all, as he had in February 1970, that he landed in jail, where police went to work on the "troublemakers," slapping, punching, and stomping on their heads, ribs, and groins. Though his face was bloody and his eyes swollen almost shut, John could see the faces of the officers, twisted with rage and hate.

While he did not respond with hate—he did not want to turn into what they were—it was a long time before John could see a police officer and not feel fear and bitterness. Gradually, however, he was able to forgive, understanding that racism hurts everyone.

Seed of the Church

Recipient of seven honorary doctorate degrees and numerous awards, John Perkins is known today as a man who puts the gospel to work. He began Mendenhall Ministries and Voice of Calvary, ministering to the whole person. His vision for transforming people and communities has taken shape in the Harambee Christian Family Center and the Christian Community Development Association (CCDA), bringing blacks and whites together in partnership for the sake of the gospel.

Let justice roll on like a river, righteousness like a never-failing stream! (Amos 5:24, NIV).

Watchman Nee

China—May 30, 1972

Watchman Nee and six of his young preachers-in-training spread out through the Chinese village of Mei-hua to preach the gospel. The villagers, however, were interested only in preparing to celebrate the feast of their god, Ta-wang (Great King) with the accompanying gambling, fireworks, and revelry.

Li Kuo-ching, Nee's youngest preacher and a new believer himself, became frustrated. "What's wrong? Why won't you believe?" he shouted to the crowd.

A villager shrugged. "Why should we? We have Ta-wang. His feast day is two days away. He's very dependable. For 286 years Ta-wang has sent sunshine for his feast day."

"Then I promise you," cried Li, who was only sixteen years old, "our God, who is the true God, will make it rain on Ta-wang's feast day."

News of Li's challenge spread rapidly. It was like a contest. "Agreed!" said the people. "If it rains on Ta-wang's feast day, then your Jesus is indeed God."

When Watchman Nee heard it, he was horrified. Li was young and inexperienced. Was he putting God to a reckless test? What if God did not choose to send rain on the feast day? Then no one would listen to them preach about Jesus. But then Watchman Nee recalled Elijah's challenge to the prophets of Baal. He and his assistants got excited. They felt confident that the God of Elijah whom they preached would send the rain.

Before breakfast was over on Ta-wang's feast day, rain was cascading down. After that, the villagers were eager to hear the gospel of Jesus Christ.

A Name and a Mission

Twenty-two years earlier Watchman Nee's mother lay awake listening to the night watchman make his rounds. Lin Huo-ping desperately wanted a baby boy. The Ni family already had two girls but no male heir, so important in Chinese culture. "O God," she prayed, "I will give this baby back to serve You, if You will only give me a son."

When Ni Shu-tsu ("He who proclaims his ancestor's merits") was born on November 4, 1903, in Swatow, China, there was a big celebration. True to her word, Huo-ping dedicated this child to God's service. As the child grew into a young man, he wanted a name that reflected his mission in life: preaching the Word of God.

Lin Huo-ping told her son about the night she lay awake listening to the watchman and the promise she had made to God. "How about Ni To-sheng?" she suggested. "To-sheng means 'the watchman.'" And that is how Watchman Nee got his name.

Watchman Nee was greatly influenced by Christian missionaries, especially Margaret Barber, an Englishwoman. But he was troubled that the foreign missions were divided by denominations—Presbyterian, Christian Missionary Alliance, and so forth. Watchman thought all Christians in each city should unite as one true local church under Jesus Christ. As a result of his teaching, many house churches were established, called "Church Assemblies," completely free of foreign connections. But even though Watchman's desire was unity, many who were drawn to these assemblies were drawn away from other churches—and so there were hard feelings and criticism. This movement, however, spawned many of the house churches that continued a faithful Christian witness even after the Communists expelled all foreigners.

Seed of the Church

In 1952, the Communists arrested Watchman and charged him as a "counterrevolutionary" and with corrupting the minds of young people. However, by this time he had helped establish about four hundred local house churches in China and thirty more elsewhere in Southeast Asia. Many of his writings, such as *The Normal Christian Life* and *Sit, Walk, Stand*, continue to inspire Christians all over the world. The Communists held him in prison for twenty years until he died on May 30, 1972.

Under his pillow, he left the following note: "Christ is the Son of God who died for the redemption of sinners and resurrected after three days. This is the greatest truth in the universe. I die because of my belief in Christ."

Wang Zhiming
China—December 29, 1973

Wang Zhiming's story can't be understood apart from the cultural and political upheavals occurring in China during the twentieth century. He was born in 1907 in Yunnan Province, just after the Boxer Rebellion in which as many as twenty thousand Chinese Christians were killed, as well as several Western missionaries. Nationalistic fervor and a desire to be rid of Western imperialism took many forms during Zhiming's lifetime—including the development of the Three-Self Patriotic Movement claiming to be China's indigenous Christian church.

To many Chinese, Christianity was the cultural arm of Western imperialism. If Christianity was to survive in China, reasoned some Chinese Christian leaders, it must divorce itself from Western influence and root itself totally in Chinese thought and culture. Thus the Three-Self Patriotic Movement was born, incorporating principles of self-sufficiency: Self-Support (financial), Self-Leadership, and Self-Propagation. Today known as the Three-Self Church—the only Protestant denomination recognized by the Chinese government—it is controversial to most Western Christians, as well as to many Chinese, who feel that government controls inhibit true evangelization and freedom of religion.

During this time, however, Wang Zhiming was a simple pastor with a heart to minister among the approximately three thousand Christians in Wuding County, Yunnan. Educated in mission schools, Zhiming taught school for ten years and served as an evangelist for five years before being elected chairman of the Sapushan Church Council in Wuding in 1944, then ordained a pastor in 1951. By 1954, the Communists had won the civil war with Chiang Kai-shek, and all Western missionaries had left China. Zhiming loved his country and did his best to be loyal to the communist government, but he refused to take part in "denunciation meetings" and did nothing to foment hatred against foreign governments or peoples.

From 1966 until 1976, the Gang of Four unleashed the so-called "Cultural Revolution" intended to wipe out all vestiges of "the old" and replace it with "the new"—a scheme which rained cruelty, evil, and inhumanity upon their own people. The Red Guard, the young "enforcers" of the cultural revolution, sought to root out religion wherever they found it. Churches were closed, worship was forbidden, and Bibles confiscated and destroyed. Wang Zhiming dared to criticize the Red Guard—and in May 1969 he was arrested with his wife and children and put in prison. (Wang's wife was released after three years in prison, but two of his sons remained in prison for nine years and another reportedly committed suicide while incarcerated.)

Four years later, at the age of sixty-six, Zhiming was brought out of prison on December 29, 1973, and executed publicly at a mass rally of more than ten thousand persons. Meant to unite the people against a "religion" that transcended the nationalistic spirit, the rally instead broke into riotous groups, and the executioner was assaulted by sympathetic Christians among the crowd.

As the Cultural Revolution crumbled, the policy to wipe out religion was modified. The Three-Self Church was officially recognized, but under strict government controls (while independent house churches and other denominations were declared illegal and suffer continued pressure and persecution). In 1980, Wang Zhiming was "rehabilitated" by the state (i.e., the charges against him declared false) and his family was compensated for their sufferings.

In 1981, a memorial gravestone was dedicated at Sapushan Church, near the village in Wuding County where Wang Zhiming pastored for nearly twenty years. His statue also stands in a niche over the entrance to Westminster Abbey, representing the witnesses who gave their lives as Christian martyrs during the twentieth century.

Seed of the Church

As the Scripture says of the Saints, "They will rest from their labours, for their deeds follow them."

—Inscribed on a memorial to Wang Zhiming,
the only monument in China known to commemorate
a Christian killed during the Cultural Revolution

I heard a voice from heaven saying, "Write this down: Blessed are those who die in the Lord from now on. Yes, says the Spirit, they are blessed indeed, for they will rest from all their toils and trials; for their good deeds follow them!" (Revelation 14:13).

Archbishop Janani Luwum
Uganda—February 16, 1977

In 1877, the Church Missionary Society of the Anglican Church sent missionaries Wilson and Shergold-Smith to Uganda, where they were welcomed by King Mutesa I. But under his son, Mwanga II, Christians suffered severe persecution. However, the church continued to grow rapidly through indigenous evangelization. In 1935, a revival spread throughout eastern Africa. People were paying their debts, asking forgiveness, and reconciling with old enemies.

Meanwhile, Uganda became a British Protectorate around 1900, and then regained its independence in the 1960s. Prime Minister Milton Obote took full control of the government in a palace coup. In 1971, Obote's army chief of staff, General Idi Amin, staged a military coup of his own and took over as "president for life."

Both Protestant and Catholic clergy tried to work respectfully with the government, even as they strengthened their flocks for possible persecution. The Anglican Church prepared to celebrate its Centennial in 1977, including a play about the three young pages martyred by King Mwanga, to correspond with Martyrs Day on June 3.

But Idi Amin was determined to stamp out all traces of dissent. People were disappearing at a rapid rate and turning up dead without benefit of trial or conviction. On Sunday, January 30, Bishop Festo Kivengere preached a sermon on "The Preciousness of Life," denouncing the violence and charging the government officials in the congregation to not abuse their God-given authority. It was a challenge that did not go unanswered.

The Wreck That Wasn't

The following Saturday, February 5, government soldiers burst into the home of Archbishop Janani Luwum in a predawn raid, on the pretext of looking for a stash of weapons. They found nothing, and Luwum wrote a note

285

to President Amin protesting the way the search was carried out and asking for an opportunity to meet with the president to convey the deep concerns of the religious community with the heightened repression and killings. To Luwum's surprise, Idi Amin invited the archbishop and other religious leaders to a meeting in Kampala on Wednesday, February 16, "to talk about their concerns."

That evening, Festo Kivengere, who had accompanied his archbishop, returned alone with shocking news: Janani Luwum had been detained! The delegation had been kept waiting many hours, then had been told to go home—except for Janani Luwum. When Kivengere and the others refused to leave, saying they would wait for their archbishop, they were ordered to leave at gunpoint. "That," said Festo Kivengere with a heavy heart, "is when we knew that our archbishop had been arrested."

All night long people gathered at the Luwum home in Kampala to pray. Mary Luwum insisted on being driven to the building where her husband had been taken into custody, but no one could tell her what he had been charged with or where he was.

People were still on their knees praying when someone ran into the room with the morning paper. The frontpage headline read in bold letters: Archbishop Killed in Car Crash. A picture of a wrecked car accompanied the story. Mrs. Luwum began to weep. But many in the room were suspicious. That wrecked car looked familiar, like one that had been wrecked weeks ago. Many of the Archbishop's friends believed that Janani Luwum had refused to sign a confession of any wrongdoing, so was taken somewhere and shot.

The Christians in Kampala urged Festo Kivengere to flee. If Idi Amin was so bold as to kill the Archbishop, they knew Kivengere would be next. The Kivengere family managed to escape out of the country, traveling over the mountains to Kenya.

The archbishop's body was delivered to his native village in a sealed coffin for burial. The villagers pried open the coffin; that's when they discovered the bullet holes.

Forty-five thousand people gathered for a memorial service for Janani Luwum in Kampala at the site where the martyred bishop, James Hannington, was buried. During Festo Kivengere's exile, he wrote a book about his own journey toward forgiveness: *I Love Idi Amin — The Story of Triumph Under Fire in the Midst of Suffering and Persecution in Uganda.*

In His Own Words

"While the opportunity is there, I preach the gospel with all my might, and my conscience is clear before God that I have not sided with the present government which is utterly self-seeking. I have been threatened many times. Whenever I have the opportunity I have told the president the things the churches disapprove of. God is my witness."

—Archbishop Janani Luwum

Chet Bitterman

Columbia—March 7, 1981

When Pope John XXIII was installed in the Vatican in 1958, he called for an end to Catholic-Protestant tensions around the world. In South America, where evangelicals and Protestants had been denounced and persecuted for decades by the Catholic hierarchy and local vigilantes who saw them as "traitors," the Pope's declaration ushered in an era of grudging tolerance at first, then genuine respect and cooperation.

But terrorism as a tool of political change continued to create an undeclared war between right-wing government factions and leftist liberation movements—with both Catholics and Protestants often caught in the middle. In 1980, three American nuns and a Catholic lay worker were murdered in El Salvador by a right-wing government faction because they were helping street children left homeless by the war—and thus seen as "aiding the rebel cause." In Guatemala, nine priests on a right-wing hit list were killed in as many months. That same year in Guatemala, terrorists from the leftist Guerrilla Army of the Poor gunned down twenty-eight-year-old John Troyer, a Mennonite missionary.

To heed the call to missions in South America during the twentieth century was to face the very real threat of terrorism. Wycliffe Bible Translators, in its mission to make God's Word available to all language groups, faced this reality head-on. In 1975 the mission voted not to yield to terrorist demands under any circumstances. To give in to demands might save one missionary hostage—and put thousands of others at risk.

With Bible translation came literacy; with literacy came education; with education came better farming methods that helped many poor in the outlying villages. Educated peasants thought for themselves and did not readily pick up arms to join the Marxist guerrillas. To M-19, one of Columbia's most notorious guerrilla groups, that meant Wycliffe Bible Translators and its Summer Institute of Linguistics (SIL) had to go. M-19's leaders devised a plan: to kidnap Al Wheeler, the director of Wycliffe's office in the capital city of Bogota, and hold him hostage until all the Bible translators left the country.

The Wrong Hostage

On January 19, at 6:30 A.M., hooded terrorists burst into the SIL residence in Bogota and herded the twelve adults and five children into the living room, where they were bound and gagged. "Wheeler! Where's Al Wheeler?" they demanded.

The missionaries could only shake their heads. Wheeler wasn't there.

"You then!" The guerrilla leader pulled a young American to his feet. Chet Bitterman and his wife and two children had been in Columbia only a few years. But the terrorists shoved Chet into a car at gunpoint and roared away. His wife and the other missionaries were bewildered. Why had they taken Chet? What did the guerrillas want?

The answer came four days later in a written demand: "Chet Bitterman will be executed unless the Summer Institute of Linguistics (SIL) and all its members leave Columbia by 6:00 P.M. February 19."

The missionaries all agreed: they could not capitulate. Prayer chains formed across the world as February 19 came . . . and went. Other deadlines were set, then passed. The terrorists sent letters and photos from Chet to local newspapers to prove he was being treated well. In a letter published on the front page of a Bogotá newspaper, a Catholic priest pleaded: "We want to ask the kidnappers to free this man who had dedicated his life to the extremely noble task of translating the Bible into an Indian language. We can't become . . . indifferent to the pain of our Protestant brothers. We esteem and respect them." The Wycliffe missionaries were hopeful that Chet might be released unharmed.

Then came the dreaded news, a messenger banging on the gate: "They've found Chet's body in a [mini]bus!" It was March 7. Chet had been held hostage forty-eight days.

What went wrong? But even in her grief, Brenda Bitterman prayed with friends, "Lord, thank you for choosing Chet. We know you don't make mistakes."

Seed of the Church

According to Cam Townsend, founder of Wycliffe Bible Translators, more than two hundred people from around the world volunteered to take Chet's place.

In His Own Words

"If something is worth living for, isn't it worth dying for?"

—Bernie May, past president of Wycliffe Bible Translators

Randy Alcorn

Portland, Oregon—1989—present

As one of the founding pastors, Randy Alcorn had seen his congregation grow into a substantial church in the twelve years he and his wife, Nanci, ministered in the Portland, Oregon, suburb. He made a good salary, and as a burgeoning author, was receiving book royalties. He also served on the board of a crisis pregnancy center, and he and his family had opened their home to a pregnant girl, helping her find an adoptive home for her baby.

Walking with this young woman through the plight of her unplanned pregnancy heightened Randy's concern for all the other babies who were dying from abortions. He began to participate in peaceful nonviolent "rescues" at abortion clinics, which led to his arrest on a number of occasions followed by short stays in jail.

When an abortion clinic won a court judgment against him and several other protesters, Randy told the judge, "I'll pay anyone anything I owe them, but I'll not hand over money to people who would use it to kill babies."

The court's response was to garnish his wages, requiring the church to send a quarter of his wages each month to the abortion clinic.

Randy resigned from his ministry to protect the church from the choice of paying the abortion clinic or defying a court order. In addition, he assigned all his book royalties to Eternal Perspective Ministries, which employed him at minimum wage—an amount the court could not legally touch. "On the positive side," Randy recalls, "our family had been living on only a portion of my salary from the church, and we'd just made our final house payment a few months earlier, so we were out of debt." Still, there was the possibility the court could take their house and all other assets in the $8.2 million suit against Randy and his codefendants, even though their actions hadn't involved any violence or property damage.

But the night before the trial, Randy's attorney called to say, "I don't know how to explain this, but I just received a fax from the abortion clinic. They want to drop you from the lawsuit."

What a relief! Their house was safe and their girls, nine and eleven, could continue attending the private Christian school they loved. But why had he been dropped from the suit? The only reason Randy and his attorney could come up with was that, as a pastor, he'd received considerable press, and the abortion clinic preferred dropping his name, thereby ending the ongoing coverage of his moral objections to abortion.

Out of the Mouths of Babes . . .

After hearing the offer, Randy's eleven-year-old daughter said, "Daddy, if the abortion clinic thinks they'll be better off without you on the case, it's a good sign God wants you there." His younger daughter agreed. And that night Randy told his dumbfounded attorney they would remain on the lawsuit.

Through numerous lies and unfair maneuvers and a blatantly prejudicial judge, the abortion clinic won their suit of $8.2 million against Randy and his codefendants. But the clinic never got Randy's house, and an anonymous donor paid his children's tuition to get them through school.

Seed of the Church

During the thirty-day trial, three abortion clinic employees quit. One explained, "I don't know what happened. It's like I suddenly woke up and realized we're killing babies here. That's not what I want to do with my life."

In addition to many other projects, in 2013, Eternal Perspective Ministries—the organization Randy started and works for—was able to give away 39,458 books to organizations and individuals for ministry needs, distributed $477,615 from book royalties to other worthy organizations, and funded the translation of Randy's book *Why Pro-life?* into French, Albanian, and Bosnian, to help reach people worldwide with the truth about the unborn.

The Lord watched over the other defendants, and none of them were devastated by the judgment. Though one lost approximately $30,000 in retirement monies, the Lord was faithful to provide and more than made up for any loss of income.

In His Own Words

"What others intended for evil, God intended for good (Genesis 50:20). We began a wonderful new ministry and took that minimum-wage salary. All of our assets, including the house, were in Nanci's name. (She reminded me I should be nice to her). Before any lawsuits were filed, I'd removed my name from bank accounts and checkbooks. By the time we were done, legally I owned absolutely nothing. And for the first time I began to understand—to truly know—what God means when He says, 'Everything under heaven belongs to me' (Job 41:11)."

—Randy Alcorn

Part 5

Communism: Persecution by Design

Over the centuries since the church was founded, nearly seventy million people have been martyred for being Christians.[1] In the West, the mention of Christian martyrs often evokes images of early believers remaining faithful while hungry lions tore them apart in Roman arenas . . . or perhaps brave reformers enduring the Inquisition's rack only to be burned at the stake . . . or maybe dedicated missionaries witnessing to hostile headhunters.

However, another enemy of the church rivals the lethality of all the Roman emperors, the barbarians on the frontiers of civilization, the hordes of the great Khans, the Nazis, or even adherents of hostile religions. And that is Communism, which in China, North Korea, and Vietnam is still persecuting and killing Christians today.

In their voluminous and scholarly work *The Black Book of Communism*, Stephane Courtois and associates estimate the total number of victims of Communism worldwide, from the Russian Revolution in 1917 to the Soviet war in Afghanistan in 1989, to be between 85 and 100 million.[2] The means of death ranged from war and starvation to torture and execution. Of that number, researchers David Barrett and Todd Johnson claim that 23.3 million were Christians who died in the Soviet Union alone.[3] As with other persecutions, some were offered the opportunity to renounce their faith, while others were merely rounded up because they were Orthodox, Mennonites, Catholics, Baptists, or Seventh-day Adventists; stripped of their possessions; and sent to Siberia where they died in a forced labor camp. But that number—23.3 million—is equivalent to one-third of all the Christians martyred throughout history.

Perhaps the free world was too weary after World War I to pay much attention to the atrocities of the Russian Revolution. Perhaps Russian Orthodox Christians in the Soviet Union seemed too remote and "unlike us" for westerners to heed their hue and cry. Perhaps the Mennonite refugees who escaped seemed too insignificant to get concerned over why they were fleeing. Perhaps it was just a matter of poor communications: We didn't really know what was happening until it was too late.

This is not to say there wasn't concern in the West about the spread of Communism. It was only the imminent threat of Hitler that enticed Churchill to support Stalin during World War II. And certainly, after the war, a strong anticommunist sentiment swept the United States, somewhat fueled by reports of persecution, but other objections to Communism seemed to attract the most attention.

- Geopolitically, the free world feared communist expansionism as Eastern Europe and most of Asia embraced Marxism. And in the third world, from Africa to Cuba, Communism co-opted nationalistic struggles to throw off colonialism.
- Militarily, of course, the Cold War raged with its threat of MAD—"mutually assured destruction" by a nuclear war.
- Economically, Communism promised struggling third world peoples security: "From each according to his ability to each according to his need," while painting capitalism as a greedy oppressor/exploiter.
- Theologically, everyone knew that Communism was atheistic, accusing capitalists of using religion as an "opiate of the people" in order to fleece its citizens. Most people could see that Communism substituted Karl Marx as the messiah, *Das Kapital* for the Bible, and Lenin's tomb as the sacred shrine.
- Personal liberty was essentially absent in communist countries, and that was distasteful to those in the free world. Added to this were ongoing reports of the horrors of the gulag, banishment to Siberia, and the gruesome torture of dissidents—oftentimes Christians.

With these concerns in mind, many westerners dedicated themselves to opposing Communism. However, after a time, the reports of persecution in communist countries were dimmed by constant denials. Add to this the kangaroo court an overzealous Joseph McCarthy made of the Senate, then the dishonesty and folly that surrounded the Vietnam War, and the intolerable terror of a seemingly never-ending Cold War, and many westerners began looking for a way we could just "all get along." To some churches in the West, "Give peace a chance!" seemed a far more noble cause than stirring up a fuss about the thousands of Christian Indians and eight hundred pastors murdered by the Communist Shining Path in Peru during the 1980s.

Theoretically, the church is not supposed to defend or attack any political party. The church was born in a hostile, even dangerous, environment, and it often thrives in the same. There was truth in the indictments against greedy capitalists. Militarily, MAD was mad, and it was hard not to see the great superpowers in a struggle for world domination that left no party honorable. As for the theological battles, some westerners may have appeased themselves with the promise that the truth would ultimately triumph. We in the West certainly wanted to hang on to our freedoms and privileges, but world history had been dominated by dictators, so why be so concerned about "restrictions" in the USSR or China? Torture of dissidents was terrible, but perhaps some brought it on themselves, and besides, how many stories of "occasional" excesses like hanging people by their thumbs or exploding them with a fire hose can one take if it occurred some time ago on the other side of the world and there's nothing now the average person can do about it?

What people in the free world didn't seem to take sufficient note of, however, was that in the middle of the debates, in the middle of the Cold War, millions were dying, many of them Christians and many of them as martyrs.

But the carnage continued. Even after the fall of the Soviet Union, people are still dying for their beliefs under Communism. According to *New York Times* reporter Nicholas D. Kristof, "Secret Communist Party documents just published in a book, *China's New Rulers*, underscore the grip of the police. The party documents say approvingly that 60,000 Chinese were killed, either executed or shot by police while fleeing, between 1998 and 2001. That amounts to 15,000 a year, which suggests that 97 percent of the world's executions take place in China."[4] He goes on to note that many of these are Christians.

A recent report based on firsthand evidence published by Christian Solidarity Worldwide summarized the plight of Christians in China as follows:

Christians described how they were beaten with fists, batons and poles, hung from the ceiling and tied in excruciating positions. Some were tied for hours on end with their arms bound diagonally across their backs, their thumbs secured with wire and, in some cases, with weights attached to increase the pain. Others were tied up in the shape of the crucifix and left hanging in agony for hours. One believer gave eyewitness evidence of the use of actual crucifixes in torture, saying that detainees (not necessarily Christians) are tied onto the crosses and leaned at an angle against the wall for periods as long as a whole day. The impact on the internal organs is horrific as the strain causes them to spiral into chaos. Other torture involved excessive exposure to the elements. One man was heard calling out the name of Jesus and was picked up by four guards and thrown to the ground repeatedly until he died.

Frequent recent arrests, accompanied by torture, were reported. Hundreds of Christians suffer daily in the gruelling labour education camps in China. Others are released after arrest and torture on payment of heavy fines.[5]

Tribulation

It must be bad enough if you or your church is being persecuted while over the hill or in the next city you know there is peace, as may have been the case in some ancient locales. But how much more frightening it must be when throughout the land—your whole "world"—Christians are being hunted and persecuted and there is no place to flee, no safe haven. Perhaps those who experience such horrendous, ongoing persecution wonder whether they are in the middle of the Great Tribulation of Revelation 7:14.

The question naturally arises, How can they remain faithful? How can they resist denying Christ to save themselves, their families, or even to die without enduring more pain? Perhaps the answer is in the commitment of a martyred African pastor in Zimbabwe. Can we affirm it with him?

I'm a part of the fellowship of the unashamed. The die has been cast. I have stepped over the line. The decision has been made. I'm a disciple of His and I won't look back, let up, slow down, back away, or be still.

My past is redeemed. My present makes sense. My future is secure. I'm done and finished with low living, sight walking, small planning, smooth knees, colorless dreams, tamed visions, mundane talking, cheap living, and dwarfed goals.

I no longer need preeminence, prosperity, position, promotions, plaudits, or popularity. I don't have to be right, or first, or tops, or recognized, or praised, or rewarded. I live by faith, lean on His presence, walk by patience, lift by prayer, and labor by Holy Spirit power.

My face is set. My gait is fast. My goal is heaven. My road may be narrow, my way rough, my companions few, but my guide is reliable and my mission is clear.

I will not be bought, compromised, detoured, lured away, turned back, deluded or delayed.

I will not flinch in the face of sacrifice or hesitate in the presence of the adversary. I will not negotiate at the table of the enemy, ponder at the pool of popularity, or meander in the maze of mediocrity.

I won't give up, shut up, or let up until I have stayed up, stored up, prayed up, paid up, and preached up for the cause of Christ.

I am a disciple of Jesus. I must give until I drop, preach until all know, and work until He comes. And when He does come for His own, He'll have no problems recognizing me. My colors will be clear![6]

Notes

1. David Barrett and Todd Johnson, "Evangelism through Martyrdom: 70 Million Christians Killed for Their Faith in 220 Countries across 20 Centuries," *World Christian Trends* (Pasadena, Calif.: William Carey Library, 2001), global diagram 16.
2. Stephane Courtois et al., *The Black Book of Communism* (Cambridge, Mass.: Harvard University Press, 1999), x. (First published by Robert Laffont in France in 1997 as *Le Livre Noir du Communisme: Crimes, Terreur, Repression.*)
3. David Barrett and Todd Johnson, "Global Top Ten Lists on 145 Major Missiometric Categories," *World Christian Trends* (Pasadena, Calif.: William Carey Library, 2001), "Martyrs," list 5.
4. Nicholas D. Kristof, "God and China," *New York Times,* November 24, 2002.
5. Christian Solidarity Worldwide, P.O. Box 99, New Malden, Surrey KT3 3YF, UK. Press release dated December 8, 2000. Published by Jon Dee in the "Persecuted Church Collection." Used by permission. www.persecutedchurch.com.
6. Louise Chapman Robinson, veteran African missionary and former president of the Nazarene Foreign Missionary Society, claims this statement was found among the papers of a Zimbabwean pastor after he was martyred.

The Witnesses

Victims of Eastern Lightning

China—1989

"A little truth is a dangerous thing." "A wolf in sheep's clothing." "A little white lie." As these common sayings attest, danger doesn't always appear with flashing warning lights, but often comes disguised in half-truths. This is true of cults all over the world that masquerade in the cloak of Christianity.

In 1989, Zhao Wei Shan broke away from the denomination founded by Witness Lee in China and started a new sect called "Church of the Everlasting Foundation," calling himself "The Powerful One." A short while later he teamed with a woman named Deng, whom he called "The Almighty One," and the name of the group became "The Church of the True God." Eventually the group adopted the name "Eastern Lightning," taken from Matthew 24:27: "As lightning that comes from the east is visible even in the west, so will be the coming of the Son of Man" (NIV).

Eastern Lightning teachings have many similarities to Christianity, but like all cults, they have added their own teachings that supersede or even deny biblical truth. The EL divides God's work into three stages:

• **The Era of the Law:** God was called "Jehovah," and humankind became aware of their sins through the law.

• **The Era of Grace:** God revealed himself through Jesus, and sin was forgiven by believing in Jesus' death and resurrection.

• **The Era of the Kingdom:** But Jesus went back to heaven, so is now distant. Today God is revealed through "The Almighty One"—Christ has "come again" for the second time as the "female Christ," whose work is to speak judgment to God's church, conquer the whole universe, and reign over all the earth.

Eastern Lightning has penetrated twenty provinces in China and gained over a million adherents, using various tactics to lure unsuspecting Christians away from their home congregations and families, especially targeting those in the "house church" movement, seeking to destroy it from within. They maintain control of their "converts" through submission to a strict hierarchy, sexual temptation, drugs, and violence.

Glimpses

October 1998: Pastor Xiao Peng, age thirty, was alarmed by EL teachings in She Qi County, Henan Province. He spoke boldly against this cult and taught his church members how to defend the truth and resist false teaching. One evening someone came to his door and said the pastor was needed outside the village—but it was a trap. Xiao was attacked with steel pipes and cut with knives about the face. Discovered bloody and mangled, missing one ear, he was rushed to the hospital but is badly disfigured for his stand for the truth.

October 2001: Zhou Dian Yu, a widow living in Shanxi Province and a zealous Christian, thirsted to know more about Christ. She attended a training for lay Christian leaders sponsored by Eastern Lightning, eagerly received the new teachings, and was sent back to her church. Fortunately, the church pointed out the errors and helped her back to the truth of the gospel. Zhou decided to return the EL books she had received . . . but she never returned. Her body was discovered the next day in a house, dead of coal fumes.

March 2002: A young woman named Zhang Song Yun, a member of Eastern Lightning in Henan Province, tried to persuade her elderly Christian mother to join the group. When her mother refused, Zhang tried to gouge out her mother's eye with her fingers. When that failed, she sent her son to break his grandmother's arms.

A Word of Wisdom

"A lie which is all a lie may be met and fought with outright, but a lie which is part a truth is a harder matter to fight." —Alfred, Lord Tennyson

---

[Paul wrote,] "These people are false apostles. They have fooled you by disguising themselves as apostles of Christ. But I am not surprised! Even Satan can disguise himself as an angel of light" (2 Corinthians 11:13-14).

Abuk Ajing

Sudan—February 22, 1990

Abuk Ajing was only fourteen when the government's Islamic forces swept through her village in 1990. For months—years—the Sudanese government had been unleashing its troops on the villages and towns of southern Sudan, forcibly removing people from land wanted for agriculture or oil and torturing or killing those who resisted. Government forces kidnapped young women and forced others to accept Islam—or face torture, mutilation, or death.

Many of the villagers fled to safety, but Abuk was not able to escape. Soldiers grabbed her and said, "You will come with us."

Fearing what would happen if she was taken away from all she had ever known, Abuk boldly refused. "No! I will not."

Angered at her refusal, the soldiers demanded that she repeat the creed of Islam: "There is one God; Allah is his name, and Muhammad is his prophet."

Most Sudanese Christians know that such a day will come: Convert to Islam—or suffer the consequences. Had Abuk's Christian family talked about what to do? what to say? But now she was alone, surrounded by hard-faced men with guns. All she had to do was repeat those words, and maybe they would let her go.

Yet again Abuk exhibited a boldness unusual for a young girl. "No! I will not."

The soldiers reacted savagely. Ripping off her clothes, they tied her with cords so she could not move. Helplessly, she watched as they drew their long knives and held them in one of the village fires until they were hot and glowing. *Oh Jesus!* she prayed. *Help me to get through this torture!*

Again and again the hot knives were applied to Abuk's chest, shoulders, and back. Unbelievable pain wracked her young body. *Jesus, help me to endure!* When the soldiers tired of their handiwork, they beat the helpless girl until she fell unconscious and then left her for dead.

Scars of Suffering

Ten years later, in 2000, two American mission workers visited Abuk's village and noticed an attractive young woman with a toddler on her hip. Her face betrayed suffering beyond her years, beyond anything the two foreign women could imagine. Would she tell them her story?

The young woman nodded and gave her guests two broken chairs outside her mud hut, while she sat on a piece of tin. The little boy in her arms hid his face, as if the white faces of the visitors looked like ghosts.

With the help of an interpreter, she began to speak. She was twenty-four years old. Her name was Abuk Ajing. At the age of fourteen . . .

At the end of the story, Abuk gently pulled down on the top of her dress, revealing the deforming scars the scalding knives had left on her chest. Without proper medical care, her scars are often infected. She lives with continual pain.

But she does not speak as though she wishes she had answered differently. There is determination in her eyes, a well of self-discipline in her spirit. This is what it means to be a Christian in Sudan. There comes a day when one must choose: Embrace Islam and deny Christ . . . or refuse to deny Christ and embrace suffering.

Seed of the Church

God has not forgotten us. Evil is departing and holiness is advancing. These are the things that shake the earth (Hymn by Sudanese Christian Mary Alueel).

With the strength God gives you, be ready to suffer with me for the proclamation of the Good News (2 Timothy 1:8).

Rómulo Sauñe
Peru — September 5, 1992

Since 1970, communist terrorists, calling themselves the Shining Path, murdered between 25,000 and 30,000 people, including thousands of Christians and some 800 pastors in their attempt to take over Peru. Thousands of other civilians were caught in the cross fire as the government tried to stop the terrorists and capture their leader, Abimael Guzmán Reynoso.

On September 5, 1992, a band of these terrorists set up a roadblock high in the Andes to intercept an Indian pastor, Rómulo Sauñe. While Quechua Christians were not enthusiastic about the Peruvian government, most refused to join the terrorists because of their violence. Sauñe had done much to unite the Christians across denominational lines, helping translate and sell over forty thousand Bibles. He revived the rural churches with vibrant worship and Scripture songs written to traditional music.

Sauñe had become a pastor to pastors even as the Shining Path tortured and executed more Christians in an attempt to force them to join the revolutionaries.

Now, as the dilapidated truck stopped at the roadblock, the guerrillas opened fire. Within moments twenty bodies lay in the road. After finding Rómulo Sauñe, his brother Rueben, and three of his nephews among the dead, one guerrilla radioed to his commander, "We got him!" Then they left.

Family Legacy

Rómulo was killed while returning to Ayacucho from his mountain village of Chakiqpampa, where he had been encouraging the believers and visiting his grandfather's grave. His grandfather, Justiniano Sauñe, had been one of the first in his village to accept the gospel back in 1950. When the Shining Path came, the Sauñes would not recant—not even when the terrorists raped Rómulo's grandmother and burned the family home. Finally, the Shining Path came for Justiniano.

Rómulo's brother, Joshua, recalls the event: "One Sunday, standing before his people, he said, 'This is the last Sunday that I am before you. Next Sunday, I'm not going to be here because the Lord has called me home.'

"The next day, he was pulled from his house. Many times in the past the Lord had warned him to escape as the terrorists were coming to kill him, and he did so. But this time the Lord told him, 'They are coming to take your life, and you are coming with Me.'

"When my grandfather told the Shining Path that the only solution for our country was found in Jesus Christ, they started to kill him. They took out his eyes, cut out his tongue, and finally chopped his heart from his chest before he died. He was eighty-five years old and still defending the faith."

At first Joshua wanted to avenge the deaths of his two brothers, his grandfather, and nine other relatives. Why had God let this happen? His people had suffered so much. If God couldn't protect them, he would take up arms against the Shining Path. But when Joshua actually saw the bodies of his family members, God changed his heart, and he realized that Satan was his real enemy. And the most powerful offense against Satan was the love of Christ. Joshua Sauñe is now the president of the Quechua Evangelical Church of Peru with more than two hundred indigenous congregations.

Seed of the Church

Rómulo's death did not go unnoticed. Braving the threats of the Shining Path, two thousand people paraded through the streets of his home city, Ayacucho, singing "Onward Christian Soldiers" and carrying banners declaring, "Ayacucho for Christ" and "For me to live is Christ, to die is gain." Abimael Guzmán Reynoso, head of the Shinning Path is now in prison.

[Jesus said,] "I tell you the truth, unless a kernel of wheat falls to the ground and dies, it remains only a single seed. But if it dies, it produces many seeds. The man who loves his life will lose it, while the man who hates his life in this world will keep it for eternal life" (John 12:24-25, NIV).

Tim Van Dyke and Steve Welsh

Colombia—June 19, 1995

January 16, 1994, was a lazy Sunday morning at *Finca Esperanza* (Hope Academy), the boarding school for children of missionaries with New Tribes Mission in Colombia. For the weekend, several of the eighty students had gone into Villavicencio, the town an hour away where some parents served as logistical support for missionaries out with the tribes, operated the guesthouse, or were in language study. Some kids took friends into town for a visit. But seventeen-year-old Donna Miller stayed at school where her parents were cooks.

Suddenly, Donna's mother turned from the window and ran to the phone. She dialed 1-1-1 to ring the emergency warning on all the school phones—in the dorms, the cafeteria, the classrooms, and all the other family houses. Guerrillas were coming! She'd seen them approaching up the dirt road that ran through the campus.

Everyone locked their doors, but it wasn't long before threats from the heavily armed members of the Revolutionary Armed Forces of Colombia—four men and one woman—herded everyone outside into a small gymnasium, where the woman and a man stood guard while the other three insurgents searched the campus.

Donna's first fear as she took her place with her back to the wall in the room with fifty other students and staff was that they were being lined up for a firing squad. But then the guerrillas passed around leaflets and launched into angry propaganda speeches explaining their cause. Would they be lecturing us if they intended to kill us all? Donna thought. Hopefully not! Nevertheless, "Uncle" Steve Welsh—the school's beloved maintenance man—was tied up with a rope. Had he resisted? What was going on?

The guerrilla in the doorway kept asking where Donna's father and the two pilots were. Donna's dad was gone. He had left the day before to help some friends living in a remote area build a house. But the missionary pilots, who flew their planes from the adjacent airstrip, should be around somewhere. The guerrillas were insistent. They wanted Donna's dad (a cook), maintenance man Steve Welsh, and the two pilots.

Finally, when the other three guerrillas returned from their search without the pilots or her dad, they pointed to Tim Van Dyke, acting principal for the school. "We'll take him!" They grabbed Tim and yanked the rope holding Steve Welsh. Neither Steve nor Tim had a chance to say good-bye to their wives or children before they were dragged out of the gym. Then the guerrillas ordered everyone to stay put.

Silence ensued after the door slammed until someone began softly singing a praise song. That broke the spell. After an hour or so, a couple of the men peeked outside. The guerrillas were gone. Everyone emerged, and the teachers notified the Colombian army.

No Ransom

New Tribes Mission immediately organized a contingency team. The beautiful school that had served the missionary children so well had to be abandoned. It was just too close to contested territory. Intense prayer was solicited from believers around the world.

Within two weeks, the guerrillas made radio contact, demanding ransom for the release of Tim Van Dyke and Steve Welsh. New Tribes Mission never pays ransom. To do so would only encourage other kidnappings. Still, contact with the kidnappers increased. In May, the guerrillas allowed Steve to talk over the radio to assure the mission that he and Tim were alive. Then, before summer ended, contact diminished. In the fall, the help of new Colombian government officials and international organizations such as the Red Cross raised hopes. But by spring, the guerrillas had cut off contact, though in April two sightings of Tim and Steve came in, reporting them in good condition.

Then on June 19, in a clash on a jungle trail between the Colombian military and the insurgent guerrillas, Tim and Steve were executed with bullets through the backs of their heads, presumably to create a diversion so the guerrillas could escape.

Ever since the attack, Donna has been "super cautious," always locking her doors and feeling wary when out of the house. She's married now, to a fellow student from *Finca Esperanza*, and the fact that her dad could have been kidnapped and killed has brought them much closer. But the deepest impact for Donna has been the hundreds of people who were saved as a result of hearing the story of Tim and Steve and knowing, as she says, "That they would have given their lives if it had brought only one person to Christ."

Orson Vila
Cuba—May 24, 1995

In 1990, when the Soviet Union unraveled, Fidel Castro's grip on Cuba weakened as well. No longer could his foreign comrades subsidize his crippled showcase economy. Being point man for Communism in the Western hemisphere, was suddenly as conspicuous as standing in a pillory. He needed a way to improve his image at home.

Previously Castro had opposed Christianity not only on ideological grounds but also because he didn't want to waste any of his regime's valuable resources on building new churches or repairing old ones. But why not loosen the restraints on house churches that weren't expecting to build new buildings. Such benevolent approval should raise the popularity of the aging dictator, and besides, people were already meeting in house churches without permission anyway.

But Castro did not know what he unleashed. Bibles, tracts, and children's Bible stories were distributed openly, and the gospel message was being preached with great power by fearless evangelists. Young Communists converted to Christ and began tearing up their party-membership cards and throwing them in the streets. Soon the revival among both Protestants and Catholics led to the establishment of over three thousand new house churches. The Assemblies of God churches in Cuba, which previously claimed only seven thousand followers, experienced some of the most rapid growth until there were nearly fifty thousand members, most of them young professionals disillusioned by economic hardship and ideological emptiness but inspired by the transforming power of God.

Quite Some "House" Church

In the province of Camagüey, eighty-five new house churches sprang up. Pastor and evangelist Orson Vila led one of the largest, with a congregation of twenty-five hundred people meeting in shifts in his backyard. Some Cubans were so spiritually hungry that they waited in line for twenty-four hours for prayer and counseling with Pastor Vila. Many other pastors in Cuba were seeing a similar revival, but because Pastor Vila's ministry grew so large, it drew the attention of Castro's regime as a "spiritual threat."

Communist officials ordered the closing of 85 of the 101 house churches in that province, Pastor Vila's church among them. But he refused. He had been imprisoned before for preaching the gospel—something he had been doing for twenty-three years—and he was not about to quit now that God was pouring out his Spirit in revival.

On the morning of May 24, 1995, at 5:30 A.M., some fifteen police, special brigades, and state security agents surrounded Pastor Vila's home with police vans, patrol cars, and a cargo truck. They arrested him, confiscated all church equipment, and took him to the courthouse. But as he was being interrogated, some five thousand Christians from all the churches in the city surrounded the building and proclaimed, "Christ lives!" followed by choruses such as "Cuba for Christ!" and "The walls shall fall!"

Nevertheless, Pastor Vila's lawyer was not allowed to provide a defense, and according to Amnesty International, he was subsequently sentenced to eighteen months for "disobedience" (in violation of article 147) and for holding "illegal meetings" (in violation to article 209). He carried out the first part of his sentence at the Cerámica Roja Prison in Camagüey province and was later moved to "Las 40" Penitentiary, also in Camagüey.

Word went out around the world concerning his incarceration, and thousands of believers began praying. Amnesty International declared him a prisoner of conscience. His fellow prisoners asked him if his conviction were a punishment from God. "No," he answered, "God loves prisoners, and sent me to you to tell you about Jesus." Soon many became Christians, and a church was started in prison. On the outside, by September, Pastor Vila's congregation had doubled, meeting in other locations.

Finally, Pastor Vila was released on March 2, 1996, having served only half of his sentence. Four days later, he was preaching again in Camagüey.

Peter and the other apostles replied: "We must obey God rather than men!" (Acts 5:29, NIV).

Dave Mankins, Mark Rich, and Rick Tenenoff
Colombia — September 10, 1996

On January 31, 1993, armed guerrillas burst into the homes of three New Tribes missionary families simultaneously in Púcuro, deep in the Darién jungles of Panama. They held Mark Rich, Dave Mankins, and Rick Tenenoff at gunpoint while their wives—Tania Rich, Nancy Mankins, and Patti Tenenoff—packed a few personal belongings for their husbands and then watched as they were marched off into the night with their hands bound behind their backs.

Tribal leaders had initially invited the missionaries to Púcuro, a village of approximately three hundred Kuna people in the southeastern part of the country, about fifteen miles from the Colombian border. In addition to studying the Kuna language and culture, the missionaries were involved in linguistic analysis, teaching the people to read and write in their own language, and administering medical assistance. The missionaries also translated the Bible and taught Bible studies to interested Kuna residents.

Within hours of the kidnapping, the guerrillas made radio contact with NTM and demanded a $5 million ransom. It was soon determined that the guerrillas, members of Revolutionary Armed Forces of Colombia (FARC), had taken the men over the boarder into Colombia. Following the kidnapping, the wives and families came to the United States, and the New Tribes Mission (NTM) set up a crisis management committee.

Just before Christmas 1993, the kidnappers proved their hostages were still alive by allowing Dave, Mark, and Rick's voices to be heard on the radio. But then in January the guerrillas broke off communication.

The crisis committee did everything possible to find out what had happened to the missionaries: pursuing leads, questioning suspects, launching a huge media campaign, and pressuring the Colombian and U.S. governments.

NTM says that early in 1996, it reestablished contact with the guerrillas again with hope that progress was being made toward the release of the men. But in the middle of the year, contact was again cut off. At about that time a defector from the guerrillas told a Colombian army officer he knew where the men were being held. He later led troops to the camp. However, apparently while fleeing the military in fear, the guerrillas decided that Dave, Mark, and Rick were a liability and dispatched them along a jungle trail in the hills of northern Colombia.

But New Tribes Mission, the waiting wives and children, and the thousands of praying Christians were not told about the deaths. Efforts continued to find and rescue the men. In November 2000, Colombian police arrested José Milcíades Urrego Medina, known as "Commander Rigoberto," the second in command of the FARC unit that kidnapped the men. But he refused to give investigators any information about the missionaries.

Slowly, however, rumors of their survival were discredited while reports of their death mounted until on September 10, 2001, the crisis committee and the wives of Dave Mankins, Mark Rich, and Rick Tenenoff agreed that, given the available evidence, it was time for the families to acknowledge that the men were dead and gain some closure to the 1993 kidnapping.

How Could This Happen?

Nancy Mankins admits that she spent weeks sprawled across her bed awash in wads of Kleenex and gallons of tears feeling sorry for herself. "Here we had turned over our lives, promised to go to the ends of the earth to spread God's Word, and now this?"

We often do not understand what God is doing. We don't have the wisdom or perspective to understand. But we do know God is good, just, and at work to draw all people to himself. Choosing to believe these facts, Nancy says, "We are not always able to choose our circumstances, but nobody can take away my choice of how I'm going to get through them."

Truly God is good to . . . those whose hearts are pure. But as for me, I came so close to the edge of the cliff! My feet were slipping, and I was almost gone (Psalm 73:1-2).

Mother Teresa

India—September 5, 1997

Small as she was, Mother Teresa lifted the dying woman into a wheelbarrow and trundled the flickering life to the hospital. But when the hospital staff saw that rats and maggots had eaten away much of the woman's body, they refused to take her. "We can do nothing for her," they said. "We only have room for people who might get better."

But the Catholic sister wearing the white sari with blue stripes stood her ground and insisted until the hospital finally admitted the dying woman.

Mother Teresa shook her head sadly. "No one should die alone and unloved," she told the other Missionaries of Charity. "We need a home where the very ill can die in peace." She went to city officials and asked for help in finding some place to care for the dying. They showed her some rooms that travelers had used who came to visit the temple of Kali, a Hindu goddess. The rooms were filthy and needed cleaning. But Mother Teresa immediately accepted. She named the new home Nirmal Hriday, "Place of the Immaculate (Pure) Heart," and went to work cleaning it up. It opened on August 22, 1952, and was soon full of men and women whom no one else wanted to help.

Some of the neighbors were angry. They thought a Catholic mission was defiling their Hindu temple. One day a group of tough young men blocked Mother Teresa's way. "If you don't leave, we will kill you!" they threatened. Mother Teresa shrugged. "If you kill me, I will just get to Heaven sooner," she said. Puzzled that she wasn't afraid, the young toughs backed off.

Missionaries of Charity

Mother Teresa was born Agnes Bojaxhiu on August 26, 1910, to Albanian parents living in Skopje, the capital of Macedonia. Agnes's father, a builder, died when Agnes was only eight years old. But even though her mother had to work hard to support herself and her children, she had a cheerful spirit and taught her children to care about the poor. "If you decide to do something, do it gladly," she said. "Otherwise, do not take it on at all."

The Catholic Church was an important part of Agnes's life all through her childhood. She became involved in the Sodality of Mary, a group for young people that learned about missionaries in foreign lands and raised money to help the poor. Their motto was: "What have I done for Christ? What am I doing for Christ? What will I do for Christ?" Agnes decided that she wanted to serve Christ by devoting her life to missions.

At the age of eighteen, she applied to the Order of Loreto Nuns, which sent missionaries to India. In January 1929, she arrived at the Loreto Convent in Darjeeling, India, as a novice. She chose the name of Sister Teresa, after Saint Thérèse, the patron saint of missions. After taking her final on May 14, 1937, Sister Teresa was sent to the Loreto Convent in Calcutta, where she taught school to wealthy Bengali girls.

But right outside the convent walls was a *bustee*, or slum. Teresa's heart went out to the hungry children, the sick and elderly dying right in the street, the lepers that no one would touch or help. The sisters tried to bring some children into the convent to educate them, but convent life was too different from what they were used to. Sister Teresa realized if she wanted to serve the poor, she would have to go out and live among them instead.

Receiving permission from the Pope to leave the convent, Sister Teresa began living among the poor, dressed in a simple, cotton sari, teaching the children in the street and comforting the sick and dying. She was joined by some of her former pupils who wanted to serve in the same way. In 1950, the tiny nun formed a new order called the Missionaries of Charity, adding a fourth vow of serving the poorest of the poor.

As head of this order, she became Mother Teresa. In 1960 the work expanded to other parts of India; in 1965, to Venezuela—until today there are more than five hundred centers around the world staffed by the Missionaries of Charity. In 1979, this humble nun received the Nobel Peace Prize, using the prize money to further "the work."

When Mother Teresa died on September 5, 1997, she had become a symbol around the world of "giving a cup of cold water in Jesus' name."

The King will tell them, "I assure you, when you did it to one of the least of these my brothers and sisters, you were doing it to me!" (Matthew 25:40).

Raheela and Saleema

Sheikhupura, Punjab Province, Pakistan—July 8, 1997

As girlfriends do around the world, seventeen-year-old Saleema gave her friend Raheela the best gift she could think of: a Bible. Raheela, raised in a Muslim family, was curious. Soon she was humming the Christian songs Saleema was always singing, and even teaching them secretly to her little sister. Encouraged by Raheela's interest, Saleema invited her friend to a Good Friday service. There, Raheela heard for the first time that Jesus had died on the cross, taking the punishment for *her* sins. Even though the Koran mentions Jesus and calls him a great prophet, she had never heard the Good News!

Joyfully, Raheela accepted Jesus as her Lord and Savior. She couldn't keep it to herself; she told her family even though she knew they would be terribly upset. Upset? Hardly the word. According to strict Islamic Shari'a law, converting to another religion is blasphemy—punishable by death. Trying to "save" their daughter, Raheela's parents tried to beat it out of her, but she refused to deny her love for Jesus. So even though she was only sixteen, her parents decided to marry her to a Muslim man and take care of the problem. Distraught, Raheela ran away.

305

Reheela's parents showed up at Saleema's home, accusing them of hiding their daughter. But Raheela was nowhere to be found. The next thing Saleema knew, the police arrived and arrested both her and her parents. The charge: converting a Muslim. Their pastor, Arthur Salim, was also arrested. For three days, Saleema, her parents, and the pastor were interrogated, beaten, and tortured. The guards put Saleema and the pastor into a cell together, removed their clothes, and tried to force them to commit adultery. When they refused, they were beaten again. Finally, they were released.

A few weeks later, however, Raheela was discovered hiding in a women's shelter. The family was furious. They had to restore the family's honor. On July 8, 1997, Raheela's brother, Altaf, dragged her into the street, gun in hand, and publicly executed her. Then he turned himself in to the police.

A Murder Charge

Saleema was devastated by the death of her friend. But her troubles were only beginning. Once again the police showed up at Saleema's house. To her astonishment, Raheela's family was charging her with "causing" the events leading up to her friend's death! Again Saleema was confined in the local jail and abused by her jailors. Red chili powder was forced into her vagina, she was severely beaten with a rubber hose and a leather belt, and raped by four of her guards.

Finally, Saleema was released on bail on August 7, 1997. Pakistani Christians surrounded her and her family for the legal process ahead. Pastor Salim and his family had to flee to avoid further persecution. Suffering from the effects of her ill-treatment, Saleema missed a couple of court hearings . . . but finally, after two years of wrangling with the Pakistani court system, Raheela's family dropped the charges against her. Two years after Raheela died because she refused to deny her newfound Savior, Saleema—now nineteen years old—was legally free.

But in her soul and spirit, she had been free all along. Falsely accused, abused by her captors, persecuted for her faith . . . Saleema shared in Christ's sufferings. And was found worthy.

In Their Own Words

If you promise to carry your cross, it will be a life full of thorns, mountains, and difficulties. But no matter how big the mountain, Jesus will help you overcome!

—Saleema, age nineteen

[Jesus said,] "If you refuse to take up your cross and follow me, you are not worthy of being mine. If you cling to your life, you will lose it; but if you give it up for me, you will find it" (Matthew 10:38-39).

House Church Pastor
China—1998

When the Eastern Lightning cult in China first began recruiting members, their first tactic was temptation, using money tucked in books about their teachings; then they used coercion and violence against those who rejected their teachings. Sexual temptation and reputation damage was used in yet a third stage. But the cult is learning from its failures and is becoming more sophisticated in its use of persuasion and deception to delude and confuse Christian believers. Read. . . .

"My Testimony"—by a young pastor from Anhwei

I am a young brother who had been deceived by the Eastern Lightning cult for one month. During the time when I was deceived, I served them with great effort. In order to serve this cult, I was an enemy to the senior pastor who ministered to our church; I accompanied false teachers of the cult to spread errors in many churches, attacking and slandering those brothers and sisters who had realized the truth about the EL. . . .

During that one month, I attended more than a dozen training sessions to listen to the teaching of the cult and to receive the "truth." I was one of their key candidates to be trained and boasted about. . . . If it were not for God's restraining in every way, I could have gone very far with them to "preach the Gospel" in many other areas to poison people. Imagine that! If that had been the case, I probably would never have had a chance to come to my senses. It is so scary even to think back! . . .

Before the teaching started, I suggested inviting a certain older brother to come. I realized we who were present at the meeting had not believed long, and we had no experience with any heresies, nor did we have a solid understanding of the truth, so I thought we should have the older brother come and help discern whether this teaching was right or wrong. But [my friend] Zhang stopped me strongly, saying, "Don't let the older man come here. It's for his benefit—because this teaching is God's judgment. It is different from what has been taught before, and it is hard for people to receive. Many old servants of God will not accept this teaching because they love position and are bound by old ideas. . . . They may even resist or slander, closing the door of all churches under their control. By doing this, they will become blasphemers of the Holy Spirit, and consequently suffer eternal death. . . . So we'd better keep the older brother uninformed. It's for his benefit."

This brother heard from EL that today's Christians are "just like the Pharisees in Bible times": "[The Pharisees] had learned from the Scripture that a

Messiah was coming, and had pictured him according to the 'letter' in the Scripture. But when Jesus did come, they found what they had learned did not match His reality. . . . We who live today have never seen Jesus either. We could only imagine Jesus' second coming through the 'letter' of the Bible. So now that Jesus has truly come back, are we going to repeat what the Pharisees did, and to limit Jesus by 'the letter' and reject the Almighty One?'"

The pastor continues:

> They didn't allow us to examine their behavior, saying, "The Pharisees couldn't find any flaws in Jesus' teaching, but they could easily find His faults in His behavior, such as the disciples not washing their hands before eating, Jesus' eating and drinking with sinners, healing the sick on Sabbath days, etc. It's the same with us today. If you set your minds on finding our faults, you certainly will. Because the time has changed, so have our working styles." . . . This is how they justify and cover their lies, slanders, immorality, and deceptiveness. . . .
>
> Once, I accepted their teaching, but I never had any peace throughout that one month, and my hands and body could not help trembling. This had never happened while I followed Jesus. Other people also experienced the lack of peace and intensive battles in their hearts at the initial stage. Thank God! He preserved a desire for truth in my heart. So later I stayed home and quieted myself for several days. After I studied the Bible, I realized that the teaching of the female Christ was all false and could not stand examination. It is all errors that have come from the devil. Therefore after I realized the truth, I wrote down my experience briefly, so that everybody can also see the reality.

Of this you can be sure: No immoral, impure or greedy person—such a man is an idolater—has any inheritance in the kingdom of Christ and of God. Let no one deceive you with empty words, for because of such things God's wrath comes on those who are disobedient. Therefore do not be partners with them (Ephesians 5:5-7, NIV).

Ayub Masih

Pakistan—April 27, 1998

Bashiran Bibi followed her youngest son, Shazad, as they threaded their way through the narrow walkways of Sahiwal Central Jail. It had been so long since she had seen her son, Ayub Masih.[1] Sentenced to death? How could that be! He was just a student at a Bible college—*had* been a student before his arrest, that is—but that was years ago. At first, it all had seemed like a big

308

mistake that would surely get sorted out during a hearing. Finally, he had been tried, convicted, and sentenced to death on April 27, 1998. His crime? "Blaspheming" the prophet Muhammad. Law 295-C of the Pakistani penal code made "blasphemy" a crime punishable by death. His sentence was later suspended pending appeal, but after waiting another three years, the High Court turned down his appeal. On August 22, 2001, he filed his final appeal to Pakistan's Supreme Court—his last hope.

Shazad stopped abruptly before a barred doorway cut into the sand-colored bricks. "Ayub!" he called into the gloomy interior of a cell. A tall figure moved quickly into the patch of sunlight on the other side of the iron bars. His dark hair had grown long, and his beard was full. But Ayub's face lit up when he saw his mother and brother.

Bashiran's heart fluttered with relief. Her son could still smile.

Law 295-C

Ayub Mashi's problems began on October 16, 1996, when he attended a community meeting to defend his Christian parents' property rights from Muslim extremists who were attempting to confiscate their home. Ayub's neighbor, Muhammad Akam, later claimed Ayub said, "If you want to know the truth about Islam, read Salman Rushdie." (Rushdie's novel, *The Satanic Verses*, contains "blasphemous" comments against the prophet Muhammad, earning Rushdie a fatwa, a religious decree by Iranian leaders, calling for his death.) Ayub denies making any blasphemous statement, but shortly after the meeting, he was beaten by a mob, arrested, and charged with blasphemy.

Ayub's case was registered without proper investigation, based merely on a statement by Muhammad Akam, fabricated apparently to force the Christian families to drop claims to their land. The very day Ayub was arrested, fourteen Christian families were evicted from their homes and their lands appropriated. Ever since, Muhammad Akam, Ayub's accuser, has taken up residence as a squatter in Ayub's family home.

At the courthouse on November 6, 1997, Muhammad Akam fired a gun at Ayub, narrowly missing him. Though security was tightened—the trial was continued in the prison, where Ayub was denied the right to a defense—the shooter was never charged. An Islamic mullah offered an award of ten thousand American dollars to anyone who killed Ayub Masih. And, in February 1999, two fellow prisoners attacked Ayub, trying to kill him. From then on, he no longer went for exercise with the other prisoners when they were let out of the cells.

His cell was fourteen feet long and five feet wide, partially open to the sky. Winter nights could get very cold, and in summer, temperatures could be as high as 129 degrees Fahrenheit. He had an open toilet and a cement bed about eight inches off the floor covered by a mat, sheet, and pillow.

Ayub Masih suffered from stomach problems and had become very weak. When Ayub's family visited him in jail, however, he was able to tell them, "This cell can't stop me from loving my Lord Jesus Christ." He read his Bible daily and prayed for his enemies.

Pakistan's president, General Pervez Musharraf, proposed a change to Law 295-C that would punish anyone bringing false charges. If charges proved false, the person bringing them could face the same punishment that the accused would face if convicted. However, since 9/11 and the War on Terrorism, other priorities have preoccupied Pakistan.

Nevertheless, God answered the prayers of thousands of praying Christians around the world, and on August 16, 2002, Ayub was released.

Can anything ever separate us from Christ's love? Does it mean he no longer loves us if we have trouble or calamity, or are persecuted, or are hungry or cold or in danger or threatened with death? . . . No, despite all these things, overwhelming victory is ours through Christ, who loved us (Romans 8:35-37).

---

1 The name *Masih* is not a last name but something of a caste name meaning "Messiah." Hence, under Pakistan's so-called blasphemy law, many Christians with this name have been arrested: Anwar Masih, Ashiq Masih, Gul Masih, Habib Masih, Manzoor Masih, Pervez Masih, Ranjha Masih, Rehmat Masih, Shafiq Masih, Salamat Masih, as well as Ayub Masih.

Pastor Abram Yac Deng

Sudan—1998

If you had traveled to Sudan with The Voice of the Martyrs field workers in May 1998—VOM's eighth trip to the Sudan with blankets, food, survival packs, and Bibles for the hundreds of thousands of people displaced by Sudan's twenty-year civil war—you would have had the opportunity to meet Abram Yac Deng (*Pastor* Abram, though he was only twenty-four years old).

You barely notice the tribal markings that scar his forehead. What you notice is Pastor Abram's wide welcoming smile, his white teeth in sharp contrast to the pure African blackness of his skin. That he can smile at all is something of a miracle. Shortly before your arrival in his village of Ayien, thirty-eight thousand people—most of them Christians—had been attacked by government soldiers in the nearby town of Turalei. Men and women had been driven from their homes and beaten; some had died. Their homes had been torched and destroyed. Many children were abducted—the boys forced to learn and submit to Islamic doctrine, the girls sold as slaves and subjected to sexual bondage.

Pastor Abram knows it is only a matter of time until the Islamic raiders come to *his* village.

The Church of Ayien

Your heart swells when you realize that four hundred people pack into Pastor Abram's simple church each week. Pastor Abram introduces you to

Andre, one of his church members. You notice that Andre's hands are horribly disfigured. At your questioning glance, Pastor Abram quietly informs you and your group that Andre barely escaped with his life from a burning church, set on fire by Muslim soldiers intent on purging Sudan of the Christian religion and routing potential members of the Sudanese People's Liberation Army (SPLA). "Ninety- nine members of Andre's village died in that church fire," Abram tells you soberly.

You also meet several women, among them Elizabeth Ading Deng and Abuk Goch and her children. They have so little compared to your multiroom home back in the States, your car with its heat and air-conditioning, your closet full of clothes, and your bank account. Yet their smiles are warm and welcoming. You have come in Jesus' name, and your visit says someone cares about their suffering.

Pastor Abram's eyes keep straying to the bundles of Bibles you have brought, lapping up the sight of them like a man parched with thirst. He pulls out his own small Bible, barely holding together within its red cover, the pages worn and tattered. And you learn a startling fact: Abram Yac Deng has the only copy of a Bible in his entire congregation. Yet he has been faithfully teaching the Word week after week to people hungry to know about the love of God.

But seeing the hundreds of Bibles provided by The Voice of the Martyrs mission, Pastor Abram can hardly contain his joy. Now every household in his congregation will have a Sudanese Bible. Many can't read. But already he is imagining literacy classes for men, women, and children, using the Scriptures as their textbook.

And so you say good-bye to your new friends. Your life will never be quite the same. Could you live in the midst of such poverty and danger and still be strong in your faith, as they are?

You heard about the danger. You saw its results in Andre's disfigured hands. But still, you aren't quite prepared when next you hear news from the church of Ayien: *Four days after your visit*, the Islamic raiders swept down upon this village. Pastor Abram was shot in the head at close range, killing him immediately. The church was torched and seriously damaged. Elizabeth Ading Deng and Abuk Goch were dragged away into slavery; two of Abuk's children were also kidnapped, along with twenty-two others from the village. Nearly one hundred villagers were murdered. And the Bibles that had brought them such hope and joy . . . all were destroyed in the fire.

Nothing in all creation will ever be able to separate us from the love of God that is revealed in Christ Jesus our Lord (Romans 8:39).

311

James Jeda
Sudan—1998

For the last two decades—since 1983—Islamic militants from northern Sudan have been waging *jihad* (holy war) against their fellow Sudanese in central and southern Sudan in an effort to create a wholly Islamic state. Sudan's oil-rich areas, claimed by the Government of Sudan (GOS), also account for the bombing of villages and forced removal of thousands of families—and for the West's strange silence in the wake of massive religious persecution, abduction and slavery, imprisonment, torture, and genocide.

On returning from a visit to Sudan in 1998, an American Episcopal priest said, "What we saw and heard and touched is the material for nightmares, a human hell."

Nineteen percent of the population of southern Sudan is Christian. Over two million people have been slaughtered by war and genocide. Five million have been displaced into refugee camps and live in mind-boggling poverty. Mission and relief agencies such as International Christian Concern, Faith in Action, The Voice of the Martyrs, and World Concern have been trying to address the desperate needs for food, shelter, clothing, and medical attention—and in the process uncover story after heartbreaking story . . . for the real story of Sudan can only be told one man, one woman, one *child* at a time.

Out of the Fire

The relief volunteers found him in a refugee camp in southern Sudan, clinging to a meager existence with his only remaining relative, his grandmother. Rags barely covered the boy's thin body. Sorrow and suffering clouded his eyes. When asked about his story, he pulled up his shirt to reveal large burn scars covering the right side of his body from his armpit almost to his navel and along the inside of his right arm.

James Jeda was only nine or ten years old when Islamic raiders attacked his village. In the ensuing chaos, he watched in horror as his mother, father, and four brothers and sisters were butchered. James was among those who were not killed but taken prisoner.

That night, in the raiders' camp, James was ordered to gather wood for a fire to cook the evening meal. As the dry wood blazed into a hot fire, the soldiers asked James to tell them the names of any "rebel soldiers" [Sudanese Peoples Liberation Army (SPLA)] in the area. James shrugged; he didn't know. Then the soldiers demanded that he say, "Allah is great! And Muhammad is his prophet!"—thereby declaring himself a Muslim.

Still numb with shock and grief at the deaths of his entire family, James somehow found the fortitude to speak. "That would not be possible, because I am a Christian."

Enraged, the soldiers picked up the little boy and threw him into the fire for which he had gathered wood. Thinking they were finished with him, the raiders packed up their weapons and left. But somehow he managed to roll out of the flames and hide in nearby bushes till the raiders were gone, then run to safety.

Doctors in relief hospitals grafted skin over the third-degree burns, but he still does not have full use of his right arm. The pain of the burns has gradually healed, but the pain in his heart over the murders of his parents and siblings will take longer to heal.

Seed of the Church

"We should be as concerned about the persecution of Christians in Sudan as we are about our neighbors down the street. Maybe in some respects more so because America has had a privileged position in the world."

—Chuck Colson, Founder, Prison Fellowship

It would be better to be thrown into the sea with a large millstone tied around the neck than to face the punishment in store for harming one of these little ones (Luke 17:2).

Cassie Bernall and Rachel Scott
Columbine, Colorado—April 20, 1999

At 11:19 A.M. on April 20, 1999, Eric Harris and Dylan Klebold opened fire on their fellow students at Columbine High School. By 11:35 A.M., twelve students and one teacher were dead and twenty other students wounded. Harris and Klebold then turned their guns on themselves.

Traumatized victims, anguished families, and a stunned public still ask, "Why? Why, why, *why?*" As the news stories unfolded, a picture of two isolated and troubled teens emerged, with a long list of names of people they disliked (only one was actually injured in the massacre) and a hatred for jocks, minorities, and stupid people who actually believed in God. The carnage they planned could have been even worse: Two twenty-pound propane bombs were found in the school cafeteria. If they had exploded, all 448 people in the cafeteria might have been killed.

"Whatever It Takes"

But other stories emerged from the horror—stories of courage, faith, and hope. When the two killers entered the library and started shooting, panicked students dived under the study carrels. One of the predators singled out Cassie Bernall, a girl outspoken in her Christian faith, under one of the desks. "Do you believe in God?" he challenged. Several witnesses testify that Cassie said, "Yes"—and was shot dead. Another girl, Val Schnurr, already wounded in the shotgun blasts, was crying, "Oh my God, oh my God!" She, too, was asked, "Do you believe in God?" She, too, said yes. But as the shooter paused to reload his gun, she crawled away and survived.

One of the library witnesses was Craig Scott, whose sister Rachel—also a strong Christian—was shot and killed in the school parking lot. According to the young man who was with her (who was wounded and remains paralyzed today), Rachel tried to crawl away after being wounded. Seconds later Eric Harris came back, grabbed her by the hair, and pulled her head up. "Do you believe in God?" "You know I do," Rachel said bravely. "Then go be with him," said Harris and shot her in the head.

Rachel had been living her faith and growing as a Christian for many years. After her death, many students testified of her kindness toward those who were often ignored by others—new students, the not-so-popular, the handicapped. That's just who Rachel was.

But Cassie . . . her declaration that yes, she believed in God, was a remarkable testimony to a life redeemed. Early in her teens Cassie had dabbled with witchcraft and was being sucked into darkness and despair. But her parents, Misty and Brad Bernall—unlike Eric Harris's and Dylan Klebold's parents—stayed on her case and practiced "tough love." Two years before the horrific events of April 20, 1999, Cassie said yes to Christ's love and gave her life to him. Friends and family all say her life turned around 180 degrees. Instead of living in darkness, she became a "light for Christ."

At Rachel Scott's funeral, her pastor challenged, "The torch has fallen from Rachel's hand. Who will pick it up?" Both girls' parents have taken the stories of Columbine to schools and churches across the nation. A foundation in Cassie's name has helped build the Cassie Bernall Home for Children in Las Lajas, Honduras. A new youth center at West Bowles Community Church, her home church, also bears her name.

But their *real* legacy are the thousands of young people all across the nation who are saying yes to Jesus, committing themselves to live for Christ with the same boldness and courage as these two young girls.

In Her Own Words

"Now I have given up on everything else / I have found it to be the only way / To really know Christ and to experience / The mighty power that brought / Him back to life again, and to find out what it means to suffer and to / Die with him. So, whatever it takes / I will be one who lives in the fresh / Newness of life of those who are / Alive from the dead."

—Poem written by Cassie Bernall
two days before she was shot at Columbine,
and found after her death

[Jesus said,] "Everyone will hate you because of your allegiance to me. . . . By standing firm, you will win your souls" (Luke 21:17-19).

Pastor Li De Xian

China—1999 to the present

They had been coming on Tuesdays for months—men in shirt sleeves, women in simple print dresses holding children by the hand; old people with splayed fans to brush away the heat. As many as five hundred people gathered each week in the village of Huadu in Guangdong Province, China, to hear house church pastor Li De Xian preach the Christian gospel in an open-sided shelter.

But as the bicycles and dusty sandals began to arrive the morning of October 12, 1999, all they found of the shelter was a pile of rubble. Uncertain of what had happened or what to do, there wasn't much time to think. As soon as Pastor Li arrived, scores of Public Security Bureau (PSB) officers charged through the gathering and placed Li under arrest, whisking him away to the nearest prison.

What was so threatening about a Christian pastor teaching the Bible to eager listeners—ordinary people, transformed by the Word of God? That, according to the PSB, was exactly the problem. Pastor Li's preaching was attracting a large gathering, a group of self-proclaimed Christians who refused to join the *official*, government-sanctioned church in China: the Three-Self Patriotic Movement. But would *you* go to church where you couldn't bring your children or teach them? ("No children under the age of eighteen shall be brainwashed with religious beliefs.") Where you couldn't share the gospel with others? ("They shall not persuade and force others to believe in Christianity.")

The Voice of the Martyrs—a ministry serving the persecuted church worldwide—says, "Eighty percent of China's Christians will not be part of a 'church' which refuses to proclaim a resurrected Jesus who will return for his own. China's unregistered Christians now outnumber the 50-million-member Communist Party."

"I Will Preach till I Die"

The PSB released Pastor Li the next day with a stern warning: He would get "the beating of his life" if he showed up again to preach the next Tuesday. But Pastor Li had a simple answer: "I will preach till I die."

Three times that October he was arrested when he showed up to preach in Huadu and released the next day. But on November 9, 1999, he was once again arrested and this time held fifteen days—the longest a prisoner can be held without being charged. During this time he was not allowed to mingle with the other prisoners, for fear he would preach to them. Their fears were well founded. Li can very well say with the apostle Paul, "I want to report to you, friends, that my imprisonment here has had the opposite of its intended effect. . . . Everything that is happening to me in this jail only serves to make Christ more accurately known, regardless of whether I live or die. They didn't shut me up; they gave me a pulpit! Alive, I'm Christ's messenger; dead, I'm his bounty. Life versus even more life! I can't lose!" (Philippians 1:12, 21-22, *The Message*).

After being beaten so badly that he vomited blood, Pastor Li was released on November 24. The next Tuesday meeting in Huadu passed without incident. But the following week, the PSB once again broke up the meeting and arrested Pastor Li.

"You dare to fight against the Party?" they screamed.

Pastor Li shook his head. "I am not fighting and struggling against you. You are struggling against God, and you can never win."

Momentarily, at least, the officers were speechless. But month after month the harassment continued. Pastor Li was told if he showed up to preach in Huadu, he would be arrested. Li shows up; Li is arrested and held either overnight or for the full fifteen days. He even keeps a bag packed "for jail."

Then, for a time, the harassment stopped. But even as this book is being written, VOM got word that Li had been arrested, held fifteen days, and released . . . once more.

In His Own Words

Christ was the first to suffer. We just follow Him. There are many thorns, but we are just injured a little on our feet. This suffering is very little.

—Pastor Li to visitors from The Voice of the Martyrs a few months after the arrests and harassment began

[Jesus said,] "If they persecuted Me, they will also persecute you" (John 15:20, NKJV).

Roy Pontoh
Indonesia—January 20, 1999

According to a February 1999 U.S. Congressional Human Rights Caucus briefing, three groups of people have been systematically attacked and marginalized in Indonesia: ethnic Chinese, Christians, and moderate Muslims. Though the incidents occurred in different places, it appears well-organized outside provocateurs came in to create riots.

The violence began with harassment of the right to worship, progressed to closing places of worship, attacks on and burning those places of worship, then attacks and burning the homes of religious followers, and finally sadistic killings. At least twenty-five Indonesian churches were destroyed or damaged in January alone.

This briefing claims that the authorities—the police, the military, and even the central government—have done very little, if anything, to quell the violence. Furthermore, they often appear to be involved in discrediting the sources of the leads when outside agencies attempt to investigate the attacks.

"I Am a Soldier of God!"

The weekend Bible camp at Pattimura University on the island of Ambon had ended, and parents had arrived to pick up the 150 or so kids and adults and take them home. But there weren't enough cars for everyone, so Pastor Meiky Sainyakit and three other men went to rent a truck from the adjacent village of Wakal when a mob of Muslim extremists attacked them and pulled them from their car. One of the men escaped, but the mob stabbed Pastor Meiky and another man to death and then dowsed them with gasoline and burned their bodies.

After a while, the people still waiting at the university for rides home heard the chants from the approaching mob. In fear, they ran to hide in the university buildings, but the mob found many of the youths.

Fifteen-year-old Roy Pontoh was one of those dragged out to stand and face his accusers. "Who are you?" asked one of the mob leaders.

Trembling, Roy raised his chin and said, "I am a soldier of God!"

The attacker swung his machete at Roy, hitting and almost severing his arm. "Who are you?" the man demanded again. Roy gave the same answer and was again struck with the machete, this time gashing his shoulder.

"What is God's soldier?" the man roared.

"A soldier of God is ready to die for Christ," Roy responded in great pain.

Again the sword whistled through the air, this time slicing through Roy's stomach.

"Jesus," Roy cried as he fell to the ground.

The mob dragged Roy's body away and threw it in a ditch. Three days later, his family found it.

Seed of the Church

Though grief racked the hearts of Roy's parents and the fellow Christians who knew him, they praise God that he had the courage to remain faithful even in the face of death. Despite such widespread persecution—some say thousands of Christians were martyred on the island of Ambon in the first half of 1999—the church in Indonesia is growing at a rate of 1.25 million new believers every year.

> Since we are surrounded by such a huge crowd of witnesses to the life of faith, let us strip off every weight that slows us down, especially the sin that so easily hinders our progress. And let us run with endurance the race that God has set before us. We do this by keeping our eyes on Jesus, on whom our faith depends from start to finish. He was willing to die a shameful death on the cross because of the joy he knew would be his afterward. Now he is seated in the place of highest honor beside God's throne in heaven. Think about all he endured when sinful people did such terrible things to him, so that you don't become weary and give up. After all, you have not yet given your lives in your struggle against sin (Hebrews 12:1-4).

Graham Staines (and Philip and Timothy)

Orissa, India—January 22, 1999

Born in Brisbane, Australia, Graham Staines felt called at a young age to follow in his father's footsteps as a missionary. In 1965, he accepted a post at an old hundred-bed leprosarium in the remote village of Baripada in Orissa, India. In addition to helping the victims of leprosy, Graham fought to eradicate polio and tuberculosis and spent time translating the Bible into a local dialect.

In 1983, Graham married Gladys, an Australian woman who had come to India with other aid workers. They had a daughter and then two sons.

Harassment and attacks against Christians increased significantly in 1998, especially in the eastern state of Orissa and the western state of Gujarat. Some observers claim the violence corresponds with the rise to power of the Hindu nationalist Bharatiya Janat Party. Apparently radical Hindus in these areas considered the increasing number of Christian converts as political losses.

Dara Singh, a die-hard crusader for his religion, led a group of these radicals. He went around the countryside warning people about the dangerous intentions of Christian missionaries. Singh was wanted by the police in connection with two murders, but his supporters shielded him from capture. When he heard that some thirty tribal people had converted to Christianity, he was very outspoken in his opposition.

A Jeep Pyre

Every year, Graham Staines attended a retreat outside the village of Manoharpur, about a hundred miles from his home. In January 1999, he and his sons—Phillip, ten, and Timothy, six—made the journey. Because of limited space in the houses in the small village, Graham and his sons slept in a Jeep. At around midnight of the twenty-second, people in nearby houses were awakened by screams and saw fire enveloping the Jeep that was surrounded by a mob. But when they attempted to run to the aid of the victims inside, some claimed Hindu activists prevented them from leaving their houses. Finally, residents said, one of the extremists blew a whistle, and the attackers fled into the night. Though the villagers tried to extinguish the fire, everything had been reduced to ashes.

Initial government reports said the attack was premeditated, and blamed Hindu extremist Dara Singh for organizing it. Over a year later, more than fifty people had been arrested, finally including Mr. Singh. He was also linked to the recent murders of Catholic priest Arul Doss and Muslim trader Sheik Rahman. Later, however, Mahendra Hembram, also arrested in the government's dragnet, confessed to being the one who actually set fire to the Staines's Jeep. "While others put straw under the vehicle, I set fire to it," he said in a written confession. "All the other accused are innocent and therefore should be set free."

But was Dara Singh really innocent?

318

In the meantime, Gladys Staines had been devastated by the death of her husband and sons. How could this happen? "Initially I wanted [the guilty persons punished]. I wanted it badly," she said. "But then I saw how important it was to move on with life. What does one gain from retribution? Yes, I've forgiven them. I only hope they don't kill any more. . . . As for us, we must carry on with our lives and see that God's will is done. That is most important."

She and her daughter remain in India, continuing Graham's work and beginning construction on a new forty-bed hospital.

Finally, in September 2003, Dara Singh and twelve others were convicted of incinerating Graham and his sons.

Seed of the Church

"Martyrs are not necessarily those who are hungry to die. They are merely souls with an excessive appetite to please Christ. They would rather please him by having to die than disappoint him by selling out on key issues of obedience."

—Calvin Miller, *Into the Depths of God*

The Lord is my rock, my fortress and my deliverer; my God is my rock, in whom I take refuge. He is my shield and the horn of my salvation, my stronghold (Psalm 18:2, NIV), on a poster hanging in the Staines's home

---

Wedgwood Baptist Church
Texas—September 15, 1999

Mass shootings dominated the headlines in 1999. In April, two student gunmen opened fire at Columbine High School in Colorado killing twelve classmates and one teacher and wounding twenty others before fatally turning their guns on themselves. In May, four people were shot in a Georgia high school. Over the Fourth of July weekend a white supremacist went on a rampage in the Midwest, killing two and wounding ten before committing suicide. At the end of the month a gunman cut loose in Atlanta, killing nine and injuring twelve. In August three were shot dead in Alabama, and in another incident five were shot at a Jewish community center in Los Angeles.

But no one expected carnage to visit Wedgwood Baptist Church in Fort Worth, Texas, until Larry Gene Ashbrook, wearing blue jeans and a black jacket and smoking a cigarette, entered the church as young people were listening to a Christian rock band. He shot the janitor and two others in the vestibule and walked into the sanctuary shouting curses and threats. Then he fired some thirty rounds from his semiautomatic handgun, pausing to reload at least twice, until he had killed three adults and four teens and wounded seven others. Ashbrook also exploded a pipe bomb in the church, but it hurt no one.

Finally, when police arrived, Ashbrook sat down in a rear pew and shot himself in the head.

"See You at the Pole"

That morning had been designated as "See You at the Pole," when students gathered around their school flagpole to pray for their school and nation. The evening youth rally and concert was a follow-up.

Before this tragic event, Pastor Al Meredith had prayed that God would do *whatever it took* to expand the ministry of Wedgwood Baptist. Wedgwood is located where people had a hard time finding it, but its obscurity soon disappeared. Hot on the heels of the police and ambulances came the media as the attention of millions of people around the world turned to Wedgwood Baptist Church.

The Message

What did the world see? By the following Sunday, just four days after the shooting, the members had removed the bloodstained carpets and pews and hung flowers over the bullet holes. Then they gathered to worship God. Pastor Al Meredith said that while it was not easy to interrupt grieving for Sunday worship, "we believe it is important that we not allow the kingdom of darkness to hinder what God wants to accomplish in his people."

"Where Is God in All This?" he titled his sermon, then answered the question by directing his congregation to Romans 8:28 and saying "The sermon of my life is this: God is in control, and God loves us."

As his prime example of that truth he said, "The most obscene, despicable, evil crime in all the world happened 2000 years ago. . . . But out of that came my salvation and yours." If God could bring such great good out of something so horrible, he could work in their circumstances for good as well.

The congregation embraced that truth, and seven people gave their lives to Christ that morning.

Within days the church's Web site received tens of thousands of hits, thousands of cards and letters poured in, and fifteen thousand people attended the memorial service in the local football stadium, where the gospel was clearly presented while CNN broadcast it to millions of people around the world. As a result of viewing the broadcast, 35 people in Japan became Christians. At several schools "See You at the Pole" prayer meetings proliferated. At one, 25 accepted Christ and at another, 110. A teacher led 22 students to Christ in her classroom. And the reports continued, documenting hundreds of conversions.

We know that God causes everything to work together for the good of those who love God and are called according to his purpose for them (Romans 8:28).

Part 6

Islam: Exchanging Martyrs

Has any religion suffered more martyrs than Christianity? Yes, Islam! While there have been seventy million Christian martyrs over two thousand years, there have been eighty million Islamic martyrs in only fourteen hundred years, according to *World Christian Trends* statisticians, David Barrett and Todd Johnson.[1]

It took only two centuries after Muhammad began preaching in about A.D. 612 for Islam to spread west from its origin in Arabia to Syria, Egypt, North Africa, and Spain, and—by the end of the tenth century—east to Persia, India, and beyond. Not long thereafter, it had spread north to Turkey and the Balkans, and south to sub-Saharan Africa. Today, Islam is the fastest-growing religion in the world with nearly 1.2 billion adherents. (Nearly two billion people claim to be Christian.)[2]

Islam recognizes Moses as the giver of God's Law to the Hebrews and Jesus as a true prophet (but not the divine Son of God), but it claims that Muhammad was the last and greatest prophet, superceding all other prophets. While Muhammad had many misconceptions about Judaism, Christianity, and even the content of the Bible, he acknowledged the validity of original biblical texts—both Old and New Testaments—but claimed that the message was corrupted over time and was therefore untrustworthy. In contrast, the revelations God gave him and which he recorded in the Koran in the "eternal language of Arabic," have been miraculously preserved by Allah from error. (That is why many Muslims hesitate to translate the Koran from Arabic.)

Though there are many other moral injunctions, Islam is characterized by "the five pillars."

1. The *shahada,* or profession of faith: "There is no god but Allah, and Muhammad is his prophet."
2. The *salat,* the duty to perform five prescribed prayers each day facing Mecca.
3. The *sawm,* or fasting from eating, drinking, or sexual intercourse, is required from dawn to sunset during the month of Ramadan. This practice is to encourage physical and spiritual discipline.
4. The *zakat,* or almsgiving to express devotion to God. This obligatory charity (virtually a tax) reminds Muslims of their moral duty to assist the poor, the orphans, and widows, and in so doing purifies one's own wealth.
5. All physically and financially able Muslims are to make a *hajj,* or pilgrimage, to Mecca at some time during their life. Numerous rituals accompany the pilgrimage, including the wearing of seamless white garments.

While these characteristics are certainly incompatible with Christianity (or Judaism), they do not reveal the cause for such enmity between the two religions. And while the angel of the Lord said in Genesis 16:11-12 that Abraham's son, Ishmael (and his descendants, including Muhammad), "will be against everyone, and everyone will be against him. Yes, he will live at odds with the rest of his brothers," that is a prophecy, not an explanation.

Militant Religions

Some Muslims say Islam has a sixth pillar: jihad, or holy war. Technically, the word in Arabic means "holy struggle," to expend one's all to please God. Most modern Muslims understand this to apply primarily to living a virtuous life and helping other Muslims, but it can also mean fighting to defend other Muslims or the faith itself. Today, a minority of radical Muslims emphasize this more-militant element of jihad, even to the point of aggressively and violently extending the faith. And there are numerous references in the Koran that can be read that way. Here are just a few, though other translations render the passages in somewhat milder terms.

- Slay them [infidels] wherever you find them. Drive them out of the places from which they drove you. Idolatry is more grievous than bloodshed. But do not fight them within the precincts of the Holy Mosque unless they attack you there; if they attack you put them to the sword. Thus shall the unbelievers be rewarded: but if they mend their ways [become Muslims], know that God is forgiving and merciful (Sura 2:191, Dawood).
- Fight against them [non-Muslims] until idolatry is no more and God's religion reigns supreme. But if they desist, fight none except the evil-doers (Sura 2:193, Dawood).
- Warfare is ordained for you, though it is hateful unto you; but it may happen that ye hate a thing which is good for you, and it may happen that ye love a thing which is bad for you. Allah knoweth, ye know not (Sura 2:216, Pickthall).
- We shall cast terror into the hearts of those who disbelieve because they ascribe unto Allah partners, for which no warrant hath been revealed. Their habitation is the Fire, and hapless the abode of the wrong-doers (Sura 3:151, Pickthall.) ["Partners" refer to the Christian Trinity, which Islam abhors.]
- How many a city We have destroyed! Our might came upon it at night, or while they took their ease in the noontide" (Sura 7:4, Arberrry). [The "We" is Allah, who often refers to himself in the plural even though Islam claims he has no partner.]
- Prophet, make war on the unbelievers and the hypocrites and deal rigorously with them. Hell shall be their home: an evil fate (Sura 9:73, Dawood). [The word translated "make war" is *jihad*.]

Muslims who claim that violent expansion is not intrinsic to Islamic doctrine say that these passages (and other similar ones) are inaccurately translated or taken out of context. However, while more mild interpretations may be reassuring, the history of Islam suggests that from the beginning they were not always understood in peaceful terms.

Even within Muhammad's lifetime, Muslims made two military forays northward into the Byzantine Empire, attempting—unsuccessfully at the time—to conquer Constantinople. (Not until 1453 did the Ottomans bring Islamic rule to Constantinople/Istanbul.) Within ten years after Muhammad's death, Muslims had conquered Palestine and most of Persia, Iraq, Syria, and Egypt. By 733, only a hundred years after Muhammad's death, an Islamic state stretched from India, through the Middle East, across North Africa, and up into Spain.

It appears that jihad in practice, at least, had a distinctly militant application from the very beginning. However, Muslims who object to the militant characterization of their religion claim that Islam was not itself spread by the sword but that the conquering armies of Arabia and other Islamic countries merely opened the way for the vanquished peoples to hear the message and freely embrace Islam.

Christianity began on a different note. While John's Revelation does say the King of kings will triumph over the forces of evil at the end of the world in what seems like military terms, it appears to be a supernatural victory in which Christ never calls on his human followers to take up physical weapons. Paul wrote, "The weapons we fight with are not the weapons of the world" (2 Corinthians 10:4, NIV). In fact, no New Testament passage prescribes physical warfare as a tool of evangelism or even for the Christian's self-defense. When the soldiers came to arrest Christ and Peter drew a sword, Jesus told him to put it away and rebuked him with, "All who draw the sword will die by the sword" (Matthew 26:52, NIV). Shortly thereafter Jesus explained to Pilate, "My kingdom is not of this world. If it were, my servants would fight" (John 18:36, NIV), effectively ruling out violence as a means of spreading or defending the church.

However, by the time Muhammad came on the scene, nearly six centuries later, Christianity already had compromised Christ's renunciation of force. In fact, as early as 408, Augustine justified coercion and violence to force repentance (see page 48), as well as to wage "just" wars. So, it is no surprise that Christ's "servants" were prepared to fight for the kingdom when it seemed threatened by Muslim invaders.

Whereas Islam seems to have employed violent conquest from its beginning, perhaps even mandated by its scriptures, it was only in its corruption that the church abandoned Jesus' teachings and the values of the apostles to endorse war in the Middle Ages.

Flash Points

Palestine, which at first had been under Greek rule after Alexander the Great conquered it and then Roman rule, became officially "Christian" shortly after Constantine legalized Christianity in 313. Called "the Holy Land" by Christians from then on, it became the focus of Christian pilgrimage, which produced a golden age of prosperity and security.

The advance of Islam west through Palestine, across the north of Africa and up into Spain, and north toward Constantinople (which did not fall for eight hundred years) was essentially a protracted conquest of hitherto Christian lands with the expected death of tens of thousands of Christians who saw themselves as merely defending their homes from invaders. When the Arabs invaded Morocco, for instance, they slaughtered thirty-five thousand Christians, whose blood was literally flowing through the streets.

After Muslim Arab armies invaded Palestine and captured Jerusalem in 638, the majority of the population converted to Islam. "People of the Book"— as Muslims designated Christians and Jews—were allowed freedom of worship and self-rule in their communities. However, in 1009 al-Hakim, who was a Fatimid Khalif of Egypt, ordered the destruction of many churches, including the Church of the Holy Sepulcher in Jerusalem. This and the restrictions on pilgrims and taxes understandably galled the Catholic Church. In 1074, during an era of corrupt popes, Pope Gregory VII proposed leading fifty thousand volunteers to help the Christians in the East and possibly to liberate Jerusalem. Finally, in 1095, in response to desperate appeals from Eastern emperor Alexius Comnenus, the new pope, Urban II, preached a stirring sermon at Clermont.

"A horrible tale has gone forth," he said. "An accursed race utterly alienated from God ... has invaded the lands of the Christians and depopulated them by the sword, plundering, and fire." Toward the end, he made his appeal: "Tear that land from the wicked race and subject it to yourselves." The crusaders succeeded in capturing Jerusalem in 1099, but not without horrendous atrocities. When a town called Ma'arrat Nu'man was conquered, 100,000 people were killed and the town burnt to the ground. Jerusalem fared little better with 65,000 to 70,000 slaughtered at the al-Aqsa mosque.

Subsequent Crusades attempted to extend "Christian" control, but within the next two hundred years, Islamic fighters drove out the Europeans and regained control of the Holy Land, thereby "winning" the Crusades. Nevertheless, Islam has never forgotten the great offense of the Crusades.

The Ottoman Empire, which ruled from about 1300 to 1921, when it was defeated by the British in World War I, was the next powerful Islamic presence in the Middle East, resulting in widespread martyrdom of Christians. The defeat of Constantinople heralded the dawn of a new era of warfare using heavy cannon bombardment. As was common after a long siege, victorious soldiers poured into the city killing, raping, looting, burning, and enslaving. When Sultan Mehmed finally entered the city, he went straight to Haghia Sophia Church and ordered it converted to a mosque. Then he ordered a stop to the killing.

The Ottomans continued their conquest, colonizing Greece, all of the Balkans, Romania, Bessarabia, and Hungary, only to be stopped at the outskirts of Vienna in 1529. But perhaps the worst atrocity befell Armenia.

Although Armenia accepted Christianity in the fourth century, by the latter half of the nineteenth century, this buffer state, sandwiched between Russia, Turkey, and the Persian Empire, was under control of the Ottoman Turks. Fearing that the hierarchy of the Orthodox Church might inspire a revolt, the Turks welcomed Protestant evangelical missionaries until they saw how many Muslims were converting to Christianity. Then the Ottoman Turks turned on all Christians in Armenia, imprisoning thousands of converts. Still fearing an uprising at the end of the century, government soldiers killed 100,000 Christian Armenians.

Then during World War I, claiming that the Armenians were helping Russian invaders, the Turks launched a genocidal attack against the Armenians on April 24, 1915. After killing as many as 600,000, they attempted to drive the remaining Armenian population out into the desert. Before they were finished, approximately 1.5 million Armenians had been killed out of the total population of 2.5 million.

Most true Christians would like to disassociate themselves from the "Christian" Serbs responsible for massacring Croats and Muslims during the Bosnian Civil War from 1992 to 1995. In many ways, most people in the country were not strongly religious, it was merely a means of distinguishing one ethnic group from the other once the war started. However, much of the Islamic world saw the atrocities as more war crimes by Christians.

On September 11, 2001, as though trading martyrs, Islamic terrorists dove hijacked airliners into the World Trade Center towers, the Pentagon, and a Pennsylvania field killing three thousand victims, not necessarily Christian martyrs but a strike against the American "infidels," as far as radical, fundamentalist Muslims were concerned.

For many Americans, oblivious of the sectarian conflicts that have been raging throughout the world, the 9/11 attack was a wake-up call. We had presumed previous international terrorism was the work of a tiny minority of extremists who are always present in society. Suddenly, as reporters began doing background stories, the public learned that the minority wasn't so tiny and that the actions of terrorists were an extension of a sector of Islam that had been systematically persecuting thousands of Christians and other non-Muslims in Afghanistan, Algeria, Egypt, Indonesia, Pakistan, Saudi Arabia, Somalia, Sudan, and other nations either with Islamic governments or powerful, radical Islamic contingents.

Unfortunately, too often we have been silent in the face of these persecutions worldwide. But it may help us to know that several countries, even some with considerable hostility toward the United States, have responded when Christians have mounted a concerted campaign on behalf of imprisoned Christians in their countries. Therefore, it is critically important to remain informed by organizations such as Voice of the Martyrs and do our part to contact officials with concern when the lives of fellow Christians—or anyone being persecuted for their religious beliefs—are at risk.

Returning to Jesus' Ethic

As Christians, what should our attitude be as tensions between Islam and Christianity continue to rage? Perhaps Jesus' words bring the most hope: "Love your enemies! Pray for those who persecute you! In that way, you will be acting as true children of your Father in heaven. For he gives his sunlight to both the evil and the good, and he sends rain on the just and on the unjust, too. If you love only those who love you, what good is that? Even corrupt tax collectors do that much. If you are kind only to your friends, how are you different from anyone else? Even pagans do that" (Matthew 5:44-47).

Loving one's enemies will not necessarily save our own skin, since persecution comes with the territory of following Christ. The reason that Jesus gave for loving one's enemies was not that utilitarian; it had a more eternal goal: to "be perfect, even as your Father in heaven is perfect" (Matthew 5:48).

Notes
1. David Barrett and Todd Johnson, "Evangelism through Martyrdom: 70 Million Christians Killed for Their Faith in 220 Countries across Twenty Centuries," *World Christian Trends* (Pasadena, Calif.: William Carey Library, 2001), global diagram 16.
2. David Barrett and Todd Johnson, "Global Adherents of the World's Nineteen Major Distinct Religions," *World Christian Trends* (Pasadena, Calif.: William Carey Library, 2001), table 1–2.

The Witnesses

Zeba
Pakistan—1999

Situated between the volatile borders of Iran, Afghanistan, and India, Pakistan has endured British colonialism, three major wars, military regimes, and corrupt governments. In recent years, militant Islamic groups have been trying to force Muslim Sharia law as the law of the land, which would intensify the already severe persecution against the country's 1.7 percent Christian population.

But those are only facts and figures. The face of persecution in Pakistan today can perhaps be understood by meeting a young girl named Zeba.

Too Much Suffering in a Short Life

"Here. Memorize these verses. How can you be so ignorant of Islam?"

Trembling, twelve-year-old Zeba shook her head. She tried to be respectful toward the master of the house where she was employed as a servant, but he kept drilling her about Islam. "I-I can't. I am a Christian, you see."

The man's eyes snapped fire. "Insolent girl! You dare to talk back to me?" The slap came out of nowhere, sending Zeba to the floor. He jerked her up and hit her several more times before stalking off.

Zeba tried to hide the marks from the beating from her mother and father—it would only upset them. Her family needed the money she brought home from her job as a household servant. But after the third beating, she broke down and told her mother what was happening.

What was a mother to do? She could not stand idly by while her child was being mistreated. Gathering her courage, Zeba's mother draped a long scarf around her jet black hair and shoulders, walked to her daughter's place of employment, and asked to see the master of the house. When the man appeared, Zeba's mother explained that she was raising her daughter as a Christian and would he please stop trying to convert her to Islam?

Infuriated, the man slapped Zeba's mother so hard she fell down, then kept kicking her until she lay crumpled and motionless on the ground. He stomped off—but within minutes returned with a can of fuel, which he poured over the unconscious woman. And then he struck a match.

The horrifying death of Zeba's mother devastated her family. Zeba's oldest sister, Aseema, was so consumed with grief that she stopped eating and died two months later. Zeba's father, Sharif, already impoverished, borrowed money in order to keep his family alive—but the subsequent debt threatened to keep him in servitude to the lender with no hope of paying off the principal.

Hopeless? No. Zeba shed many tears over the death of her mother, but several months later asked to be baptized. Dripping wet, her smile was a witness that her faith was still strong and sure. Hearing of this family's plight and their steadfastness in the face of such grievous persecution, a generous donor provided money through The Voice of the Martyrs (VOM) to pay Sharif's debt. The mission, which serves the persecuted church worldwide, also set up a sewing-and-literacy school for girls like Zeba, who otherwise would be forced to bow to Islam just to keep their jobs. Zeba learned to read and write in the VOM school, using the Bible as her curriculum, and graduated in the fall of 2001.

Today Zeba has a dream: she wants to become a Bible teacher and tell her own people about Jesus. Meanwhile, using the sewing machine and cloth given to her at graduation, this young teenager is helping to support her family. Beyond a shadow of a doubt, Zeba knows that she belongs to the family of God worldwide.

God has combined the members of the body . . . so that there should be no division in the body, but that its parts should have equal concern for each other. If one part suffers, every part suffers with it; if one part is honored, every part rejoices with it (1 Corinthians 12:24-26, NIV).

Kamerino
Sudan—2000

The overwhelming suffering in modern Sudan can hardly be comprehended. Hundreds of thousands of innocent civilians, many of them Christians, have been decimated by two decades of bloody civil war between the Government of Sudan (GOS), determined to impose Islamic rule on all Sudanese, and the Sudanese Peoples Liberation Army (SPLA). As with all wars, religion, politics, power, and greed for land and oil run roughshod over the lives of ordinary families who just want to make a living, feed their families, and worship God in peace. Ordinary families like Kamerino's.

A Grandmother's Story

She was getting on in years, the age when a grandmother should be able to rest, watching her grandchildren tumble and play with the freedom of childhood and grow up into strong men and women, who can care for their elders. But that was before the Islamic government soldiers descended on their village in southern Sudan, burning and killing and taking captives who would end up as slaves in the households and harems of the rich.

Now she was raising her grandson, Kamerino, as best she could. But with so many breadwinners dead or captured, the village was starving to death, bit by bit, day by day. So what could she do when he asked permission to venture away from the village with three of his friends—boys like himself—to look for food? Fear leaped into her heart. She didn't want him to leave the village.

Their world was not safe. But she knew his stomach pinched with hunger. Maybe the boys could find some edible plants or roots.

But as the afternoon sun sank lower and lower in the brassy Sudanese sky, the grandmother knew something was wrong. The boys should be back by now! Several adults headed in the same direction the boys had taken earlier that day—a landscape of tall, dry grasses and stubby bushes and trees.

Anxiously Kamerino's grandmother waited along with the other villagers. Suddenly the searchers appeared in the distance—but no lanky boys trotted alongside. Wait—they were carrying something . . . someone . . .

It was Kamerino, moaning in shock and pain. His body was covered with fresh third degree burns. Stifling the urge to wrap her protective arms around him, the grandmother motioned the rescuers to bring her grandson into a small "hut" made of concrete blocks, where they laid him on a piece of green plastic tarp. Someone gave him water to drink through parched lips. But no one knew what else to do. There was a mission hospital, but it was fifty miles away! The grandmother knew she could never carry him that far.

Kamerino tugged on her skirt. "The soldiers—" he croaked. Gradually the story came out. While hunting for food, the boys saw GOS soldiers in the distance—and by their shouts knew they'd been seen. The boys ran into a field of tall grass, hoping to hide. But the next thing they knew, the soldiers had surrounded the field and set it on fire. In panic, Kamerino's friends ran through the flames, hoping to escape. But by the gunfire he heard, Kamerino knew they had only met another death. He chose the fire.

Clutching her pain to herself, the grandmother kept watch over the boy. Flies gathered on his raw flesh faster than she could wave them away. The burns began to smell. Whenever Kamerino moved, he cried out in pain. But still he lived.

On the eighth day, a head poked into the shelter. "Come quickly! Missionaries! A big truck!" The grandmother ran. Later she would learn that they were a team from The Voice of the Martyrs, delivering blankets and other supplies to displaced families. For now, all she knew was that they had a truck. Wheels. To take Kamerino to the hospital.

The VOM team sprang into action. Supplies were rearranged in the truck, and Kamerino was placed gently inside. "We need to get him to the hospital fast," she was told as she climbed in beside her grandson.

God had sent help just in time. Today Kamerino's grandmother watches proudly as the boy attends a Christian boarding school. Although scarred for life, he is growing into a fine young man. Her legacy. She knows God spared his life . . . for a purpose.

The Lord said to Satan, "The Lord rebuke you, Satan! The Lord who has chosen Jerusalem rebuke you! Is this not a brand plucked from the fire?" (Zechariah 3:2, NKJV).

The Four Evangelists

China—2000 (all names have been changed)

The Eastern Lightning cult in China has used many devious means to lure new Christians away from their foundations to accept "the female Christ" as "The Almighty One," Christ who has "come again." But in recent years, EL has begun targeting Christian leaders, and their tactics have gotten more subtle and subversive.

Divide and Conquer

A pastor of a house church in Henan Province—we will call him Pastor Chiang—was aware of the Eastern Lightning heresies and some of their coarser tactics, such as trying to marry into the family of an influential Christian leader, or if that didn't work, seducing a single son in an attempt to blackmail the elder with threats of damage to his family's reputation. But what Pastor Chiang didn't know is that an Eastern Lightning "spy" had been quietly infiltrating his own church for nine months, biding his time and learning the weak points of the leaders that might be used to advantage.

This unassuming "spy"—we will call him Yang—came to the church as a "new Christian with a heart to serve God," but who lacked knowledge of the Bible and needed the wisdom of elders. Of course the sisters and brothers were quite willing to disciple this new believer who seemed so eager to learn. Yang was very meek, admitting his shortcomings and willingly submitting to correction. He learned all the praise songs and prayed aloud "in Jesus' name." After the sermon, he would be very loud in his praises: "The Lord is merciful to us, for we have never heard preaching as good as this!"

In February 2000, Pastor Chiang was called away for three months to minister in another place, leaving the church in the hands of other leaders. This was Yang's golden opportunity. Coming to the brother who had been put in charge, Yang said, "I've just returned from Lanzhou [Gansu Province], where I was visiting my brother. Hundreds of people have never heard of the Way, the Truth, or the Light! I've never been trained to teach or preach—will you go and speak to them the truth and fundamentals of the gospel?"

Such a call could not be refused! And this brother had been in the church for almost a year, so they didn't suspect sabotage. A team was put together—two men, two women—to go minister in Lanzhou. When they arrived by train, three "brothers," two of them from Lanzhou, met them and embraced Paul, the team leader, with flattering words: "I have seen you before in a vision! The Lord told me you were coming to teach us God's Word—and now you are here! Praise the Lord! God knows our needs!"

The third man said he had come from Xian in obedience to a vision: "The Lord gave me a vision that there would be two female disciples coming from the northeast to revive the church in Xian. Our need is so great! Are there not four of you? Will you not come with me to minister in Xian?"

The team members at first refused to split up, but the pleadings and "visions" and flattery of their ministry overcame their caution. The two sisters got back on the train with Yang and the man from Xian, while the two brothers stayed in Lanzhou. In Xian, a woman met them who said she had arranged a meeting and they must hurry; but another woman said she too had arranged a meeting! What to do? Unwisely, these sisters allowed themselves to be separated once again in order to teach at both meetings. (The same tactics of "need" and "flattery" were being used to divide the brothers back in Lanzhou until each was ministering alone.)

Once separated, the team members were moved from place to place under the guise of desperate ministry needs. Each one continued to receive excessive praise—though the promised crowds of hundreds turned out to be a handful of EL members. And then . . . the brainwashing and indoctrination began.

Seed of the Church

"Dear fellow workers, no matter when, no matter where, coworkers must not separate."

—a letter written by one of the four evangelists who
thought she would never return home alive

[Jesus] called his twelve disciples together and sent them out two by two, with authority to cast out evil spirits (Mark 6:7).

Johannes Mantahari

Indonesia—2000

"Johannes! Johannes! Wake up!"

Eighteen-year-old Johannes Mantahari groggily open his eyes. Could it be morning already? No . . . the room was still dark, the birds quiet. But the hand shaking his shoulder was insistent, the voice urgent.

"Laskar Jihad troops—headed this way! Run! Run!"

Johannes bolted awake. Not taking time to put on a shirt or wrap food for a journey, the young man joined others in his village moving swiftly between their thatched roof homes to disappear into the surrounding jungle on Halmahera Island.

Too late! Running feet surrounded him. Lashing out with his hands and feet, Johannes tried to fight them off. But there were too many, and he tasted dirt as he was thrown facedown to the ground. Johannes could feel about five of the radical Muslim warriors pinning him to the ground. Out of the corner of his eye, he made out about five more lurking above him with swords drawn. Twice that many surrounded their victim so that he could not escape.

"So!" leered one of his captors. "You are one of these Christians? What do you say now—are you ready to become a Muslim?"

"No!" said Johannes through gritted teeth. He could barely move.

"No?" Johannes heard the swish of a sword. "Convert, you infidel—or die."

Johannes had thought about this moment. What would he do if given that choice by the radical Muslim group that had been terrorizing Indonesia in recent years? He was ready with his reply. "If I die, I will go to heaven to be with Jesus."

"Then die, infidel!" screamed one of his attackers.

Again the swish of a sword, and Johannes felt the sharp tip graze his temple and slice into his left shoulder and forearm. Then another sword slashed deeply into the back of his neck. Then more slices on his back and legs. Bleeding profusely and barely conscious now, Johannes was only vaguely aware of being covered with large banana leaves and a match being struck.

Then all was quiet. *I'm dying,* he thought. *Jesus! Help me!*

Suddenly his mind cleared and with a surge of strength, Johannes threw off the barely smoldering leaves—they were too green to burn—and staggered into the jungle, heading for a cave he knew about.

Stranger in the Night

Johannes bandaged his wounds as best he could with leaves and vines to stop the bleeding. When it was safe to leave the cave, he stumbled through the jungle for eight days, but found no one to help him. Finally he collapsed from exhaustion, certain he would now take his last breath. With that last breath he again cried out: "Jesus, help me!"

Suddenly he felt the touch of a hand on his arm. The touch was firm, reassuring, peaceful. Johannes tried to twist around to see who his benefactor was, but in the dark night could see no one. "Who is it?" he shouted with the last ounce of his strength. "How did you get here in the middle of the jungle? I have seen no one for days!"

Sitting up, Johannes looked all around him. The person with the comforting touch had disappeared. But he felt an unusual warmth and surge of energy flow through his body. Staggering to his feet, Johannes stumbled on.

How long he walked after that, Johannes did not know. But suddenly he heard a familiar voice. "Johannes! Is that you?" It was his brother-in-law. He had been found!

Johannes had stopped the bleeding on many of his wounds—but hundreds of maggots were squirming in the deep, pus-filled gash on the back of his neck. His brother-in-law employed the best remedy he knew: pouring kerosene over the wound to kill the loathsome creatures.

Today, twenty-year-old Johannes, studying to become an evangelist, bears the scars of the night he was confronted with the choice: Convert to Islam—or die. To him the scars are badges of honor for Jesus. And he believes it was Jesus who comforted him in the jungle and gave him the strength to carry on when he was ready to give up.

In His Own Words
"I forgive them as our Father in heaven forgives us."
—Johannes Mantahari, speaking of the Laskar Jihad troops who nearly killed him

---

[Jesus said,] "If you forgive those who sin against you, your heavenly Father will forgive you. But if you refuse to forgive others, your Father will not forgive your sins" (Matthew 6:14-15).

Safeena
Pakistan—2000

Officially, Pakistan has been cooperating with the United States to root out terrorism since the terrible events of September 11, 2001. But as we know in our own country, laws by themselves do not change hearts. Discrimination and persecution by the Muslim majority against the tiny minority of Christians in Pakistan (2 percent) continue unabated.

Statistics mean little to truly understand what a Christian family might endure in a Middle Eastern or Asian country in the twenty-first century. So for a few brief moments, put yourself in the sandals of the Christian parents of a teenage girl named Safeena. . . .

The Strength of a Teenager

Jobs are scarce and pay meager in present-day Pakistan—especially if you are a despised Christian, a "second-class citizen." Like many other poor families, you finally face the inevitable: your fourteen-year-old daughter will have to take a job as a household helper with one of the wealthy Muslim families in town to help support the family.

You are apprehensive, but brown-eyed Safeena assures you. "They are very nice to me, Father. Why, they practically treat me like their own daughter!" How could they help it? Safeena is sweet tempered, with dancing brown eyes and a smile that lights up her face. And she has been taught to cook, keep a clean house, and treat laundry with care. Yes, her employers *should* realize they have gold in their household helper.

But your parent's heart can't help noticing that one of the sons in the family likes Safeena a bit *too* well. His eyes follow her; he goes out of his way to speak to her. Still, you are shocked when his parents indicate that he would like to marry Safeena. But . . . he is a Muslim, and she is a Christian! Yes, well, they hedge, she would have to convert.

333

Now Safeena comes home looking troubled. "They beg me to renounce my foreign religion and convert to Islam," she tells you. "But I tell them I cannot. I am a Christian." At first the pressure is beguiling. They love Safeena! They want her to become a *real* part of their family. But when she continues to refuse, the pressure becomes sharp. Safeena wants to quit her job, but . . . what will your family do without the income she brings in?

Oh, how you regret it now! For one day the son decided that if he couldn't have Safeena one way, he would have her another. Following her up to the roof of the family home where she was hanging up the laundry, he caught her alone and raped her. Totally shattered, Safeena ran home to your sheltering embrace. She quit! She couldn't go back.

Her weeping shatters your own spirit. Then anger wells up inside—but with no place to vent. How could such a thing happen? Surely, even his parents could not condone such a beastly act! You pace back and forth, considering criminal charges against the young man. But before you can do anything, the police show up at your door. They have a warrant for the arrest of your daughter, Safeena. Arrest?! Yes, she has been charged with stealing from her employers' home. The police tear your home apart, looking for missing jewels. They find none, but they take *your* jewel: Safeena.

Safeena is locked up in the local jail for one month. You are nearly beside yourself, feeling helpless and enraged, unable to protect your little girl–woman. But it gets worse. The son came to the jail and was left alone with your daughter—and he raped her again. And the guard raped her too.

Now Safeena is out of jail on bail. But she feels so much shame. Rape carries a terrible stigma in Pakistan—for the woman. Who will want to marry her now? She is still facing charges of theft . . . all because she refused to deny her faith in Jesus.

You feel humbled by your own daughter. Safeena is trying to rejoice, even in her sufferings. She is trying to see God's hand at work in the harsh realities of her circumstances. She truly understands what it means to "count the cost" to follow Jesus.

Do we?

Seed of the Church

"You never know how much you really believe anything until its truth or falsehood becomes a matter of life and death to you."

—C. S. Lewis

Don't let anyone look down on you because you are young, but set an example for the believers in speech, in life, in love, in faith and in purity (1 Timothy 4:12, NIV).

Sonmin Grace Church

Tajikistan—October 1, 2000

Ever heard of Tajikistan? Perched above Afghanistan's northern border, Tajikistan gained its independence when the Soviet Union was dismantled in 1991. But since "independence," Tajikistan has endured a five-year civil war between its neocommunist government and Islamist-inspired opposition. In 1997, rival factions signed a peace agreement, but ongoing clan warfare sometimes spills over its borders.

The World Factbook estimates that 80 percent of Tajiks are Sunni Muslim, 5 percent are Shi'a Muslim, and 4 percent are Christian (primarily Orthodox). The people have only had the complete Bible in the Tajik language since 1992. In general, Christian groups have been more tolerated than in many Muslim-dominated countries—but let's look at one "story behind the story" of a Korean mission in the capital city of Dushanbe to catch a glimpse of what it has cost a group of Christians to share the Good News in Tajikistan.

"Illegal Missionary Activity"

1990s: Sonmin Grace Church, a Christian congregation made up of ethnic Russians, Tajiks, and Koreans, is formed by a South Korean mission. The church rented a large, three-story building, where several dozen church members lived together in community. The third floor was turned into a sanctuary able to seat at least two hundred worshippers.

November 1999: The Committee for Religious Affairs of the Tajik government informed the church that it was in danger of losing its state registration because of its evangelistic outreaches into towns across the country. Three different times police raided services, confiscated "illegal missionary propaganda," and interrogated church members.

August 9, 2000: Three South Korean students associated with the Sonmin missionary center in Dushanbe were detained by local police in the town of Kurgan-Teppe and accused of "missionary activity" for passing out leaflets, then expelled from the town.

September 30, 2000: The U.S. Embassy in Dushanbe evacuated all its personnel from Tajikistan because of confirmed "threats against foreigners." Resident foreigners were advised to observe extra caution.

Sunday, October 1, 2000: With Pastor Yun Seop Choi traveling abroad, a guest speaker brought the morning message at Sonmin Grace Church. As the offering was being collected, witnesses say, a stranger came in and left a bag on one of the rear pews. A few minutes later, the bag exploded, tearing doors off their hinges, shattering the windows, and turning the furniture into splinters. Two worshippers were killed immediately and scores wounded. As the panicked congregation scuttled down the two flights of stairs, another bomb on the first floor went off, sending bodies hurtling in different directions. All together ten people died and seventy were injured, some seriously.

(Two persons sustained burns over two-thirds of their bodies and one man was blinded in both eyes.)

By the end of the day, the police had arrested twelve people—all leaders of the church! All were interrogated, not just about the bombing, but about why they had become believers in Jesus and what plans they had to evangelize others. Eventually all church leaders were released without any charges, though several had been beaten.

October 6, 2000: Pastor Yun Seop Choi returned to Tajikistan and was reunited with his congregation. Many wept as he came into the room.

October 30, 2000: Two students at the Dushanbe Islamic Institute were arrested and charged with the bombing. According to witnesses, church members saw and recognized them. The investigation also linked the two to two other bomb attacks elsewhere.

July 13, 2001: Twenty-five-year-old Mustofokul Boymurodov and twenty- two-year-old Sadriddin Fatkhuddinov were convicted and sentenced to die by firing squad. The sentence is being appealed. According to a Sonmin Grace Church member, "Christian believers are in favor of life and generally oppose the death penalty," stressing that church members did not lobby for any particular sentence, though several gave witness at the trial.

Meanwhile, Sonmin Grace Church is attempting to rebuild its life and ministry.

We are pressed on every side by troubles, but we are not crushed and broken. We are perplexed, but we don't give up and quit. We are hunted down, but God never abandons us. We get knocked down, but we get up again and keep going (2 Corinthians 4:8-9), circled on a blood-stained page of the Bible of an elderly woman killed in the bombing

---

Mai-Ling

China—2000 (all names have been changed)

The two female evangelists looked at one another uncertainly. What should they do? They had already left the two brothers on their evangelism team back in Lanzhou in response to an urgent request from the city of Xian to come here to minister. But no sooner had they arrived than they were presented with a schedule conflict.

The first woman who met them at the train station said she had arranged a meeting where they would be teaching. But a second woman said, "I have also arranged a meeting. Hurry! What should we do? It's a terrible waste to keep two good preachers together." So as not to disappoint their hosts, the two evangelists agreed to split up for the evening—one going to the first meeting, the other to the second.

They did not know they would not see each other again for five months.

Build Them Up; Then Tear Them Down

The fourth evangelist on the ministry team from Henan Province—we will call her Mai-Ling—was told the meeting was in a suburb of Xian, but in reality she was taken to a town named Weinan. The next day there was "a desperate need" in Tongguan.

Moving constantly, Mai-Ling hardly had time to think. But God seemed to be using her. At least her hosts kept telling her, "Your sermon was the best we have ever heard. We would like to invite you to preach in still another village."

On the fourth day, as Mai-Ling was presenting the gospel message, two men in the congregation began to disrupt the meeting. "Don't listen to her! She is a demon." The men rolled around on the ground, hit people, broke things, and shouted to drown her out. This went on for days. Convinced the two men were demon possessed, and pressured by members of the congregation to cast them out, Mai-Ling tried to lay hands on the two men and several times prayed for the demons to leave "in the name of Jesus!"

But the men just mocked her. "Why do you still pray in Jesus' name? Don't you know Jesus' name became useless long ago?" Others in the congregation—unknown to Mai-Ling, all of them were members of the Eastern Lightning cult—joined in the mocking. Mai-Ling began to doubt. Was it true the name of Jesus was powerless?

Some people suggested they take a collection and confine the men in a mental institution. "How much money do *you* have?" they asked Mai-Ling. They kept asking until she had given everything she had with her, more than a thousand RMB (about $120). Now she was penniless—and dependent on her hosts for every need.

Two weeks went by. As Mai-Ling lost confidence, a "brother" named Wang Enguang from Zhejiang Province came into the meeting. Immediately the "possessed" men started to shout: "The light! The true light! I'm afraid!" Their bodies jerked and stiffened, then became calm.

"The demons have been cast out!" people cried. "Hallelujah! This is the truth!"

Mai-Ling felt humiliated and defeated. She sat down, while "Preacher Wang" took over and step by step began preaching the doctrines of Eastern Lightning: The Jews do not accept the truth because they are still in the Era of Law; Christians do not accept the female Christ because they still linger in the Era of Grace; but the Era of the Kingdom has come!

For months Mai-Ling became more and more confused. She could not escape; she had no money and her shoes and day clothes were removed each night. But when she was enticed with flattering words by Wang Enguang to "forget her husband" (who was not a Christian) and go to bed with him, Mai-Ling knew she was being asked to commit adultery. She refused, and from that time on she looked for a way to escape . . . finally walking over the Tongguan mountains, begging her way onto buses, weeping copious tears when she was finally reunited with her family and home congregation.

337

She was the last of the four evangelists to escape Eastern Lightning.

In human form he obediently humbled himself even further by dying a criminal's death on a cross. Because of this, God raised him up to the heights of heaven and gave him a name that is above every other name, so that at the name of Jesus every knee will bow, in heaven and on earth and under the earth, and every tongue will confess that Jesus Christ is Lord, to the glory of God the Father (Philippians 2:8-11).

Idris Miah
Bangladesh — ca. 2000

Dark shadows gathered between the simple thatched dwellings as night fell. Idris Miah left his supper, slipped into the night, and gathered with other men at the appointed time and place. It was time to put a stop to the traitor in their midst.

In first-world countries, people dated their letters 2000-plus. Celebrations marking the twenty-first century had come and gone; computer technology and the wonders of e-mail linked humankind as never before; "ecumenism" and "tolerance" for religious plurality were smug bywords of Western democracies.

But here in a typical village in Bangladesh, the men gathered by twos and threes in the shadows until they were twenty-five strong. Their purpose: to attack their neighbor Abu and teach him a lesson. Christians would not be tolerated in *their* village. They were Muslims! Allah was the true God and Muhammad was his prophet! Who did Abu think he was, turning his back on Islam and following a *Western* religion?

Keeping to the shadows and walking quietly, Idris Miah was near the front of the pack as the villagers neared Abu's home. Suddenly he stopped. He could hear someone talking—they had not counted on Abu having company. Had he gotten wind of their plan and gathered others to help him? What should they do now?

Idris listened. Abu was praying! In a loud, clear voice, Abu was praying for the entire village by name. "Oh, Jesus, forgive them for what they are about to do!"

"Someone has told Abu about our plan!" someone hissed in Idris's ear.

"Well, that won't stop us!" muttered another.

As one, the group of men rushed Abu's house. But just as suddenly, the front-runners stopped, while others bumped into them. Idris tried to move forward, but it was like an invisible barrier surrounded Abu's house. Confused and frightened, the men dropped back and melted away into the night.

Lying beside his wife and sleeping children, Idris could not get what happened out of his mind. Wide awake, he kept thinking about Abu's prayer.

Father, forgive them, for what they are about to do! Did they really not know what they were doing? If Abu knew what had been planned, why hadn't he run or defended himself? What kind of God preached *forgiving* one's enemies?

Beside himself, Idris got up and once more made his way to Abu's house. The house was dark and silent. Tentatively, then more insistent, Idris knocked on the door.

A sleepy Abu opened the door. "Idris! What are you doing here at this hour?"

Idris Miah had only one question. "Tell me! Who is Jesus?"

Praying for the Enemy

The two men talked for hours. As dawn lit the sky over the village, Idris returned to his wife and children. "I have become a Christian!" he announced. "I asked Jesus to forgive my sins. Now I belong to Jesus! Jesus has saved me!"

Seeing the joy in Idris's life, his wife and children gave their lives to Jesus too. But within days, Idris was fired from his job. His children were forced out of school. But Idris is not bitter. No one can take away the joy of Jesus from his heart. And like Abu, he prays for his enemies, because it was Abu's prayer that opened his eyes.

[Jesus said,] "Love your enemies and pray for those who persecute you that you may be children of your Father in heaven" (Matthew 5:44-45, NIV).

Pastor Emmanuel Allah Atta

Pakistan—October 28, 2001

Sarapheen met her husband, Emmanuel Allah Atta, for the first time on her wedding day, July 7, 1973. As the custom in Pakistan dictates, her parents arranged her marriage. As nominal Christians, they chose a young man also from a Christian family. But Sarapheen soon discovered that her new husband wanted to become a pastor and dedicate his life to serving the Lord Jesus Christ. A new excitement percolated within Sarapheen's spirit. She wanted to join her husband in serving the Lord. Shortly after they were married, Emmanuel led Sarapheen to personal salvation in Christ.

The next few years were challenging for the newlyweds as Emmanuel went to seminary, then an evangelist training school in Hyderabad. He was ordained in 1985, and became pastor of the Church of Pakistan, a Protestant congregation that met in St. Dominic's Catholic Church in Bahawalpur. For many years, Muslims and Christians lived peacefully side by side in this city—even though the Catholics and Protestants together comprised a mere 3 percent of the population in Pakistan.

In the meantime, children were coming along in the Atta family—eventually five daughters and one son. "We had a pleasant marriage," says Sarapheen, "and because we often prayed together, we never fought. Our life together was fantastic. My husband was very kind, and he never abused me in married life. He was a good example of a pastor. I will never forget his kindness, and I will miss him."

Had a pleasant marriage? Will miss him? Hidden in the past tense lies Sarapheen's new reality—a reality that took them by storm on October 28, 2001.

The Final Sermon

The Protestant congregation met for the "early" service at St. Dominic's Church. The praise and prayer service had been so joyful, the service was running late. Pastor Emmanuel did not mean to delay the Catholic mass, but he couldn't cut his sermon short. The whole world was anxious in the wake of the Islamic terrorist attacks on the United States on September 11—just a month and a half earlier. Tensions had increased between Muslims and Christians in Pakistan. Fervently, he encouraged his congregation of seventy-five persons to "pray without ceasing" during the troubled times ahead. "As you faithfully pray," he said passionately, "you will grow closer to God and stronger in spirit."

As he concluded his sermon shortly before 9:00 A.M., three men dressed in long, black shalwars and brandishing Kalashnikov automatic weapons stormed into the church and up the aisle. "Throw your Bible down!" one of them ordered Pastor Emmanuel.

The pastor pulled his Bible close to his heart and turned away. "I will not!"

"Allah Ahkbar!" shouted the gunman. "God is great!"—just as he opened fire with his automatic weapon, pumping bullets into the pastor's back. The pastor's long white robe grew red with bloodstains as he fell to the floor.

The other terrorists opened fire on the congregation, pumping over five hundred rounds into the screaming crowd for six long minutes. When they finished their vicious work, fifteen church members were dead, plus a Muslim security guard who'd been standing watch at the front gate. There was no discrimination among the victims. The beloved pastor, men, women, children, a two-year-old child . . . dead.

Sarapheen's face crumples when she talks about the death of her beloved husband, but the tears include tears of joy. "Our Lord told us that in his name we would suffer," she says. "It is an honor and privilege that my husband is a martyr for Jesus."

Four-year-old Kinza says her daddy looked right at her as he fell to the ground "and went to sleep." When asked where her daddy is now, Kinza says simply, "He's in heaven with Jesus."

In His Own Words

The following is the text from which Pastor Emmanuel preached the morning he died.

Please don't despair because of what they are doing to me here. It is for you that I am suffering, so you should feel honored and encouraged. When I think of the wisdom and scope of God's plan, I fall to my knees and pray to the Father, the Creator of everything in heaven and on earth. I pray that from his glorious, unlimited resources he will give you mighty inner strength through his Holy Spirit (Ephesians 3:13-16).

Park Ho-Bong

North Korea — 2001 (All names have been changed.)

Mrs. Kim knew the moment he walked in the door. A mother always knows when something is not right with one of her children, even when he is grown. Anxious, she asked, "What's wrong?"

Kim Joon-Hee made no reply. But his lips were pressed together, his eyes narrow, as though he could hold it in, whatever was troubling her oldest son. She rose and stood before him. "Please tell me, my son. What is wrong?"

"Nothing." His reply was clipped, and he pulled away from her.

But Mrs. Kim was a mother and she did not give up. "Joon-Hee, you cannot hide it from me. Something terrible has happened. You must tell me."

"I cannot believe—!" he blurted, then shook his head, too upset to speak further.

But bit by bit, the patient mother drew the story from her son. . . .

In Cold Blood

They were walking down the street together, two friends coping with an ordinary day in one of the world's remaining communist countries. In spite of the severe famine that had been crippling North Korea for the past six years, Kim Joon-Hee and Park Ho-Bong had the future before them . . . maybe they would marry, raise a family, get decent jobs. Intent on their conversation, they didn't notice the two police officers in their brown uniforms with red trim until they stood before them.

The policemen ignored Joon-Hee, but fixed their steely gaze on Ho-Bong. "You are a Christian!" one of them spat. Bewildered, Joon-Hee looked at his friend, expecting a protest. But none came, even when the officer struck Ho-Bong, knocking him to the ground. *What is happening here?* Joon-Hee thought in a panic. The next moment the other officer took his pistol out of its holster and pointed it at Ho-Bong's head. Frozen in fear, Joon-Hee realized his friend was looking up at him, straight into his eyes. Ho-Bong's face was calm, but his eyes were pleading—not with the policemen, but with Joon-Hee.

341

And then the policeman pulled the trigger. . . .

Joon-Hee's voice broke. "I knew what Ho-Bong was saying to me with his eyes, Mother. He wanted me to believe the same thing he did." The tears spilled over at last. "They executed Ho-Bong right in front of me because he was a Christian. But . . . I do not even know what a Christian is! I don't understand any of this."

Mrs. Kim's head dropped into her hands. "I understand."

"How could you possibly understand why they killed my friend?"

She lifted her head. Mrs. Kim had never dared to tell her son, for fear his fate might be the same as Park Ho-Bong. In North Korea, Christians had been forced to worship underground since Kim Il Sung, "the Great Leader," took control of the country in 1948. But it was time. "Because I am a Christian, too." As Joon-Hee's eyes widened in astonishment, Mrs. Kim gently told her oldest son about how God had sent his only Son into the world to die on a cross, taking the punishment for our sins so that all who believed in him could be saved for eternal life.

"God allowed you to witness the martyrdom of one of His brave children, my son. As those bullets hit his heart, a seed was planted in yours."

"He wanted me to believe!" Joon-Hee cried. "I do! I believe!" With her arm around her son, Mrs. Kim's heart nearly burst with joy as Joon-Hee prayed and asked Jesus Christ into his heart. God had not forgotten her son, but had allowed someone else to tell—no, live!—the gospel right in front of her son's eyes.

In His Own Words
"Bless them."
—Park Ho-Bong's last words before he was executed in the street

---

God so loved the world that he gave his only Son, so that everyone who believes in him will not perish but have eternal life (John 3:16).

Methu and Adel Barege (and Christien)
Indonesia—July 2001

Indonesia. To most of us in the western world, the name invokes romantic images of lush islands in the Pacific, sandy beaches, warm breezes, quaint villages, and handsome brown-skinned people. But for Christians living among the overwhelmingly Muslim population, the past few years have been a living hell.

Radical Muslims in Indonesia have been conducting jihad, or "holy war," against villages that have established Christian churches, especially in the Muluku Islands and in Sulawesi. When a village is attacked, churches, businesses, and homes are burned; those who resist are beheaded, and others are forced to convert to Islam or suffer severe consequences. Since 1998, the number of Christians who have lost their lives to Islamic jihad has passed the ten-thousand mark.

A Living Hell

Methu Barege was about to go out of his mind. Falling to his knees beside the dead bodies of his eight-year-old son, his mother, and his mother-in-law, he wept in desperation.

Methu, his wife, Adel, both their mothers, and their two children had fled into the jungle the previous day when jihad troops had attacked their village of Ceru on the island of Doi in January 2000. Methu and other villagers, armed with machetes and sticks, had tried to defend their town but were soon overwhelmed. The attackers headed for the Christian church, doused it with gasoline and lit it on fire, then began burning people's homes as the villagers fled.

On the second day out, the Barege family had been surrounded by hostile troops in the jungle. In the panic and confusion, Methu had managed to escape. After nightfall he crept back, feeling around in the dark for his family—only to find bodies. But Methu could not find the bodies of his wife and ten-year-old daughter, Christien. Were they dead? Had they escaped? Had they been kidnapped? Hope and dread twined their fingers around his heart. Two months went by before Methu finally learned Adel and Christien were still alive!—kidnapped by the same troops that had killed the rest of his family.

But their captors told Methu there was only one way he could be reunited with his wife and daughter: He had to convert to Islam. Methu resisted; the soldiers pressed, mocking Jesus, calling him a pig with long, lice-infested hair. They threatened: If he chose Jesus, he would die. Then they changed tactics, offering Methu money and property if he would remain with them as a Muslim. Methu still shook his head. "Even if you offered me a pile of gold as high as I am, I would never join Islam."

Methu saw his wife and daughter only long enough to tell them his decision. "I will wait for you even if it takes ten years," he told his wife tearfully.

Later that same year, Methu received a letter from Adel, telling of her constant abuse and humiliation. She had married a Muslim farmer—the only way to get some protection from the constant threats. But, she wrote, "you have only one true wife, and I have only one true husband."

The situation seemed hopeless, but Methu continued to pray daily in spite of his great heartache. Then, fourteen months after he had last seen his wife and daughter, Methu received incredible news: Adel had escaped her Muslim captors and made her way back to her home village of Manado. Rushing to join her, Methu realized something was wrong: "Where is Christien? Why did you leave her behind?" Tearfully Adel told him they could not both escape, and Christien had told her mother to "go ahead."

For three months, Methu tried to rescue his daughter without success. Then, in July 2001, Christians and Muslims met together in the village

343

of Dama for a "reconciliation meeting." Making his way through the large crowd, Methu spotted his young daughter. In the press of all the people, no one noticed as father and daughter slipped away.

Oh, what joy! Reunited with his family by the God he refused to deny, Methu Barege is now studying to be an evangelist.

In His Own Words

"I never want to be disowned by Jesus." —Methu Barege

[Jesus said,] "If anyone denies me here on earth, I will deny that person before my Father in heaven" (Matthew 10:33).

Todd Beamer
United States—September 11, 2001

When President George W. Bush addressed Congress on September 20, 2001, just nine days after terrorists attacked America downing the World Trade Center towers, punching a hole in the Pentagon, and slamming Flight 93 into a remote Pennsylvania field, he said, "In the normal course of events, presidents come to this chamber to report on the state of the Union. Tonight, no such report is needed. It has already been delivered by the American people. We have seen it in the courage of passengers, who rushed terrorists to save others on the ground— passengers like an exceptional man named Todd Beamer."

Present in the chamber was Todd's wife, Lisa, mother of their two children and pregnant with a third.

Todd Beamer, a thirty-two-year-old dedicated Christian, had boarded the Boeing 757 for an 8:00 A.M. flight from Newark, New Jersey, to San Francisco, but its departure was delayed. A few minutes after nine, when the late Flight 93 was finally in the air and approaching its cruising altitude, United Airlines control radioed all its airborne pilots and warned them of potential "cockpit intrusion."

According to Dennis Roddy, a columnist with the *Pittsburgh Post-Gazette*, approximately forty minutes into the flight, "three of the highjackers stood up and put red bandanas around their heads. Two of them forced their way into the cockpit. One took the loudspeaker microphone—unaware it could also be heard by air traffic controllers—and announced that someone had a bomb on board and the flight was returning to the airport. He told them he was the pilot, but spoke with an accent."

Soon, however, the man with the apparent bomb strapped around his waist with a red belt ordered everyone—including the flight attendants—to sit down.

It was a hijacking!

The terrorist pulled the curtain between first class and coach, but not before Todd saw two people lying on the floor outside the closed cockpit door. A flight attendant later told Todd she thought they were the pilot and copilot, perhaps dead.

Beginning at about 9:20, various passengers managed to make cellular or in-flight telephone calls to family and friends, telling of their plight. In so doing, they learned of the holocaust enveloping the World Trade Center towers and the Pentagon hundreds of miles behind them. It didn't take them long to realize that the hijackers of their plane had similar plans. However, possibly unlike the passengers on the other flights, they had time to resist!

At about 9:45, Todd Beamer made phone contact with Lisa Jefferson, a General Telephone Electronics (GTE) supervisor, and told her of the hijacking and related various details of what was then happening: Two of the hijackers were in the cockpit with the door locked behind them. The man with the bomb remained in the passenger section of the plane.

"We're going down!" he shouted at one point, then said in a calmer voice, "No, wait. We are coming back up. No, we're turning around."

Later he told Jefferson that several of the passengers had decided to jump the hijackers, beginning with the guy with the bomb. "I don't think we're going to get out of this thing. I'm going to have to go out on faith," Beamer said. "Will you pray with me?" They recited the Lord's Prayer, after which Todd said, "Jesus, help me." Then, after getting Jefferson to promise that she would call his family and tell them of his love for them, he turned away from the phone, leaving the line open.

The last words Jefferson heard from him were, "Are you ready? Okay. Let's roll!"

Officials say Flight 93 crashed at 9:58 A.M., but no one on the ground was hurt.

Being There

Later, Lisa Beamer found this quote from Teddy Roosevelt in Todd's desk: "The credit belongs to the man who is actually in the arena, who strives valiantly; who knows the great enthusiasm, the great devotions, and spends himself in a worthy cause; who, at worst, if he fails, at least fails while daring greatly; so that his place shall never be with those cold and timid souls who know neither victory nor defeat."

Be strong and courageous! Do not be afraid of them! The Lord your God will go ahead of you. He will neither fail you nor forsake you (Deuteronomy 31:6).

345

Veronica Bowers (and Charity)

Peru—April 20, 2001

At the age of seventeen, Veronica (Roni) Luttig made a vow to God that she would not date anyone unless he wanted to be a missionary. She was attending Piedmont Bible College in North Carolina at the time, because she had heard God's call to missions.

Finally, a young man who had been raised in Brazil by godly missionary parents and was planning to be a missionary himself asked her to go rollerskating. Roni not only became a true friend of Jim Bowers, but also finally married him on November 23, 1985.

Finishing school was delayed by a term in the Army so Jim could take advantage of the GI bill, but after graduation, they applied to the Association of Baptists for World Evangelism (ABWE) as missionaries and were sent to Iquitos, Peru.

After many years of waiting, however, doctors told them that if they wanted to have children, they had better consider adoption—possibly a two-to- five-year process. In the meantime, in the summer of 1994, they went to Peru to build a houseboat so they could become riverboat missionaries on the Amazon. But to their delight, they were selected that fall as adoptive parents for Cory, a wonderful baby boy. Six years later, Roni and Jim Bowers adopted Charity, their second child.

Shot Down

For some time, the U.S. State Department had assisted the Peruvian government with drug interdiction, specifically by providing CIA-operated reconnaissance flights to detect drug-trafficking aircraft. At about eleven on Friday morning, April 20, 2001, a U.S. reconnaissance plane detected a small Cessna 185 float plane in Peruvian air space seemingly coming from Brazil. Initially, it didn't appear to have filed a flight plan, so a Peruvian Air Force jet fighter—guided by the Americans—intercepted and shot it down.

In the plane were Jim and Roni Bowers, their two children, and missionary pilot Kevin Donaldson, an experienced flier in the Peruvian Amazon, a region where ABWE pilots had been active for fourteen years. The Bowers were returning to their home in Iquitos, Peru, from the border town of Leticia, where they had gone to get documents for their newly adopted infant daughter at the nearest Peruvian consulate.

Donaldson *had* filed a flight plan (proved later with a copy). He had never left Peruvian airspace and had been in regular radio contact with the tower at the Iquitos airport. In fact, he had already received some landing instructions. Furthermore, the fighter did not fire a warning shot or give any other signals to land before opening fire.

The bullets from that attack wounded Donaldson in both legs, yet he bravely guided the flaming Cessna down onto the Amazon River where it bounced and then flipped over.

Jim Bowers and his eight-year-old son, Cory, were uninjured, but Roni and baby Charity were both dead from direct bullet wounds from the Peruvian fighter.

After balancing for a half an hour on the capsized wreckage of their plane, the three survivors were rescued by a local Peruvian in a dugout canoe, who took them to the village of Pevas. It was one of the fifty villages along a lush two-hundred-mile stretch of the Amazon where the Bowers regularly made stops with their houseboat to set up a volleyball net, read Bible stories and show Christian films off the boat's generator, dispense simple medicine, and lead Bible school.

The Peruvian and American governments have since offered· sincere apologies and assured the mission that pilot Donaldson bore no responsibility for the incident. The fault lay entirely with government negligence in failing to follow interdiction guidelines.

In Jim Bowers' Own Words
"I've been asking God to help me not feel so sorry for myself, and Cory. God has granted that request with a real peace in the midst of our empty longings for our two precious girls. 'The Lord gave (nineteen wonderful years with a beautiful person, seven fun months with a perfect baby), and the Lord hath taken away; blessed be the name of the Lord,' said Job when he lost his children [Job 1:21, KJV]. You've asked God to help me have Job's perspective and your prayers are being answered."

—Jim Bower

Dayna Curry and Heather Mercer
Afghanistan—November 14, 2001
"Lord, send me to the hardest place on the face of the earth," Heather Mercer had prayed, and God may have answered her prayer in giving her an opportunity to serve in Afghanistan with the German-based relief agency Shelter Now International.

Dayna Curry grew up in the wealthy Nashville, Tennessee, suburb of Forest Hills, where as a teen of divorced parents she seemed to find her passion in serving others through her church. While in college at Baylor University in Waco, Texas, she volunteered for short-term service projects in third-world countries.

Divorce had also fractured Heather's comfortable home. Seeking meaning, she excelled in school, but at the age of fifteen, she found in Jesus Christ the salvation she so desperately needed, and thereafter her life was never the same. She wrote of living in total abandonment for Jesus and a desire to "experience fully the power of Jesus Christ."

347

Six years younger than Dayna, Heather also went to Baylor University in Waco, Texas, and it was while they were there that they joined the Antioch Community Church. Their interest in missions grew, especially fueled by learning of the poverty and suffering of the orphans and widows in Afghanistan, and they both volunteered for a short-term mission trip to Afghanistan in the summer of 1998. A year later, Dayna moved to Afghanistan to work with Shelter Now.

A year and a half later Heather decided to join her there. Heather's parents were so upset over their daughter going to such a faraway country, especially one with no diplomatic ties with the U. S., that her mother wrote letters to Congress and the State Department asking if there was a legal way to prevent Heather from going to Afghanistan.

Dayna and Heather were the only single girls on the team, so they ended up sharing a house together in Kabul.

Imprisoned by the Taliban

Because Afghanistan's Taliban regime required women to cover themselves from head to toe when out in public, Heather and Dayna followed those rules, but they were often spat upon and persecuted by Islamic fundamentalist men. The children, however, followed them as though they were passing out candy, and the women often received their help, though cautiously. Publicly the girls confined themselves to their relief work, but privately they spoke of the love of Jesus with those who seemed willing to listen.

To one particularly eager family, they showed the JESUS film on August 3, 2001. Apparently, it was a setup. Taliban police raided the house, arresting Heather and Dayna along with four German and two Australian aid workers. The charge: preaching Christianity—a crime under Taliban law. The police also searched the Shelter Now offices, where they confiscated Bibles in the local Pashto and Dari languages and a book entitled *Sharing Your Christian Faith with Muslims*. "We will punish them according to law—if they are found guilty, they will be hanged," declared Taliban Chief Justice Maulawi Noor Mohammad Saqib.

Then came the September 11 terrorist attacks on America by Afghanistan-linked al Queda operatives and the ensuing War on Terrorism. The Taliban moved the prisoners from prison to prison—five in all—during their confinement of more than a hundred days, at one point locking them in a steel shipping container without heat or blankets.

On November 14, anti-Taliban forces freed the eight aid workers from a prison in Ghazni, and shortly after midnight three U.S. Special Forces helicopters picked them up from a field outside town and whisked them to their respective embassies in Pakistan.

Both Dayna, age thirty, and Heather, age twenty-four, say they hope to go back to Afghanistan. "If we are going to see the glory of God and local communities of believers established [among Muslims]," says Heather, "it's going to mean people standing up in the midst of persecution and saying, 'Yes, I follow Jesus.' And it will cost people their lives."

Jesus said to the disciples, "If any of you wants to be my follower, you must put aside your selfish ambition, shoulder your cross, and follow me. If you try to keep your life for yourself, you will lose it. But if you give up your life for me, you will find true life" (Matthew 16:24-25, a favorite passage of Heather Mercer)

Guizhen Zhang

Shandong Province, China—June 2001

The following letter, smuggled out of a Chinese prison in 2001, speaks for itself:

In Her Own Words

My name is Guizhen Zhang. I am a 43-year-old woman.

In the evening of November 29, 2000, my family was sleeping and I was awakened by a loud noise in the yard. I turned on the light, and Baode Li [a police officer] and a group of people suddenly broke in and started ransacking the house. One of them yelled at me, "Get up now, and come with us."

I asked him, "What crime did I commit?"

"You'll know when the time comes."

Then they pushed and pulled my husband (Yuejin Li) and me by force into their police car and took us to the Dingtao County police station.

The next day I was taken to the detention house to be interrogated. There were four people there directed by Baode Li. He stared at me with contempt. "Do you know why you were arrested?"

"No, I don't," I replied.

He yelled back fiercely, "It is because of you believing in God. [He cursed at me.] You're so stubborn, you deserve a good beating." With this, he slapped me hard several times. I was so dizzy that I was seeing stars, and my ears were ringing. He shouted at me while he was slapping me, "Kneel down!" He kicked me and knocked me down to the floor. "Are you going to tell us why you believe in God? Shameless woman, you're worthless running around from here to there."

They forced me to raise my cuffed hands up for more than an hour. Whenever I couldn't hold up my arms any longer and they fell, the police would kick at my waist, hit my head hard, twist my ears, and pull my hair. My hair was pulled out and my ears hurt so bad as

349

if they were cut by a knife. I began to scream. However, they didn't stop their interrogation.

"Who else believes in God beside you?"

"Just my husband and me."

Pa-de Li scolded me viciously, calling me terrible names. "You shamelessly refused to confess. Wait and see what we will teach you under forced labor."

Four of them kept cursing and beating me for more then three hours till I was lying on the floor motionless like dead, black and blue all over. Even so, they still didn't stop torturing me and kept yelling, "This _____ is very stubborn and needs to be labor-educated. As soon as we put her under labor-education, we'll win the victory."

This torture lasted till it was getting dark when they let me go back to the cell. My cell is closed all day with a disgusting smell, because the inmates are not allowed to leave to use toilet. It is not a place for human beings. In the morning and evening, we are only given a bowl of watery noodle soup and a half steamed-bread. At noon we get cabbage boiled in water. I am starved every day, but still I have to pay five yuan for the meal there.

Three days later, Baode Li and the other four policemen took me to Jinnan Women Lao Jiao [Re-educated through Labor] Camp. I was sentenced to two years and I am currently serving out my term. I was accused of "Believing on God." I remain guilty.

—Guizhen Zhang, written in June 2001

Seed of the Church

"Our churches in China are undergoing persecution; your churches in the West are undergoing delusion."

—Samuel Lamb, Chinese Christian, a prisoner for twenty years

Keep your conscience clear. Then if people speak evil against you, they will be ashamed when they see what a good life you live because you belong to Christ. Remember, it is better to suffer for doing good, if that is what God wants, than to suffer for doing wrong! (1 Peter 3:16-17).

Kim Joon-Hee

North Korea—2001 (All names have been changed.)

A river, deep and wide, stood between Kim Joon-Hee and his goal, but he was determined. His mother wanted a Bible so she could teach her sons the way of Jesus, but no one they knew in North Korea had one—or was willing to admit it if they did. But Kim Joon-Hee had heard that there were Bibles in

China, and that people from "outside" were willing to help Christians get more.

The Yalu River rode the entire northern border between North Korea and China. If you had permission to cross the border into China, there were bridges. If you didn't have permission—which Joon-Hee did not—you had to cross secretly.

Following a name and address he had been given, Kim Joon-Hee made his way to the house of a Chinese Christian and asked for help locating a Korean Bible. He recognized the bland expression, the guarded eyes. Why should they trust him? He was a North Korean, where to be a Christian was a potential death sentence. But maybe if he shared his testimony . . .

Five Thousand Bibles

And so he told them the story of his friend, Park Ho-Bong, who had been cruelly executed right before his eyes by two policemen who stopped them on the street—accused of being a Christian. "I didn't understand what it was all about—and then my own mother confessed that she, too, was a Christian. As she told me the gospel story, I realized how my friend could die so peacefully and willingly—because Jesus had died willingly for us. I asked Jesus to come live in my heart and was nearly bursting with joy—even though I had seen my friend murdered on the street that very day.

And then, just as suddenly, Kim Joon-Hee had begun to weep. "What's wrong? What's wrong?" his mother had asked, confused at this sudden change of mood.

"My brothers!" Joon-Hee had cried. "They do not know Jesus! We must tell them!"

As Joon-Hee's younger brothers came home that day, they had discovered their mother and older brother crying together. Now *they* wanted to know what was wrong! And so Joon-Hee told them what had happened that day. "Now you, too, should receive Jesus Christ as your Savior!" he told them.

Kim Joon-Hee had been a Christian only a few hours when he led his own brothers to salvation. He had never seen his mother so happy. After years of praying for her sons in secret, in one day all her children had come to know Jesus too.

"But all she knows about the Bible is what others have told her," Joon-Hee concluded. "We need Bibles in North Korea! Can you help?"

Gladly, the Chinese Christians joined the hunt for a Bible in the Korean language. Finally a miniature book was placed in front of Joon-Hee. Opening the book, words he understood leaped off the pages! "The Holy Bible"—written in Korean!

"Where can I get more of these?" he cried excitedly. His new friends shrugged. This was the only copy they could find. But Christians in the "free" world might be able to help, they said. Joon-Hee took heart. "I need 5,000 of these Bibles," he said boldly. "I will be back in one month to pick them up."

The copy of the Korean Bible had been printed by The Voice of the Martyrs, an organization begun by Richard Wurmbrand to help the persecuted church around the world. By the time Kim Joon-Hee crossed the Yalu River the second time, VOM had hurriedly printed 2,800 copies of the miniature Bible ready for him to take back into North Korea, with a promise for 2,200 more. Full of hope, Joon-Hee promised he would be back—knowing full well what the consequences would be if he was discovered.

Seed of the Church

"As those bullets hit his heart, a seed of hope was planted in yours."
—Mrs. Kim to her son Kim Joon-Hee following the execution of Park Ho-Bong

"O death, where is your victory? O death, where is your sting?" . . . How we thank God, who gives us victory over sin and death through Jesus Christ our Lord! (1 Corinthians 15:55-57).

The Javid Family
Pakistan—October 28, 2001

Even the Muslim population of Bahawalpur was shocked at the massacre that took place at St. Dominic's Catholic Church during the early morning Protestant worship service on October 28, 2001—and they feared the worst. Surely the Christians would retaliate for the ghastly murder of fifteen innocent victims!

The city had reason to worry. Anger and bitterness rose quickly out of the shock and sorrow—especially among the young people from Christian families. The two eldest daughters of Pastor Emmanuel Allah Atta shook with rage at the senseless killing of their father, right in the pulpit! When some of the older teen boys started talking about taking vengeance, they were ready to cheer them on. But even in her grief, their mother Sarapheen took them to the Bible. "As Christians, we must forgive [the terrorists]," she told her six children. "Jesus told us to love our enemies."

"True Pakistanis"

Seventeen-year-old Khurum Javid and his thirteen-year-old sister Kanwal also had reason to be full of bitterness. That Sunday morning the entire Javid family all came to the Protestant worship service to give thanks to God for their new car. After the bloody massacre, as the dead were accounted for, the rescuers made a chilling discovery: *eleven* of the fifteen persons killed were from the Javid family. Eight of them were discovered in a heap in the corner of the sanctuary. It was obvious that the older family members had tried desperately to shield the children—to no avail. Of the entire family, only Khurum and Kanwal and two grandparents remain. Yes, the young people had good reason to want revenge.

But Christian leaders in the city rallied quickly, calling people to prayer. They got the young people together and persuaded them to cool their tempers. Yes, the perpetrators should be brought to justice, but nothing would be gained by taking vengeance into their own hands; it would only make the situation worse.

Several days after the massacre, Christians and Muslims met together in a "reconciliation meeting." Peear Muhammad Abrahim, an Islamic mullah, got up and praised Christian restraint in Bahawalpur. "These Christians have demonstrated what it means to be true Pakistanis!" he declared.

But the wheels of justice grind slowly. Several suspects have been arrested in the case—though some witnesses insist that the men in custody are not the ones who committed the crime.

Meanwhile, life must go on for the children of Pastor Emmanuel, for Khurum and Kanwal Javid. But it is not easy. Tensions in Pakistan have heightened since the terrorist attacks in America, and since the Pakistani government has officially supported the U.S. in denouncing and rooting out terrorism. In a country that already treated Christians as second-class citizens, denying them many rights enjoyed by the Muslim majority, how does a family survive when the breadwinner has been killed?

"Please pray for me," Kanwal Javid told The Voice of the Martyrs (VOM) team which came to the church in Bahawalpur soon after the massacre to help the families of the victims. "I want to study medicine. Pray that God will give me strength and courage to overcome adversity, and that He will give me the wisdom, finances, and ability I need to do advanced studies."

A girl, a Christian minority, an orphan, a Pakistani . . . Kanwal Javid has many obstacles to overcome to reach her goal. But out of the tragedy, she and the other victims of the massacre at Bahawalpur are learning a new reality: that the family of God is worldwide and that other Christians do care.

We have worked wearily with our own hands to earn our living. We bless those who curse us. We are patient with those who abuse us. We respond gently when evil things are said about us. Yet we are treated like the world's garbage, like everybody's trash—right up to the present moment (1 Corinthians 4:12-13).

Lai Kwong-keung
China—2001

The Communist Chinese government recognizes only two Christian churches: the Protestant "Three-Self Movement" and the "Catholic Patriotic Association." Reportedly, they have a combined membership of about eighteen million. However, between forty and eighty million people belong to the underground church in China. These independent house churches refuse to register with the State because of government interference.

Many representatives for the independent house churches claim that the Communist state sanctions the Three-Self Patriotic Movement in order to control, restrict, and ultimately eradicate religion. Apparently, Communist authorities fear that unregulated religion will increasingly become a serious alternative to Communist ideology.

The stifling nature of the government's control is evident in these (among other) regulations:

- A permit must be obtained from the county Religious Affairs Bureau in order to establish religious meeting points. No unauthorized meeting points are allowed.
- Christian believers must actively cooperate with the government to carry out thoroughly the Party's religious policies. . . . They shall not persuade and force others to believe in Christianity. They shall not brainwash teenagers under eighteen with religious beliefs. They shall not bring children to religious activities.
- Christian believers shall not preach their religion outside the church buildings and specific places which have been designated for religious activities. They shall not preach itinerantly. They shall not receive self-proclaimed evangelists into their homes, churches, or meeting points.

With Peter and the apostles, many house church Christians say, "We must obey God rather than human authority!" (Acts 5:29) and therefore insist on independence.

The Shouters

One network of house churches in China is known as the "Shouters," having gotten its name from the practice of repetitiously shouting, "O Lord Jesus." This denomination, with historical ties to the Local Church movement, founded by Witness Lee, claims close to half a million members in southeast China, but the government banned it as a cult in 1995. Because the government restricts Bibles, the Shouters sought to import copies of a version known as *Recovery Version New Testaments,* published by the Local Church.

Two representatives for the church, Yu Zhudi and Lin Xifu, approached Lai Kwong-keung, a Christian businessman and asked him to smuggle the Bibles in for them. Lai was a Hong Kong resident, not a mainland Chinese citizen, and Hong Kongers still enjoy religious freedom even though the territory reverted to Chinese rule in 1997. So there was some hope he could succeed. However, in May 2001, Lai and Yu and Lin were arrested after bringing 33,080 Bibles into China in two clandestine shipments.

All three were convicted and fined the equivalent of $18,000 each. Yu Zhudi and Lin Xifu were sentenced to three years in prison. Lai initially was charged under anti-cult laws, which human rights activists feared could carry a death penalty.

President Bush was planning to visit China in late February 2002, and when he heard of Lai's case, he asked the U.S. State Department to look into it. U.S. ambassador to China, Clark T. Randt, mentioned Lai in a speech on January 21, saying China should "abide by the international norms of behavior."

On January 28, 2002, the charges against Lai were reduced to "illegal sales of foreign publications," and he was sentenced to two years in jail. Then the government granted him "medical bail" to return to Hong Kong for treatment for hepatitis.

In His Own Words

"How can I believe in a Jesus who has to listen to leaders in Beijing?" asks an underground preacher from Henan province. "My Jesus does not have any masters."

An angel of the Lord came at night, opened the gates of the jail, and brought them out (Acts 5:19).

Pastor Marson Lindo Moganti
Indonesia—2001

Based on the island of Java in Indonesia, Laskar Jihad is one of the largest Muslim extremist groups in the world. Recruiting radical young Muslims into its militias, training them in camps hidden in island jungles, Laskar Jihad thumbs its nose at the Indonesian government and regular army, waging jihad, or holy war, against Christians and other non-Muslims on the various islands of Indonesia at will.

On the Maluku Islands—a cluster of small islands like stepping-stones between Borneo on the west and New Guinea on the east—over two hundred Christian churches have been destroyed since October 2000. But God uses even persecution and jihad to prune and purify his people. . . .

Lukewarm to Burning

In November 2001, Laskar Jihad troops on the island of Sulawesi attacked and destroyed Calvary Presbyterian Church in the village of Sangginora. Correction: they destroyed the *building*. But Marson Lindo Moganti, the pastor of Calvary Presbyterian, was anything but defeated. He told aid workers from The Voice of the Martyrs he believes God allowed the building to be burned "because the hearts of our church members had turned far away from God, and they were in a lukewarm condition."

But since the attack, the congregation of two hundred has swollen to five hundred persons attending services. Church members are now "counting the

355

cost" of what it means to be a Christian. Revival has stirred the hearts of the people, deepening their prayer life and worship. The fire of God burns in their hearts and in their love for one another.

The Christmas Massacre That Wasn't

That same year, seven thousand jihad troops reportedly surrounded the city of Tentena in central Sulawesi, home to sixty thousand villagers and refugees, pledging to "wipe out the Christians" during the Christmas season. But this is the information age, even in Indonesia, and word of the potential massacre spread to Christians and ministries around the world. Christians prayed; they e-mailed, faxed, and spread the word to others to pray. They contacted their own governments as well as the Indonesian government, urging government intervention to prevent the massacre.

Violence against churches and Christians in Indonesia had gone virtually unchecked in the years 1999, 2000, and 2001. But in response to the public outcry around the world, the Indonesian government sent twenty-four hundred regular army troops to protect Tentena, averting the crisis. And on December 18, 2001, Christian and Muslim leaders in central Sulawesi met to sign a government-sponsored peace plan. A similar event took place in February 2002, in the Maluku capital of Ambon.

Christian refugees who have seen family members killed, their homes and churches burned, and have been chased from their villages in the jihad are understandably cautious. Will the peace plan last? What are the intentions of Laskar Jihad and other radical Muslims in the islands? When aid workers ask what they can do, one answer stands out: Pray. Their best weapon is prayer—the prayers of Christian brothers and sisters across the world . . . including the prayers of those who read this book.

Seed of the Church

"God's revival is now burning in the hearts of the congregation, and we now have more intimate worship with the Lord."

—Pastor Moganti of Calvary Presbyterian Church
in Sangginora, central Sulawesi, Indonesia

Since you are like lukewarm water, I will spit you out of my mouth! You say, "I am rich. I have everything I want. I don't need a thing!" And you don't realize that you are wretched and miserable and poor and blind and naked. I advise you to buy gold from me—gold that has been purified by fire. Then you will be rich. And also buy white garments so you will not be shamed by your nakedness. And buy ointment for your eyes so you will be able to see. I am the one who corrects and disciplines everyone I love. Be diligent and turn from your indifference (Revelation 3:16-19).

Martin and Gracia Burnham

Philippines — June 7, 2002

Martin Burnham was born in Wichita, Kansas, on September 19, 1959, to Paul and Oreta Burnham. In 1969, his parents volunteered with New Tribes Mission (NTM) and began serving in the Philippines. Later, Martin graduated from Calvary Bible College of Kansas City, Missouri, and Wichita Aviation Education Center. He also completed missionary training with NTM and in 1983 married Gracia Jones from Arkansas.

Together the young couple joined NTM and went to the Philippines, where Martin served as a missionary pilot. His parents were still missionaries on the islands. Martin and Gracia's three children—Jeff, Mindy, and Zach—were born in the Philippines.

In May 2001, to celebrate their eighteenth wedding anniversary, Martin and Gracia took a brief vacation at Dos Palmas Resort off Palawan Island in the southern Philippines. On Sunday, May 27, rebels from the Abu Sayyaf Group (ASG)—with links to Osama bin Laden's al Qaeda terrorism network—attacked the resort, kidnapping several people, including Martin and Gracia and another American, Guillermo Sobero. The Abu Sayyaf whisked the captives to Basilan Island, an ASG stronghold.

Early in the ordeal, the Philippine military surrounded the hostages and their kidnappers, who had holed up in a hospital, but the Abu Sayyaf escaped with more hostages, including Filipina nurse Ediborah (Deborah) Yap. In the ensuing months, Mr. Sobero's beheaded body was found. The guerrillas killed other captives but allowed most to go free. From November 2001, only the Burnhams and Ms. Yap remained hostage.

In June 2002, the Philippine military launched "Operation Daybreak" to hunt down the Abu Sayyaf rebels believed to be hiding in the jungles of the Zamboanga Peninsula.

On June 7, the jungle was so dense and the rains so heavy that the soldiers virtually stumbled upon the guerrillas as they were taking a midday break. The ensuing firefight left Martin Burnham and Ediborah Yap dead, and Gracia with a bullet wound through the thigh. She was successfully evacuated to a hospital for recovery.

The Ordeal

Before leaving Manila to reunite with her children in the States, Gracia shared this report with Jody Crane, the field chairman of NTM-Philippines.

> Martin was highly respected by every one of the ASG. In the beginning, they laughed in disbelief at how he responded to being a captive and their terror, but as time went on, they were awed of his confident faith in the Lord Jesus. Martin always graciously offered to carry things for the ASG and for the other hostages. Though a guard chained him to a tree each night for the whole year, Martin showed

the love and compassion of Christ throughout this year of terror to both his captors and the other hostages.

He had lengthy discussions about the claims of Christ with all the ASG guards and hostages. On one occasion, he was having a very serious talk with Abu Sabaya [the guerrilla leader] about God's judgment on sin. I was in the background motioning to Martin to "cool it," but he very gently continued sharing the truth of Christ with Sabaya.

One day after an exhausting hike all day, we strung our hammock and sat in it. Martin said, "It's been a very hard year, but it has also been a very good year." We then began thanking the Lord for everything: our hammock, our boots, for every believer that we had ever met and could remember, and all the people we knew were praying for us. [Over five thousand signed up with NTM to receive regular e-mail updates and pray.]

Then the Lord reminded us of Psalm 100:2, which says, "Serve the Lord with gladness: come before His presence with singing." We had often sung. Martin said, "We might not leave this jungle alive, but at least we can leave this world serving the Lord with gladness."

The last thing we did before lying down for a noontime nap was to pray together.

Seed of the Church

Under what other circumstances could Muslim terrorists have been enticed to listen to the gospel for a year, and in a manner that they came to respect?

I want you to know, dear brothers and sisters, that everything that has happened to me here has helped to spread the Good News (Philippians 1:12).

Pastor Rafiq
Bangladesh — 2002

In February 2002, *The Voice of the Martyrs* magazine published a letter from a church leader in Bangladesh. His own words tell the story of what it means to answer God's call to ministry in parts of Southeast Asia. . . .

Much Fruit

I live in Bangladesh, and God has called me to evangelize Muslims. For the past 16 years, I have been doing this difficult ministry. God has given us much fruit, and many Muslims have converted. However, we do experience much persecution. We know this will continue as long as we are on Earth, and we choose to continue preaching the gospel every day that we can.

There have been many attempts made on my life from the fundamentalist Muslims who are angry about the gospel message being preached. But still I love these people very much. Jesus tells us to love our enemies and do good to them who hate us. The highest good we can do to anybody is to share the gospel message that can save their soul. . . .

One night when I was asleep in the home of one of my evangelists, nine men came to kill me. Two of them had guns. They demanded that the evangelist give me to them, so they could kill me. The evangelist refused to hand me over, so the men beat him and started to break off pieces of his bamboo-and-grass house. Then they forced their way into the house to drag me out. During all this time, I was sound asleep. One of the men with a gun found me sleeping on the floor. He kicked my head with his foot. I stood up and tried to walk, but it was very dark and I wasn't fully aware of what was happening. They took me outside and tried to fire their gun at me. I prayed, "Lord Jesus, save us!" Immediately we saw some light that seemed to come from heaven. This bright light made our persecutors very afraid. They all ran away and said that an angel had come from heaven to save the "Christian preacher."

In one of our outreach areas, 150 Muslim families have become Christians. The area Muslim leaders gathered together and decided to hire a professional hit man to kill me. He was paid half the $900 (U.S.) before the job and would receive the other half after I was dead. He came to my office and put his hand into his bag to pull out his gun. He started to raise his gun and point it at me. I was reminded of Psalm 91:15: "He will call upon me, and I will answer him; I will be with him in trouble, I will deliver him and honor him."

Before his arm could be extended to point the gun at me, his whole arm froze in place. He could not move his arm! He became afraid and started to cry. I got up from my chair and came near to him and asked him what happened. He started telling me the whole story, but he still could not move his arm. He asked me to pray for him. This is just like Jesus told us to do: Pray for those who persecute you. I prayed for him and explained the gospel to him. God healed his arm, and this former murderer accepted Christ into his heart.

I continue my ministry with confidence that no one can take my life before the Lord's appointed time. I am willing to die for the gospel, but I know this will only happen when God plans for it. The first chapter of Second Thessalonians teaches us that we must have faith and love as we fight the spiritual battles for the souls of men. We must endure trials of many kinds in this lifetime for the sake of the gospel, so that we can tell as many as we can about Jesus.

In His Own Words
"To love in this way is not humanly possible. It is only possible as we let the love of Jesus live and grow in our hearts and overflow to love as He loved us."

—Pastor Rafiq (not his real name)

A new command I give you: Love one another. As I have loved you, so you must love one another (John 13:34, NIV), the Bible verse Pastor Rafiq has taken as "the motto of my life."

Winifred Ritchie
Pakistan — March 17, 2002

In a world increasingly divided by ethnic groups, politics, race, and religion, the Protestant International Church (PIC) in Islamabad, Pakistan, was a haven for Christian diplomats, aid workers, missionaries, teachers, employees of international corporations, refugees from Afghanistan, and visitors from many countries. A half mile away, security at the U.S. embassy in Islamabad had been tight since the terrorist attacks of September 11, 2001. In the wake of those attacks, attendance at Sunday morning worship at the PIC had shrunk to about half— from 150 to around 75—as diplomatic missions and international corporations sent employees and family members home.

But Many Stayed

On Sunday morning, March 17, 2002, eighty-one-year-old Winnie Ritchie, a former teacher in Chicago who now teaches English to Afghan refugees in Pakistan, settled into her seat on the left side of the nondenominational church. With her were two fellow ESL (English as a Second Language) teachers: Tammy, age thirty-one, from The Evangelical Alliance Mission (TEAM); and Laura, a new teacher from Guam.

The congregation sang "This Is Holy Ground," and a visiting pastor was in the middle of his sermon when Winnie heard a commotion at the door and suddenly saw "three round black things in the air." Instinctively, Winnie and her companions dove for the floor, age notwithstanding. They huddled under the sparse protection of the metal chairs they'd been sitting on, and Winnie pulled her clothes over exposed areas of her body as explosion after explosion ripped through the church. For a few minutes it was impossible to know what was happening as smoke filled the interior of the church amid the sound of breaking glass, crashing debris, and screams.

And then . . . silence. As the smoke cleared, Winnie saw one of the round black objects lying on the floor only a few feet away. A grenade . . . that hadn't exploded. She was splattered with blood—but she could find no wounds. Laura, however, was holding her middle, and a deep gash on Tammy's arm bled freely. Helping her younger companions, Winnie stumbled toward the door, over bodies and body parts. Looking back, she saw that the brass chandeliers had crashed to the floor and all the windows had blown out.

At the hospital, Winnie helped an American woman who was covered with bad cuts from flying glass. She continued to be her calm, efficient self until a fellow ESL worker came hunting for her to see if she was all right—and suddenly the tears began to flow.

It was not the first time Winnie had faced death up close and personal. The first was when she'd been nearly killed in an automobile accident that killed her husband during the Afghan war with Russia. And yet Winnie had stayed on. "Retiring" was not in her vocabulary. She was a teacher, and Afghan refugees needed teachers.

At day's end, five were listed as dead—Rabia Edward (Pakistan); Anwar Baizar (Afghanistan); Barbara Green (American embassy); Kristen Green, Barbara's teenage daughter; and an unidentified person. At least forty more were injured, some critically.

Keep On Keeping On

Word spread quickly through the ESL team to family and supporters in the United States and Canada that Winnie Ritchie had been injured in the blast. To allay everyone's fears, this plucky teacher sent the following e-mail to her son Joe Ritchie, who had recently returned to Chicago from Afghanistan:

"Just a quickie to let you know that I am OK. This A.M. during the middle of our preaching service a bomber came into the church and threw a number of hand grenades. At least five have been killed. That number will rise. Many were injured. All my colleagues are OK. Some wounded but not too seriously. I hit the floor and under chairs and waited it out. The inside of the church is demolished. Life is changing fast and more changes will have to be made. . . . All for right now. Love you very much, Mom."

In Her Own Words

I'm not afraid, but I think we have to be alert, and be a little more cautious. We try to just keep on going as normally as we can.

—Winnie Ritchie, survivor of the PIC bombing

God has not given us a spirit of fear and timidity, but of power, love, and self-discipline (2 Timothy 1:7).

Villagers of Soya

Indonesia—April 28, 2002

Since January 1999, bitter sectarian fighting between Muslims and Christians in the Maluku Islands of Indonesia has killed nearly ten thousand people. Local Indonesians—both Christians and Muslims—have repeatedly said the violence in the former Spice Islands was precipitated by outside provocateurs, even trained combatants. Now officials in Southeast Asia agree that al Qaeda operatives, part of the terror network blamed for the September 11, 2001, attacks in the United States, played a major role.

At the height of the conflict in 2000, Jafar Umar Thalib, the leader of the militant Muslim organization, Laskar Jihad, called for all Muslims to wage a holy war against Christians in Maluku. Thousands of young Muslims from all over the country heeded that call, including many from Malaysia, Pakistan, and even Afghanistan.

The Indonesian government seemed so sympathetic to the Muslim extremists or so impotent to enforce peace that a small, long-dormant group, the Maluku Sovereignty Front, that had advocated separating Maluku from the rest of Indonesia, rose up to defend Christians. Their militancy, however, only gave Muslims excuses for attacking Christians.

A Fragile Peace

Finally, after growing weary of the fighting, moderate Muslims and Christians reached a peace deal on February 12, 2002. However, the agreement did not address the disarmament and removal of outside agitators, nor the apparent inequity with which the government dealt with Christians and Muslims—after all the violence, not one person had been sentenced to jail during the three strife-torn years.

On Thursday, April 25, 2002, the fifty-second anniversary of a failed independence bid by the Maluku Sovereignty Front, Alex Manuputty, raised a separatist flag, again advocating an independent state. Manuputty and sixteen supporters were promptly arrested and charged with subversion.

The next day, Jafar Umar Thalib, commander of the violent Laskar Jihad, addressed a crowd, urging Muslims to ignore the peace agreement. "Use bombs and fire them at the enemy," he said, according to a recording of his speech. "There can be no reconciliation with non-Muslims. We will fight them until our last drop of blood."

Early Sunday morning, April 28, Laskar Jihad made its move, wearing military-style uniforms. Well armed and carrying grenades and bombs, they descended on the Christian village of Soya, near Ambon, in Maluku. Thirteen Christian villagers—including a six-month-old baby and a two-year-old boy—were killed. The Islamic militants injured six other people and destroyed thirty homes and a church building.

Is Enough, Enough?

Fearing Indonesian authorities would do nothing, the leaders of twelve church groupings on the islands appealed for protection to the United Nations secretary-general, Kofi Annan, on Monday.

Finally, the government acted by issuing orders for the dissolution of the separatist Maluku Sovereignty Front, *and* the expulsion of Laskar Jihad from the islands. On May 4, with the cabinet's approval, police arrested Laskar Jihad's commander, Jafar Umar Thalib, saying his speech directly incited the deadly attack on the Christian villagers of Soya. But what will it take to disarm and then deport his militant organization?

Furthermore, when Indonesian vice president Hamzah Haz, the leader of the country's largest Islamic political party, visited his "Muslim brother" Thalib in his cell as a gesture of Islamic solidarity, one wonders whether the government is committed to establishing peace or not.

Pray this way for kings and all others who are in authority, so that we can live in peace and quietness, in godliness and dignity (1 Timothy 2:2).

Sources

The authors consulted the following primary sources in researching material for this book.

Anderson, Gerald H., ed. *Biographical Dictionary of Christian Missions*. Grand Rapids: Eerdmans, 1998.

Braght, Thieleman J. van. *Martyrs' Mirror*. Scottdale, Penn.: Herald Press, 1660, 1950.

Brother Andrew with John and Elizabeth Sherrill. *The Narrow Road: Stories of Those Who Walk This Road Together*. Grand Rapids, Mich.: Fleming H. Revell, 1967, 2001.

Brother Andrew with Verne Becker. *For the Love of My Brothers*. Minneapolis, Minn.: Bethany House Publishers, 1998.

Christian History Interactive. Carol Stream, Ill.: Christianity Today International, 1997.

dc Talk and The Voice of the Martyrs. *Jesus Freaks–Stories of Those Who Stood for Jesus, the Ultimate Jesus Freaks*. Tulsa, Okla.: Albury Publishing, 1999.

Douglas, J. D., and others, eds. *Who's Who in Christian History*. Wheaton, Ill.: Tyndale, 1992.

Foxe, John. *Book of Martyrs*. Middleton, England: Edwin Hunt, 1563, 1833.

Hefley, James and Marti. *By Their Blood–Christian Martyrs of the Twentieth Century*. Grand Rapids, Mich.: Baker Books, 1979, 1996.

Jackson, Dave and Neta. *Hero Tales: A Family Treasury of True Stories from the Lives of Christian Heroes*, 4 vols. Minneapolis, Minn.: Bethany House Publishers, 1996, 1997, 1998, 2001.

———. *On Fire for Christ: Stories of Anabaptist Martyrs*. Scottdale, Penn.: Herald Press, 1989.

Morgan, Robert J. *On This Day: 365 Amazing and Inspiring Stories about Saints, Martyrs and Heroes*. Nashville, Tenn.: Thomas Nelson Publishers, 1997.

Shea, Nina. *In the Lion's Den: Persecuted Christians and What the Western Church Can Do About It*. Nashville, Tenn.: Broadman and Holman Publishers, 1997.

Sidwell, Mark. *Free Indeed: Heroes of Black Christian History*. Greenville, S.C.: Bob Jones University Press, 1995.

Tucker, Ruth A. *From Jerusalem to Irian Jaya: A Biographical History of Christian Missions*. Grand Rapids, Mich.: Zondervan Publishing House, 1983.

Woodbridge, John D., ed. *Ambassadors for Christ: Distinguished Representatives of the Message throughout the World*. Chicago: Moody Press, 1994.

In addition, they consulted numerous specific sources for each individual story. Sources for each "Witness" may be found at http://daveneta.com/support-pages/fearnotsources.html.

Index

About the Authors

Dave and Neta Jackson, husband-and-wife writing team, are the authors or coauthors of more than 120 books that have sold over 2.5 million copies. They are best known for Neta's award-winning Yada Yada Prayer Group series and their forty-volume Trailblazer series for young readers and Hero Tales series for families. They make their home in the Chicago area. Find them at www.daveneta.com, www.trailblazerbooks.com, www.facebook/DaveNetaJackson, and www.twitter.com/DaveNetaJackson

CPSIA information can be obtained at www.ICGtesting.com
Printed in the USA
LVOW08s0914230214

374813LV00001B/43/P